T4-AKE-978

ISDN, DECnet®, and SNA Communications

RELATED TITLES

C Programmer's Guide to NetBIOS
W. David Schwaderer

C Programmer's Guide to Serial Communications
Joe Campbell

Data Communications, Networks, and Systems
Thomas C. Bartee, Editor-in-Chief

Data Communications Testing and Troubleshooting
Gilbert Held

Digital Communications
Thomas C. Bartee, Editor-in-Chief

Micro-Mainframe Connection
Thomas Wm. Madron

PC LAN Primer
The Waite Group

Reference Data for Engineers: Radio Electronics, Computer, and Communications, Seventh Edition
Edward C. Jordan, Editor-in-Chief

Telecommunications Networks: A Technical Introduction
Robert J. "Bert" Murphy

Understanding Data Communications, Second Edition
Revised by Gilbert Held

Understanding Local Area Networks
Stan Schatt

The Waite Group's UNIX Communications
Bart Anderson, Bryan Costales, and Harry Henderson

Handbook of Computer-Communications Standards, Volume 1: The OSI Model and OSI-Related Standards
William Stallings

Handbook of Computer-Communications Standards, Volume 2: Local Network Standards
William Stallings

Handbook of Computer-Communications Standards, Volume 3: Department of Defense Protocol Standards
William Stallings

UNIX Networking
Stephen G. Kochan and Patrick H. Wood, Editors

ISDN, DECnet®, and SNA Communications

Thomas C. Bartee

A Division of Macmillan, Inc.
4300 West 62nd Street
Indianapolis, Indiana 46268 USA

FIRST EDITION
FIRST PRINTING—1989

International Standard Book Number: 0-672-22512-3
Library of Congress Catalog Card Number: 89-61052

Acquisitions Editor: *James S. Hill*
Development Editor: *C. Herbert Feltner*
Manuscript Editor: *Albright Communications, Incorporated*
Production Coordinator: *Marjorie Hopper*
Illustrator: *Don Clemons*
Indexer: *Northwind Editorial Services*
Technical Reviewer: *Thomas C. Bartee*
Keyboarder: *Jeanne P. Wagner*
Compositor: *Shepard Poorman Communications, Incorporated*

Printed in the United States of America

Trademarks

All terms mentioned in this book that are known to be trademarks or service marks are listed below. In addition, terms suspected of being trademarks or service marks have been appropriately capitalized. Howard W. Sams & Company cannot attest to the accuracy of this information. Use of a term in this book should not be regarded as affecting the validity of any trademark or service mark.

ACCUNET, 3B, 3B 20D, ESS, 1A ESS, 1ESS, 4ESS, 5ESS, 1PSS are trademarks and AT&T, SLC 96, and UNIX are registered trademarks of American Telephone and Telegraph.

Apple, AppleTalk, and Macintosh are registered trademarks of Apple Computer, Inc.

CompuServe is a registered trademark of CompuServe Services, an H & R Block Company.

DEC, DECnet, and VAX are registered trademarks and RSX, PDP-11, ThinWire, and DDCMP are trademarks of Digital Equipment Corporation.

DMS, DMS-100, DMS-100/200, and DMS-250 are trademarks of Northern Telecom Limited.

Ethernet and Xerox are trademarks of Xerox Corporation.

IBM, IBM AT, and Personal Computer AT are registered trademarks and CBX, Netview, Netview PC, Personal Computer XT, and Rolm are trademarks of International Business Machines Corporation in the United States and/or other countries.

MCI is a registered trademark of MCI Corporation.

NEC and NEAX are registered trademarks of NEC America, Inc.

Telemail is a registered trademark of General Telephone and Electronics Corporation.

Overview

Contents

Preface

Communication is now entering a new era. The development of advanced voice facilities is proceeding in parallel with the accelerated expansion of computer-to-computer systems, PC networks, local area networks, leased-line dedicated networks, and a multitude of other facilities. Making sense of this explosive growth is a major challenge. Fortunately, the new systems are based mostly on standards which have been written by international standards organizations or by major computer companies (such as DEC and IBM).

This book is dedicated to clear explanations of the new systems and how the standards are used in the new and existing systems. Included are

- a look at the standards organizations from the inside—how they operate and interrelate
- digital communications—its potential and limitations
- IBM and DEC—what's happening now and what's planned for the future
- communications management—a new field that's growing up fast
- circuit, message, and packet switching—their structures, operations, and impact

The first chapter, "An ISDN Primer," presents an introduction to and overview of some of the most important topics in modern communications. One of the authors, Robert Linfield, was assistant director of the National Telecommunications Institute of America (NTIA) and is known as an authority on the politics of communications and the international organizations. Don Glen, coauthor and also from NTIA, is known for his standards expertise, and coauthor Evelyn Gray, also from NTIA, is a respected editor and writer in the communications area. This chapter provides you with the knowledge to understand the giant strides forward now being taken and even gives information on digital versus analog systems and computer usage in communications equipment.

The second chapter, by Don Glen, gives the most lucid explanation of the present telephone system and how it is structured I have ever read. I cannot tell you how pleased I was when I first read this material. You will be dazzled by his insights and clarity as this complex subject is presented.

Chapter 3 describes packet communications systems and is by Tony Michel who is with BBN, a major manufacturer of packet switches and other communications equipment. The fundamentals of packet switching are fully explained and you will find a carefully worked out description of the advantages of packet systems. This chapter is a model of careful reasoning and has a tutorial approach which makes everything crystal clear.

The next chapter gives an overview of packet-switching standards. Here, Don Glen has presented the first really lucid look at present standards, how they work, and why they are as they are. His continuing involvement with standards committees gives you information which cannot be found elsewhere.

Chapter 5 presents the new world of communications as viewed by the Bell Operating Companies. C. A. Cooper, who is a district manager with Bell Communications Research, tells how the network operators are facing the future and what is being done to improve present systems and provide new services and features. Since all these companies are part of a worldwide development and all companies must interface and still compete, this material gives fascinating insight into what is planned. The importance of existing equipment cannot be denied because of the billions of dollars invested in it. His remarks on how capabilities can be expanded for only a few dollars more is a real eye-opener.

Chapter 6 explains some of the technical considerations involved in making the changes necessary to move to all-digital systems from our present situation. There are millions of twisted pairs in existence and these must play a part in any future development. Just what can be done—and how—is the subject of this chapter by Victor Lawrence, AT&T department head, and Professor Syed Ahamed, senior member of the IEEE. This is a work of obvious authority.

Chapter 7 is an introduction to the management of communications systems. This is a new and exciting area and the overview and considerations presented here make an important contribution to a rapidly developing subject. Paul Brusil and Claude LaBarre, both contributors to many standards and specifications efforts, are established management experts in this new area.

Clearly a major subject in communications is the IBM SNA system. As the major product of the world's largest data processing company, SNA cannot be ignored and must be a major consideration in any work on this subject. The seven IBM authors who prepared the material in Chapter 8 have done an exemplary job of explaining SNA and placing it in perspective.

The final chapter gives you an overview of DECnet, DEC's family of communication systems. Radia Perlman, designer of algorithms and protocols, carefully explains and documents the use of international standards in the DEC system. Chapter 9 is a major contribution to our understanding of how DECnet fits in the overall scheme of things.

Appendixes A, B, and C, compiled by the authors of Chapter 1, provide an exclusive look inside the organization, structure, and processing of standards, including a reprint of the question that led to the ISDN concept.

Appendixes D and E, written by the authors of Chapter 7, present additional views of the organization and processes of international standards bodies as well as details of various efforts to implement specifications.

In all, this book presents a rare opportunity to discover what currently exists in communications and what is being developed. I know of nowhere else that this level of expertise can be found and it is with pleasure I introduce the work of this distinguished group.

Thomas C. Bartee
Editor

Chapter 1

An ISDN Primer

Robert F. Linfield
Donald V. Glen
Evelyn M. Gray

Chapter 1

THE INTEGRATED SERVICES DIGITAL NETWORK (ISDN) concept is believed by many to be the communication means for the future information age. Several interconnected national ISDNs can provide a high-performance, multiservice, digital network for global communications.

This chapter introduces the developments in telecommunications technology—from analog to digital—that make the efficiencies and economies of an ISDN possible. We also explore technical and policy considerations: Why is an ISDN needed? How is it expected to evolve? What problems will it cause? Who is working on them?

Additional information is presented in the Appendixes at the back of the book. Appendix A provides a description of the organization, structure, and processing of standards, known as Recommendations, within the CCITT. Appendix B is a reprint of Question 1 of CCITT Study Group XVIII, initiated in the late 1970s, which led to the ISDN concept. Appendix C is a description of the Open Systems Interconnection (OSI) reference models of the International Organization for Standardization (ISO) and the CCITT.

A need to move information is growing worldwide. Increasingly, the information transfer must be rapid and inexpensive, between points near or far. In response, a global effort is under way to establish a digital network that will transport voice and nonvoice information as needed—the ISDN. One or a number of ISDNs might evolve in each country from existing network(s). In the United States, several ISDNs could emerge from existing telecommunications systems.

Digital technology makes the ISDN concept feasible. Telephone systems in the United States and abroad are using digital technology to improve and expand capabilities. Traditionally analog nonvoice information, such as facsimile and television, is becoming more dependent on digital transmission. New services such as videotex and teletex already use digital transmission techniques.

The marriage of digital technology and information transfer is important to multibillion dollar industries—banking, product distribution, insurance, manufacturing, medicine, and travel reservations—with their own extensive private telecommunication networks. Office automation, dependent on digital systems, is an integral part of these industries.

A potential ISDN configuration may consist of the concept illustrated in Figure 1-1. The U.S. ISDN(s) may interconnect to non-U.S. ISDNs, International Record Carriers (IRCs), value-added networks (VANs), and private networks, including local area networks (LANs). Initially, the U.S. ISDN will use in-place equipment to handle digital bit-streams. As the network and services evolve, the ISDN will include communication equipment that permits integration of voice and nonvoice services. Subscribers of each network, public or private, will be able to communicate with each other. Variable transmission rates dependent on a user's need will be available on demand. Although all ISDN services have not been defined, they are expected to include digitized voice, data transfer between computers, facsimile, graphics, video, and other services such as telemetry (in energy management and security monitoring), videotex, electronic mail, and data base access for work processors—in all, a broad scope of information services in an information society.

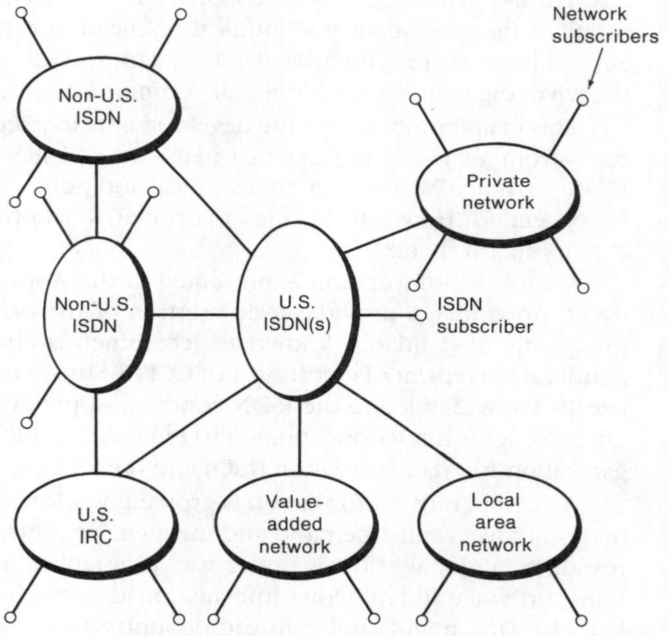

Figure 1-1. Potential ISDN configuration.

Standards for an ISDN are being developed by the International Telegraph and Telephone Consultative Committee (CCITT) of the International Telecommunication Union (ITU), an agency of the United Nations. The United States and other countries are working to define the ways that subscribers will have access to an ISDN. Contributions to the CCITT are made through a coordinated effort by these countries. In America, the U.S. CCITT Joint ISDN Working Party is the focal point for ISDN effort by government and industry.

Many issues need to be resolved before the ISDN becomes a reality. The U.S. communications environment is unique because of the many common carriers, public and private networks, and multitude of different services. The following questions need to be answered:

- What should be the geographical or network boundaries of the U.S. ISDN(s)?
- Where do the public, private, cable TV, and local networks fit within an ISDN?
- How will all these networks interconnect to the ISDN or to each other?
- How will the U.S. ISDN(s) interconnect with foreign ISDNs?
- Who, or what, will manage, set standards for, control, and operate an ISDN?

Why an ISDN?

Primary reasons for establishing ISDNs are the economy and flexibility made possible by integrating emerging new services with existing services. It is more efficient to use and reuse existing networks than to build a separate network for each service. With digital technology, communication resource sharing among services has become feasible.

Three factors motivating an ISDN are

- technological developments that make possible expanded capabilities
- the lower cost of offering new equipment and services (because of digital technology and digital network characteristics)
- the demand and subsequent availability of new or expanded services

Combining these three factors results in economic benefits through service integration.

Merging of Two Technologies

The groundwork for the ISDN may have begun four decades ago with the onset of convergence between two technologies. Starting with the 1940s, computers and communications technologies were two distinct areas of development. With time, these technologies have become dependent on each other.

During the past four decades, communication technology in such fields as microwave radio, cable, satellites, and telephone switching systems developed on a separate but convergent course with computer technology. Electromechanical computers were in existence when the first electron-tube computer (Electronic Numerical Integrator and Calculator or ENIAC) came into being. It was followed by solid-state computers that used transistors and integrated circuits (ICs). Eventually, switches controlling telephone lines required computers for control and to provide new customer services. Concurrently, computers accessed by telephone lines required higher data rates and digital networks. A data terminal that at one time was limited as a human interface to a computer now contains communications and computing ability. The communications and computer industries converged and aided each other. Differences between data processing and communications have become less distinct: communications now use extensive computer control and computer services have communication embedded within them.

Figure 1-2 illustrates the overlapping of the communications, data communications, and data processing industries, by showing dollar totals (in billions) for each of the three industries for the years 1970, 1975, 1980, and 1985.

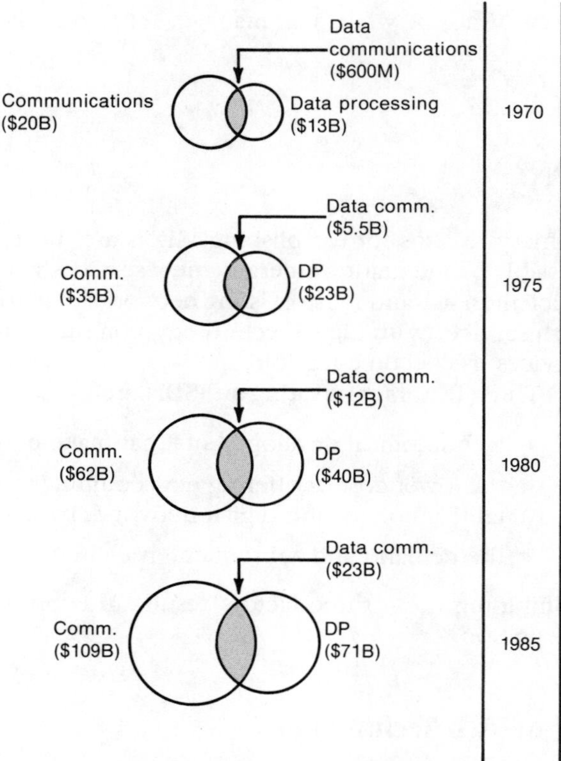

Figure 1-2. Growth of data communications industry.

Figure 1-3 shows the changing composition, by percent, of the U.S. workforce from 1860 to 1980. Stage I was mainly an agricultural economy, stage II an industrial economy, and stage III is the information economy.

As our society becomes increasingly involved in information services, the use of communications increases, and the efficiency of digital communications becomes more important to us. Improvements in communications technology become very significant as we try to improve our nation's productivity to compensate for rising labor costs.

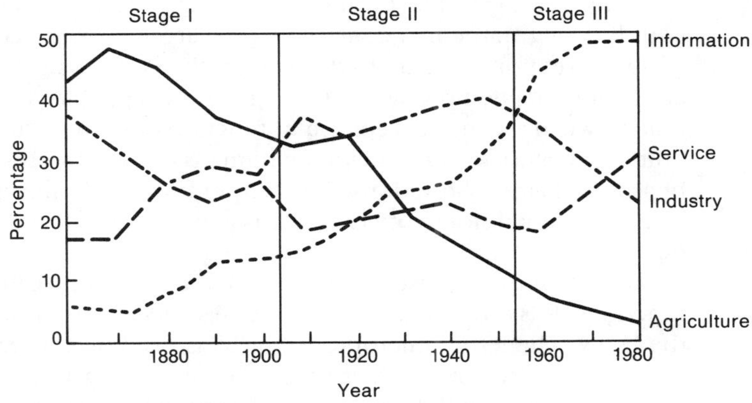

Figure 1-3. Changing composition of U.S. workforce.

Technology Advancements

One of the reasons for the merging of telecommunications and data processing is that individual electronics components have increased in capacity and speed while decreasing in cost. These simultaneous developments have made it easier to add a small, inexpensive chip to a terminal or a telephone to provide enhanced capabilities.

To understand the nature of these enhancements, it is necessary to understand the basic elements of a computer. Figure 1-4 illustrates the fundamental structure found in all computers, ranging from large supercomputers to microcomputers.

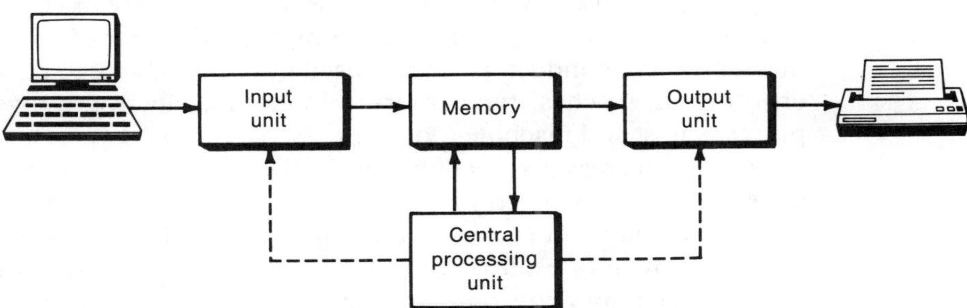

Figure 1-4. Basic structure for large computers and microcomputers.

Each computer consists of three basic units:

- central processing unit (CPU)
- internal memory
- input/output (I/O) capability

The CPU performs arithmetic, logic and control functions, manipulating and directing traffic in a computer. The direct memory contains the programming instructions that are performed by the CPU. It also contains the data that are being operated on by the CPU. The I/O capability is the communications link between the internal computer functions and the outside world. The input unit is the interface through which humans can control the computer with keyboards and tape instructions. The output unit is the interface for recording results on external storage media such as paper, magnetic tape, discs, or solid-state devices.

Microcomputers use different chips to form the CPU, memory, and I/O functions. It is the chip unit that underlies telecommunications technology and the ISDN. The term "microprocessor" has been used to mean the CPU.

Microcontrollers, such as those used in microwave ovens and other home appliances, contain the CPU, memory, and I/O functions on one chip. The limited instructions and memory requirements to control a microwave oven allow integration of the three functions.

The tremendous advances made in semiconductor technology since the development of the vacuum tube and transistor have completely revolutionized the computer industry. In 1946, ENIAC had 18,000 vacuum tubes and weighed 30 tons. Reliability was not its strong point. The microcomputer of today is extremely small, yet more powerful. It has the same three elements (CPU, memory, and I/O capability) that ENIAC had, but is composed of complex circuits on thin wafers of silicon as small or smaller than the end of a finger. It is 20 times more powerful than ENIAC and extremely reliable. These microcomputer advances are the result of miniaturization and mass production.

With the introduction of the transistor in the 1950s, and subsequent higher densities of transistors and complete circuits on a wafer chip, came lower per-unit costs of production and a flourishing digital technology. Integrated circuits or chips have invaded almost every segment of society—home, office, factory, hospitals, and entertainment centers. As the technology has advanced, so have its applications. Although computer companies use over 40 percent of all chips produced, semiconductors are also used in air conditioners, refrigerators, cameras, digital watches, typewriters, telephones, electronic toys, stereos, airplanes, autos, and machine tools.

One of the reasons that chips are used in so many devices today is that they are small in size with very large capacity. Figure 1-5 illustrates the increasing density of component circuitry on a chip and the decreasing cost per memory bit. The growth of electronics capabilities is characterized in one way by the number of components on a single chip. In 1960, one discrete device (transistor) was encapsulated in a package. Today, very large scale integrated (VLSI) circuits contain several million transistors and related components on a chip within a package.

Figure 1-5 also shows the declining average price of memory devices that store bits of information. This has enhanced data communications and data processing services through digital technology at a lower cost. According to U.S. Department of Commerce data, the average price per memory bit dropped from two cents to less than one one-hundredth of one cent (1983 value) in a little over a decade and is continuing today.

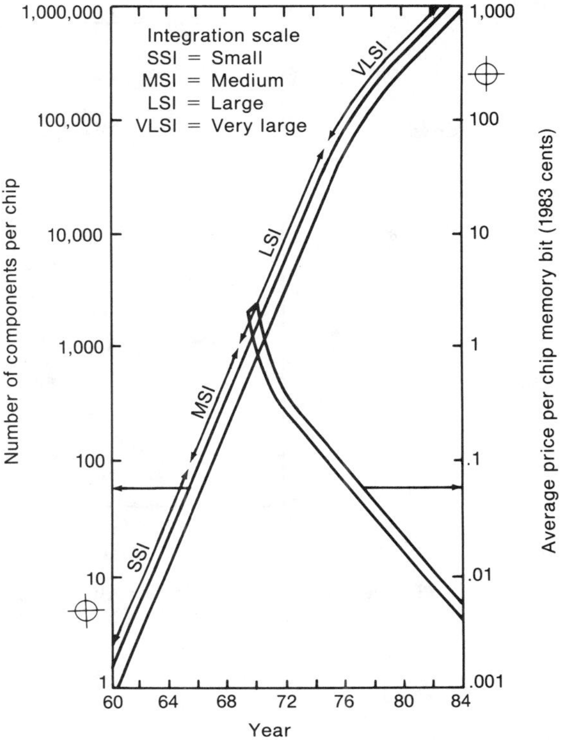

Figure 1-5. Trends for increasing density of components and decreasing cost of memory.

Market Size

According to the U.S. Department of Commerce, chip technology is now used in the production of more than $200 billion worth of goods and services in the United States alone. As more uses have been found for semiconductors, international demand for chips has skyrocketed. Production of semiconductors has doubled every year during the 1970s. Total world sales increased from $1 billion to $21 billion.

The value of U.S. production and consumption of all chips per year is graphed in Figure 1-6.

The use of semiconductors should increase even further in the 1980s and 1990s. The U.S. Department of Commerce expects that the world market for semiconductors exceeded $50 billion by 1988 and will exceed $200 billion by the end of the century. A learning process in utilization and economy of scale have assisted this trend in consumption.

The use of integrated circuits has also made possible the manufacture of many new products such as personal computers and pocket calculators. For personal computers, the 1988 market was $20.9 billion, with an expected increase to $32 billion in 1990.

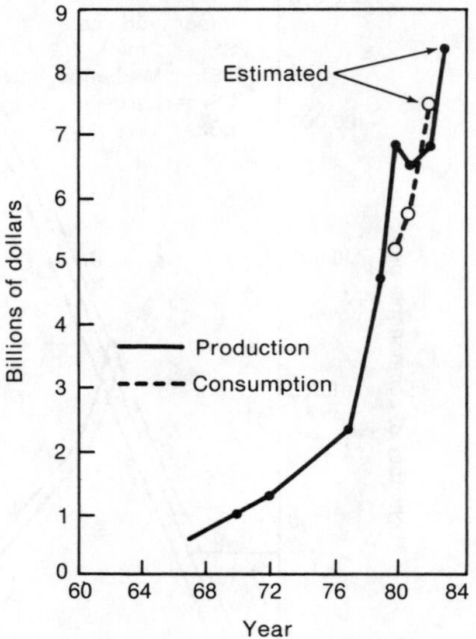

Figure 1-6. Value of U.S. production and consumption of all integrated circuits (chips).

Users of Communications Services

There are several major industries that require voice and nonvoice communication services on a large scale. A few of the obvious ones to mention are

- banking
- insurance
- manufacturing
- distribution
- reservations services
- medical
- office automation

These industries are sizable, and each has a significant impact on the U.S. economy. To illustrate size and to show the extent to which they are involved in data communications, two industries have been chosen for illustration: banking and office automation.

Banking. The size of the banking industry as a whole can be illustrated with Department of Commerce statistics: for 1982, commercial banks had assets of over $1,800 billion. Savings and loan institutions had an additional $708 billion in assets (U.S. Department of Commerce 1983). In 1980, electronic data processing equipment in banks handled more than $250 billion of data transactions over telecommunication lines. An American Bankers Association 1979 survey showed that as a rule, large banks with over $500 million in deposits had the most extensive telecommunications facilities: facsimile, Wide-Area-Telephone Service (in-WATS), electronic funds transfer, telecommunications for security and alarm systems, switched wideband or digital service, word processing equipment, computer terminal systems, telephone bill-paying service, etc.

The total annual domestic telecommunication expense for the commercial bank industry was over $866 million in 1979, compared to $788.4 million in 1978 and $626.6 million in 1977.

Computer World and other journals have reported savings in time and money when banks have automated certain teller functions and used EFT (electronic funds transfer). Further costs can be saved for the banking industry by using an ISDN for its sizable data communications operations because there would be no need for banks to buy or build separate networks for each type of data transfer application: with an ISDN, voice and nonvoice would be transmitted over the same network.

The Office Automation Industry. Office automation, which is part of all these industries that rely heavily on data communications, is a big industry in itself. According to estimates, U.S. spending for advanced office gear quadrupled from 1981 to 1986, going from $3 billion in 1981 to an estimated $12 billion in 1986. U.S. shipments of gear that can be linked to form electronic offices, or automated offices, should grow 34 percent per year through 1990. Office automation is still growing as our information society develops. In 1980, 60 percent of $1.3 trillion paid out for wages, salaries, and benefits in the United States went to U.S. office workers.

New Services. Accompanying the increase in capability of individual components has been an increase in applications of those components. Customized software (programs) have made possible a wide range of telecommunications products and services. These new service requirements have created an increased demand for an ISDN. A partial list of such new services would include

- distributed processing
- electronic mail
- EFT
- teleconferencing with data and facsimile
- mixed services (teletext and video) in one network

As our information society grows, as technology develops, as component prices fall or stabilize, our use of communications goods and services will increase to maintain productivity levels and offset the rising cost of labor. ISDN efficiencies can assist in this effort by making efficient use of transmission network(s) for a variety of telecommunications services rather than building a separate network for each type of service. While the emphasis within this section has been placed on data communication and processing, one should not dismiss the importance of voice communications. Voice is expected to maintain 80 percent to 90 percent of the communications traffic for many years.

Telecommunications Primer

Defining any telecommunications network is a difficult task. This is particularly true today when networks are becoming more complex, are performing more functions, and providing additional services daily. The material in this section is intended for the reader who may not be completely familiar with some terminology, or aware of various facets of telecommunication network operation. While not intended to be exhaustive, the terms and concepts in this section will assist understanding the description of ISDN(s) in the next section.

The air of communications is used to transfer information between two or more individuals or "things." *Telecommunication* means to transfer information at a distance. A telecommunication system such as a telephone network provides economical information transfer to many separated users. This is because the telephone network uses *switches* so that many intermittent users can share the same resources or elements.

The resources include

- *terminals* such as the telephone
- *switching nodes* such as the nearest telephone exchange
- *transmission links* or *paths* among terminals and nodes

A simple telecommunications network is shown in Figure 1-7.

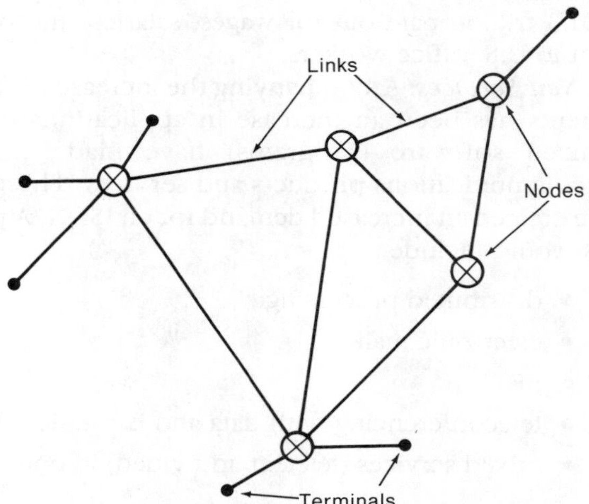

Figure 1-7. A telecommunications network.

Basic Communication Concepts

The intent of a communication is to transfer information between two, or among a number of, points. The communication may be a face-to-face conversation or a telecommunication over a telephone. It also could be the sending or receiving of a letter, watching television, reading a book, attending a lecture, or an art exhibit. Each of these communications requires a minimum of three common elements. They are a *source* generating information and placing it on a transmission *medium*, which relays the information to the *receiver* (Figure 1-8). The medium can be the air we breathe, communication lines of metallic wire, or the postal service that conveys letters and packages.

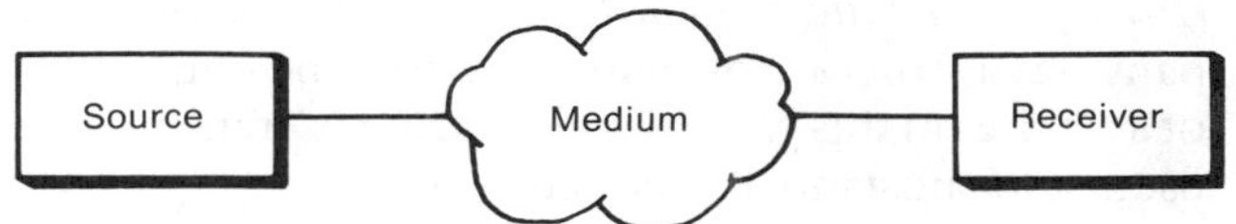

Figure 1-8. The three components needed for a communication.

The information transferred over any medium can be called a *message*. In data communications it is also called *data*.

Message communications involve a combination of message source, medium, and receiver that compose a communications *network*. In a communications network (also called a system) the emphasis may be on voice communications or on nonvoice applications. In a voice communications network, the source and receiver can be telephone instruments with communication lines in between. In a nonvoice network, the source and receiver can be a teleprinter, video display terminal (VDT), computer, or facsimile (fax) machine. Generically, these devices are called *data terminal equipment (DTE)*. Again, the transmission medium can be a communication line or a satellite in stationary orbit provided by a telephone company. In either example, the source and receiving units provide a user interface and media conversion device to the system for a human operator (Figure 1-9). Although the communication lines are usually telephone lines, they may also be wires or cables installed as private network media apart from the telephone company. An installation such as this might exist where a company decides to be responsible for its own communications lines.

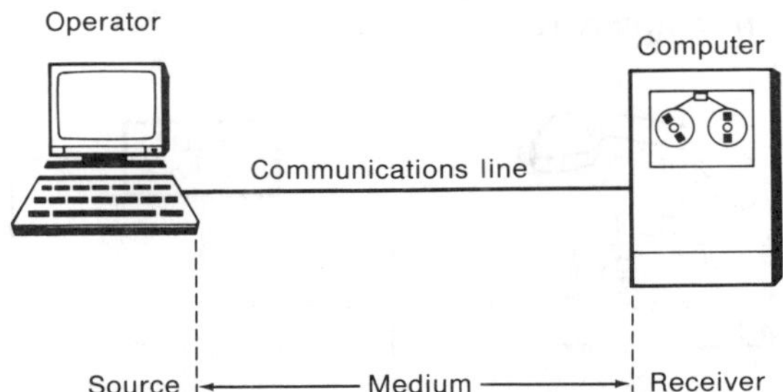

Figure 1-9. Operator interface with communications network.

Whether part of a telephone company installation or not, the installation of communication lines is expensive. The installation of a separate wire between each pair of users within a communications network, and especially through a telephone switching company with millions of customers, would be prohibitive. For example, in Figure 1-10 there are twenty-one wires interconnecting only seven users. Therefore, switches are used to overcome logistical impossibilities and expense. They are part of the transmission network. Switches can be located at company locations or at telephone company central or trunk offices. At company locations, the switches are called *private branch exchanges (PBXs)* or *private automatic branch exchanges (PABXs)*. The telephone company has a structure of switches across the country to serve the user needs. Use of switches in this way enables sharing of transmission resources between many users and substantially reduces costs.

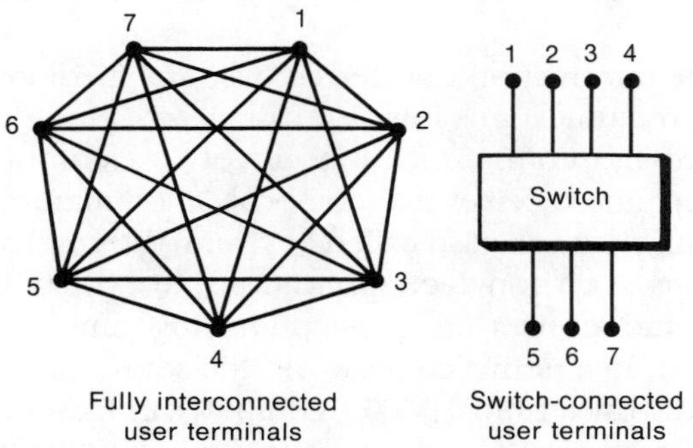

Figure 1-10. Fully interconnected and switch-connected users.

A simple telephone call illustrates the source, medium (including switch), and receiver concepts just described. In this example, another idea is introduced. Something must tell the switch to behave in a certain way to make the connection between two specific users that are the source and the receiver. This instruction is called switch *control*, which takes place when a telephone is dialed or pushbuttons are depressed, and *signaling* is generated to control the switch remotely (Figure 1-11).

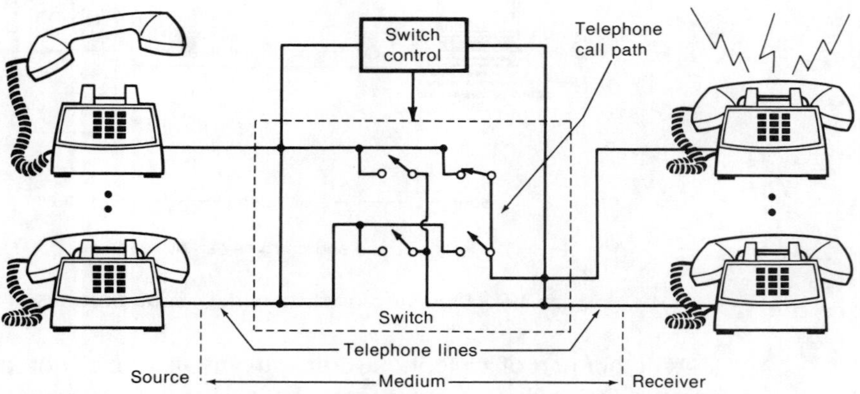

Figure 1-11. Placement of call by telephone switch control.

A telephone call is originated as follows:

1. An individual at the source lifts the handset off the cradle to start the call. This is called going *off-hook* and is detected at the local telephone office.
2. The local telephone office returns a dial tone signal heard by the caller on the source phone.
3. Rotary dialing or pushbutton depressing by the caller provides instructions to the switch phone.
4. A connection is established through the switch to the receiver and ringing is initiated. A ring-back signal is heard at the source telephone.
5. The receiver handset is lifted off the cradle and conversation may commence.

There are many other elements that go into making a telephone call but the relative context of a source terminal (in this example, a telephone), transmission medium (telephone lines and switches), and receiver terminal (another telephone) applies to all communications networks.

The telephone conversation that takes place in this example also provides insight to data communications. Normally, the individuals at each end take turns speaking. This is called *half-duplex transmission*—the medium carries conversations in either direction, but on an alternating basis. Other examples of half-duplex operation are police radio calls and tennis volleys.

If the callers could understand each other while talking at the same time, without attempting to take turns speaking, this would be *full-duplex operation*. Most telephones can operate in this manner and the caller can be interrupted by the listener by speaking at the same time. Full-duplex operation is simultaneous transmission in both directions over the same medium. Other examples of full-duplex operation are two-way streets and man/computer communications.

A *simplex communication* takes place when the caller at the source does nothing but talk while the individual at the receiver does nothing but listen. Radio and television broadcasts and one-way streets are other examples of simplex operation.

In voice or nonvoice communications the medium is called a *channel* that extends from the source to the receiver. Simplex and half-duplex channels require only two wires at the DTE, while four wires are usually needed for full-duplex operation. Under certain conditions, two wires can be used for full-duplex operation in data transmission.

An analog signal can be represented as a continuous though changing waveform (Figure 1-12). In the case of the transmission of a human voice over the telephone system, the sound waves consisting of fluctuating air pressure are converted within the handset to electrical form. (Remember, the source generates information and places it on a transmission medium.) Media conversion takes place through this mechanism at the source and in its inverse form at the receiver so that the original voice is reconstituted. The waveform characteristics of the voice transmission are contained within certain frequency limits determined by the telephone company circuits. The limits are generally 300 to 3,400 cycles per second (3,400 Hz). While adequate for analog voice communication they limit the data rate for nonvoice communication.

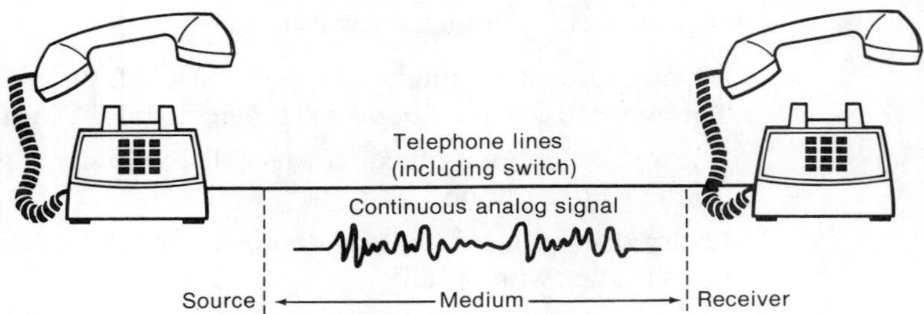

Figure 1-12. Analog signal on a telephone line.

A digital signal is not continuous and can have only discrete values. The most common digital signal is a string of pulses having only two, or *binary*, values such as on/off, light/no light, and 0/1. Digital communication is the transmission of these binary digits, or *bits*, over transmission channels. This is the language of the data terminal and computer.

For a long time, digital signal channels were not available from telephone companies (also called *common carriers*); analog channels were therefore used for digital data transmission. To send digital signals over analog channels, a device called a *modem* is needed. Modem stands for *mod*ulator-*dem*odulator and is a device that converts digital signals to analog form at the source for transmission over analog channels, and reverses the process at the receiver. Figure 1-13A depicts the conversion of digital 0s and 1s to analog 0s and 1s between a terminal and a computer. The ability to convert between analog and digital signals is called *encoding* and the transmission speed is expressed in bits per second (b/s). The modem is called a *data set* in the Bell System. Generically, modems are called data circuit-terminating equipment or DCEs.

It is also possible to convert analog voice to digital form using a *cod*er and *dec*oder or *codec* for transmission over digital lines (Figure 1-13B). Use of this voice conversion process is important to ISDN, since digital channels can now be used for both voice and nonvoice transmission.

With encoding techniques, it is possible to send data bits over analog voice communication channels at such common values as 300, 1,200, 4,800, or 9,600 bits per second. The ability to send data at a high rate makes it possible to improve communication efficiency and reduce costs through a technique called *multiplexing*.

Assume that a company regional office in Denver has eight terminals that can send data information at 1,200 b/s to a headquarters computer in Chicago (Figure 1-14A). On a per-terminal basis, 8 leased phase channels and 16 modems (one at each channel end) are needed to transfer data. Each telephone line transfers data at the rate of 1,200 b/s through each modem. Acquiring two multiplexers and two modems that can transfer information at 9,600 b/s over one 9,600 b/s telephone line will result in significant monthly and annual operating cost savings (Figure 1-14B). Introduction of digital telephone lines in the concept shown in Figure 1-14 permits removal of the modems that are needed for compatibility with analog telephone lines.

Information that is transferred between source and receiver often is in the

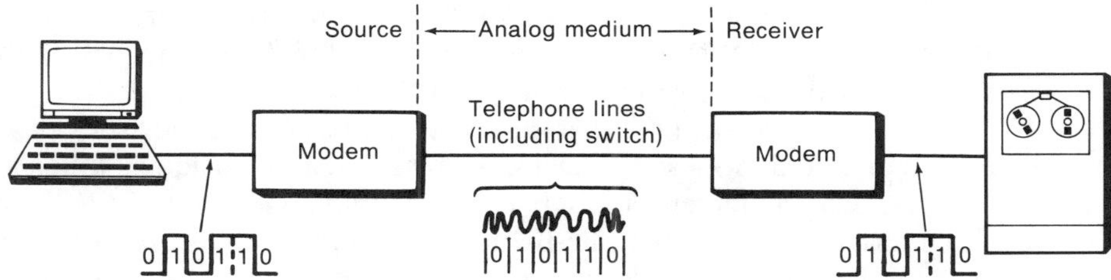

A. Modern conversion of digital signals for transmission on analog channels.

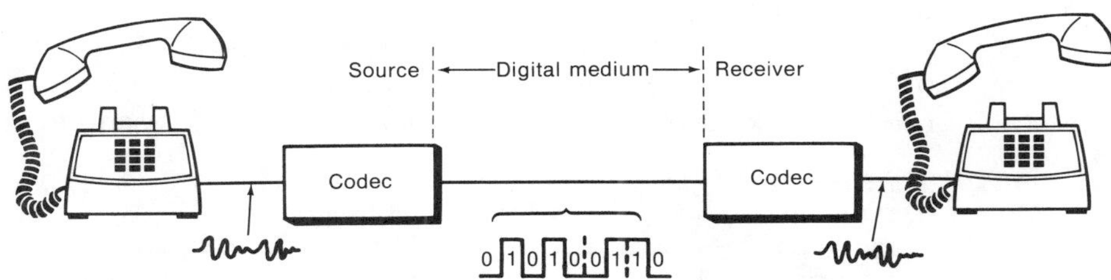

B. Codec conversion of analog signals for transmission on digital channels.

Figure 1-13. Conversion of signals for transmission.

form of bits that convey digital information. They are sent in groups of 5, 6, 7, or 8 bits that represent a *character* on a keyboard. (A character is a letter, figure, punctuation, or other sign contained in a message.) One of the most common character sets for keyboards is called the ASCII (American Standard Code for Information Interchange) code. The ASCII code is usually associated with *asynchronous transmission* where characters are sent one at a time at an intermittent rate dependent on the dexterity of the keyboard operator. Each set of character bits must be individually synchronized with the transmission rate of the system, for example at 300 b/s or 1,200 b/s. However, asynchronous transmission wastes transmission time because of its start-stop nature. *Synchronous transmission* has a constant time interval between characters or bits and is a more efficient means of transferring information at faster rates. ASCII characters can be sent synchronously as well as asynchronously.

Before data or character transmission can take place, certain physical connections must be made, as for example, between a modem and a telephone company line. Another very important connection is between the modem and data terminal. This is called an *interface*. Essentially, it is a boundary between two dissimilar devices. Definitions, in the form of standards, are made to state what the voltage, timing, and sequence of operation shall be across a boundary connector for data and control signals. RS-232-C is an example of such a definition. Physically, it is a standard for the small connector on the back of a DTE which is connected through a small cable to another connector at the modem. The RS-232-C designation is one interface standard for data transmission from the Electronic Industries Association (EIA). Other interface standards have been defined by the EIA in the United States, and by international standards organizations. Defining functions of interfaces is a major activity of standards organizations such as EIA, American National Standards Institute (ANSI), the CCITT, and International Organization for Standardization (ISO).

A simple example that describes the basic characteristics of a terminal connected to a modem for data transmission can be listed as follows: the DTE has an ASCII character set, operates half-duplex, with an RS-232-C interface ("to the modem," which is implied). Transmission is asynchronous at 300 b/s.

Acoustic couplers are a special form of interface, but the maximum possible data rate that can be sent is lower, such as 300 b/s. Acoustic couplers allow the use of a telephone handset as a connection to telephone lines that are used as transmission channels.

One last concept to be introduced is the *protocol*. A protocol is a rule, or set of rules, that initiates and maintains communications in a network. There are rules to make a phone call, and there are rules for sending and receiving

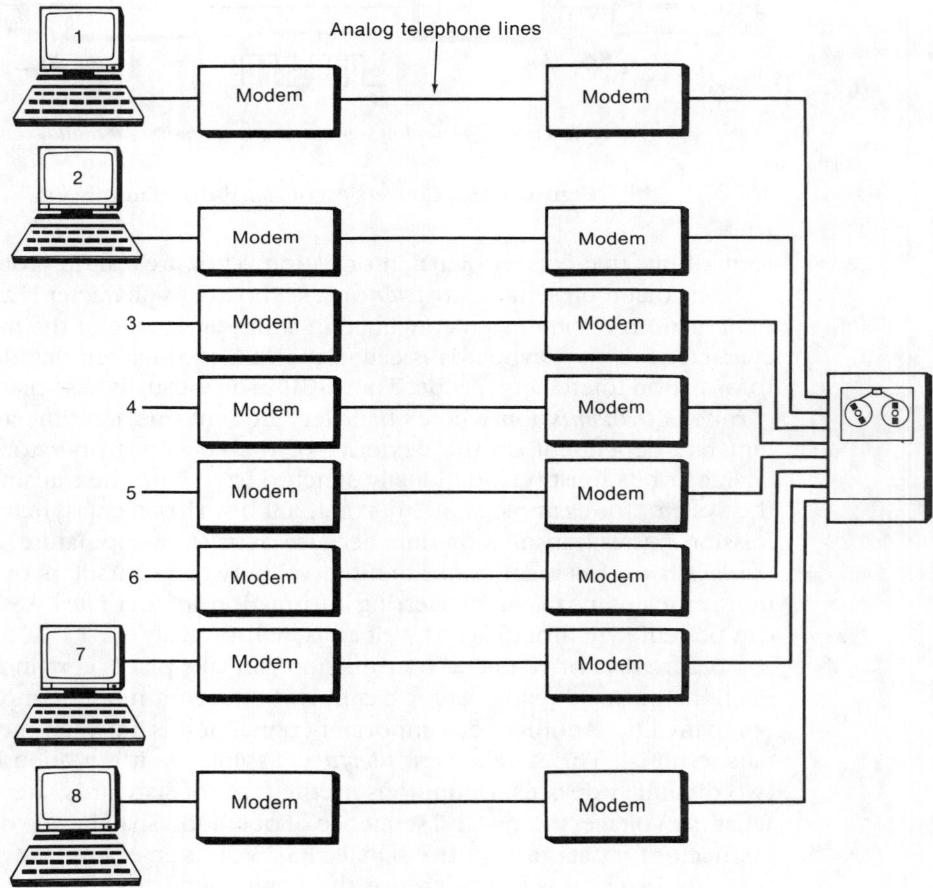

A. Individual modems and lines for each terminal.

Figure 1-14. Eliminating modems and telephone lines through multiplexing.

nonvoice information such as data. To place a phone call it is necessary for the dial tone to be heard before dialing after going off-hook. Similarly, with data transmission, certain steps such as acknowledgments between source and receiver are part of the protocol procedure. The RS-232-C interface defines not only a physical connector, but also the protocol encompassing certain procedural steps necessary to establish and maintain a connection.

Communication System Elements

This section examines the elements that have been mentioned within the context of explaining basic communication concepts. These elements are the many different kinds of communication terminals that are available to the user, the transmission media and switching facilities that are in use by common carriers, and the use of so-called "dedicated" networks. Each has a bearing on the future of ISDNs.

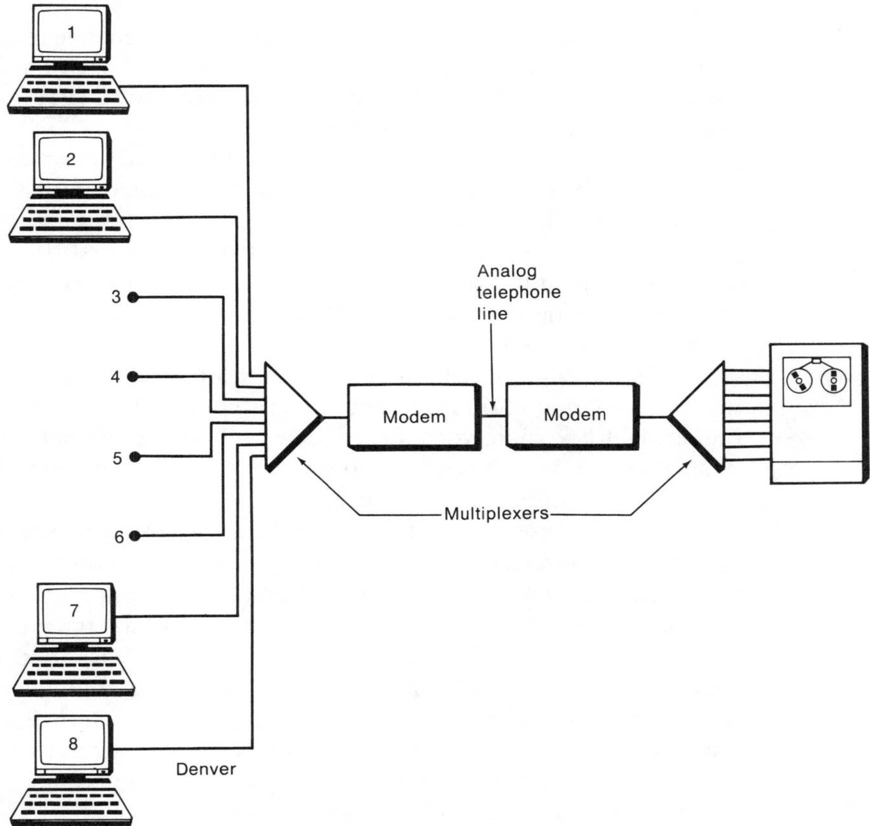

B. Replacement of modems and lines with multiplexers.

Figure 1-14. (cont.)

Terminals

So far there has been reference to types of user terminals: telephone, teleprinters, and VDTs which also have been called CRTs (cathode ray tubes). These are among the simplest available for information exchanges between locations, and can be categorized as voice, data, and graphics terminals.

Voice Terminals. Voice terminals can encompass telephones with multiple keys when many lines are connected to a telephone at a business location. The keys are used to select the lines for outgoing or incoming calls.

Associated peripheral equipment can include automatic call distribution (ACD), automatic dialer telephones, and telephone answering machines.

Automatic call distribution is used by the airline industry to respond to reservation requests. When all ticketing agents are busy, the caller is put on "Hold" and then is served by the first available agent. Other users of ACD are credit card companies (credit verification), and the banking and insurance companies.

Automatic dialing makes use of "intelligence" in the form of microchips built into a phone. Preprogrammed numbers can be dialed by pushing a single button.

More exotic voice terminals are available which change (digitize) the analog voice signal to digital form for storage on a memory device such as a disk that stores digital bits. Devices for voice store-and-forward (VSF), speech recognition, and voice response are on the market.

VSF is like an electronic voice mailbox. Improved communications are possible in a company where messages can be retained until the recipient can receive them. Time is saved through VSF in two ways. First, three out of four phone calls do not reach the intended party on the first try. Second, the VSF system can direct the voice messages to more than one recipient. The digitized voice bits on a memory storage disk can be sent, received, or redirected in voice form under computer control.

Speech recognition allows the recognition of specific spoken words of an individual. Recognition of certain words is applicable in air traffic control training, in security where voice prints are matched with a person's pronunciation of specific words, in battlefield control of weapons, and in sorting packages by routing that is under voice control.

Voice response is useful where an entry function is performed on a keyboard and a chosen set of words is orally required to prompt the user. Particular applications for voice response are in personal banking such as credit card verification, account status requests, and electronic funds transfer.

Data Terminals. Data terminals are frequently classified on the basis of characteristics and may be labeled as dumb, smart, and intelligent. Characteristics— and costs—frequently overlap. Common characteristics are a video display and keyboard provided for each terminal. After that, the extent of microprocessor computing and control power designed into a terminal determines operating features, flexibility in usage, and cost.

The major operating differences are that the dumb terminal is connected to a computer or retrieval service and acts as an electronic typewriter. A computer memory provides data for display to this person-machine interface. The smart terminal is able to operate, to a limited extent, by itself (*stand-alone*) without connection to a computer. The intelligent terminals have all the characteristics of smart terminals, but with additional features. Intelligent terminals have much more significant stand-alone ability because of extensive microcomputer power and memory storage.

Perhaps the best example of an intelligent terminal is the personal computer (PC), or microcomputer, with communications ability. Microcomputers and PCs are available that can communicate asynchronously and synchronously, and have extensive programming capability.

Point-of-sale (POS) terminals and *automatic teller machines (ATM)* provide a data transmission function. The POS records the sales transaction at a department or supermarket while the ATM handles a financial transaction between a bank and a customer.

Teleprinters (Figure 1-15) are a kind of terminal device usually associated with sending telegrams. They have an alphanumeric keyboard for sending (usually asynchronously), a printer for receiving, and a communications interface. Teleprinters, or teletypewriters, are being replaced by VDTs. Still, they retain a part of the marketplace because of cost effectiveness where a printed copy is required. A VDT with a printer is more expensive than a teleprinter by itself. A low data speed is dependent on maximum print speed that is determined by how characters are formed on a page, either mechanically or under electronic control.

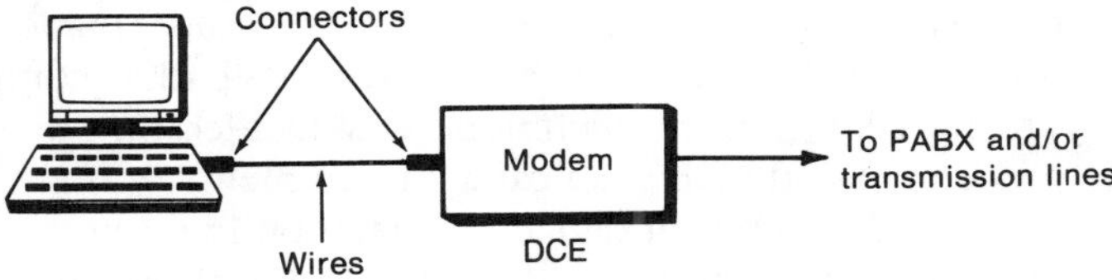

Figure 1-15. Interconnection between a terminal and modem through an interface.

Some models of teleprinters (and PCs) are popular for their portability. They are lightweight and carried as briefcases by traveling business people. Sometimes an acoustical coupler is built in and information can be transmitted by using the hotel room telephone, and sometimes a telephone jack is available. The receive-only (R-O) printer does not have a keyboard, but shares many characteristics of the teleprinters that do.

Graphics Terminals. Graphics terminals frequently include facsimile, although charts and graphics information can be generated and displayed on video displays. Facsimile enables accurate transmission of photographs, weather maps, signatures, and written or printed matter. For electronic mail distribution, the original graphic material is scanned by reflected light, electronic beams, or lasers, converted to electronic signals, relayed over transmission lines to a remote location, and recreated. In early units, the facsimile signals that are sent for transmission of an $8\frac{1}{2}'' \times 10''$ document could be expected to take several minutes—for example, 3 or 6 minutes. This is no longer true. Some analog units can send a page of text in less than a minute. Most digital facsimile units can send a page in less than 90 seconds. The image reproduction quality, or resolution, is related to the transmission speed—the higher the resolution, the longer the transmission time. Extremely short transmission times with high resolution are possible on digital machines when high-speed data transmission lines are available from a common carrier.

The problem of compatibility that has existed is being overcome and shows the value of standards. It was once impossible to send a message unless the same model facsimile machine from a particular manufacturer was used at both ends of the transmission. Now because of adherence to CCITT Groups 1, 2, and 3 Facsimile standards developed by international agreement, most of the new facsimile devices are interoperable and usage is rapidly growing.

Transmission, Transmission Control, and Connectivity

Currently, transmission signals on telephone lines can be analog or digital. A combination of both is likely when a circuit is completed across the country. Analog transmission links between telephone offices are the result of previous technology and capital investment. Digital transmission is an answer to more recent economic need: wire cable is expensive and below ground it is often difficult to find room for additional wire without tearing up streets. More efficient transmission over wire and other media was needed.

In 1962, AT&T introduced digital transmission to solve this problem. It is called *pulse code modulation (PCM).* Transistors made this technology possible due to their low cost and low power dissipation compared to vacuum tubes. The initial cost of this technique was justified on the basis of performance improvement and savings in capital investment.

As the number of digital transmission lines increased, it was apparent that additional cost savings would accrue if digital switches were to take the place of analog switches at telephone offices. Because costly conversions are needed at the analog and digital interfaces of the switch, switches now being installed by the telephone company are digital.

PCM is a technique that enables voice that has been changed into an analog signal to be changed to a digital signal. In the original AT&T version, the analog signal is sampled at 8 kHz, encoded at 8 bits/sample and transmitted at 64,000 b/s (64 kb/s). After traveling through switches and transmission lines to the telephone office nearest the receiver, the encoded voice signal of 64 kb/s is decoded and smoothed by filtering to analog and then returned to voice form (Figure 1-16). There are other kinds of analog-to-digital (A/D) and digital-to-analog (D/A) conversion schemes, but PCM is the most common. Bartee (1987) covers PCM and other conversion schemes, and their quality, in detail.

The one 64 kb/s digital signal just described is usually multiplexed with 23 other signals for sending through switches and transmission lines. The 24 digital voice signals are combined for efficient transmission over wire pairs in a cable or other media. Combining of the signals through time sharing is called *time-division multiplex (TDM).* The 24 channels of 64 kb/s with added framing bits (to delineate a group of bits) are sent at a data rate of 1,544 kb/s or 1.544 million bits per second (Mb/s). This is a T1 carrier and is a standard in North

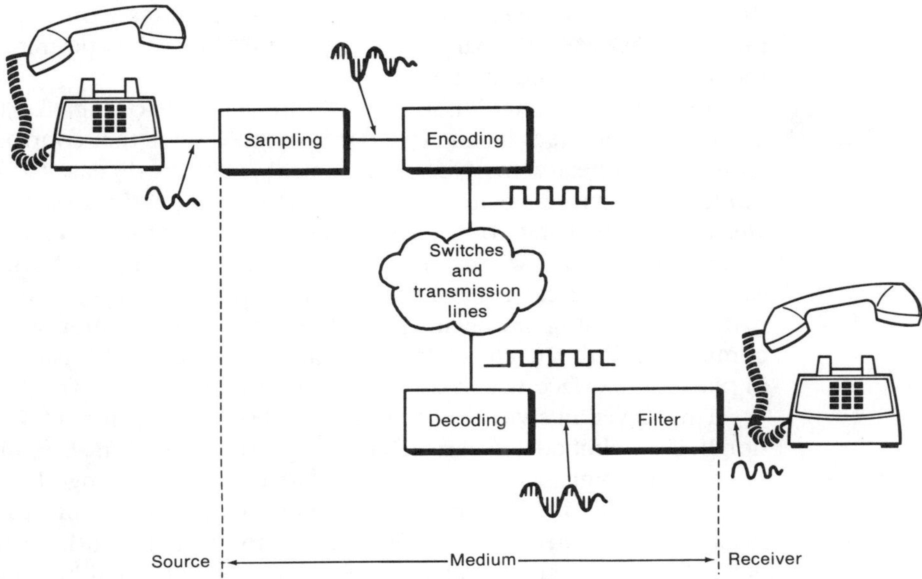

Figure 1-16. Digital transmission of voice for one channel.

America. Higher orders of TDM, such as 48 (T1C carrier) or 96 (T2 carrier) voice circuits are also sent over cable. The European standard combines 32 channels in a similar way, resulting in an overall rate of 2.048 Mb/s.

Previously, the circuits that had been designed for analog voice transmission used a process called *frequency-division multiplex (FDM)* to transmit multiple conversations over a single channel. Since its introduction, TDM has proven more efficient at shorter distances and is replacing FDM.

Switches were introduced earlier as part of the medium, and signaling was introduced as part of the control of the switches. The evolution of switching is based on three eras of technology: manual, electromechanical, and electronic. All three types of switches have survived simultaneously, although each type has predominated during a given period. Until recently, the number of telephone lines controlled by electromechanical switches has predominated, but that is changing in favor of electronic switches. Electromechanical switches are of two types, the "step-by-step" and crossbar. Both of these types are automatically controlled for routine functions by wiring logic, or *hardwired*. However, it is difficult or impossible to make wiring modifications for control of these switches. Beginning in 1965, electromechanical switches were replaced in public telephone networks by computer-controlled electronic switching systems (ESS). (Computer-controlled PBXs were available in 1963.) Hardwired, also called hardware, control of switches has changed to programming instruction sets linked to computers. This software control of switches also aids in flexibility in offering services to the public and is called *stored program control (SPC)*. For example, with SPC, "800" service is now feasible and allows a customer to receive calls without charge to the calling party.

SPC is a set of instructions stored in computer memory to set up calls handled by the switches. Solid state technology, based on VLSI circuits for microprocessors and smaller and cheaper memory, has permitted combining the telephone and computer.

Electronic switches based on SPC can be analog or digital. These switches can be considered as having two parts: the SPC units that control the switches and the switches themselves. The control is always digital, its only operating mode. An electronic switch, however, can be designed for switching analog (*a space-division switch*) or digital signals (*a time-division switch*).

Space-division switches provide a physical path through metallic or solid state contacts for each signal through the switching system. The signal on the path can be analog or digital. Space-division mode operation was chosen to be compatible with the electromechanical telephone plant (installations) already in place to interface with existing customer equipment.

Time-division switches use high-speed solid-state circuits. Digital information being switched is separated and assigned to time slots. (Recall TDM.) Using memory, the signals in time slots are shifted and interchanged with other time slots as needed to switch the travel path of the information bits to a destination. Because of this mechanism, the time-division switch handles only digital signals and cannot handle an analog signal unless that signal has been previously converted. In practice, most modern switches are a combination of space- and time-division design with signal conversion at the appropriate interface.

Signaling fast enough to control these computerized switches efficiently was needed to realize their potential. The Bell System responded with a system called *Common Channel Interoffice Signaling (CCIS)* to transfer control information between switches. Conventional analog signaling systems pass the control information, in the form of tones, within the same path that later carries the voice conversation (see Figure 1-11). This is called *in-band signaling*. In contrast, the CCIS sends the information over its own separate data network for control of many voice and data circuits (Figure 1-17). This is called *common-channel signaling (CCS)*. Essentially, a complete transparent subnetwork controls the switches by transferring control information between SPC processors at locations that are called *signal transfer points (STPs)*. With CCIS, phone calls and data message services are connected faster and more efficiently, thus saving time and operating expense. This also permits more service offerings to the customer.

Connectivity of voice and nonvoice terminal equipment at user premises depends on various transmission facilities such as wire pairs, coaxial cable, microwave radio, fiber optics, and geostationary satellites. Telephone offices are connected to these media to provide customer services. Cables consisting of hundreds of wires provide connections in a metropolitan area. Coaxial cables, radios, satellites, or combinations of both make the connections over long distances.

The block diagram of Figure 1-18 shows the basic elements of a telecommunication system that connects a source to the receiver through the various transmission media. At the users' premises, the equipment can consist of computers, terminals, modems, and PBXs. The modems and PBXs may be maintained by the user or telephone company at the customer's discretion. Typically, customer equipment is connected to the local telephone office switch via the *local loop* (also called *subscriber loop*) which usually consists of two wires. Other equipment can be digital multiplex equipment that can combine up to 96 voice channels for transmission to user locations. This digital connectivity uses the same voice digitization techniques (PCM) as the T-carrier system.

New digital technology permits half-duplex operation on wire pairs that looks like full-duplex to the user. High-speed data bursts are sent in alternate directions between the user and local office in a "ping-pong" fashion. This is called *time compression multiplex (TCM)* and is being tested extensively and successfully. TCM is part of the technological evolution to ISDN.

The metro/interoffice facilities between the local telephone office and another telephone office within a metropolitan area consists of many wire pairs in a cable used for transmission of the T1 carrier (24 voice channels), T1C carrier (48 voice channels), T2 carrier (96 voice channels).

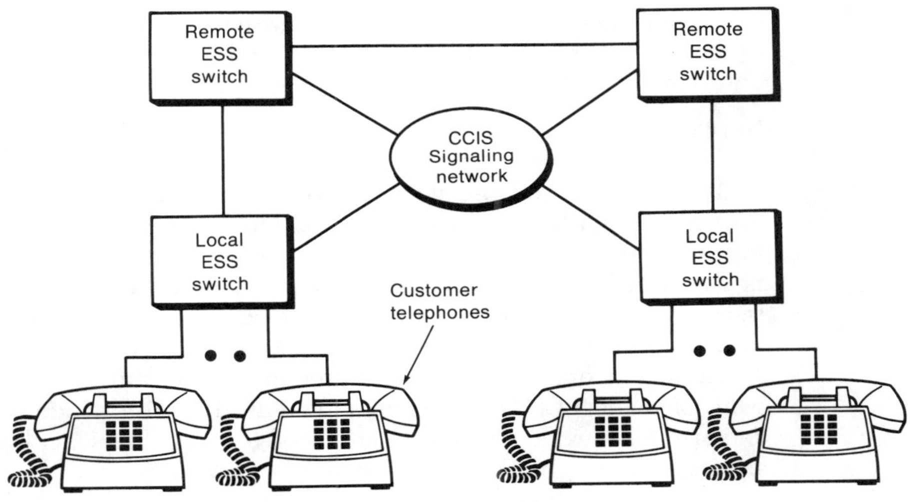

Figure 1-17. A separate network for control of the telephone system.

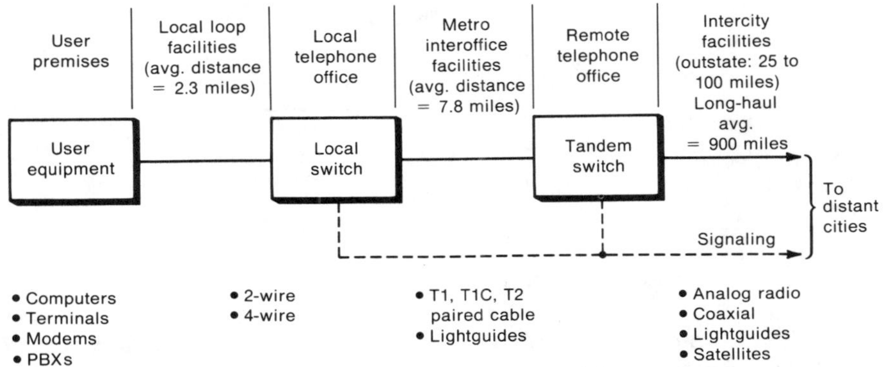

Figure 1-18. Telecommunication network elements and facilities *(after Skrzypczak et al., © 1981 IEEE).*

The intercity facilities for connectivity may consist of analog microwave radio, coaxial cable, lightguides (also referred to as fiber optic cable and optical waveguides) and satellites. All are capable of extremely high-capacity message transmission.

The reason for using analog radio over long distance is that it is still more economically advantageous over 250 miles (400 kilometers) than some form of digital communication. In contrast, digital connectivity has been proven less expensive for local loops and metro/interoffice facilities.

Fiber optic links have been installed in many locations: between Oakland, San Francisco and Sacramento; and between Washington, D.C., New York, and Boston.

Satellites are another important facet of long-haul digital connectivity. A number of satellites such as the WESTAR and COMSTAR have been in geosynchronous orbit for years. They are capable of carrying thousands of voice circuits simultaneously. New satellites with greater capacity such as the TELSTAR 3 series are also actively used.

Networks

At times there is overlapping terminology in communications that may be confusing. "Network" is one of those words. One use of the word network actually involves the technologies that are used to set up circuit paths for communication networks: circuit, message, and packet switching. A second use relates to transmission services that are provided as public or private networks. A public network is "plain old telephone service" (POTS) available to the general public. A private network may consist of leased lines for exclusive use of a large company. Elements of POTS are shown in Figure 1-18. To provide services, public and private networks can use circuit, message, or packet switching (Figure 1-19), and can use switched and nonswitched (leased) lines.

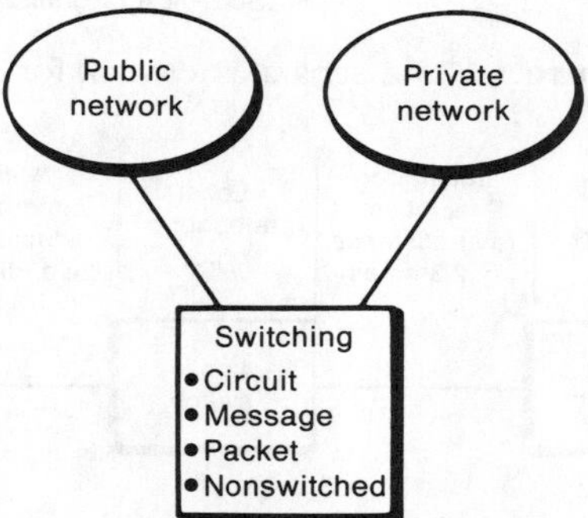

Figure 1-19. Public and private networks can use similar technology.

A *circuit-switched* or *line-switched network* provides service to subscribers by way of a dedicated path between two users. Telephone lines, switch connections, and other facilities are allocated on an exclusive basis for the duration of the call (Figure 1-20A). A telephone call is an example of circuit switching. The complete message (voice or nonvoice) travels without apparent delay between the source and receiver.

A *message-switched network* stores entire messages at switch locations for transmission on circuits when message channels and the called terminal become available. Each switch location has a memory disc for message storage and subsequent forwarding (store-and-forward) to the next nodes. (Figure 1-20B). (In data transmission a *node* is a location that interconnects data transmission lines.) Telegram service is an example of message switching. Delays between sending and receiving can accumulate as the complete message is stored at each successive node while awaiting transmission to the next node. Messages are not transmitted in "real time" as in circuit-switched transmission. Message switching is used where tradition or procedures require that a hard copy be provided for record purposes such as in military communications. Messages are usually sent and received on teleprinters at each user location.

A *packet-switched network* is a form of message switching. However, each message is divided into small units called *packets* (Figure 1-20C). After the message is broken up at the first node, each packet travels independently to the destination node where it is reassembled in proper order. Each packet has its own destination address. Packet switching is a store-and-forward technique, except that the storing is of very short duration compared to message switching. An important point is that the packets shown in Figure 1-20C can be mixed with many other packets. This permits more effective use of resources (transmission media and other facilities) than with the other switching techniques. Packet switching can be used for voice communications. Examples of packet-switched networks are Telenet and Tymnet. (See Chapter 3, "Packet-Switched Networks."

CCITT Recommendation X.25 provides the functional guidelines for implementing packet switching. There are many X.25 packet-switched networks in existence within the United States and abroad. Not all are compatible because Recommendation X.25 is not yet complete in all details and networks deviate in some aspects.

Services are a set of functions provided over a network's facilities. In the ISDN concept, one network could provide many services. Services may be switched or nonswitched (private or leased lines). Both service types are related to technical and pricing parameters provided by a carrier. Technical parameters to be selected by a customer willing to pay a fee for their use includes *bandwidth* (meaning capacity or range of transmission speeds, such as Hertz or bits per second and described as low-speed, voice-grade, or wide-band). Quality of transmission is another parameter because some voice and nonvoice channels are better than others.

A network can also be a series of points connected by communication channels and can refer to the public-switched telephone network (PSTN) or a private network dedicated to the use of one group of customers. Other network names are circuit-switched data network (CSDN) and packet-switched data network (PSDN).

Representative service offerings include those offered by AT&T Information Systems (formerly American Bell), American Satellite, GTE Telenet, Tymnet, and Western Union.

AT&T Information Systems/Net 1000 provides public-switched and private line services over a nationwide packet-switched communications network. Services are for data transmission, data processing, programming, and network management. A uniqueness of this VAN (value-added network) is the feature that enables dissimilar computers and terminals to communicate with each other.

A VAN is a network formed by leasing lines from traditional common carriers to interconnect computer-controlled switches at different nodes. Added features are offered through this arrangement and packet switching is an integral part. GTE Telenet and Tymnet are examples of other carriers basing services on packet-switching technology.

American Satellite, RCA Americom, Satellite Business Systems, and Western

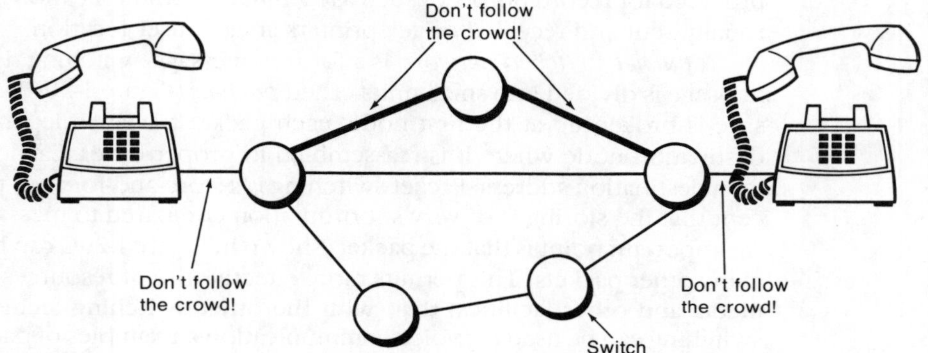

A. *Circuit switching with dedicated physical path.*

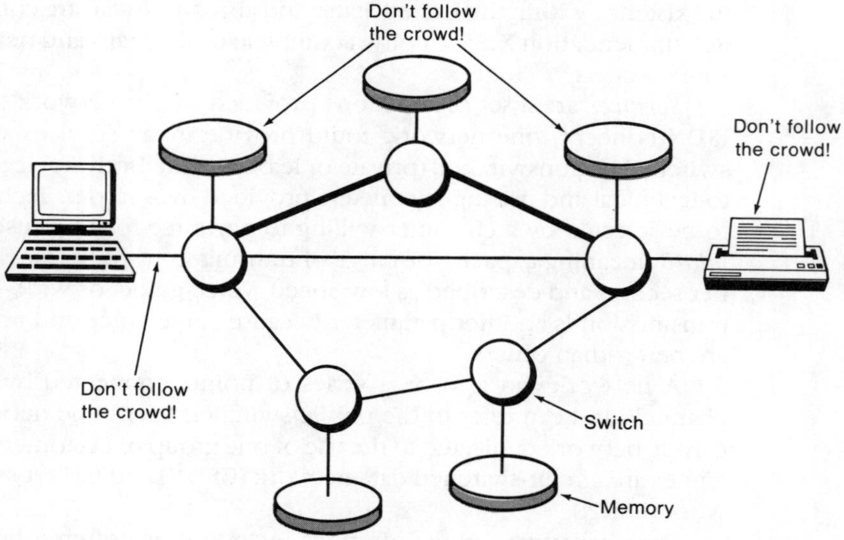

B. *Message switching with temporary memory storage for complete message relay.*

Figure 1-20. Circuit, message, and packet switching.

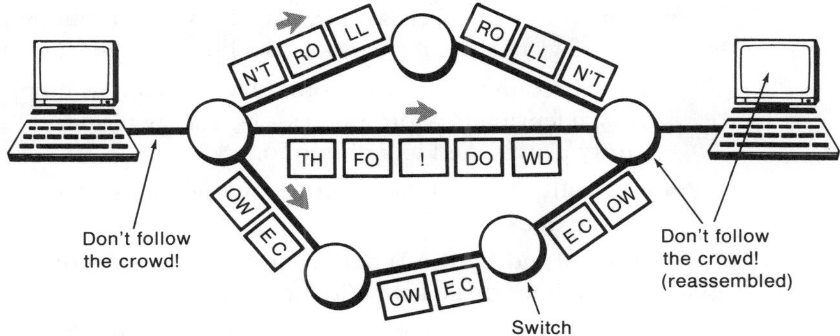

C. Packet switching with limited size message packets.

Figure 1-20. (cont.)

Union are examples of companies that offer private line services over satellite facilities. The main attraction of using satellite channels for long-haul is the lower cost compared to terrestrial circuits. The investment cost of a satellite system is the same whether the message travels 200 or 2,000 land miles. This makes satellite usage economically attractive over longer distances for large volumes of traffic.

Western Union also offers a service that is similar to the public telephone system with an important difference. While the public telephone system is voice-oriented with telephone terminals, the Western Union service uses teleprinters in a similar way for text transmission. Teleprinters, which have been traditionally used, and display terminals communicate with each other on a message basis. This service is called Telex II since it incorporates the Teletypewriter Exchange Service (TWX) that was formerly owned by AT&T. On a technical basis, it is a message-switched, low-speed (110 b/s), half-duplex service that uses ASCII code for the teleprinters and terminals.

Just as video game machines are dedicated computers given to a single function, Telex is a good example of a *dedicated network* where a system may be used for a single purpose. Cable TV (CATV) is also a dedicated network. Facsimile Service from Graphnet, Incorporated was formerly a dedicated network. This was a VAN using store-and-forward techniques to transmit digitized graphic images (facsimile) on the network. Graphnet later added digital data communications services using its store-and-forward facilities base so that it was no longer a one-purpose, dedicated network.

Telemail, offered by GTE Telenet, uses packet switching and can accept messages from many kinds of data terminals that would normally be incompatible. Incompatibility is overcome through speed and protocol conversion. GTE Telenet has announced intentions of providing interfaces for facsimile, voice store-and-forward (voice mailbox), and high-speed data transmission. Adding these services makes it a nondedicated network that encompasses the ideas of the ISDN.

Local area networks (LAN) are another class of system. LANs are

- high-speed, private networks for voice and nonvoice applications

- limited in geographical size, usually within a building or a number of buildings in a small area such as a business park or university campus
- an interconnection of multiple devices such as computers, data terminals, teleprinters, word processors, energy monitors, alarm systems, security alarms, and video monitors
- normally, but not necessarily, independent of common carrier telephone lines
- unregulated by the Federal Communications Commission (FCC) if no phone lines or digital radio are used
- based on media such as twisted wire pair, multiple wire cable, coaxial cable, fiber optic cable, or digital radio

A LAN is usually designed and built with a certain physical connection pattern, known as *topology* in mind. The topology has three basic forms: *star*, *ring*, or *bus* (Figure 1-21). Star topology has a central switch making terminal-to-terminal (point-to-point) connections for information transfer. The PABX is an example of a central switch. With the ring topology, information is transferred in one circular direction between points without a control switch. In bus topology, one or more cables interconnect devices for information transfer, without a central switch but under a distributed control mechanism.

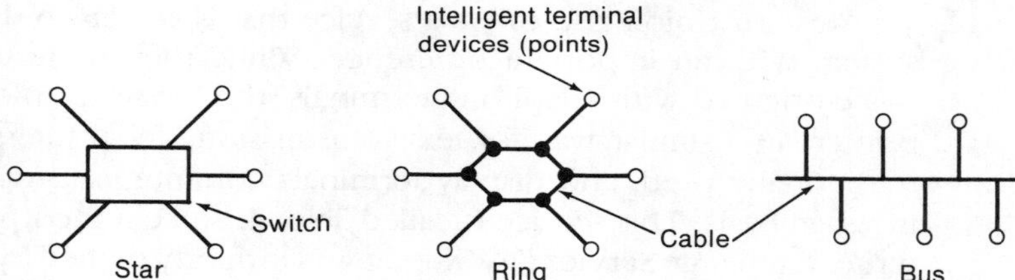

Figure 1-21. Basic LAN physical patterns or topologies.

Messages from different terminals travel over the same medium (resource sharing) when using a ring or bus topology. A contention exists to determine which message has precedence to be sent. Protocols based on standards resolve the contention. The use of microprocessors in LANs permits progress to be made in the distribution of network control and interfacing. LAN standards have been developed by the Institute of Electrical and Electronics Engineers (IEEE) Project 802 technical committee. More than 50 companies market LANs in various topologies and with different degrees of user participation, hardware sales, and installation. Applications for LANs are in office automation, business data processing, personal computing, real-time voice, and video.

ISDN

ISDN is a concept that is nearing reality. It is designed to provide a broad range of user communication needs through a total digital communication system.

Many necessary components already are in place. The current digital telephony and digital data communication networks that are now in existence are essential elements for evolving to the ISDN.

Telephone networks have already evolved through two distinct states, and are now embarking on the third. The three network states are called Integrated Analog Network (IAN), Integrated Digital Network (IDN), and ISDN.

The IAN stage was dependent on switched networks providing voice or voice-simulated (e.g., modem conversion of data) services by managing costs through the application of analog transmission and analog-switching technology.

The IDN stage is dependent on switched networks providing voice or voice-simulated services by minimizing costs through the application of digital transmission and digital-switching technology.

The ISDN stage depends on switched networks providing user-to-user (end-to-end) digital transparency where voice and nonvoice (e.g., data) services are provided over the same transmission and switching facilities.

When one assumes the collective wisdom of the network providers, the network users, and the network manufacturers it appears that the public switch network (PSN) of the future will be an ISDN.

The CCITT (1985) defines ISDN as a "network, in general, evolving from a telephony integrated digital network, that provides end-to-end digital connectivity to support a wide range of services, including voice and non-voice, to which users have a limited set of standard multi-purpose user-network interfaces."

Standards for various ISDN capabilities are in various stages of completion. Different standards organizations have completed a substantial number of recommendations concerning ISDN and this work is continuing. This standardization process has now reached the point where a number of manufacturers are developing and testing product lines to offer ISDN features, functions, and interfaces.

Features and functions associated with ISDN include

- end-to-end digital service
- standardized access interface structures
- 2B+D for small users (B = 64 kb/s, D = 16 kb/s)
- 23B+D for large users (B = 64 kb/s, D = 64 kb/s)
- well-defined basic services and supplementary services

Users perceive potential benefits such as

- faster and more complete information access
- increased productivity and better time management due to new services (e.g., voice mail)
- ease of adding new services
- reduced cost due to voice and data integration in local access areas
- simplified network management and control
- reduced operation and maintenance costs due to standardized system interfaces

Some potential problems with narrowband ISDN are

- high development costs
- evolution from voice network not the solution for data
- implementation too late for LAN users
- obsolescence when broadband ISDN is introduced

Problems may also arise because narrowband ISDN is vendor-driven, not market-driven. (See Bartee (1985) for a detailed discussion of the technical aspects of ISDN.)

CCITT View

The discussion in this section expresses essentially a CCITT view as portrayed in CCITT draft Recommendations and related documents. The United States is a participant and makes contributions to CCITT proceedings, but the CCITT ISDN approach reflects a strong influence of European administrations where the provision of communication services is a government monopoly. The U.S. view differs, for example, in the sense that there will be a number of different competing service providers.

The original ISDN concept was based on the premise that a digital public telephone network would be transparent to the type of information being transmitted—whether speech, facsimile, or bulk data. It was assumed that the ISDN would be based on the public telephone network. This rationale implied that an ISDN network would be a digital successor to the public telephone network. In the United States, this led to the idea of "multiple ISDNs" with similar characteristics and interconnection of these networks. As CCITT studies have progressed, recognition has been made that this may be an oversimplified approach. In the real world it may be necessary to be aware of the types of information being transmitted. Now the concept has been introduced that a limited set of multipurpose user-network interfaces will be used to interconnect users with the ISDN. "An ISDN" would then be a conglomerate of mutually interconnected networks not necessarily having the same characteristics, with subscriber access via standard ISDN interfaces.

The predominant characteristic in ISDN planning is that a broad range of voice and nonvoice services will be supported. These services will be integrated through digital connectivity between users. Services such as telemetry, security monitoring, electronic mail, electronic funds transfer, voice, facsimile, graphics, videotex, bulk data transfer between computers, and nonbroadcast video are intended to be available through an ISDN. The ISDN services are expected to use public and leased data channels, network interconnection, and circuit- and packet-switched facilities. Media will consist of wire pairs, coaxial cable, fiber cable, and satellite systems. Message switching does not appear as part of the current planning.

A fundamental principle underlying ISDN service integration is that the interfaces between the user and the network will be defined and kept to a minimum (Figure 1-22). Currently, there are many interfaces for connecting between a customer terminal and a network. Many would be eliminated as the ISDN interfaces become defined and implemented. An interface such as RS-232-C could operate in an ISDN environment but would need an adaptor. Such an interim solution will eventually be phased out. Another key principle is that bearer services (facilities such as circuit- or packet-switched channels provided by a carrier) be limited. The premise is that the communication carriers would provide the user with a minimum number of standard channel services over circuit- and packet-switched facilities.

Figure 1-22. A minimum number of user/network interfaces are planned for the ISDN.

The ISDN recommendations define functional groupings of user equipment and various reference points between these groupings, as indicated in Figure 1-23. The major functional groups are terminal equipment (TE), terminal adapter (TA), network termination 2 (NT2), and network termination 1 (NT1).

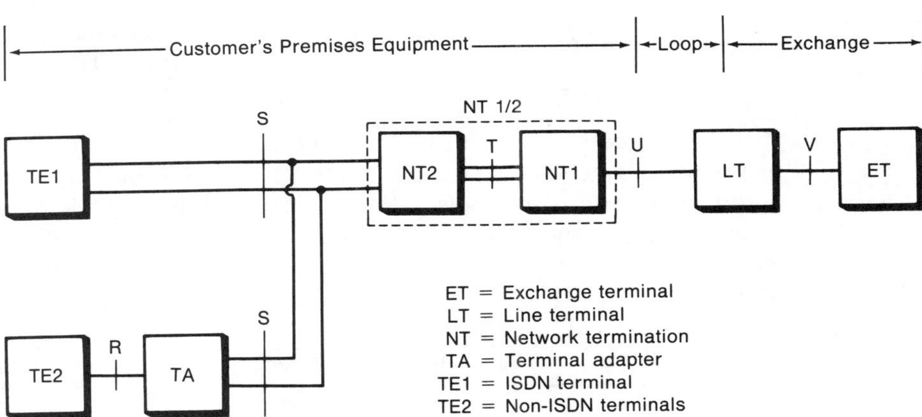

Figure 1-23. Interface recommendations for ISDN.

Terminal equipment (TE) includes devices that generate and receive information (e.g., a personal computer). Terminal adapters (TA) convert non-ISDN interfaces to an ISDN interface. Any TE2 can therefore be connected to ISDN through a suitable TA. In the figure, reference point R refers to the interface between the TE2 and the TA. Network terminations NT1 and NT2 provide distinct functions, but may be combined in a PABX or LAN. NT2 refers to on-premises switching or other intelligence that is employed by the user for communication. PABXs and LANs may contain NT2 functions. NT2 functions are separated from TA or TE1 functions by reference point S.

NT1 functions are restricted to connect the users' equipment to the digital subscriber transmission system. Reference point T designates this separation between NT1 and NT2 functions. NT1 and NT2 functions may be combined as a single functional group, which is designated at NT1/2. Such a configuration is indicated in Figure 1-23.

In the United States, the NT1 function is considered customer premises equipment, whereas in most other countries it is considered part of the network. Reference point U has been designated as the attachment between an NT1 and the digital subscriber line system.

The reference points R, S, T, and U are defined for basic and primary access in North America in Table 1-1. These interfaces provide the functions required to match the subscriber's terminals to the network. These are layer 1 functions in the Open System Interconnection (OSI) model as described in Appendix C.

Table 1-1. North American ISDN Reference Points

Reference Points	Basic Access	Primary Access
R	Existing interfaces (e.g., RS-323)	Same as basic
S	4-wire, 144 kb/s (2B+D), 192 kb/s (2B+D+overhead)	Same as basic
T	Same as S for basic	4-wire, 1.54 Mb/s (23B+D+overhead)
U	2-wire, echo canceler	4-wire transmission system (e.g., T1)

User's access to ISDN is by way of interface structures. There are two principal structures denoted as the basic interface and the primary interface. These interface structures and their channel types are listed in Table 1-2. The two primary interface structures correspond to primary rates of 1.544 Mb/s which is in common use in the United States and 2.048 Mb/s which is in more common use in Europe.

Table 1-2. ISDN Interface Structures

Basic	Primary
2B+D, where B = 64 kb/s and D = 16 kb/s	23B+D or 30B+D, where B = 64 kb/s and D = 64 kb/s

In addition, even higher H channel rates have been defined for higher speed data, fast facsimile, video teleconferencing, and the like. They include

$$H_0 = 384 \text{ kb/s}$$

$$H_{11} = 1{,}536 \text{ kb/s}$$

$$H_{12} = 1{,}920 \text{ kb/s}$$

Still higher rates are being considered for broadband ISDN, which we will explore soon.

The ISDN is being designed in such a way that current service dedicated networks may be integrated into "an ISDN" where appropriate and cost-effective. Dedicated facilities to be integrated are those of the telephone networks, circuit- and packet-switched data networks, and telex. Private line, PBX, and LAN networks are not expected to be integrated, although they will be interconnected to the ISDN (Figure 1-24). The evolution is expected to take one or two decades. This evolution will probably take place according to national or geographic boundaries based on national priorities or needs. Facilities that are already in place are to be part of this transition. The present digital networks are to be the basis for the integration of services based on economic considerations and technological evolution. Equipment is not being discarded except through obsolescence. The 64 kb/s PCM digital signal, the T-carriers, stored program control, and user-network signaling are to be an integral part of the ISDN.

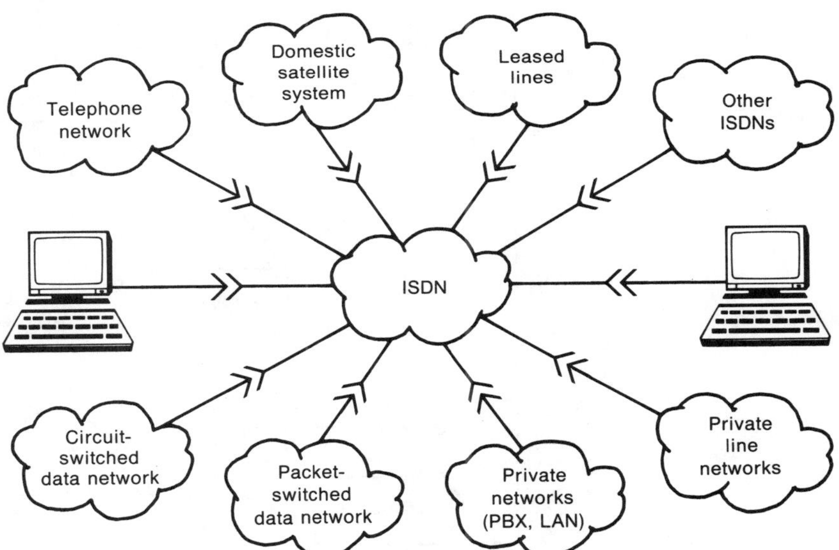

Figure 1-24. Interim interconnection of dedicated networks and ISDN(s) via interfaces.

Other factors influencing the integration and evolution to an ISDN are the competitive and regulatory atmosphere that exists in a country. The United States has many providers of communications facilities. Other countries have one—an organization of Post, Telegraph, and Telephone (PTT)—that acts as the sole common carrier. The multiplicity of carriers in the United States implies multiples or a conglomerate of ISDNs in the United States. For the last 15 years, competition in telecommunications has been increasingly encouraged. Restructuring AT&T and its subsidiaries will influence ISDN development in the United States.

Capabilities

In the United States, AT&T and other carriers have recognized the need for flexibility in designing the ISDN so it will provide the many services that have been defined and others that are still unforeseen. The following view of ISDN in the United States is based on papers from AT&T.

An example of the wide range of bit-rate information requirements for various services is shown in Figure 1-25. The message characteristics for alarm services are very different from requirements of bulk data, facsimile, and video. The alarm services have very low average bit rates (10 b/s), and short message lengths. The full-scan video at the other end of the scale requires 1.5 to 6 Mb/s depending on available transmission techniques. The message density ranges from very intermittent or "bursty" to continuous. Message lengths vary from a hundred to billions of bits. Planning for this range of user needs is a formidable task.

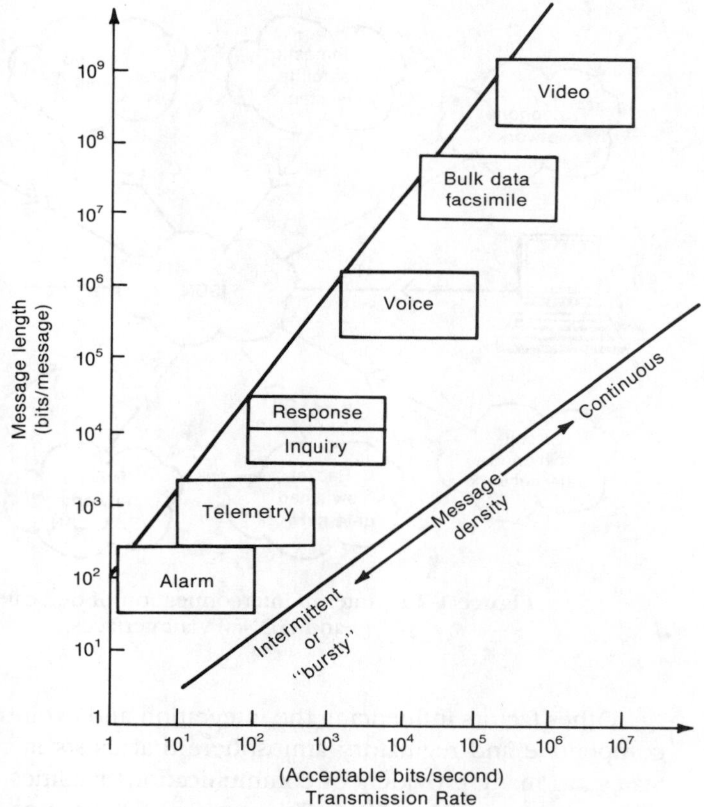

Figure 1-25. Range of message lengths, density, and transmission rates for ISDN planning *(after Skrzypczak et al., © 1981 IEEE).*

A customer will have access to an ISDN through a standard interface of two 64 kb/s B-channels (Figure 1-26). A 16 kb/s D-channel also is to be available to the customer for signaling and low-speed data. The Customer Controller provides a standard interface protocol from the customer premises to the multibandwidth *digital pipe*. The dynamically assigned bandwidth of the pipe is variable and will depend on the customer's needs for each transmission. The variable bandwidth concept is also used for circuit- and packet-switched transmission between the serving center, other networks, and other customers. Services that will be included are teleconferencing, video conferencing, facsimile, computer connections, and data base networks (Dorros 1983).

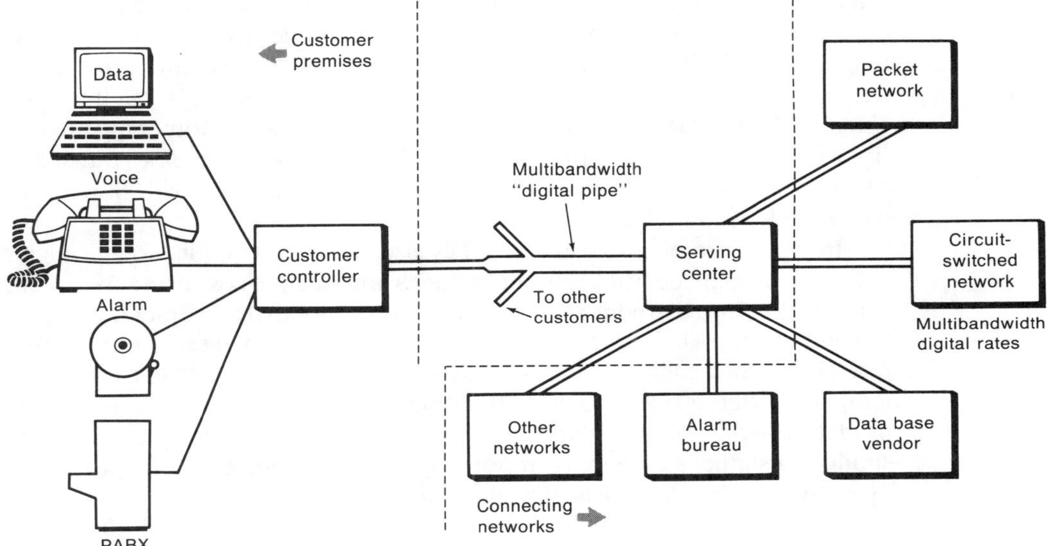

Figure 1-26. ISDN approach in the United States *(after Dorros, © 1983 IEEE).*

In the transition toward the ISDN, AT&T has announced that end-to-end, digital connectivity will be introduced using major portions of its present network. This is possible because the system can be converted to handle digital signals. Capabilities will be installed for transmission of voice and nonvoice services.

One is Circuit Switched Digital Capability (CSDC). The CSDC will allow users to send and receive analog voice and digital data alternately on the same customer connection, the local loop. A second capability is called Local Area Data Transport Service (LADTS) which is intended for two types of users: the occasional user who does not require voice communications while accessing a data base, and another user who requires voice communications while accessing a data base. A third capability, Data Bridging, is intended to transmit digital data, such as graphics or teleconferencing, from one user location to another or to many (point-to-point and multipoint). Basic packet-switched service for private networks on shared switches will be available soon. Enhanced services (such as packet assembly, disassembly, and data storage) have been announced at AT&T Information Services/Net 1000. Other U.S. carriers such as GTE Telenet and Tymnet are also offering competitive packet-switched services.

The U.S. networks are examples of evolution toward integrated digital network facilities from the in-place quality telephone service. France, in contrast, has leapfrogged a generation of analog technology to go to advanced digital transmission and switching. In 1971, the telephone system in France was considered obsolete. Now it is considered by the French to be one of the most modern in the world as the result of establishing a national priority, coupled with massive investment and development plans. New equipment embodies the latest technology in the TELEMATIQUE program of the French PTT. Extensive installation of digital switches, transmission, and common channel signaling are basic elements in the modernization process. Only digital switches are expected to be installed in the future, with many time-division switches already in place. Nearly 50 percent of the local network and 25 percent of the long-haul network were already digital five years ago (Dorros 1983). A satellite service, Telecom 1, will offer digital services to large business customers via earth stations near the customer's premises. The French packet network, Transpac, has been in operation since 1978 and has been interconnected to U.S. packet networks, Telenet and Tymnet, since 1979.

In Japan, progress toward the ISDN is also based on digital technology. Metallic wire is in place now, with lightguides and satellites expected to play major roles in the future. A videotex service such as CAPTAIN (character and pattern telephone access information network system) has been in service since 1979. A model network called HI-OVIS (high interactive optical visual interactive system) will offer services to 10,000 subscribers. Services to be offered on the model network include alarm services, telemetry, teletext, videotex, and facsimile. Facsimile is extremely important in Japan because written Japanese ideography (Kanji) is fairly easily sent on fax.

The United States, France, Japan, and other countries—including Canada, the United Kingdom, Italy, and West Germany—all are contributors to the evolution toward an ISDN. Evolution in each country is based on different geographical, political, economic, and regulatory influences. Nonetheless, there is a commonality in the sense that the developing technology is exportable for international trade. Extensive penetration of the U.S. facsimile market has been made by digital machines made in Japan and sold under American and Japanese brand names. Digital switches made in France and the United States are being exported around the world. Computers, PBXs, video terminals, and other devices based on digital processors are part of this marketplace. Compatibility is a prerequisite for success, and standards are needed.

Standards

Although many national and international standards organizations contribute to the development of ISDN standards, the original one is the CCITT. (See Appendix A.)

The CCITT conducts work through a number of study groups. Study Group XVIII, Digital Networks, is concerned with ISDN. Various subgroups address specific questions and make recommendations which are published in a series of documents before approval by the CCITT plenary assembly that meets every four years. The VIII plenary assembly's recommendations appear in a series of volumes known as the *Red Books*. The ISDN Series I recommendations in Figure 1-27 are found in *Red Book III* (CCITT 1985). This volume includes over 450 pages devoted to ISDN recommendations.

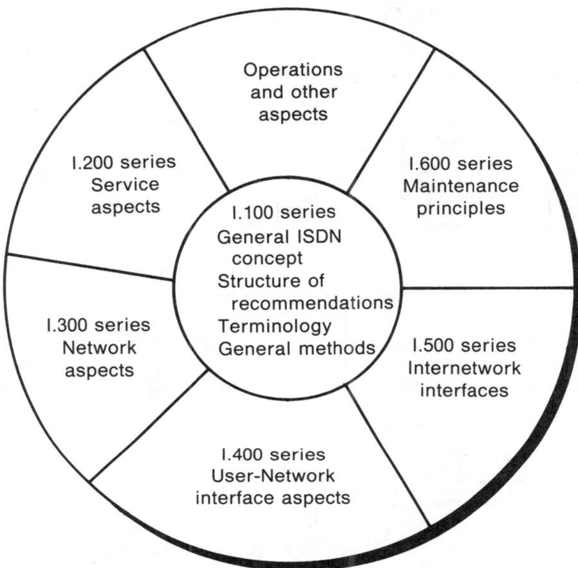

Figure 1-27. I-Series recommendations for ISDN.

In the United States, ISDN national standards are being developed by a forum known as the T1 committee. The output of this committee also provides input to the United States CCITT working groups. The T1 committee's structure and purpose are discussed later in this chapter.

Three of the CCITT draft Recommendations are highlighted here to illustrate the scope of the work.

The principles of ISDN are given in I.120. Support is given for such principles as

- voice and nonvoice services on the same network
- use of circuit-, packet-, and nonswitched connections
- use of a layered protocol structure
- recognition that ISDNs may be implemented according to national requirements

Draft Recommendation I.411 provides reference configurations and conceptual drawings for a user's physical access to a network in terms of reference points and functional groupings.

Draft Recommendation I.412 defines channel structures with respect to information and signaling transfer and access capabilities. Important principles in this Recommendation are that signaling information is carried on a D-channel (16 kb/s), separate from the main user information B-channel (64 kb/s) (Figure 1-28A). This, in principle, permits complete transparency and freedom of use of the B-channel to the user. The intent is to achieve lowest cost for the physical interface arrangements and to allow maximum standardization of terminal and other equipment with respect to the network interface. A C-channel is associated with an analog channel as a hybrid access arrangement that may be used in a transitional period while full digital access to ISDN is not yet universally available. The C-channel may carry telemetry, packet-switched data, and signaling information on the same line with analog voice (Figure 1-28B).

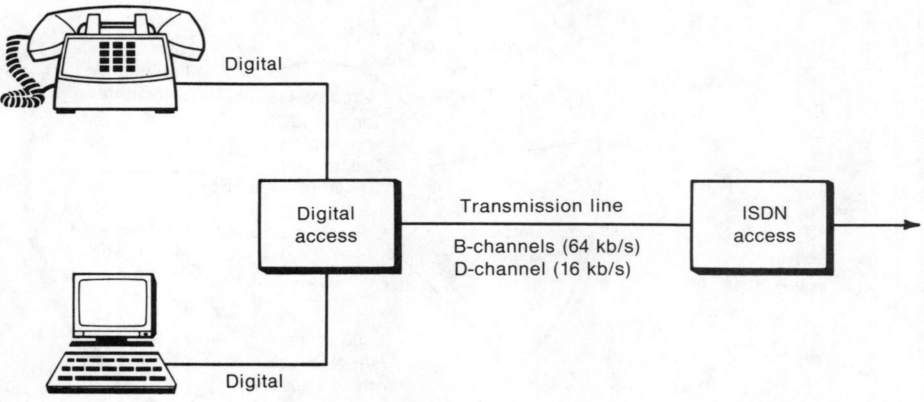

A. B- and D-channels for ISDN.

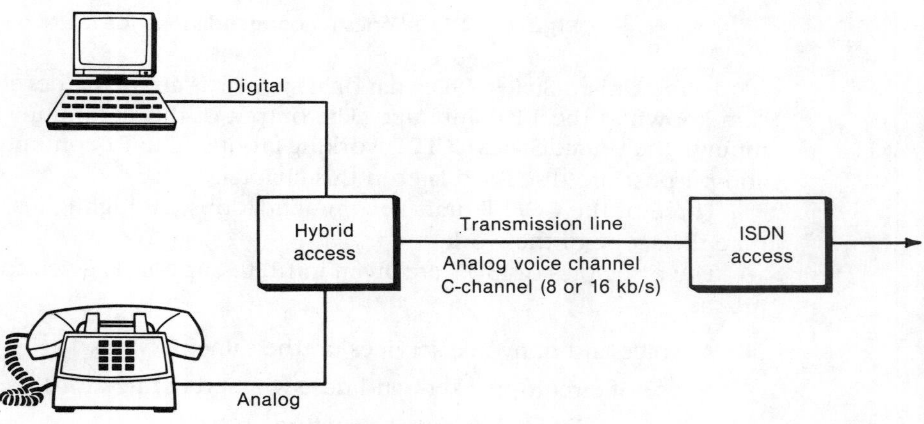

B. Analog and C-channels for ISDN (interim).

Figure 1-28. Comparison of user/network channel access arrangements for ISDN.

While the definition of the ISDN is continuing, other standards are being adopted by the CCITT that will be important to the ISDN. One of these is CCITT Recommendation X.25, which sets the criteria for interfacing subscriber data terminals to packet-switched data networks. It specifies the interface characteristics, access procedures, packet formats, packet lengths, and other parameters for operation between the user and network.

Another standard that serves as a guideline for developing the ISDN is the OSI reference model. (See Appendix C.) There are two draft proposals in existence. The first was developed by the ISO for data networking, and the second is under development by the CCITT to encompass all networks. The CCITT ISO OSI reference model is known as CCITT Recommendation X.200, Reference Model of Open Systems Interconnection for CCITT Applications.

In the past, consideration was not given by vendors to protocols, standards, or network architectures for connection with a competitor's products. A manufacturer's own set of conventions for interconnecting its equipment was often developed to gain a competitive edge. However, the ISO recognized a need for an "open" system where the terminals and computers (end-systems) of one manufacturer could be interconnected to those of another. The reference models provide a framework of standard evaluation and development for interconnections and communications between end-systems. The models provide seven layers of functional groupings of protocols. The grouping of the seven layers permits changes in one layer without disturbing others. Protocol structure development for one layer can proceed without disturbing the whole structure. (See Appendix B for details on OSI.)

Standards studies have led to a general conclusion that the ISDN concept is a practical idea. Field testing of ISDN is currently under way in many countries. The CCITT focus is on developing standard user-network interfaces on a functional basis. Defining these interfaces and interconnection standards between networks will have a number of beneficial effects. One is that manufacturers will have confidence in the long-term utility of their equipment. Another is that innovation will be promoted within the functional guideline of the standards. Nevertheless, before a user can connect to a network through a wall socket comparable to a universal telephone outlet, a number of issues remain. Some of these issues are discussed in the next section, Issues and Actions.

Broadband ISDN

During the study period 1984-1988, a taskgroup of study groups XVIII provided preliminary recommendations and guidelines for a broadband version of ISDN denoted B-ISDN. More detailed recommendations for B-ISDN are expected by the conclusion of the 1989-1992 study period.

The B-ISDN concept will be implemented some years in the future to provide a wide range of audio, video, and data applications. Both switched and nonswitched connections are supported. The B-ISDN concept will also use a limited set of connection types and multipurpose user-network interfaces to provide the range of services. B-ISDN will contain intelligence for the purpose of providing service features, maintenance, and network management functions. A layered structure will be used for specifying the access protocol. Two principal channel types are being considered by the CCITT for B-ISDN: an H_2 channel with a rate in the range of 30 Mb/s to 45 Mb/s and an H_4 channel with a rate in the range of 132 Mb/s to 139 Mb/s. Additional broadband channels may evolve during the current study period.

Issues and Actions

In the previous sections, we have attempted to explain why the ISDN concept is expected to evolve and what its implementation is likely to be. Assuming these projections are basically correct and ISDN does become a major telecommunications resource, a number of questions arise. For example, how does ISDN impact the regulatory posture in the U.S.? How are competing networks integrated into the system? Is the network control centralized or distributed? Who will administer it? What is being done and by whom to resolve technical and policy issues?

In attempting to sort out ISDN issues and categorize them, it is first necessary to define the basic premises from which these issues evolve. This is particularly important for the United States, where the regulatory environment for telecommunications differs from most other countries. Besides the national and international concerns mentioned in the last section, there are several other categories of issues that need to be explored (see Figure 1-29).

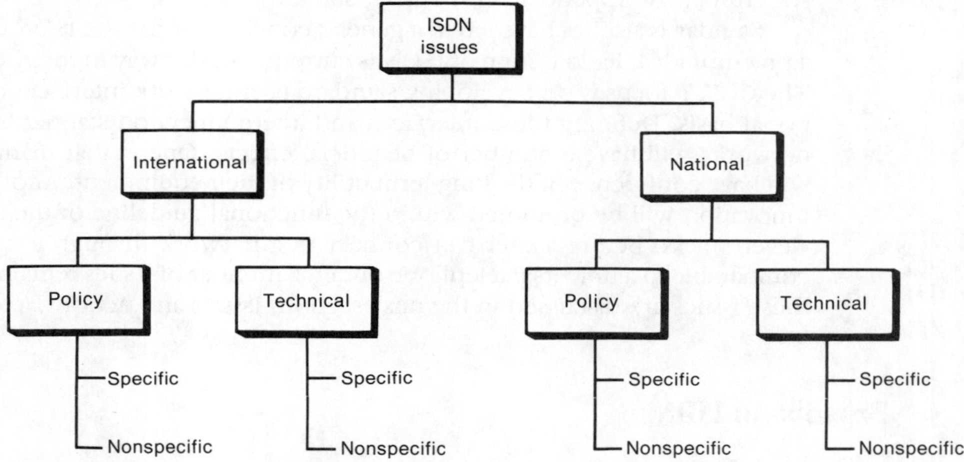

Figure 1-29. Classification of issues relating to ISDN.

Technical issues involve such matters as numbering plans, interface specifications, and signaling techniques. Such technical issues are addressed by industry working through various standards organizations.

Policy-oriented issues such as tariffs, transborder information flow, and international trade are usually addressed by the various administrations and their regulatory bodies. In the United States, this includes users and industry working in close cooperation with various government agencies to establish public policy. Agencies include NTIA (National Telecommunications and Information Administration, the principal advisor to the president on telecommunications matters); the Congress (which prepares legislation affecting telecommunications); and the FCC (which was established by the Congress to oversee the industry). Also, the courts get involved when major FCC decisions are challenged and in antitrust suits. One recent antitrust suit resulted in a major restructuring of the industry as noted earlier.

The separation into technology-oriented and policy-oriented issues is somewhat arbitrary because policy issues obviously affect technical aspects and vice versa.

Basic Premises

In order to define certain issues we must first ascertain objectives or goals that underlie all public policymaking in the United States. Perhaps the most fundamental principal is the First Amendment of the Constitution and its interpretations. For example, in 1969 the U.S. Supreme Court noted that, "It is the purpose of the First Amendment to preserve an uninhibited marketplace of ideas in which truth will ultimately prevail."

This inherently implies public exposure to diverse sources of information using multiple forms of communication media—radio, TV, telephone, etc. This need for expanding and protecting the diversity of information flowing to the public was recognized by the Congress when it passed the Communications Act of 1934 enabling the FCC to oversee its process. A primary objective of this act was to provide "a rapid, efficient, nationwide and worldwide wire and radio communication service with adequate facilities" made available "to all of the people of the United States at reasonable charges."

There have been different views on how this so-called universal, affordable service could be obtained. In 1934, a primary goal was to expand POTS to more and more users. The provisions of communication service were regulated by the FCC on the assumption that telephone service would best serve the public as a monopoly. In this way, savings accrued from combining and controlling the large-scale facilities by a single entity. In addition to the advantage of these so-called "economies of scale," the concept of universal, affordable telephone service led to a principle of rate averaging. The more profitable high-traffic portions of the network would subsidize the low-traffic portions and thereby make service available to almost everyone at a price all could afford. By the mid-1960s, POTS was generally available and new goals were established—namely to add new features and functions, thereby permitting an even greater diversity of message content, transmission services and terminals.

Beginning with the now famous Carterfone Decision in 1968 (Bartee 1986) and culminating with an equipment registration program that allows consumers to connect their own equipment to the network if that equipment conforms to certain technical standards, the FCC has consciously followed a policy of promoting competition in the terminal equipment market. The terminal equipment market's competitive potential is reflected today by the fact that there are hundreds of manufacturers and suppliers of all kinds of devices to connect to the network.

The growth of the specialized common carrier industry began in 1963 when Microwave Communications Incorporated (MCI) first filed for permission to construct a long-distance microwave system from St. Louis to Chicago. Six years later, a landmark decision by the FCC permitted MCI to begin construction and this was followed a short time later by many other applicants.

At about this same time (mid-1960s), the computer industry was developing the technology that would permit computer time sharing and remote access via telecommunications. This required more efficient communicating facilities and different terminal equipment. The FCC initiated what became known as the First Computer Inquiry to explore the issues and to assess the regulatory impact of interfacing computers with communications and of allowing common carriers to offer data processing services. It concluded that the transmission of data and the processing of data were separable and that data processing should not be regulated. However, by the mid-1970s the distinction between processing and communications became blurred as these two information industries converged. Electronic digital switches with stored program control became common and so did widely distributed computer networks. It was apparent that regulation based on a dichotomy between processing and communication was no longer feasible.

In the final decision following a Second Computer Inquiry in 1980 (FCC 1980b), the FCC adopted a regulatory distinction based on two types of service, basic and enhanced, rather than the type of technology involved. Basic services furnished by the dominant carrier, AT&T, were to be regulated and enhanced services would be unregulated. Basic services were defined by the commission as follows:

> A basic transmission service is one that is limited to the common carrier offering of transmission capacity for the movement of information. In offering this capacity, a communications path is provided for the analog or digital transmission of voice, data, video, etc., information. Different types of basic services are offered by carriers depending on a) the bandwidth desired, b) the analog and/or digital capabilities of the transmission medium, c) the fidelity, distortion, or other conditioning parameters of the communications channel to achieve a specified transmission quality, and d) the amount of transmission delay acceptable to the user. Under these criteria a subscriber is afforded the transmission capacity to suit its particular communication needs.

The commission defined an enhanced service as follows:

> The term "enhanced service" shall refer to services, offered over common carrier transmission facilities used in interstate communications, which employ computer processing applications that act on the format, content, code, protocol, or similar aspects of the subscriber's transmitted information; provide the subscriber additional, different or restructured information; or involve subscriber interaction with stored information.

The commission permitted AT&T to offer enhanced services and customer premises equipment (CPE) on a nontariffed, competitive basis provided they did so through a fully separate subsidiary to ensure that there is no cross-subsidy between the regulated and unregulated business. This separate subsidiary today was known as AT&T Information Systems.

Another conclusion of Computer II was that all customers' premises equipment should be detariffed and separated from a carrier's basic transmission service. The commission arrived at this conclusion because they "repeatedly found that competition in the equipment market has stimulated innovation on affording the public a wider range of terminal choices at lower costs."

For two decades, the concept of enhancing competition to provide marketplace regulation by reducing government involvement has been the philosophy of the FCC, the Congress, and the Justice Department. This was further demonstrated in 1982 by Congress introducing two bills (S898 and HR5158) to rewrite the Communications Act of 1934 and by the Justice Department's settlement of an antitrust suit against AT&T. Although the rewrite bills did not pass, they probably influenced the settlement of the antitrust suit, which resulted in a major restructuring of the industry under the terms of a modified final judgment by Judge Greene (1982). AT&T was to divest itself from its 22 Bell Operating Companies (BOCs) by January 1984. The BOCs could provide local telephone exchange service but not long-distance service. They could market and sell terminal equipment but could not manufacture such equipment. They had to provide "equal access" to all long-distance carriers. AT&T, in addition to providing long-distance service, could also enter the data processing field. This later service had been denied previously by a 1956 Consent Decree which prohibited AT&T from entering the unregulated telecommunications business. AT&T could not, however, enter the electronic publishing business (e.g., information such as news, weather, or sports disseminated through some electronic means like videotex). This latter restriction would be reviewed in seven years to assess competitive status. Restructuring the dominant carrier in this way was intended to reduce many of the entry barriers to new competitors.

After divestiture, the separate subsidiary requirement was applied to both AT&T and the divested BOCs. It soon appeared to the FCC that structural separation was imposing on the public excessive costs for enhanced services, and at the same time, was decreasing efficiency and innovation incentives for the interexchange and local exchange carriers. These perceived disadvantages led to the Computer III Inquiry in 1985 (FCC 1986).

As a result of the Computer III inquiry, the FCC released a report and order in June 1986. The thrust was to introduce "non-structural safeguards" as an alternative to the separate subsidiary requirement as a means of preventing anticompetitive behavior by dominant carriers offering enhanced services. These safeguards require AT&T and the BOCs to

1. provide comparably efficient interconnection (CEI) to outside vendors offering enhanced services that are potentially competitive with their own enhanced service offerings and, subsequently, submit open network architecture (ONA) plans (the BOCs, but not AT&T, must initially develop a set of Basic Service Elements (BSEs) that may be used in constructing enhanced services)
2. disclose changes in interconnection requirements in advance
3. develop (and obtain FCC approval of) procedures for allocating joint and common costs incurred in the unseparated provision of basic and enhanced services
4. provide access by others to customers' proprietary information only as requested by the customer

Open network plans were submitted by the BOCs in February 1988. By the end of 1988, they still had not been finalized, accepted, or implemented.

Based on this background, some general principles underlying U.S. communications policy can now be given. The basic premise is that information, ideas, and their means of dissemination should be available to the American people from as many sources as possible. Emphasis is on promoting a competitive marketplace for greater diversity and economic efficiency. To enhance the freedom of choice the public policy should

1. use market forces wherever possible to displace regulatory control
2. ensure equal access protection to information service providers to afford reasonable opportunity for conflicting viewpoints to be heard
3. maintain separation between information providers and information carriers
4. promote effective competition by eliminating barriers to those seeking to enter the market

The old objective of universal, affordable service is not replaced but new objectives are added: efficiency, innovation, and diversity, based on a competitive environment where customers' needs are expressed in the marketplace and where price is more directly related to cost.

With these objectives in mind, we are now in a position to categorize and explore issues that could arise from ISDN.

Issues Summary

International issues that apply to all countries and the United States fall into the categories of policy issues and technical issues. Policy issues resulting from the desire for national sovereignty include

- national security and survivability issues such as network control and restoration priorities
- issues involving the transborder flow of information including those which might affect personal privacy, internal industry development, and jobs
- international trade issues resulting from a foreign administration's desire to compete against other countries in the world markets, or to protect its internal market from foreign competition
- issues involving standards developments, e.g., ensuring that International standards do not contravene national policies or regulations
- issues raised by new technologies that may pose a threat to sovereignty and cultural identity
- fair and equitable routing and tariff regulation issues

Technical issues resulting from the need for universal, affordable services include

- interconnection issues arising due to different national networks requiring different interfaces or code and signal conversions
- issues resulting from the need for a common addressing scheme
- signaling and digitization issues affecting defense posture
- technical issues involving the development of international standards for accessing, addressing, routing, interconnection, billing, etc.
- technical issues concerning quality of service as perceived by the users

National issues follow that arise primarily from policies unique to the United States. Note that not all are necessarily ISDN-specific. Policy-oriented procompetitive issues resulting from desire to expand the "marketplace of ideas" include

- issues concerning ownership and control of certain telecommunication functions, for example, where demarcation is between transmission provider and customer premises equipment
- issues involving location of certain intelligence functions, in network or in terminal, affecting relative shares of the market accessible to common carriers on one hand and interconnect industry on the other
- issues concerning innovative services and functions and the introduction of new technologies (and who pays for impact)
- interconnection issues that arise in the United States due to the multiple networks in an ISDN structure (service provider allocation principles and routing, priorities that affect billing and ultimately a carriers revenue)
- distinctions defined by the Computer II inquiry (i.e., the basic and enhanced dichotomy as well as the necessity for boundaries between network equipment and customer premises equipment may not always be compatible with an ISDN environment)
- the issue of whether certain user features should reside in the network or in the terminal (complexity in the network favors the carrier industry whereas complexity in the terminals favors the terminal manufacturer in terms of market share)

Technical issues resulting from emphasis on increasing source diversity include

- interconnection issues resulting from multiple ISDNs in the United States, such as questions involving equal access from other networks, addressing data or voice terminals, and interfacing with non-ISDN carriers
- issues involving feature selection and carrier routing assignment, including questions on how to utilize specialized networks in a conglomerate ISDN to ensure equitable traffic distribution over participating networks
- issues concerning the performance differences between voice and nonvoice services, e.g., error rate, delivery time, and access time, and questions on charging rate for various levels of performance quality be-

cause some user performance requirements affect signal design more than network design

- issues involving technology advances such as the impact on an interface when fiber optical facilities are introduced or when bit rates change from 64 kb/s to 32 kb/s

In the United States, the telephone network provides access to nearly every business and home in the country, but these subscriber loops (primarily one twisted wire pair) are designed for 4 kHz analog voice transmission, not high-speed data transmission. This raises additional technical issues concerning access to ISDN from many potential users. Can the existing facilities handle the standard rates? What alternatives are available? How much will it cost? Who pays for the changeover? How long will it take?

International Policy Issues

National defense is a major concern to any country, and the nation's telecommunications networks are crucial to that defense posture. The impact of ISDN on this posture depends on when and how it evolves. In the United States, the interoperability beween competing networks is an obvious requirement for survivability reasons, regardless of when and how ISDN develops.

The right to personal privacy in many countries may restrict the flow of information to other countries. Countries that provide this right are reluctant to transmit protected information to countries that do not. The unregulated flow of information across country boundaries can also affect the economic growth. For example, the use of foreign data processing capabilities could restrict the growth in that area internally. Although these issues arise with any network, the worldwide scope of ISDN focuses the problem and makes it seem more urgent.

Communications between countries must be a cooperative venture. However, at the same time, many countries are actively competing in the worldwide telecommunications market. Today, the United States has about 50 percent of the world telecommunications. This market is relatively open compared to other countries that are typically much smaller and much less open to outside competition. Most countries outside North America and Japan follow recommendations of the CCITT for telecommunications equipment manufacturing and procurement. The CCITT's recommendations for ISDN will undoubtedly become the standard interface for user access throughout many countries, although each country may implement the network in any way it desires. International standards-making organizations such as the CCITT have usually recognized national needs and generally take into account the regulatory environment. This is done to allow each country to meet its administration's policies in its own way. The United States participates in these activities to ensure that industries' competitive interests are allowed.

In the United States, the ISDN could consist of many networks (voice and data, circuit- and packet-switched, basic and enhanced) interconnected and accessed by users via standard ISDN interfaces. In other countries, a single, unified network under control of a single administration may develop.

It is expected that the existence of worldwide ISDN interface standards will encourage more manufacturers to develop new terminals and enter the international market.

International Technical Issues

The ISDN concept was, in part, conceived to provide universal service in an efficient manner using available digital networks. The ISDN has been expected to evolve primarily from public telephone networks that come closest to providing universal connectivity. Although there are over half a billion telephones in the world, 90 percent are concentrated in 15 percent of the countries. Thus the global concept for ISDN remains a major issue.

In many countries, the administrations control and operate the network (e.g., the PTTs in Europe) and they also control the charges. Thus the "universal and affordable" concept is approached based on total cost of facilities. Cross-subsidies are imposed (and accepted) where necessary. In the United States, the goal of universal, affordable service has not changed, but the means of achieving it has. Market forces are replacing regulatory controls. The United States policy reflects wide consensus that the marketplace appears to be the best means of allowing new technologies (e.g., digital networks) and services (e.g., those contained within ISDN) to develop.

Because the ISDN implementation may evolve in different ways from different base networks in each country, several issues arise. One is the problem of interconnections between the networks for interoperability. This includes not only a physical gateway, but possibly code, address, and signal conversions. A common numbering scheme is desirable for international access. This raises problems in some countries where switching facilities may be unable to handle the number of digits necessary. Also, in the United States it is desirable that the numbering scheme allows for carrier selections, whereas this is unnecessary in the PTTs.

Another issue concerns the dichotomy between voice and data services. At first, one might expect that digitized voice could be handled just as data is handled because both are similar streams of bits. But there are differences and these differences could affect the cost of providing these services. The efficiency of resource utilization is a major issue. For example, the statistics of voice and data traffic are very different. The dead times between speech sounds can be used to carry other traffic. Also, voice conversations, whether their transmission is analog or digital, must occur in real time or at least essentially real time. The use of satellites, and the corresponding delay of about ¼-second associated with such circuits is disagreeable to many people and considered unacceptable by many for multihop circuits. Interactive data circuits require fast turnaround times whereas bulk data transfers can often be delayed by several minutes or sometimes hours without objection. Other quality of service measures may also differ, such as access delay, error performance, blocking probability, etc. One of the questions this data-voice dichotomy raises is whether it is better to develop an integrated network with fully shared resources and possibly nonoptimum grade of service or whether it is better to separate resources and optimize each for a particular service. In either case, an equitable rate structure is needed where multiple carriers are involved.

The routing and accounting for calls, especially incoming international calls, is another issue. The route selected could impact which carrier receives revenue. Although this is not necessarily caused by ISDN, its importance is increased as a result of the wide interest in ISDN. Both technical and policy issues are involved.

These are just a few examples that can, in part, be resolved by developing appropriate international standards. International standards for accessing ISDN, addressing, routing, interconnecting, and billing will ultimately be recommended by the CCITT, but will take time to be developed.

National Policy Issues

The ISDN concept raises a number of policy questions in the United States because of our commitment to a competitive environment. For example, how can we ensure that the CCITT process accommodates the established procompetitive policies of the United States? Competition provides the incentive to develop new, low-cost technologies, minimizes the costs of facilities and services, and provides a wider range of services at prices based on costs. For competition to develop, competing technologies must exist, be readily available to all, and be economical relative to existing service. The government policy, both economic and legal, must allow entry to competitors by reducing barriers whenever possible.

One of the underlying conceptual principles of ISDN is that it will contain intelligence for the purpose of providing service features, maintenance, and network management functions. This may not be entirely feasible in the U.S. regulatory environment where basic information transport services are regulated and enhanced services (like videotex and electronic mail) or CPE (like telephones, modems, or PABXs) are not.

The transition toward ISDN in the U.S. competitive environment will likely involve several competing networks. Are there technological, economic, or legal barriers that make multiple ISDN networks uneconomical or inefficient relative to a monolithic structure? The multiple carrier, procompetitive philosophy of the United States presents many questions concerning U.S. participation in an international ISDN.

In the United States, CPE is unregulated and considered to be separate from the network. The interface between the CPE and the network is denoted as the "U" interface which requires a new set of recommendations that are not covered by the CCITT but are being developed by standards organizations in the United States.

Still another issue involves the regulation of these networks when necessary or their deregulation when feasible. The Communications Act of 1934 gives the FCC exclusive regulatory power over interstate common carrier communications services. Authority over intrastate services is reserved for the states. The line between state and federal jurisdiction is not always clear because the same facilities may often be used for both types of service. The transition to an ISDN may be delayed in the United States unless these jurisdictional disputes are resolved. New firms may be reluctant to enter the integrated services market unless they know if, by whom, and how they will be regulated. For example, the FCC regulates some video aspects of cable, but not the common carrier services provided by the cable operator. Jurisdictional disputes raise several questions concerning availability of servicers and economic impacts which must be addressed.

National Technical Issues

As noted previously, ISDN implementation in the United States would probably consist of multiple networks provided by competing carriers. In addition to conventional wire pair, the access to an ISDN could take other forms, e.g., radio, coaxial cable, and fiber optics. The user in the United States could have a number of choices to select, including the access path, the carrier, the routing, and so forth. This selectability raises a number of technical questions concerning ISDN. How are the selections made? How are the networks interconnected? Who assigns routing? What are the cost accounting procedures? What is the impact on a numbering plan? Who administers the plan?

Two key issues affecting the ISDN's survivability and endurability during national emergencies are signaling and digitization. Signaling is important because it is the key to service integration, damage assessment, and restoral. Digitization is an issue because it is currently not cost-effective in the U.S. to use digital transmission over long distances. The network must be all-digital if restoral routing involving many tandem links is to become feasible.

Developing standards that will influence these issues include CCITT recommendations on signaling (e.g., Signaling System No. 7) and ISO standards in the OSI family. The technical communities developing these standards, CCITT and ISO, have traditionally been separated by their charters and authorities. Consequently, there is a dichotomy of standards, and often, a gray area of uncertainty at the intersection points. For example, in ISO standard 1745 (BISYNC), only the "logical connection" process is addressed; the establishment and subsequent disconnection of the physical circuit are simply referenced as "CCITT responsibilities." An ISDN implies one signaling system that does both.

Signaling is the key to integration in the ISDN because it controls the services provided by the same (shared) resources. As an example, services requiring packet switching and circuit switching will be provided by ISDN on a user selectable basis. The user's service selections, and the service features he or she desires, will be communicated to the network by the signaling system. The signaling systems currently used for circuit-switched voice and packet-switched data are substantially different because the systems are not integrated. That difference will largely disappear as ISDN becomes real.

Signaling is also a key to damage assessment and restoral in a damaged network. Restoral must be based on a knowledge of which switching centers and transmission links have survived after a disaster and how these surviving elements can be reconstituted. Signaling provides a key linkage between the control points of the network and could provide the means to collect such information.

The existing PSTN employs analog frequency modulation and multiplexing for its long-haul transmission facilities for economy reasons. Although extensive portions of the network operate in a digital mode (e.g., voice-encoded PCM), these "islands" of digital operation are generally limited to densely populated areas. At present, high-capacity digital transmission is available for direct customer use primarily in large metropolitan areas. The digital portion of the network covers a relatively small part of the geographic area of the U.S. An all-digital network is essential if many links must be operated in tandem to connect user pairs—a very likely requirement in a severely damaged network.

The ISDN concept is to provide end-to-end digital channels to the user interface that are compatible with the PCM voice digitization rate of 64 kb/s and multiples or submultiples thereof. Unfortunately, this concept will not become a reality until digital long-haul transmission becomes cost-effective. At present, it is not. A hybrid service offering (analog and digital) is being planned by CCITT Study Group XVIII as an interim measure in recognition of this problem.

In the United States, various loops, lines, and trunks currently constitute the transmission part of the telephone network. In addition to over 200 million subscriber loops, the interswitch trunks provide huge countrywide connectivity. According to some estimates, there are over 7 million trunks bundled into more than 300,000 trunk groups. The channel mileage covered by this network must be in the hundreds of millions of miles. The local loops are predominately two-wire voice frequency transmission, whereas the majority of the toll trunks are four-wire using all sorts of carrier systems. As the length of a given line or trunk increases, different systems are used because they are more cost-effective. On the long-haul trunks in the United States, analog carriers still prevail because they still cost less than other facilities. In Europe, long-haul distances are much less (typically less than 200 miles) and the transition to digital facilities is progressing at a much faster rate.

The CCITT has developed a Recommendation for encoding voice for transmission over a 32 kb/s channel. This provides an obvious cost advantage over the 64 kb/s systems in common use and extends the range over which digital T-carrier type systems are cost-effective and the rate at which the network is digitized.

Actions

We have raised a number of issues, some technically oriented and some policy oriented, and noted that not all of these issues are specifically the result of ISDN implementation but could arise from almost any future global network architecture.

Although these issues are many and complex, there is also considerable work already being done to resolve them by industry with government support in various standards organizations. In this section we will describe some of these organizations and the activities currently under way that relate to ISDN. In the limited space available we can only highlight some of these activities, recognizing that this is only a small part of the total effort.

From a regulatory and policy standpoint, the U.S. position is implemented and promulgated by legislative actions of the Congress, administrative actions of the president, actions of the Department of Justice, and decisions by the courts. Two supporting entities are the FCC, which has the regulatory authority over interstate common carriers, and the NTIA in the Department of Commerce, which advised the administration on telecommunication matters. During emergencies, the National Communication System (NCS) takes jurisdiction over many commercial network resources.

In 1983, the FCC issued a Notice of Inquiry (Docket 83-383, Adopted August 4, 1983) in the matter of ISDN. The purpose of this notice is to provide the FCC with background on ISDN developments to data and related telecommunications policy, and to discuss various issues raised by the potential implementation of ISDNs.

The NTIA and its technical research arm, the Institute for Telecommunication Sciences (ITS) in Boulder, Colorado, has, in addition to its radio spectrum policy development and management functions, several other important missions, including

1. furthering the efficient development and use of telecommunications and information services
2. promoting the development and international adoption of technical standards in the telecommunications and information industries
3. formulating and advocating regulatory, legislative, and institutional reforms to the FCC, Congress, and industry in order to promote competition and deregulation where feasible and to ensure the universal availability of basic telecommunication services.

It is with these goals in mind that NTIA participates in numerous standards activities on both a national and international basis.

The NCS is the primary U.S. agency concerned with the management and coordination of telecommunication resources and services during national emergencies. The impact of ISDN on the U.S. communications posture is, of course, a major concern of the NCS. Efforts are under way to ensure that certain interface standards will allow the emergency managers community to meet specific needs in this area including survivability, restoration, and critical user priorities.

Of the several national and international standards organizations involved in ISDN standards development activities either directly or indirectly, the primary focus is in the CCITT. Several of the technical issues have already been addressed by the CCITT and its member nations. Appendix A describes the International CCITT and the U.S. CCITT organization, which makes contributions to it and determines the U.S. position concerning various Recommendations. These Recommendations are the result of a continuing process that begins with a list of technical "Questions" prepared by the plenary assembly of the CCITT. The original list of questions on ISDN that was entrusted to Study Group XVIII is given in Appendix B. These Recommendations, along with any others completed, will be submitted to the 1988 plenary assembly of the CCITT for approval and subsequent publication in 1989 as the *Blue Books*.

In the United States, the national committee of the CCITT is headed by a representative from the Department of State. The U.S. CCITT has been divided by subject matter into five groups: regulatory matters, telegraph operations, telephone operations, data transmission and the ISDN Joint Working Party. The latter is the means whereby U.S. industry and government agencies can coordinate their inputs to the appropriate CCITT study group. An ISDN working group was formed to conduct technical studies in assigned areas in support of the ISDN Joint Working Party. This group consists of industry and government members working together to resolve many conflicting viewpoints. Contributions from this group to the CCITT are submitted via the U.S. Department of State. The process is intended to establish a unified U.S. position at the international meetings.

United States service providers recognized that methods of cooperatively planning, interconnecting, assessing, and maintaining communication networks would be needed in the postdivestiture environment, and they therefore established an industry forum so that such methods could be developed. That forum is the T1 Committee, which was created, and is administratively supported and sponsored, by the Exchange Carrier Standards Association (ECSA) and accredited by ANSI. The output of T1 is U.S. national standards and input to the United States CCITT working groups.

ECSA was organized by several of the BOCs and some independent telephone companies in August 1983—about four months prior to the divestiture. It is a private, voluntary association of the exchange carriers industry designed to accomplish two major purposes: provide a forum for and represent exchange carrier interests in standards and related technical fields affecting the industry, and act as secretariat for the ANSI-accredited T1 standards committee, "Telecommunications."

This committee was created to develop technical standards and reports supporting the interconnection and interoperability of telecommunications networks at interfaces with end-user systems, carriers, information and enhanced-service providers, and CPE. T1 is the postdivestiture entity that most nearly assumed the predivestiture role of AT&T in promoting interoperability among U.S. telecommunication networks.

The T1 committee is divided into a number of subcommittees and working groups that deal with various aspects of standardization. Since February 1988, technical subcommittees T1S1 and T1E1 are the working groups primarily concerned with ISDN. See Figure 1-30 for the working group structure.

Summary and Conclusions

We have discussed why and how ISDNs are expected to evolve and what they may look like in the future. Although there are a number of policy and technical issues, these are already being addressed by experts from industry and from

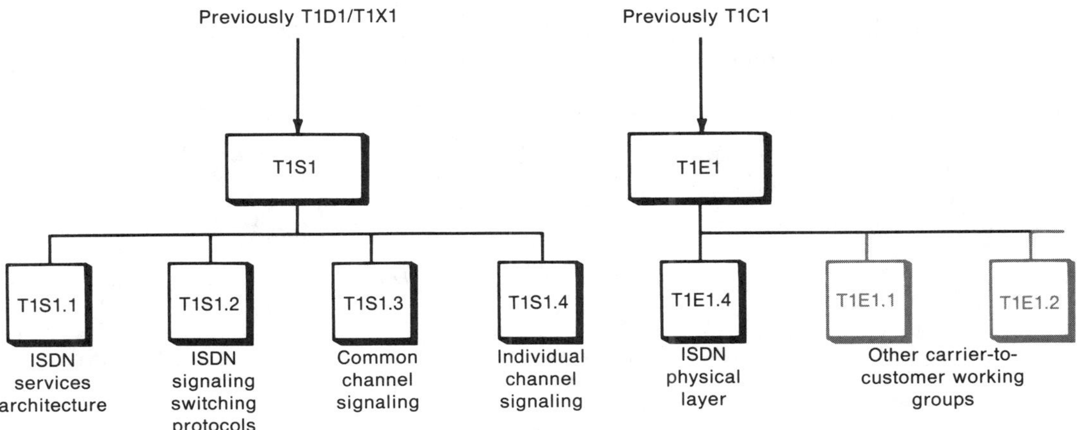

Figure 1-30. ISDN working groups in T1 organizations.

certain government agencies working together in both national and international forums.

The ISDN concept promises a number of high-performance, multiservice digital networks with potential for global communications when interconnected. While ISDN does hold promise, it is still evolving. Many serious questions remain. Will ISDN, as a distinct network, actually be realized? How soon? Will it overlay existing networks or exist primarily as digital islands?

In the U.S., the existing analog telephone plant is gradually being replaced with digital facilities. Although some of the key elements of ISDN (such as digital switching with stored program control and common channel interswitch signaling) are already in place for the long-haul network, several portions still use analog switches and in-band signaling.

Microwave facilities are still used for transmission over major portions of the long-haul network and these employ analog frequency modulation for voice and data. Although a wide variety of digital terminals is available for all kinds of uses, the basic telephone is still analog, accessing the network over analog loops. It is apparent that we face a transition period of one or two decades before an all-digital network like ISDN can become a reality.

In the future, we can expect to see many changes in the telecommunications industry. Technical advances will continue to occur, causing dramatic changes in network concepts, including ISDNs. Users will always demand new services and the new concepts will, we hope, be available at acceptable prices.

References

Bartee, T. C., ed. 1985. *Digital Communications.* Indianapolis: Howard W. Sams & Company.

———. 1986. *Data Communications, Networks, and Systems.* Indianapolis: Howard W. Sams & Company.

CCITT. 1985. Integrated Services Digital Network (ISDN). *Red Book III.* Fascicle III.5, Geneva.

Dorros, I. 1983. Telephone nets go digital. *IEEE Spectrum* 20, no. 4 (April).

FCC. 1980a. *Final Decision in the Second Computer Inquiry.* FCC 80-189, adopted April 7.

———. 1980b. *Second Computer Inquiry, Final Decision.* 77 FCC 2nd at 419.

———. 1986. *Third Computer Inquiry, CC Docket No. 85-229.* FCC 86-252. Report and Order released June 16.

Folts, H. C. 1981. Coming of age: A long-awaited standard for heterogeneous nets. *Data Communications* 10, no. 1 (January).

Greene, H. H. 1983. Opinion entered in AT&T antitrust case. District Court, District of Columbia. Civil Action nos. 74-1698, 82, 0192, and 82-025.

ISO. 1982. ISO 820. Information processing systems—Open systems interconnection—Basic reference model. *Draft International Standard (DIS) 7498.*

Skrzypczak, C., J. Weber, and W. Falconer. 1981. Bell system planning of ISDN (integrated services digital network). *IEEE International Conference on Communications* 1:19.6.1–19.6.6. Denver.

U.S. Department of Commerce. 1983. *1983 U.S. industrial outlook, for 250 industries with projections for 1987.* Available from Bureau of Industrial Economics, Washington, DC.

Chapter 2

Major Telecommunications Networks

Donald V. Glen

Chapter 2

THERE WAS A SIGNIFICANT INTERNATIONAL EFFORT to develop standards for ISDNs at the same time that events leading to the divestiture of AT&T were occurring in the United States. The ISDN standards activity continues with end-to-end digital connectivity providing the basis for a myriad of new services for home and business as the objective. The divestiture has resulted in changed telephony markets and new network architectures for the Public-Switched Telephone Network (PSTN). This chapter discusses the pre- and postdivestiture PSTN operating structure and two central office switches that are extensively used in the PSTN and have ISDN applications.

Based on digital technology, the intent of the ISDN concept is to integrate and support a wide range of voice and nonvoice applications within the same network (Figure 2-1). Standard transmission rates with a minimum of standard interfaces are intended to provide a wide variety of services. These include: telephony, circuit-switched, packet-switched, and leased-line data transfer; message handling such as telex, teletext, videotex; and image transfer such as facsimile and video conferencing.

Provisions for the ISDN also include service features and network management functions that could be supported through intelligence in the network or at the user terminal. For example, there could be a dynamic bandwidth allocation based on a user's needs. Access to an ISDN that provides the services is to be through a layered protocol structure.

The CCITT view is that the ISDN concept will evolve from existing Integrated Digital Networks (IDNs) and dedicated circuit- or packet-switched networks. As digital communication networks are just recently evolving from and replacing analog networks, the transition to an ISDN world is accelerating. Depending on the country, an ISDN could interwork with one or more non-ISDN networks or other public or private ISDNs.

With the ISDN moving toward a digital end-to-end (user-to-user) connectivity, conversion to digital equipment will continue. Concurrently, common channel signaling (CCS), specifically CCITT Signaling System No. 7 (CCITT No. 7), has been recognized as a key element of control signaling for the ISDN.

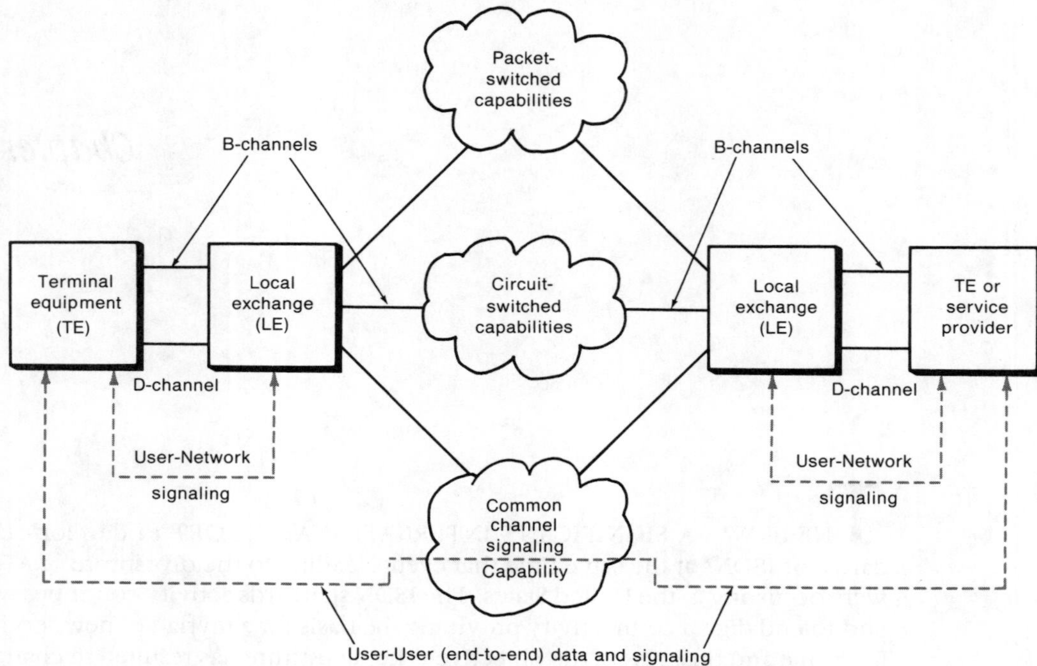

Figure 2-1. Basic concept of ISDN architecture.

The importance of this effort has been recognized as indicated by the participation of companies and governments in ISDN standards committee activities. An equally important aspect is the current state of the PSTN, particularly since the divestiture of AT&T and the Bell Operating Companies (BOCs) that occurred on January 1, 1984. For many years, prior to divestiture, a particular hierarchical network structure was developed to serve the telephony needs of the United States. Due in part to divestiture, another kind of network structure has subsequently appeared. It is based on nonhierarchical routing between exchanges and local telephone areas where, in general, services are provided by the Regional Bell Operating Companies (RBOCs) and independent telephone companies. Other elements in the present communications structure in the United States are the ongoing changes that are being engendered by decisions of the FCC and federal courts.

Traditional Network Architecture

There are two architectures to consider here for circuit-switched traffic. The first is the traditional hierarchical structure. A second, DNHR (dynamic nonhierarchical routing), was started in August 1984 and implemented by the end of 1987.

Hierarchical Switching

A hierarchical structure of "switching centers" had been developed in the United States and Canada to efficiently handle the large daily volume of telephone and data messages. In 1980, this was on the order of 600 million calls per day (AT&T 1980). As part of a switching plan, each switching center was classified according to a hierarchy of five classes based on the highest switching function performed, interrelationship with other switching centers, and its transmission requirements. The switching centers were linked to each other by trunks. The hierarchy used a tree topology to efficiently handle more than 150 million subscribers with two routing ladders (Figure 2-2).

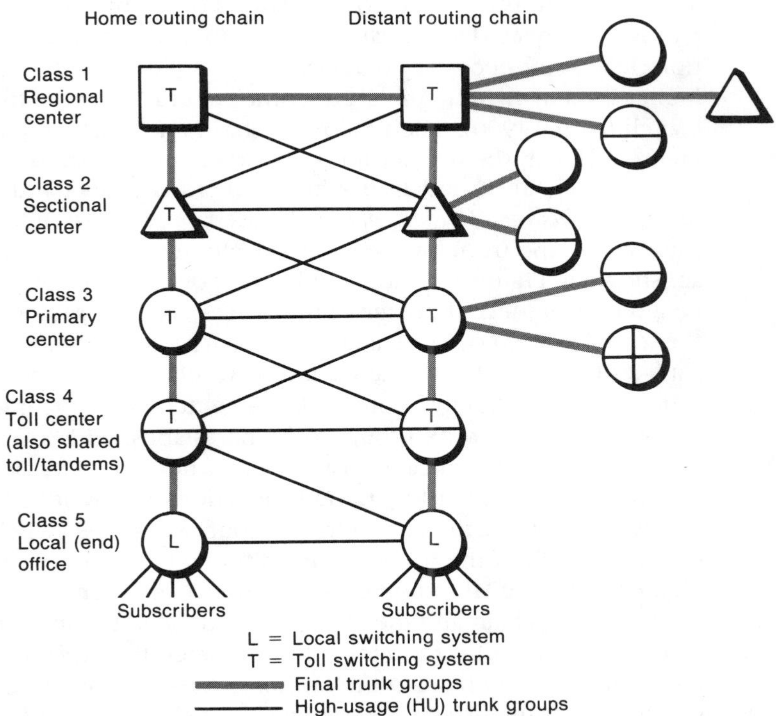

Figure 2-2. Network hierarchy and switching plan *(after AT&T 1980).*

Subscribers to the PSTN were and still are connected directly or through a PBX via two- or four-wire local loops to the local (end) switching center designated as a class 5 office. Switching centers that provide the first level of concentration for end offices and the final level of distribution for traffic terminating at end offices are *toll centers* or *toll points* (class 4 offices). Within the hierarchy shown in Figure 2-2, the higher class switch could also perform lower switching functions. For example, the class 1 regional center could perform the functions of all the lower order switching centers (classes 2, 3, 4, and 5). Class 5 offices only handle class 5 switching.

The toll centers within the hierarchy served dual functions: toll or tandem on a shared basis. This became an important distinction when the divestiture of AT&T was used to separate communications resources. *Tandem switching* refers to any intermediate switch used to establish a connection. Specifically, a tandem switch was used to interconnect class 5 end offices having insufficient interoffice traffic to justify direct trunks. Tandem switches were also used to handle overflow traffic on direct trunks between end offices. Toll switches, by that definition, could provide tandem functions.

Routing within the structure was always at the lowest level possible to minimize the cost of carrying the offered load. When both subscribers were connected to the same end office, the connection was made through that office. When each subscriber was connected to a different end office and the two class 5 offices connected to the same class 4 office, that toll center made the connection. It was not necessary that class 5, 4, or 3 offices always home on the next higher level of switch. Any class 5 office could be served from any higher level switch (AT&T 1980). The final route (basic) network architecture is shown in Figure 2-2 with the heavier lines. To prevent heavy traffic at higher levels and minimize signal degradation when numerous trunks and switches might be used, *high-usage (HU) trunks* were used between switching systems of any class where the trunks were economically feasible. Possible HU trunk groups are shown in Figure 2-2 with light lines. Various classes of switch systems could be directly connected to each of the offices via final trunk groups. For example, the class 1 office could have class 2, 3, and 4 switch systems trunked to it; the class 2 office could have class 3 and 4 switch systems trunked to it; the class 4 office would have only another class 4 switch system trunked to it.

While an HU trunk group could be established between any two offices where it was economically justified, another rule was also applied to avoid higher class switching for traffic to locations below it. The "one-level limit" rule was used to justify an HU trunk group where the switching functions performed at each of the trunk groups differed by no more than one level. (Note Figure 2-2 where HU trunk groups connect between the class 4 center in the home routing chain and the class 3, 4, and 5 centers and end office of the distant routing chain.) If traffic was low between the class 4 switching system of the home routing chain and the other offices, the one-level limit rule allowed moving the trunk groups to one higher level. Traffic loads could justify trunk groups between the class 3 primary center in the home routing chain and the class 3 and 4 centers in the distant routing chain. Other interpretations of the one-level limit rule are explained in AT&T (1980).

Another principle was also involved in the hierarchical switching structure alternate routing. High usage trunk groups were large enough to handle only a portion of the offered traffic. The switching systems redirected traffic by automatic alternate routing to a different trunk group when all circuits of an HU group were busy. Overflow calls were shifted from the most direct route to a different trunk group while the switching system attempted to stay within a two-trunk, three-switch system route. This was done so that the circuit quality provided to the subscribers remained acceptable.

Hidden Subnetworks

The telecommunications network was and is a complex system, consisting of revenue-producing networks and many subnetworks. A great amount of technology is involved in these building-block subnetworks, their functioning and interaction (Nesenbergs and McManamon 1983). These subnetworks are the Basic Synchronization Reference Frequency (BSRF—formerly Bell System Reference Frequency),the Automatic Intercept System (AIS), the Centralized Automatic Message Accounting (CAMA) system, the Traffic Service Position System (TSPS), and the CCS network (Figure 2-3). While the following brief description of the systems is based on predivestiture operation, one form or another of these subnetworks is still needed in the postdivestiture era.

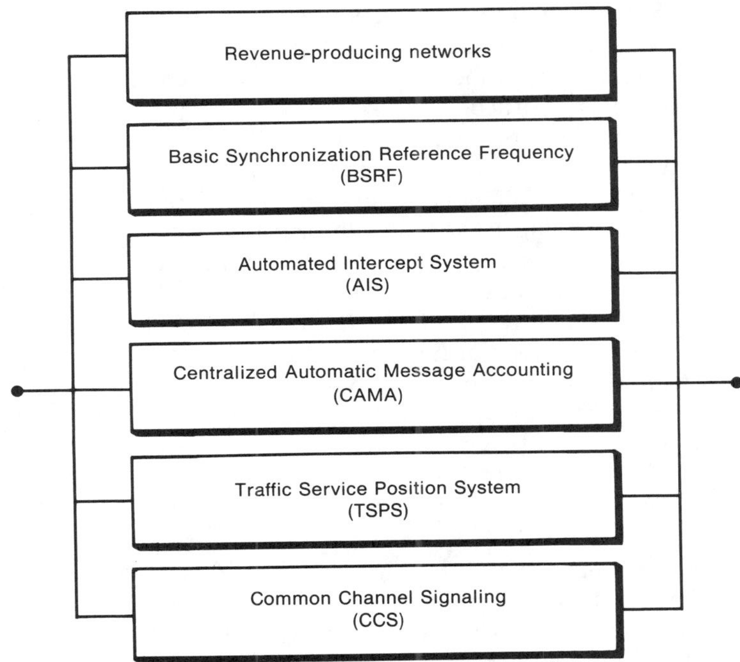

Figure 2-3. Hidden subnetworks within the communications network *(after Nesenbergs and McManamon 1983).*

The BSRF, distributed through its own subnetwork, is needed for transmission of a synchronized data stream and pulse code modulation (PCM) encoding of digitized voice. The BSRF standard with three-fold redundancy, located underground in Hillsboro, Missouri, has an error rate of less than 1 in 10^{11}. The BSRF standard is based on the Naval Observatory clock in Washington, D.C., through a LORAN-C time standard link. The standard frequency extends through class 4 and 5 offices to PBXs, remote switching units, and digital channel banks. A dividing line, based on divestiture, for distributing the BSRF now exists between the class 4 and 5 offices. Based on divestiture, the AT&T Communications domain extended through class 4 switches performing intra- and interstate switching, and the RBOCs would be responsible for distribution between class 4/5 offices and other facilities.

The AIS provides operator assistance to subscribers in the form of local (1+411) or intrastate long-distance directory assistance (1+555+1211). Since divestiture, out-of-state long-distance directory assistance is a function of a subscriber's long-distance carrier (1+NPA+555+1212) where NPA is the numbering plan area (area code). The AIS also provides occasional assistance to other operators such as resolving origination/destination conflicts by talking to subscribers and consulting data base information. Local directory assistance takes place at the class 5 end office while the remote directory assistance was with the class 3 Primary Center.

The output of a CAMA system is a prepared and mailed customer's bill. Information about a customer's call, such as the call duration, is fed from a toll or tandem switch into an accounting register. Monthly statistics are compiled to determine a customer's bill. A LAMA (Local Automatic Message Accounting) performs the same function but the recording and timing of the call are done at the local class 5 office.

The TSPS provides service for credit card, collect, and bill-to-third-number calls. Previously operator-handled, the TSPS has become mostly automated through the Calling Card Service, which enables customers to make credit card calls by dialing in the billing information without operator assistance. This new capability was made possible through modifications in the TSPS and common channel interoffice signaling (CCIS), which were key elements in the SPC network (Basinger et al. 1982; Confalone et al. 1982). The TSPS equipment was located at class 4 or higher ranking offices and gathered data from connecting trunks, (i.e., between class 5 and 4 offices) through a Remote Trunk Arrangement of a local TSPS trunk circuit (AT&T 1980).

Signaling

There are three types of signaling functions in telephony: supervisory, addressing, and call progress. These functions can be categorized as station or subscriber-line signaling and interoffice signaling. Transmission of these signals could be analog ac, analog dc, and digital. Further subdivision of signaling can be in-channel or common channel. In-channel signaling can be divided as *inband* or *out-of-band* (Bellamy 1983). In-band methods transmit signaling information in the same band of frequencies used by the voice signals (e.g., single frequency, multifrequency). Out-of-band signals use the same facilities as the voice signal but a different part of the frequency band (e.g., direct current on customer loops to recognize on- or off-hook conditions). Current usage sometimes refers to common channel signaling as being out-of-band.

Supervisory signaling involves the recognition of busy or idle states on subscriber lines and interoffice trunks, and then transmitting that information to the caller and switching system. Single-frequency (SF) tone signaling (2,600 Hz) is used in conventional in-band signaling to indicate the busy/idle state of trunk circuits between switches. *Address signaling* involves the transmission of digits of a called telephone number to a switching system or by one switching system to another. Dial pulse and dual-tone multifrequency (DTMF) signaling are used on subscriber lines while multifrequency (MF) signaling was the primary in-band system for passing address information on interoffice trunks (Figure 2-4A). Prior to 1976, most signaling between switching systems was performed by the SF/MF method. *Call progress signals* are transmitted to a caller to provide information to callers and operators relative to the establishment of a connection through a telephone network. Call progress signals are a variety of audible tone signals that indicate dialing, line busy, and ringing on the circuit (Keiser and Strange 1985).

CCS is a method that is employed in the public telephone network to exchange signaling data between processor-equipped switching systems over a network of signaling links (Figure 2-4B). The links are dedicated to control of signaling functions that are common to a number of channels.

When AT&T introduced CCS in 1976 it was known as Common Channel

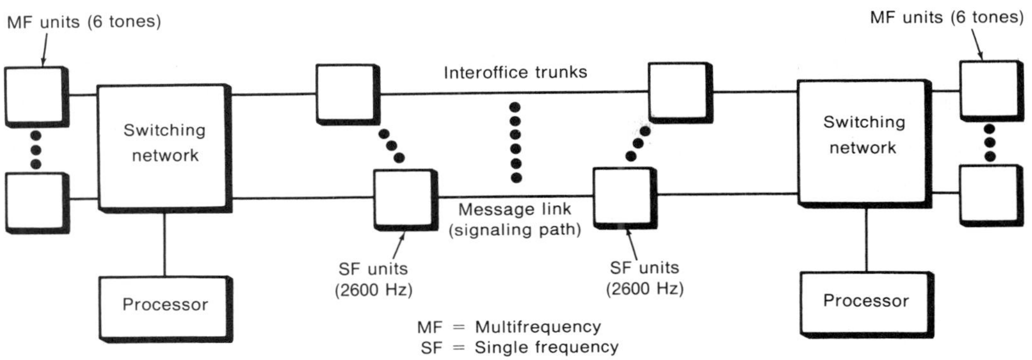

A. SF/MF in-band signaling.

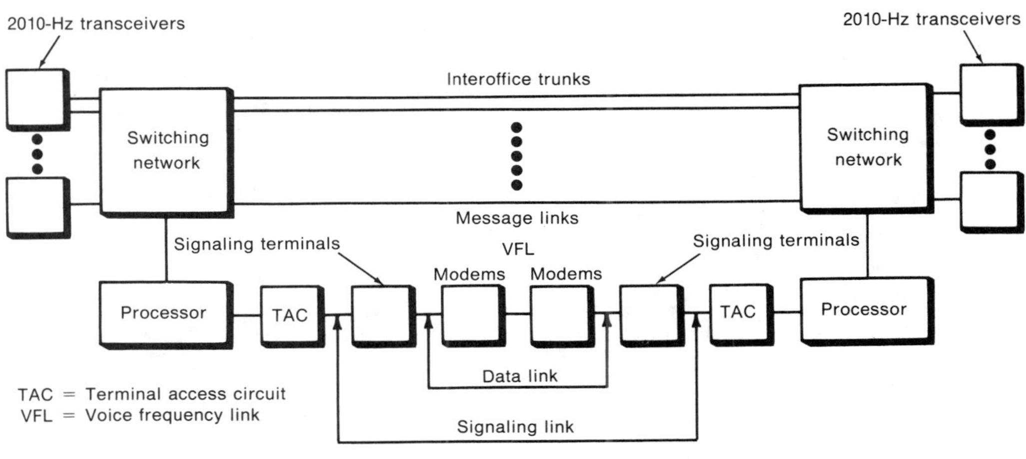

B. CCS signaling system.

Figure 2-4. In-band and common channel signaling *(AT&T 1980)*.

Interoffice Signaling (CCIS). The message format was similar to CCITT Signaling System No. 6 with the signaling information transmitted across 2.4 kb/s analog data links. The use of CCIS-improved trunk signaling between 4ESS toll switches (introduced at the same time) operating under stored program control (SPC). The introduction of CCIS increased the speed and lowered the cost of call setup and disconnect on the intertoll network (Lawser and Oxley 1987).

CCS can have three modes of operation: associated, quasi-associated, and disassociated. In the associated mode (Figure 2-5A), the CCS link closely tracks, along its entire length, the interswitch trunk groups that are served between end points. In the quasi-associated mode, the CCS links may not be closely associated with the trunk groups that are served (Figure 2-5B). In the disassociated mode, there is no close or simple association between the CCS links and the trunk groups being served. The disassociated mode permits nodes to communicate via signaling links when there are no functioning connecting trunks (Figure 2-5C).

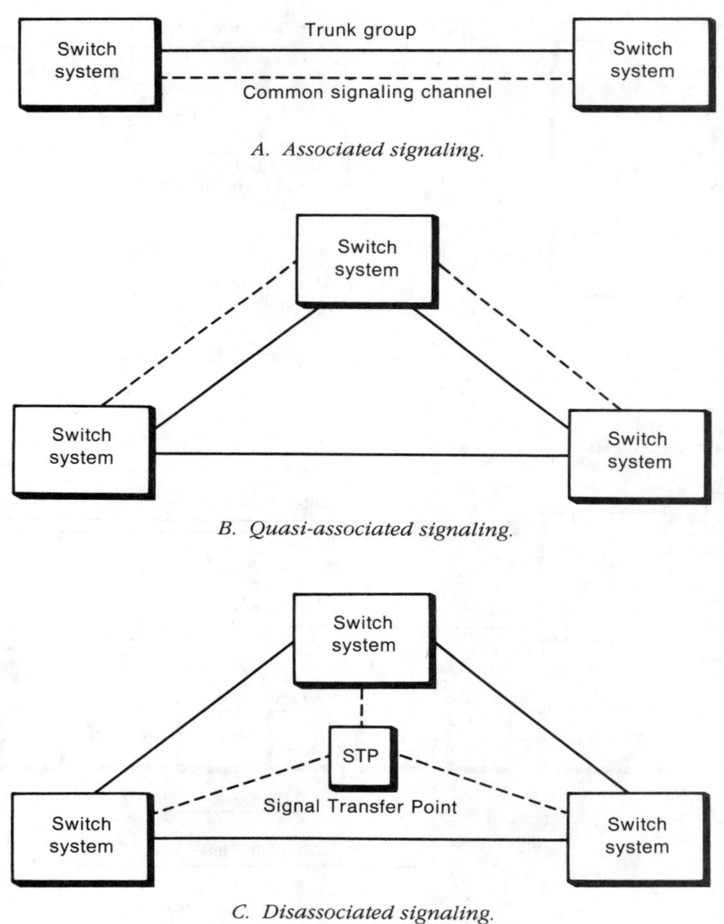

Figure 2-5. Modes of common channel signaling operation.

SPC Network

The SPC network consists of processor-controlled switching systems that are interconnected by CCS to exchange supervisory, address, call progress, and other signals. In Figure 2-6, the switching system hierarchy is shown interconnected by the CCIS network. Signal transfer points (STPs) are used in this network to concentrate signaling information and to provide access to network control points (NCPs). Information that is relevant to customer services is stored at the NCPs (Lawser et al. 1982). Traffic Service Position Systems (TSPS) are shown within the hierarchy. At the end of 1983, there were 32 STPs, 34 NCPs, and 159 TSPSs in the SPC network (Andrews 1984).

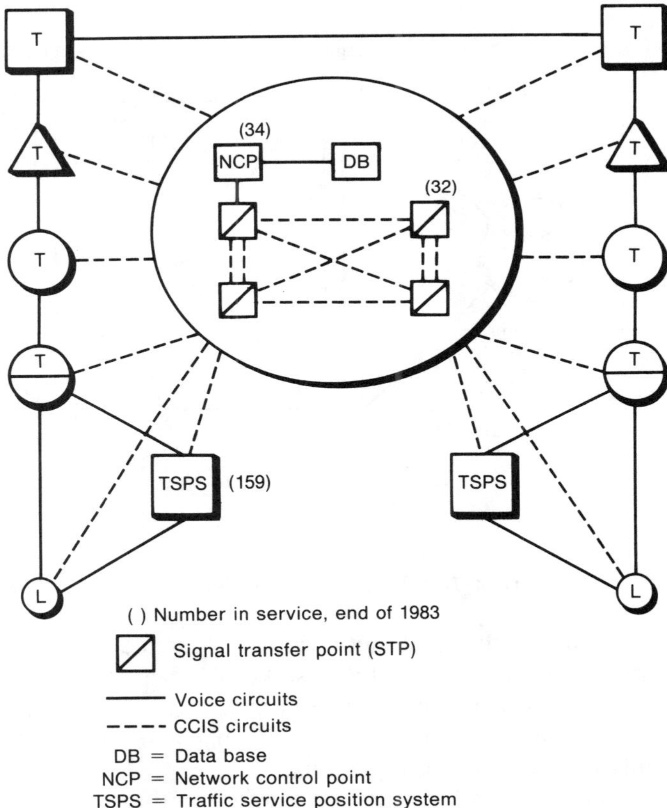

Figure 2-6. Stored program controlled hierarchical network *(after Andrews 1984).*

Access to the stored program control NCPs takes place when service calls are processed through switch offices (action points or ACPs). The ACP recognizes the need for information on how to proceed with the call and sends a CCIS direct-signaling message to the NCP. The CCIS direct-signaling message consists of the dialed number, calling customer's line [referred to as automatic number identification (ANI)] and the identity of the ACP. The ACPs can be local and toll switches, or TSPSs. The NCPs retrieve customer calling instructions pertaining to the call, analyze the instructions, and then return call-handling instructions to the ACP (Lawser et al. 1982).

Redundancy is needed since the loss of a single NCP or its associated STP would block thousands of calls. Each NCP is paired with another NCP associated with a different STP located in another geographical location. If an NCP becomes inaccessible, its mate handles the traffic load.

Access links (A-links) from a switching office to paired STPs (called mate STPs) are provided in paired (mate) links, with one link to each STP (Figure 2-7). Bridge links (B-links) are provided between mate STPs in another region. Cross links (C-links) are used to complete a signal path through the mate STP when the direct A- or B-links fail (Frerking and McGrew 1982).

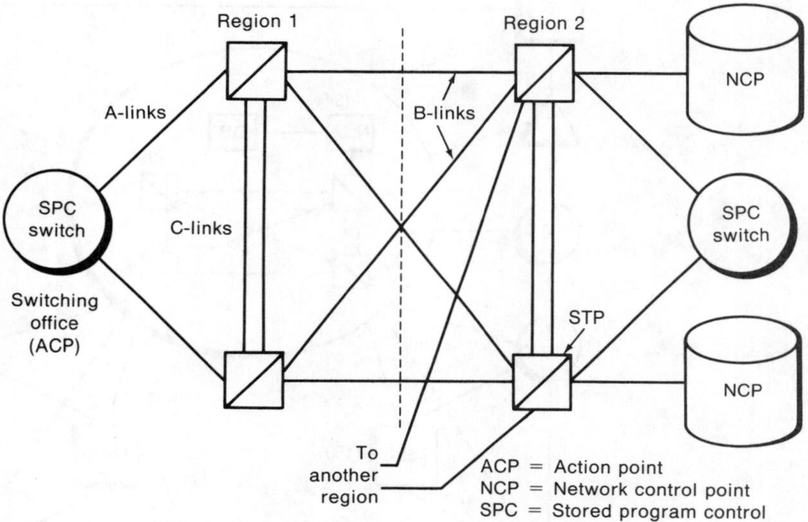

Figure 2-7. SPC network components *(after Wolfe and Martellotto 1984).*

Initially, the CCIS network was operated with STP pairs located in 10 regions across the United States. As SPC switches became prevalent and traffic volume grew, the initial 10 STP pairs were increased to 16 pairs. To improve message handling, the original 2.4 kb/s links were replaced with 4.8 kb/s transmission over analog signal links.

Other enhancements were added to the CCS network in 1985. The 2STP, based on a new processor, was introduced; 56 kb/s digital links were provided between the STPs and the ANSI version of CCITT Signaling System No. 7 protocol was augmented. This resulted in what is now known as the common channel signaling 7 (CCS7) network. The CCS7 network was almost completed in 1987 with the migration of most NCPs and the connection of 4ESS SPC switches via 56 kb/s digital links to the new network (Lawser and Oxley 1987). CCITT Signaling System No. 7 installed by other telephone companies and non-Bell carriers is called SS7.

Quasi-associated signaling has been used in both the CCIS and CCS7 networks. The STPs consist of packet data switches that use an AT&T version of CCITT X.25. The SPC structure shown in Figure 2-7 remains essentially as shown for CCS7.

New Network Architectures

The description of network architectures so far is based on the hierarchical structure that was started during the 1930s, in place in the 1950s, and continuously modified into the 1980s. The description that follows is based on current network architecture philosophy forced in large part by the divestiture of AT&T and the Bell System companies.

Background

The antitrust suit of the United States versus AT&T et al. was settled on January 8, 1982. It is called the Modified Final Judgment (MFJ) because it replaced a 1956 Final Judgment in an earlier lawsuit filed against AT&T by the United States government. A Plan of Reorganization (POR) was filed by AT&T on December 16, 1982. The MFJ was the basis for divestiture of the Bell companies from AT&T, while the POR provided the architecture of a new structure for the telephone industry. As a result, AT&T retained its long distance communication and telecommunication equipment manufacturing business (Andrews 1984). Other assets included retaining part of the Bell Laboratories. The 19 Bell System telephone companies were organized into seven RBOCs. The MFJ and POR further divided the franchised areas of the RBOCs into 161 LATAs. Eighteen other LATAs are served by other companies.

Under divestiture agreements, AT&T became an inter-LATA carrier providing communication services between LATAs. The STPs, NCPs, and interconnecting links were assigned to AT&T. Minor use of these facilities was provided by contract to the RBOCs.

The following sections will describe the inter- and intra-LATA network structures that have been established since divestiture.

Dynamic Nonhierarchical Routing

The new network structure for inter-LATA traffic has evolved from the hierarchical to a dynamic nonhierarchical (DNHR) structure. The switch systems are now classless and completely equivalent in their functions (Ash and Mummert 1984; Mocenigo and Tow 1984). Computer-controlled intelligence (i.e., SPC and CCS) that has been built into the AT&T switching and trunking network is used for DNHR. Predetermined routing patterns can be changed up to ten times per day based on measured and forecasted customer calling patterns. The changeover to DNHR started during August 1984 and was completed during 1987. Ninety-two existing 4ESS switches were affected by the changeover. Hundreds of millions of dollars are expected to be saved by AT&T in construction costs for new transmission facilities over the next ten years by implementing DNHR.

Structure

There are two parts, hierarchical and DNHR, to the new routing network structure. The conventional hierarchical structure (Figure 2-8) has a primary center switch, T3, as a traffic concentration point. The DNHR part (Figure 2-8) appears as a large network of regional (class 1) switches to the hierarchical system below it. Since the conversion of 92 4ESS switches to DNHR, an apparently classless regional structure exists in contrast to the previous conventional hierarchical structure of regional centers across the country.

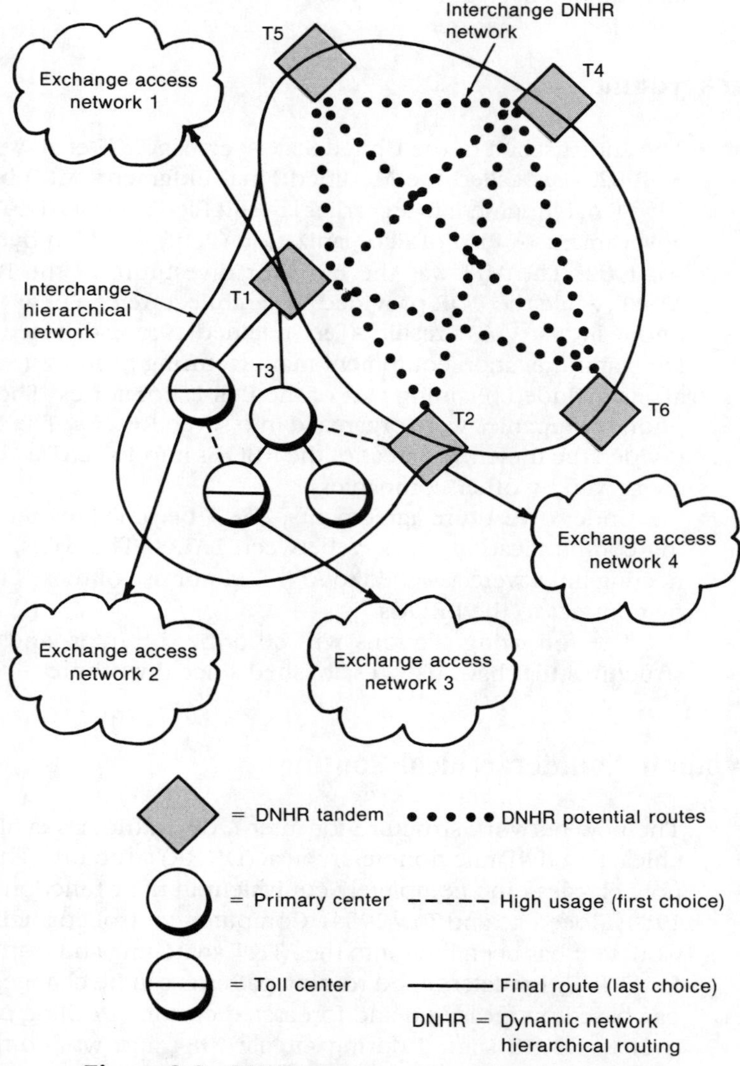

Figure 2-8. DNHR structure *(Ash and Mummert 1984)*.

Three kinds of traffic are handled by the DNHR network:

- traffic that originates in different exchange access areas, but connects to DNHR switches (originating/terminating in exchange access networks 4 and 1)
- overflow traffic from the hierarchical network (between exchange access areas 4 and 3)
- through-switched traffic loads from the hierarchical network (between exchange access networks 4 and 2)

These three kinds of traffic loads can be identified by a DNHR or originating switch that can also determine the terminating switch. No more than two trunks are to be used between originating the terminating DNHR switches for traffic that is identified as a DNHR call. Calls originating outside the DNHR network would appear to traverse at least three trunks to complete a call (e.g., one DNHR and two hierarchical trunks).

Routing

The principles of DNHR switching and routing are illustrated in Figure 2-9. An originating switch in San Diego has control of a call until it is either completed or blocked in White Plains. The switching plan uses as objectives:

1. least-cost routing with no more than three switches or two trunks involved in a call (originating, terminating, and via, a third switch between the other two)
2. predetermined optimal time-varying routing that capitalizes on idle capacity in other parts of the network (path-routing sequences that can vary ten times per day)
3. using CCS to inform the originating DNHR switch that blocking exists ("crankback") at a via switch and that another path may be attempted (real-time paths that handle overflow as a result of crankback)

For objective 3, attention should be given to the changes in the routing sequence as the day progresses, particularly for the engineered path.

Management

Network management for the DNHR is different from that used for the hierarchical structure which depended on a decentralized, multisystem, multicenter structure. Any problem between two connecting regions was reflected only in those regions.

In contrast, the DNHR requires a centralized management approach because of the classless switches, no regional boundaries, and the use of different via switches as traffic load patterns vary throughout the day. A new Network Management Operations Support (NEMOS) center receives traffic data in one centralized data base. The NEMOS automatically controls the network, in real time based on traffic measurement samples. Based on measurement and fore-

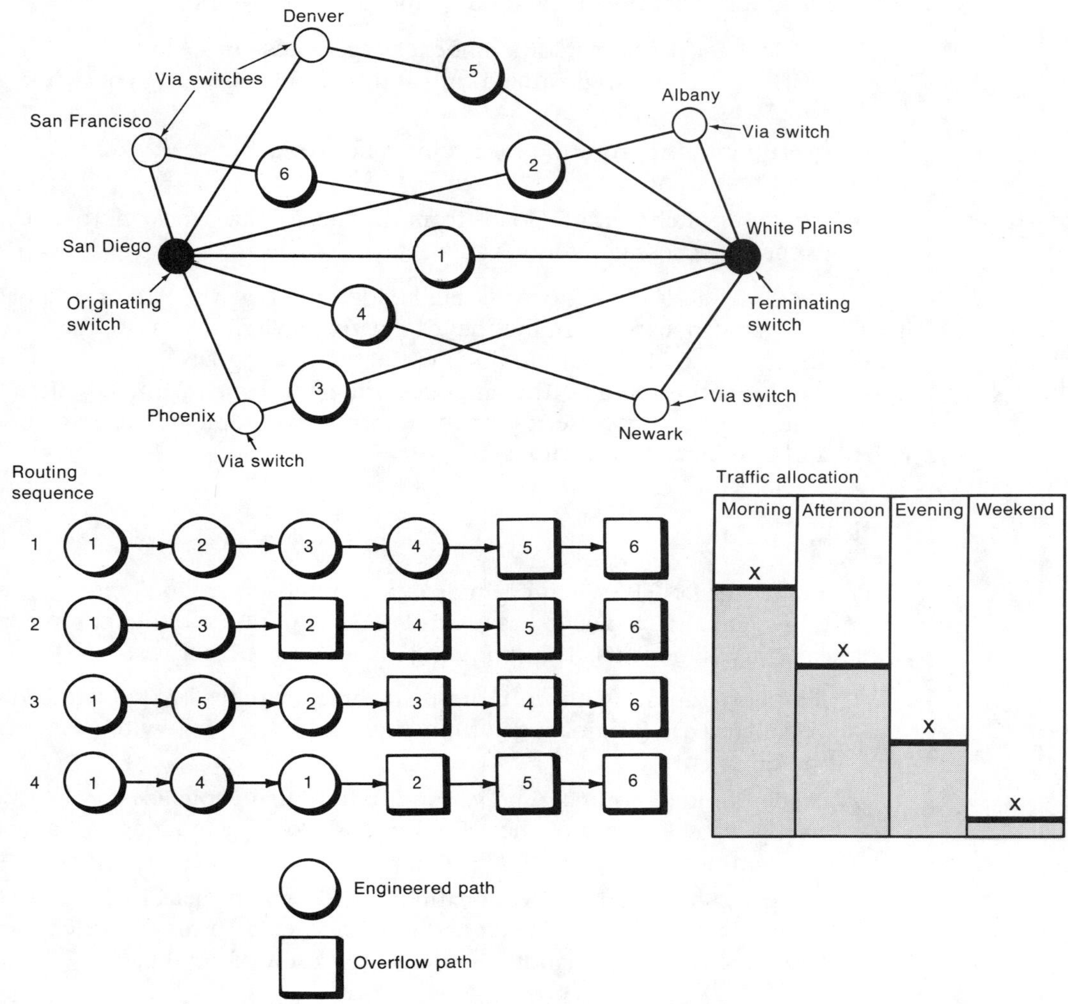

Figure 2-9. DNHR plan *(after Ash and Mummert 1984).*

casting, switch plan changes are produced semiannually; trunking is changed quarterly and also weekly if adjustments are necessary. Real-time changes are possible in response to overflow conditions. The use of CCS is integral to these switch plan, trunking, and routing changes.

The NEMOS has an automatic reroute algorithm capability that senses switch-to-switch overflow at certain levels. This information, collected every five minutes, is used by NEMOS to reroute traffic loads. The problem is approached by determining idle circuits between switch pairs. Traffic overflow from each switch pair is matched to idle circuits until all the overflows or all the idle circuits are paired. Reroute paths are removed when a switch pair falls below a particular threshold (Mocenigo and Tow 1984).

The philosophy of the DNHR network is that the administration and management are centralized, but the operation depends on distributed intelligence at the switches. The SPC, with signaling instructions sent by CCS from the NEMOS, controls the network switching.

LATAs and Equal Access

The LATAs are geographically defined areas of service responsibility where the divested operating companies and other communications carriers are authorized to route traffic. These carriers handle traffic that usually stays within state boundaries although exceptions exist. Traffic that crosses LATA boundaries must be handled by the inter-LATA carriers (Andrews 1984).

Separation of Services

Under the hierarchical structure, local tandem and toll-switching functions were often combined, for economic reasons, in a single switch within a class 4 office. According to the MFJ, all assets, including switches, were assigned to the dominant user. Generally, class 4/5 offices were assigned to a BOC, while tandems performing intra- and interstate switching were assigned to AT&T Communications. Disruption of service was avoided because sharing of assets is allowed on an eight-year leaseback plan. Under the consent decree it also has been necessary to reroute traffic that had been carried on HU trunks across new LATA boundaries between end offices.

Two conclusions can be reached from these changes. First, the inter-LATA (interexchange) carriers prevail in the areas where HU trunks were used to carry traffic. Second, more switches in the class 4/5 category have been needed to carry traffic as the intra- and inter-LATA traffic is separated before the eight-year limitation on leaseback ends. Two of these switches are described in Section 4.

Access

Prior to divestiture, the toll network (now the inter-LATA domain) as provided by AT&T and its competitors appeared as in Figure 2-10. A three-level hierarchy was used by terrestrial carriers when connecting to class 5 offices. There was only one level using time-division multiple access (TDMA) and it will likely continue to be used by satellite carriers.

For a subscriber to use a non-AT&T inter-LATA carrier it was necessary to use touchtone dialing to access a carrier. The dialing sequence used a second dial tone and required approximately 24 digits, including the caller identification number, to establish the call.

This lengthy connect dialing sequence to a carrier other than AT&T was considered "unequal" access and inferior to an 11-digit call connection that includes the 1+. Switches with SPC were modified to provide equal access for up to 999 inter-LATA carriers. Subscribers that are served by electromechanical

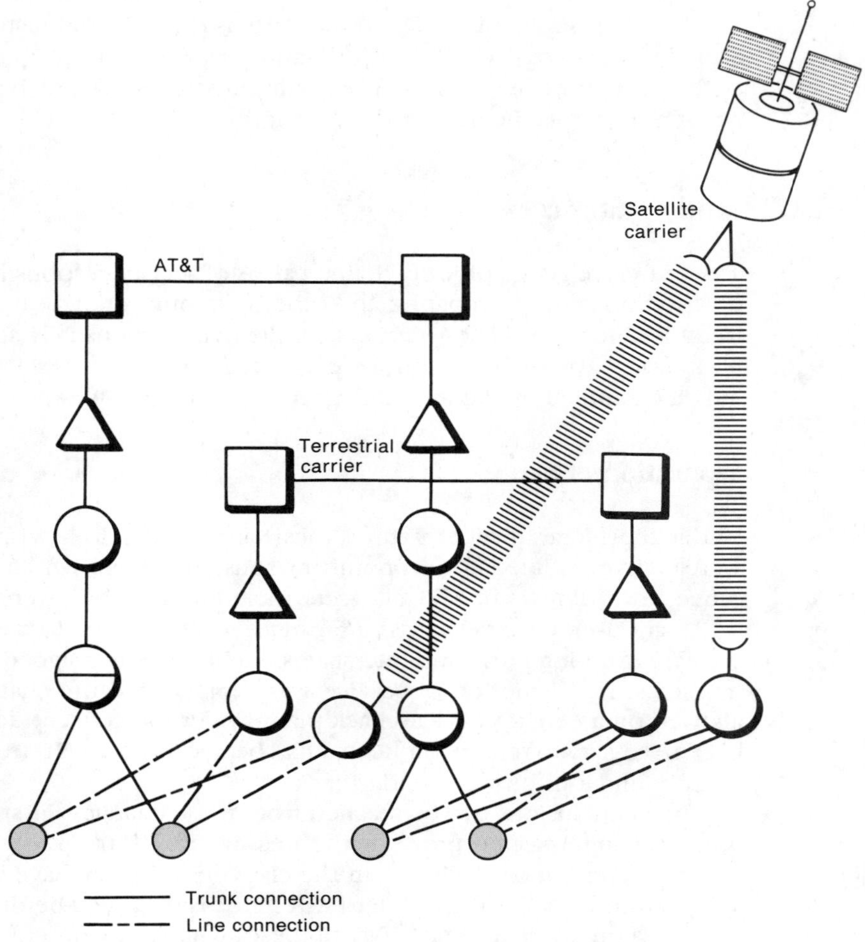

Figure 2-10. Toll networks for AT&T and other carriers (predivestiture) *(Andrews 1984).*

switches do not have the same equal access to an inter-LATA carrier until the older switches are replaced. With full equal access implementation, a subscriber can have service from any inter-LATA carrier by dialing the normal 7- or 10-digital numbers. It is also possible to override the regular carrier and select any inter-LATA carrier. This requires dialing an initial sequence of 10xxx where xxx is one of the 999 carrier selection numbers assigned to serve a LATA (e.g., xxx = 288 for AT&T).

Equal access by subscribers to inter-LATA carriers is provided through direct trunks, tandem switching, or both. Tandem switches used in this way are called access tandems (Figure 2-11). About 250 access tandems were expected to be deployed by 1987 (Andrews 1984). A switching system or facility where a LATA network is connected within the inter-LATA carrier structure is called point-of-presence (POP) or point-of-termination (POT).

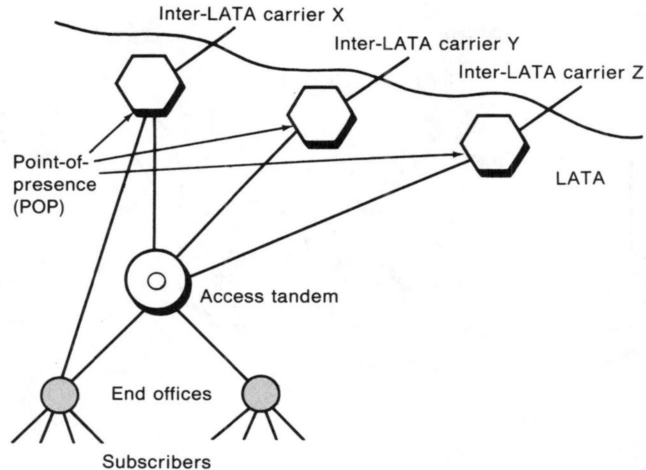

Figure 2-11. Equal access to inter-LATA carriers *(after Andrews 1984).*

Signaling and New Services

CCS links to local offices were discontinued with divestiture. At the same time, STPs and NCPs heretofore owned by the Bell System were assigned to AT&T. Other inter-LATA carriers, such as U.S. Sprint, MCI, and others are also implementing CCS that will support their services and traffic.

The RBOCs have evolved their own CCS networks. Regional STPs and LATA action points for "800" service will use CCITT No. 7. Figure 2-12 shows the inter-LATA points-of-presence for CCS and voice circuits within the LATA domain. Intra-LATA STPs are also shown as being connected to POPs, access tandems, end office, and data bases. From this it is clear that end offices that exist within the LATAs require CCS and inter-LATA carriers are part of the signaling between LATAs. Intra-LATA services include call-waiting, selective call-forwarding, call-screening, and calling-number display (Andrews 1984). Data bases for services are located in inter- and intra-LATA networks depending on the service provider.

Switch Descriptions

The two switch systems that are described in this section have a number of function attributes in common with several others. The AT&T 5ESS and Northern Telecom DMS-100 (which are described) and other switches such as the CIT-Alcatel E10-FIVE, Ericsson AXE System, GTE GTD-5 EAX, NEC NEAX 61A, and Siemens EWSD have circuit- and packet-switched applications, ISDN capability, including integrated voice and data, and common channel trunk signaling using CCITT No. 7. They are marketed in the United States for use in local, local/tandem, and access tandem offices. Based on the intra-and inter-LATA struc-

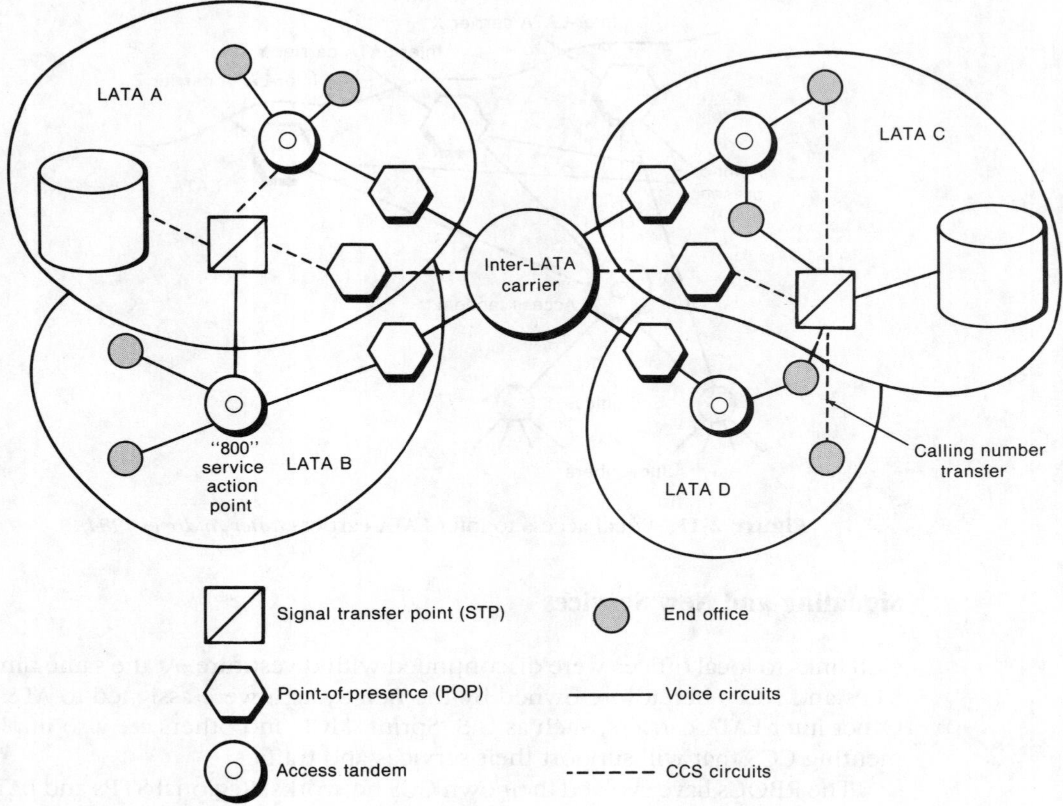

Figure 2-12. Inter- and intra-LATA signaling *(after Andrews 1984).*

tures, these switches have been, and will continue to be, installed by local and interexchange carriers. All are being manufactured or modified in the United States to meet North American switch requirements. From the information that is available, one can conclude that the architectural approaches used in all the switches will permit an adaptive approach to changing communications requirements and to the ISDN services that are emphasized by the switch manufacturers.

AT&T 5ESS

The AT&T 5ESS switch system has modular hardware and software that can be arranged to suit a customer's needs. It uses distributed processing to enable growth of capacity and capability. It has been designated to serve a range of applications and markets (Table 2-1). In some instances the 5ESS could replace older switches (step-by-step and 1ESS switches) or work in a coprocessing environment with another switch such as the 1A ESS.

Table 2-1. Market and Application Replacement Potential for the 5ESS

Application	Market: *Metropolitan*		*Suburban*		*Rural*	
Local	Crossbar tandem No. 1 crossbar No. 5 crossbar 1ESS 1A ESS	5ESS	No. 1 step-by-step No. 5 crossbar 2B ESS	5ESS	CDO No. 1 step-by-step 3ESS 10A RSS	5ESS
Toll	No. 4 crossbar 1A ESS 4ESS	5ESS	No. 5 crossbar local/toll 1A ESS	5ESS	No. 1 step-by-step local/toll	5ESS
Operator services	No. 5 crossbar Automatic Call Distributor Traffic Service Position System	5ESS	No. 5 crossbar Automatic Call Distributor Traffic Service Position System 5ESS	5ESS	Manual Traffic Service Position System/remote trunk arrangement	5ESS

This table is reprinted from Mastersteck and Spencer (1985).

The 5ESS hardware architecture has three major module components: an administrative module (AM), a communications module (CM), and one or more switching modules (SMs) including those for remote locations (Figure 2-13).

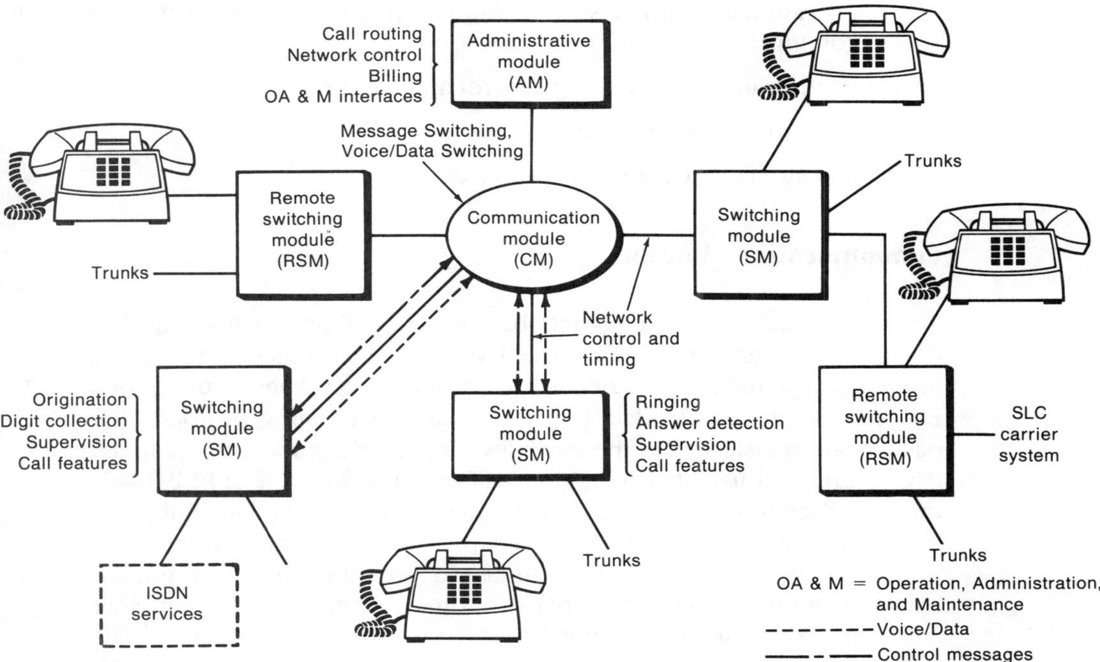

Figure 2-13. Hardware architecture for the 5ESS switch *(Johnson et al. 1984).*

Administrative Module

The AM provides interfaces required to administer, operate, and maintain the switch. The AM has dual 3B20D processors in an active/standby configuration for reliability. The active processor has control while simultaneously maintaining the standby unit. Should the active processor have a fault, the standby unit is switched into service without loss of data.

The AM performs call-processing functions such as line and trunk group routing determination for the switch modules, and the allocation of time-multiplexed-switch time slots. Call-processing support functions include systemwide craft maintenance, diagnostic control, software recovery and initialization, and certain fault recovery and error detection.

A disk memory and input/output processor (IOP) are subunits of the AM. The disk memory provides mass storage for programs and data while the IOP interfaces with support systems, video display units, printers, tape drives, and a Master Control Center (MCC). The MCC provides the interfaces for manual control of system operations and a system status display. Two craft interface languages are available for operation and maintenance functions on SPC systems such as the 5ESS. One is a language that is similar to that used in the 1A ESS. The second is the CCITT man-machine language (MML) (Carney et al. 1985; Gitten et al. 1984). The functions that are controlled by the MML (CCITT 1980) are for

1. operational purposes such as routing, traffic, tariff, and system control administration
2. maintenance of switching control and subscriber lines
3. plant installation testing
4. testing of, for example, memory dumps

Communications Module

The CM contains a message switch that transfers call-processing and administrative data messages between the other two types of modules. Messages are transferred through the CM and then to the AM and SM modules by using the CCITT Recommendation X.25 data link layer packet-switching protocol. The data packets are transferred to the modules through Network Control and Timing (NCT) links that use fiber light guides. There are two NCT links between each module. Each link carries a 32.768 Mb/s serial data stream containing 256 channels (time slots). This results in 512 channels between each module.

The 5ESS CM has a time-space-time (TST) architecture that is implemented by a time multiplex switch (to perform time-shared space-division switching) and a time-slot interchange unit (i.e., for time-division switching). The fiber-optic data links, which provide communication paths between SMs, are switched through by the centralized time multiplex switch (Carney et al. 1985; Gitten et al. 1984).

Switching Module

The SM is the expansion unit for the 5ESS switch. It consists of different types of interface equipment for line and trunk terminations, provides for call-processing intelligence, and performs the first stage of switching. There are analog and digital interface units for lines and trunks. One digital trunk line unit for interoffice trunks can terminate up to ten North American T1 lines at 1.544 Mb/s or up to sixteen 2.048 Mb/s digital lines (Carney et al. 1985). A digital subscriber loop carrier system, the SLC96, is a loop carrier pair-gain system that serves as a cable replacement or supplement that can carry up to 96 subscribers.

Equipment that is common to the SMs includes dual link interfaces (NCTs), duplicated module processors and slot-interchange units, and a digital services unit. The redundant processors control call-processing, call distribution, and call maintenance. The slot interchange unit switches 256 time slots on each NCT link (512 total). It can connect these time slots to peripheral devices or to the command module. The digital services unit provides time generation and decoding.

The 5ESS uses a computer and operating system that are an integral part of stored program-controlled networks including central office switching and switch support systems. The 3B Duplex Computer (3B20D) uses the Duplex Multi-Environmental Real-Time (DMERT) operating system. It is compatible with the UNIX operating system and also supports the C programming language. [A name change has been made and the DMERT operating system is now called the UNIX Real-Time Reliable (RTR) operating system.] Translation from the C language to CHILL has also been considered.

The 3B20D computer system is used

- in Network Control Points to provide on-line, real-time bases for STPs in the CCS network
- in packet-switched data communications networks that use CCITT Recommendation X.25, including applications of the No. 1 Packet System (1PSS) in Local Area Data Transport (LADT), ACCUNET Packet Switching Service, and CCS
- for TSPS
- as an attached processor for the 4ESS and 1A ESS switching systems to provide file storage and off-load capability
- to serve the 5ESS switch as the central processor-administrative module in addition to several other functions (Becker et al. 1984)

Software

The 5ESS software can be described in two ways: conceptual and operational. In conceptual terms, the 5ESS software architecture consists of a hierarchy of vested virtual machines where software is structured as a set of sequential abstract layers (Figure 2-14). These layers apply to all processors located within the hardware of the administrative, communications, and switching modules. The hierarchy is such that any machine, at any layer, uses the services of lower-layer machines and provides services for higher-layer machines.

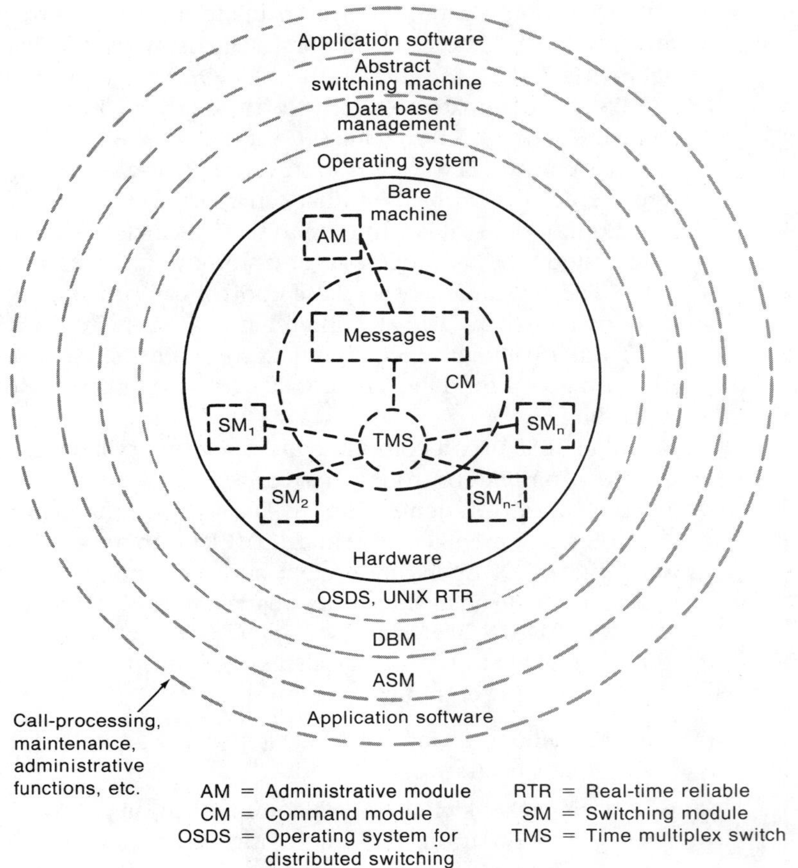

Figure 2-14. Concept of 5ESS software architecture *(Carney et al. 1985).*

The center circle in Figure 2-14 is the lowest layer of the hierarchy. It is the physical or "bare machine" and consists of the AM, SM, and CM which contains the message switch and time multiplex switch (TMS).

At the next layer, the Operating System for Distributed Switching (OSDS) runs on all processors. The OSDS in the switching modules is designed for switching applications in a distributed architecture. In the administrative module, the UNIX RTR operating system is running along with OSDS in the form of several processes. The OSDS provides five major functions (Delatore et al. 1985):

- processor isolation (hardware changes have a minimal effect on software design)
- concurrency control (the ability to handle a large number of activities as a sequence of separate tasks in a process)

- intra- and interprocessor message communication (message transmission within or between processors)
- resource scheduling (allocation of memory resources and processor time)
- timing (a time-of-day clock for billing and time-stamping and timing requests required for process control)

At the next layer (the third) of the hierarchy, the virtual machine is for the Data Base Manager (DBM). There is a collection of data bases that are located in some or all of the separate processes. The DBM supports the various data bases and distributed management of the data so that the location of the data is transparent to programs.

The abstract switching machine (ASM) is at the fourth layer of the software model. The ASM is also known as a Virtual Switching Machine (VSM). Somewhat more detail will be presented for this layer because of the interesting concepts that are considered for call processing on facility maintenance.

An analogy of the virtual machine hierarchy can be made. A conventional operating system provides a virtual machine environment to application level programs by implementing an abstraction of a bare machine. Similarly, the ASM/VSM provides high-level abstraction of the switching periphery to the switching application software (Hafer et al. 1984).

Within the VSM, there are basic resources available to the application software—the logical ports (LPs), network paths, and connectors. Also, there is a terminal process in the VSM controlling the LPs, paths, and connectors it has acquired.

Customer access channels to the switch model (Figure 2-15) may be concentrated or unconcentrated, and are used to transport customer information messages between distant terminals. The access channels are interconnected by network paths within the switch. A logical port represents an access channel to the switch. Connectors within the VSM represent an information mixer where the application of an algorithm to n input streams results in m output streams. Connectors provide the service concepts for message broadcast on a multiparty conference call. Different services may use different connectors. VSM paths in the switch model can represent

- a communication channel in the switch
- different types of communication channels
- interconnection of logical ports and connectors

Terminal processes perform various types of operations on the logical ports representing customer access channels, on the network paths, and on connectors. Operations on LPs are open and close, establishment and release (between two LPs, two connectors, or an LP and a connector), and the joining of two paths. Operations on connectors are such that the terminal process inserts a connector for the purpose of establishing a connection between LPs.

In mapping the VSM into hardware, the LP associates with the physical connection of a terminal device such as a PBX, telephone, or video display terminal to the switch. LP hardware includes the port circuitry, concentration arrange-

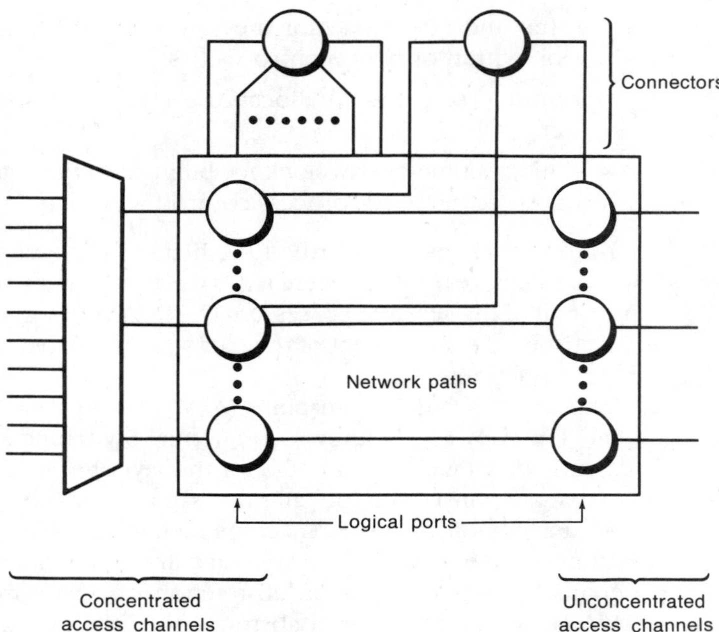

Figure 2-15. Simplified switch model *(Hafer et al. 1984).*

ment, and time-slot interchange (TSI). Paths are implemented in the TSI and TMS. Connectors are implemented in conferencing circuits (Hafer et al. 1985).

The final layer of the virtual machine hierarchy is the application software. This software provides for call-processing, maintenance, and administration.

So far this has been a conceptual description of the 5ESS software architecture. The operational software can be described as consisting of subsystem modules that communicate with each other while using specific message protocols and instructions across module interfaces. Subsystem components are shown in Figure 2-16. The switching periphery is the hardware nearest the lines and trunk ports. Routing and terminal administration is at the highest level and further removed from the hardware. As shown, all functions within the operating system (e.g., OSDS) span all processor modules.

Three major components of the call-processing software are peripheral control, feature control, and routing and terminal allocation.

Routing and terminal allocation performs call-routing and screening based on information from dialed digits and the originating line to route the call to the appropriate outgoing trunk or terminating line. The routing process provides the "link" between originating and terminating terminal process in feature control.

Feature control also consists of hardware-independent software. It is used, for example, to implement POTS, coin service, hotel/motel service, and modular CENTREX features available on the 5ESS.

Peripheral control consists of hardware-independent software that provides a set of logical primitives that are used, for example, to ring a phone, outpulse digits on a trunk, and make network connections. (Primitives are interac-

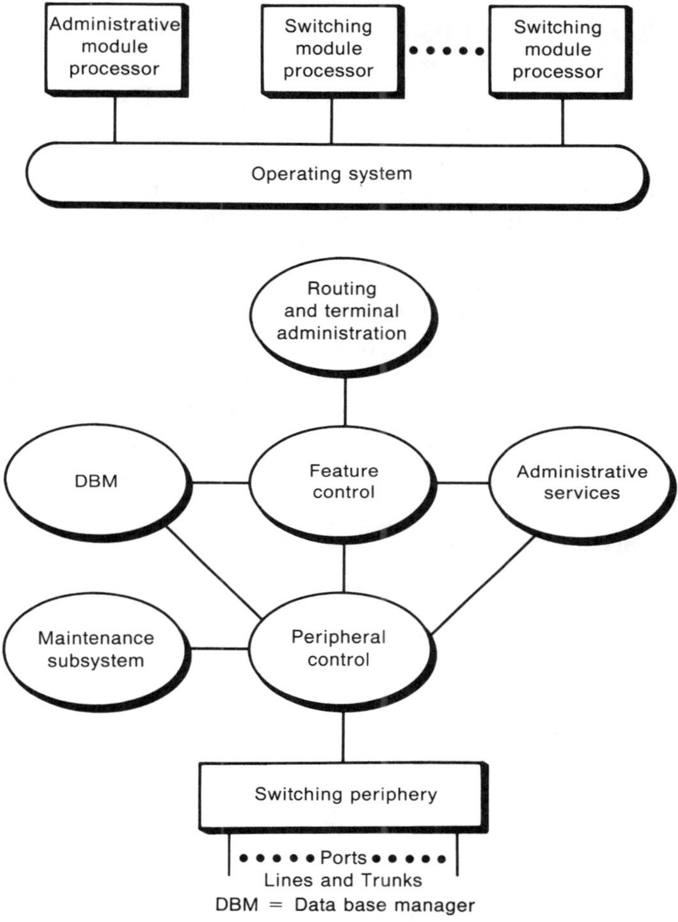

Figure 2-16. Operational software architecture for the 5ESS *(Delatore et al. 1985).*

tions between layers to convey a request, indication, response, or confirmation.)

The overall architecture of the 5ESS call-processing software was not changed because of divestiture. However, because of 5ESS end office and access tandem applications, two of the above components, routing and terminal allocation and feature control, did need modification. Enhancements were made to give each customer equal access to inter-LATA carriers on a per-call or presubscription basis. Software was added to feature control to provide new digit analysis, carrier selection and validation, and needed signaling functions.

Routing and terminal allocation was changed to allow calls to be routed to carriers (Averweg 1985).

Northern Telecom DMS-100

The Northern Telecom, Incorporated (NTI) DMS-100 family of switches is intended to provide a range of telecommunication services. The DMS-100 is a switch for use in a class 5 office. With appropriate adaptations it can provide cellular mobile services and be used as an equal access end office. A DMS-200 switch is designed for class 4 through class 1 toll centers and access tandem switch applications serving between a few hundred to 60,000 trunks. A DMS 100/200 switch is designed for local/toll operation with a combination of up to 100,000 lines or 60,000 trunks. It can serve equal access end office and access tandem switch applications. A DMS-250 is a toll switch for specialized common carriers requiring tandem switch operation. The DSMS-300 is intended to meet requirements for international gateway operations (NTI 1984).

Since the introduction of the DMS-100 in 1978, several module changes have been made without requiring a complete redesign of the DMS-100 switch.

Structure

The NTI DMS-100 switch family has a series of devices and modules assigned to four functional areas: central control complex, network, peripheral, and maintenance and administration (Figures 2-17, 2-18). Devices in the central control complex are

- message and device controller
- CPU
- program store memory
- data store memory

Network devices are the network modules (switch) and message controllers. Some of the peripheral modules are

- trunk (analog interface) circuits
- digital trunk controller
- line group controller
- line control

The input/output controllers are used in maintenance and administration.

Hardware

The central control complex is the SPC main call-processing component for the DMS-100 (Figure 2-18). A program controls call-processing, maintenance and administrative routines, and directs activity in other parts of the switch as a result

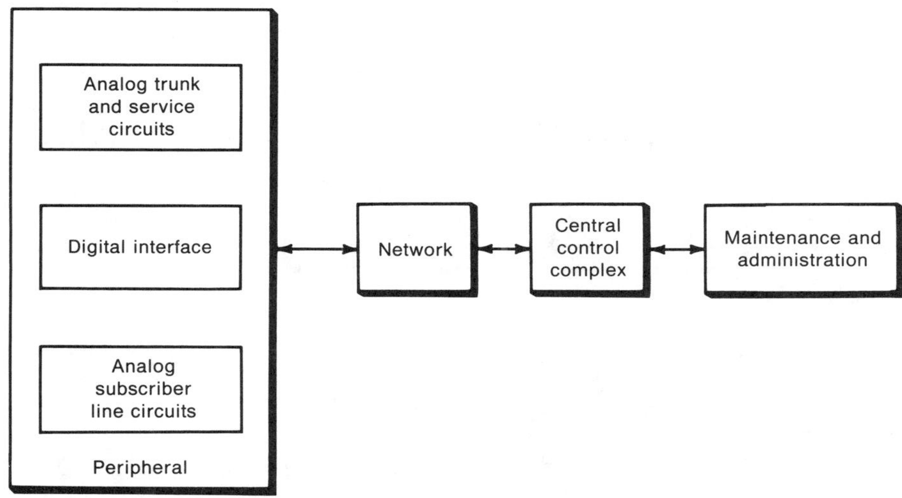

Figure 2-17. Four functional areas of the DMS-100 family *(NTI 1984)*.

of these routines. All units within the complex are duplicated. The message and device controller is a collector/distributor unit for signal buffering and routing between the central processor and peripheral equipment. The controller also contains a system clock that is synchronized to the basic reference frequency. The source clock provides timing for the switch system, peripherals, and network. The central processor unit has access to the control complex data and program store memories. It uses information within those memories to respond to network conditions by issuing commands to parts of the network. The program store memory is the repository for program instructions required by the central processor. The data store memory contains the transient or per-call type of information and customer data.

Within the network function area, the network module is the basic building block of the network units of the DMS-100. It is a four-stage time (TTTT) switch that is used to provide a voice path between an originating and terminating peripheral module. The central processor controls the voice path via messages to the network module and distributes control messages concerning the peripheral modules. There are two planes (plane 0 and plane 1) in the four-stage time switch. Both perform the same operations, but only the active side does signal processing while the other side assumes control should a fault occur.

Since being introduced in 1978 and prior to 1984, the DMS-100 family of switches has relied on four types of microprocessor-based peripheral modules: *trunk modules* that serve as interfaces to analog trunks, *digital carrier modules* for digital trunks, *line modules* that interface analog subscriber lines, and a *remote line module* that is located away from the host and performs the same duties as the line module. The peripheral module functions are call supervision, dial pulse timing, digit transmission and reception, and analog-to-digital conversion.

A series of new peripheral modules was introduced in 1984. They are *back-*

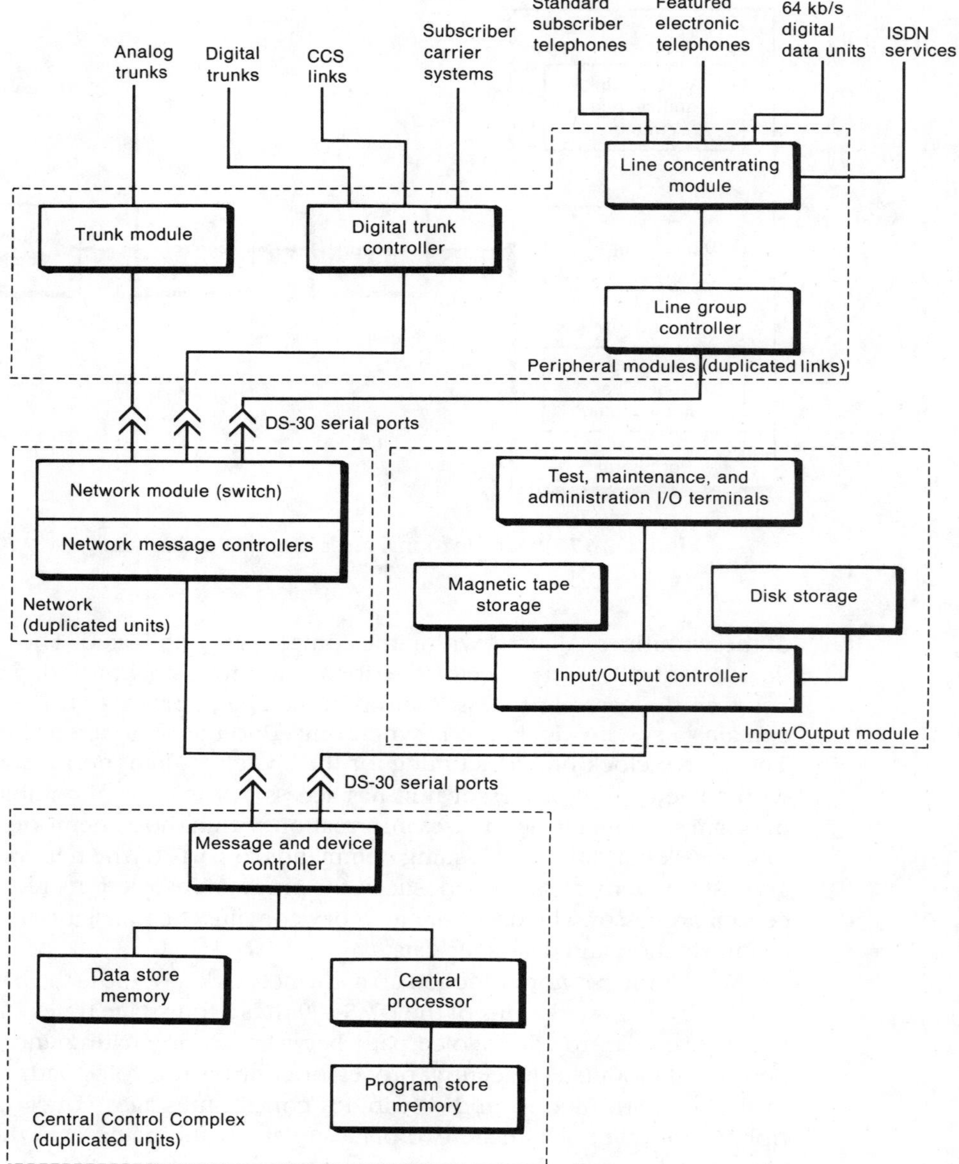

Figure 2-18. Structure of DMS-100 *(after NTI 1984; Wood 1983, 1984).*

ward-compatible modules that replace the interfaces for digital trunks and line modules. The analog trunk interface is not being replaced.

As shown in Figure 2-18, DS-30 serial ports (or DMS-X for operation to 160 Km) interconnect the hierarchical levels by conveying control messages between the central control complex, the I/O modules, and the network switching. The DS-30 port system is a Northern Telecom interface that permits module replacement without affecting other modules. The DS-30 message protocol allows the central control complex to communicate sequentially with a series of input/output and network modules. The switching network, in turn, can communicate with the peripheral modules (Wood 1984).

Within the peripheral module area, the line group controller (LGC) is called a first-tier module that controls second-tier modules, known as line concentrating modules (LCMs). Other second-tier modules that are controlled by the line group controller are line concentrators and remote switching centers. The LGC performs high-level call processing such as digit analysis and tone control. The LCM performs lower-level functions such as line supervision and digit collection. The LGC carries up to 640 PCM speech and signaling channels. Of the 640 channels, only 480 actually carry speech. The remaining channels are used for control messages, status indications, and tone distribution. A time switch within the LGC is used to direct messages and tones onto PCM channels.

The basic second-tier module, the LCM, operates under control of the LGC. The LCM provides time switching and concentration between subscriber line circuits and serial ports to the LGC.

The digital trunk controller is a variant of the LGC just discussed. It can be configured as a digital trunk controller to handle up to twenty DS-1 trunks by placing trunk call-processing software in the unit microprocessor and providing DS-1 transmission interfaces. Another variant of the LGC acts as the system interface to all common channel signaling links, including CCIS and CCS7.

Each trunk module (also a first-tier peripheral module) encodes and multiplexes incoming speech from a maximum of 30 analog trunks into a digital format. Decoding and demultiplexing is performed in the other direction of transmission within the switch. The PCM bit streams containing trunk supervisory and control signals, are combined with internal control signals, and transmitted at 2.56 Mb/s to the switch Network Module (NTI 1984; Wood 1984).

Firmware/Software

The DMS-100 family contains firmware/software that is classified into two main categories, central control and peripheral. The central control firmware/software performs functions necessary for switch operation such as high-level control of calls and system maintenance. Most of these programs are written in the Procedure-Oriented Type Enforcing Language (PROTEL). At the same time, some time-critical or maintenance operations are programmed directly in firmware. The peripheral firmware/software is microprocessor-oriented for distributed processing. It performs repetitive, time-consuming tasks such as scanning, control, and maintenance of telephone interfaces. The software in peripheral modules is written in assembly language. PASCAL is used for programming the line group and digital trunk controllers.

The software has a highly modular structure that is designed around operating functions. The different software modules accommodate the type of office (local, toll), the features required (CENTREX, CCS), and the hardware supported (trunk types, digital carriers, etc.).

Switch Implementations for ISDN

The vendors of central office switches provide similar implementation of ISDN features. While the switch architecture and software are unique to each manufacturer, compatibility with the outside communications world is required. A fundamental requirement is the ability to interwork with existing voice and data services. The AT&T 5ESS and DMS-100 are no exception.

Both are SPC switches that supported CCIS and now operate with CCS7—a requirement for ISDN. They support the basic (2B+D) and primary (23B+D or 30B+D) rate interfaces for customer access (Fishel 1986; Wong and Wood 1986). The basic rate interface is implemented through T-and U-interface line cards that relate to the ISDN T- and U-reference points. The T-interface card supports direct connections over two-wire copper pairs, not to exceed one kilometer, that are designed for intra-building applications. This is a terminal-to-network interface. The U-reference point defines the loop interface between the central office and customer premises. This interface card provides for nonloaded, twisted wire pairs at distances up to six kilometers. Both AT&T and NTI use echo cancellation technology to support full-duplex transmission of 144 kb/s of user bandwidth and additional overhead bits. The vendors also support the primary rate interface by providing terminations within the switches for the T1 carrier.

Further ISDN support is given for packet mode services, including CCITT Recommendations X.25 and X.75. Both AT&T and NTI have created a separate packet-switched network within their switches that parallels an existing circuit-switched time-division system. Processing of packets is achieved by a Packet Switch Unit (AT&T) or Packet Handler (NTI) that supports

- X.25 LAPB and packet layer procedures (PLP)
- Q.921 (LAPD) and Q.931 requirements
- X.75 signaling with packet-switched public data networks (PSPDNs)

The ISDN access arrangements occur at the 5ESS switching module and the DMS-100 peripheral module. Both switches also provide support to local area networks, CENTREX, and "800" services in which the called party, rather than the calling party, pays for toll calls.

Although these descriptions have concentrated on the 5ESS and DMS-100 because of their dominance in the U.S. marketplace, the switches from other manufacturers have been accepted with varying success.

Summary and Conclusion

Changes have occurred in approaches to telecommunications philosophy and implementation for many reasons. Two of the most important events are

- divestiture
- continuing and accelerated development of telecommunication standards, particularly those for ISDN and signaling

The traditional hierarchical structure of the public-switched telephone system has changed. It is now based on a nonhierarchical structure with dynamic routing for long-distance calls. CCS, based on CCITT signaling system No. 6 has been replaced by CCITT No. 7 as the evolution continues toward ISDN(s) through the former Bell companies and other carriers. Small non-Bell telephone companies have organized to install a signaling system based on CCITT No. 7 in rural and remote areas. Intra- and inter-LATAs and equal access for long distance exchange carriers have become a reality.

As the routing and signaling structures have changed, the market opportunities for switch manufacturers have also changed as a result of divestiture. Central office switches were previously provided by a limited number of manufacturers. Since the divestiture, and the opening of the U.S. marketplace to increased competition, a number of foreign companies have opened major facilities in the United States. Switches from CIT-Alcatel, Ericsson, GTE, NEC, and Siemens are other candidates for postdivestiture networking and ISDN applications.

The switch size from these companies ranges from 1,000 to greater than 100,000 lines with varying degrees of calling capacity. Architectural structures and software languages are different for these switches, but a common requirement is that signal format compatibility exists between central offices. One of the major problems in using these switches in an ISDN, or any other environment, is the lack of software compatibility. A diversity of switch "brands" within a common carrier requires that the software for routing, features, or applications is rewritten for each switch. This, of course, adds to system operating costs. A common software release is preferable whenever possible.

Conversely, the switches from these manufacturers were designed with a modular concept, for both hardware and software. Therefore, the ability to change or grow gracefully is an inherent function of the switches.

References

Andrews, F. T., Jr. 1984. Switching technology in a new network structure. *ISS '84, XI International Switching Symposium* (May 7–11) Florence, Italy.

Ash, G. R., and V. S. Mummert. 1984. AT&T carves new routes in its nationwide network. *AT&T Bell Laboratories Record* 62, no. 6 (August).

AT&T. 1980. *Notes on the Network*. American Telephone and Telegraph Co.

Averweg, J. L., S. J. Lueders, and M. E. Stinson. 1985. The impact of divestiture on 5ESS™ switch software. *ICC '85, IEEE International Conference on Communications 1985* (June 23–26) Chicago.

Basinger, R. G., M. Berger, E. M. Prell, V. L. Ransom, and J. R. Williams. 1982. Calling card service—overall description and operational characteristics. *The Bell System Technical Journal* 61, no. 7, part 3:1655 (September).

Becker, J. O., D. C. Opferman, and M. W. Rolund. 1984. Introduction and overview of the 3B™ computer family. *ISS '84, XI International Switching Symposium* (May 7–11) Florence, Italy.

Carney, D. L., J. I. Cockrane, L. J. Gitten, E. M. Prell, and R. Staehler. 1985. The 5ESS switching system: Architectural overview. *AT&T Technical Journal* 64, no. 6 (July–August).

CCITT. 1980. Recommendations Z.311 to Z.341, man-machine language (MML). *Yellow Book VI*. Fascicle VI.7, Geneva.

Confalone, D. E., B. W. Rogers, and R. J. Thornberry, Jr. 1982. Calling card service—TSPS hardware, software, and signaling implementation. *The Bell System Technical Journal* 61, no. 7, part 3:1675 (September).

Delatore, J. P., R. J. Frank, H. Dehring, and L. C. Stecher. 1985. The 5ESS switching system: Operational software. *AT&T Technical Journal* 64, no. 6 (July–August).

Fishel, R. A. 1986. ISDN Implementation in the 5ESS™ switch. *Globecom '86, IEEE Global Telecommunications Conference* (December 1–4) Houston.

Frerking, R. F., and M. A. McGrew. 1982. Routing of direct-signaling messages in the CCIS network. *The Bell System Technical Journal* 61, no. 7 (September).

Gitten, L. J., J. Janik, Jr., E. M. Prell, and J. L. Johnson. 1984. 5ESS™ system evolution. *ISS '84, XI International Switching Symposium* (May 7–11) Florence, Italy.

Hafer, E. H., D. M. Deruyck, A. R. Flora-Holmquist. 1984. A virtual-switching machine of the 5ESS™ switching system. *Globecom '84, IEEE Global Telecommunications Conference* (November 26–29) Atlanta.

Johnson, J. W., N. J. Burzinski, J. A. Davis, and J. Sharpless. 1984. Integrated digital services on the 5ESS™ system. *ISS '84, XI International Switching Symposium* (May) Florence, Italy.

Keiser, B. E., and E. Strange. 1985. *Digital Telephony and Network Integration.* New York: Nostrand Reinhold Company.

Lawser, J. J., R. E. LeCronier, and R. L. Simms. 1982. Generic network plan. *The Bell System Technical Journal* 61, no. 7 (September).

Lawser, J. J., and P. L. Oxley. 1987. Common channel signaling network evolution. *AT&T Technical Journal* 66, no. 3.

Martersteck, K. E., and A. E. Spencer, Jr. 1985. The 5ESS switching system: Introduction. *AT&T Technical Journal* 64, no. 6 (July–August).

Mocenigo, J. M., and D. M. Tow. 1984. Managing a network that won't sit still. *AT&T Bell Laboratories Record* 62, no. 6 (August).

Nesenbergs, M., and P. M. McManamon. 1983. An introduction to the technology of intra- and interexchange area telephone networks. *NTIA Report 83-*

118 (March). Available from National Technical Information Service, Springfield, VA, Order No. PB 83-241893.

NTI. 1984. *Planning guide, DMS 100/200 family* (December).

Wolfe, R. M., and N. A. Martellotto. 1984. Telecommunications data base application with the 3B™20 processor. *ISS '84 XI International Switching System Symposium* (May 7–11) Florence, Italy.

Wong, C. L., and R. Wood. 1986. DMS-100 evolution, and ISDN perspective. *Globecom '86, IEEE Global Telecommunications Conference* (December 1–4) Houston.

Wood, R. 1983. DMS-100 technology evolution. *Telesis* 10, no. 3.

———. 1984. DMS-100 peripheral evolution. *ISS '84, XI International Switching Symposium* (May 7–11) Florence, Italy.

Chapter 3

Packet-Switched Networks

Anthony Michel

Chapter 3

A COMPUTER NETWORK IS A COLLECTION OF MACHINES connected by communications links to permit sharing of information, resources, and processing power. Since the first experiments with computer networking in the mid-1960s, great progress has been achieved, and now in the late 1980s, powerful networks are commonplace and are an important part of most computer systems. In the two decades since the first packet network, the Arpanet, began service, this approach has been widely adopted and is the mainstay of most modern data communications systems today. In the future, integrated digital networks such as those based on ISDN will begin to enter service and the packet mode of service will be an indispensable part of these networks as well.

Communications should be singled out for separate study and separate subsystems should be built for the communications portion of a system because communications problems have much in common, regardless of the systems application. Most users and system designers would willingly be rid of the complexities of communications. The communications problem is to provide a path for moving information which is accurate (doesn't corrupt the data) and timely (doesn't unduly delay the transmission). At the same time, the user wants a channel which is flexible (imposes few restrictions on user's behavior) and efficient (most of the channel's capacity is available to the user). The user's desire—a dedicated, trouble-free, instantaneous channel to every possible destination—is hard to achieve, and practical systems achieve these goals with varying success.

Figure 3-1 shows the elements of a modern data communications system. The users are data systems such as computers or terminals, and are called hosts, terminals, or subscribers. The communications are provided by a communications subnetwork, which, in the best cases, takes on most of the burden of managing the communications problem. The figure shows the subnet as a collection of one or more switches which find and maintain paths from origin to destination across the subnet, using trunks as links between the switches. The circuit connecting the subscriber into the subnet is the local loop or subscriber loop.

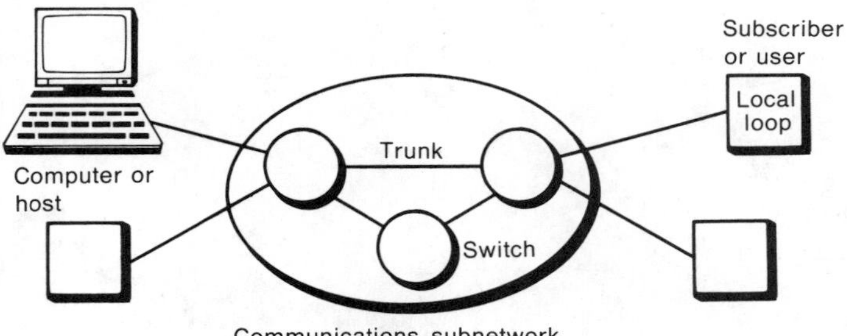

Figure 3-1. Communication system elements.

Packet-switching describes a large class of data communications systems. Figure 3-2 shows a packet-switching system in which information is grouped into blocks, or packets, by the sender, transmitted and then reassembled into the original form by the receiver. Streams of packets from many users can be processed at the same time and many conversations can be handled by the system simultaneously. In packetized form, the data can be handled within the system efficiently, data errors can be controlled, and flow rates into and out of

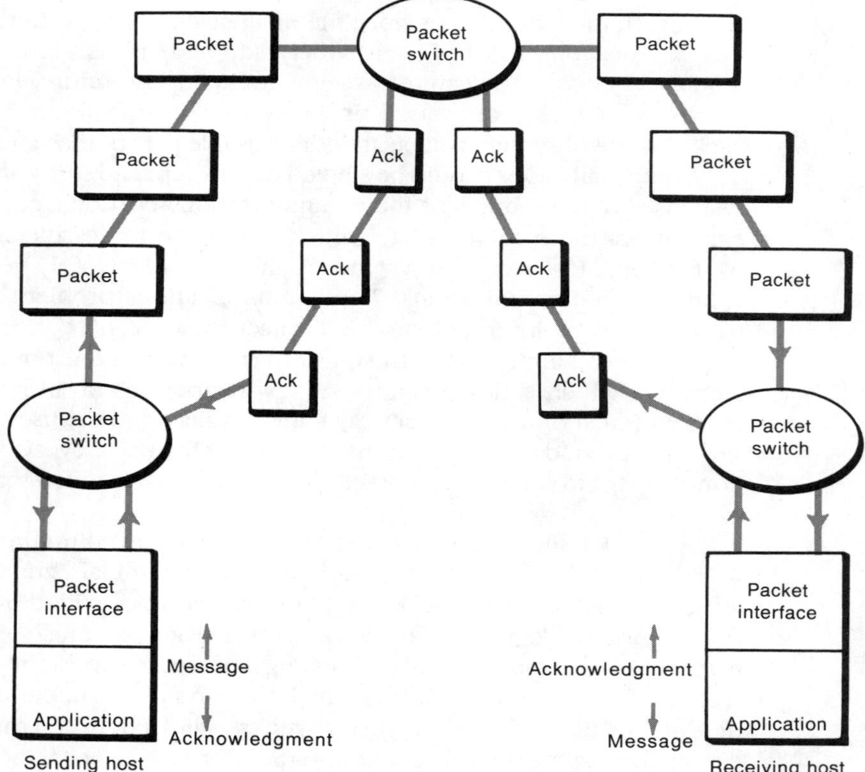

Figure 3-2. Packet switching.

the system managed. Packet systems are well suited to computer communications, which require error-free, low-delay performance, and which must share the communications facility among many users simultaneously.

Data Communications

Computer communications can be grouped into two classes, as shown in Figure 3-3. One class is *terminal to computer*, the other is *computer to computer*. With modern systems, it is rare to find simple direct links between terminals and the central computers or even between sets of computers. Even so, the distinction remains. The difference arises from the pacing of the communications. In terminal-oriented systems, a human is involved. Human users may sit and think for long periods, relative to the computer's time scale, and then, without warning, type some characters and expect a speedy response. The human thinking process establishes the communications patterns. In computer to computer systems, no human is directly involved in the transmissions, so the machines may set the pace. However, without a human in the loop to manage flow and error control, the requirements on the communication system are severe. It must not make any errors and it must adapt its behavior automatically to changing conditions. This combination of requirements—for responsive, low-delay transmissions on one hand and flexible, error-free paths on the other—is not well met by traditional telephone-type voice-oriented communications systems. This is the motivation for packet switching.

Packing Information into Blocks

To simplify the problem of organizing the data, many communications systems break the user information into blocks. Each block may then be separately man-

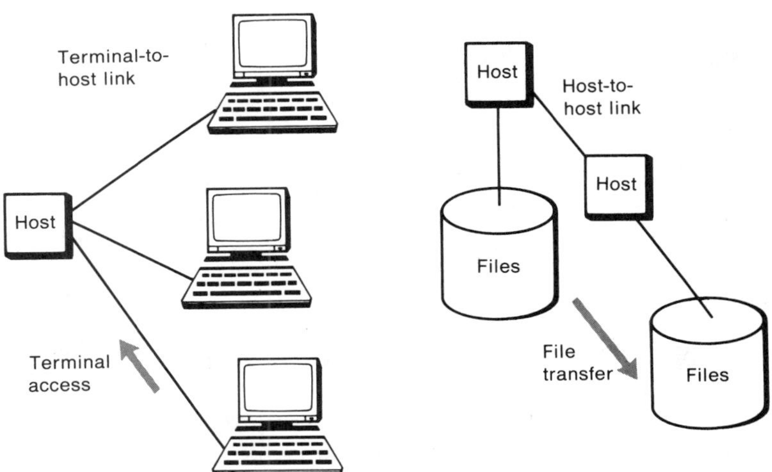

Figure 3-3. Data communications systems.

aged and accounted for by the communications subsystem. As we shall see, in circuit-oriented systems, the communications subsystem is unaware of the block structure and cannot use it to advantage. Other systems, such as the message- or packet-switching system in Figure 3-4, impose fairly strict control on the block structure, and use it to good advantage to obtain efficient, economical performance. Inside a computer, information is stored and processed in units such as individual characters (bytes), disk memory blocks, and files. A communications channel should take advantage of this basically corpuscular nature. In addition, typical behavior of a computer is to alternate processing and communications of a sequence of blocks. During data transmission, it's advantageous to have a high-capacity channel to minimize the transmission delay. However, during processing and other idle intervals, it is desirable to have a way to use the capacity elsewhere so it's not wasted. Low-delay communications channels have a great benefit for computer systems and their supporting communications. When the channel delay is sufficiently low, the recipient can explicitly acknowledge each message as it is correctly received. This allows the sending system to be assured of correct delivery which, in turn, means that the communications system need not take responsibility for unconditionally delivering the message.

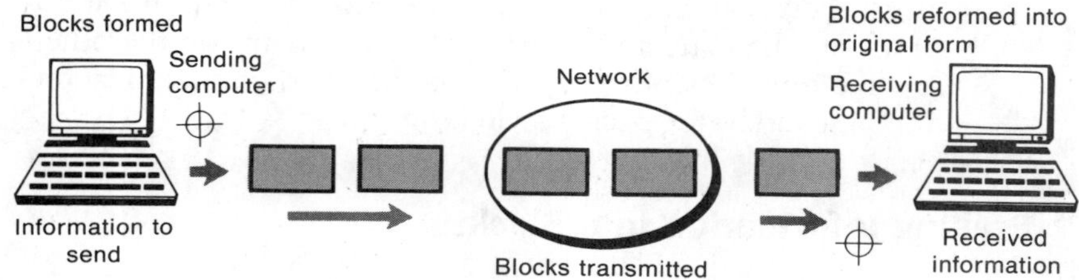

Figure 3-4. Sending data as blocks.

Capacity, Delay, and Transparency

A useful measure of the performance of a data communications system is its *capacity* in bits or characters per second. A high-capacity system will move data faster than a low-capacity system. A related idea is *efficiency* which measures how much of the capacity is available to the user versus how much is consumed by the system itself for control purposes or simply lost. The useful capacity of a system may be much less than the theoretical capacity if the user makes poor choices in the way that data is submitted for transmission. For example, in block-oriented systems, small blocks are usually less efficient than large.

Delay is a measure of the time needed for a communications system to move data from the sender to the receiver. No system can transmit information instantaneously, but comparable systems vary greatly in how much time they add to irreducible speed-of-light delay. In general, systems which manipulate the user data, for archiving, accounting and so forth, add more delay. Next to accuracy, delay is the most important aspect of system performance from a user's point of view.

A third basic idea for data communication is *transparency*. A transparent system is able to transmit data exactly as presented by the user. Some systems are not transparent because they use some data patterns or character codes for internal system control. Such systems are often harder to use.

Errors, Overloads, and Busy Signals

Three problems afflict all data communications systems: errors, overloads, and the inability to complete a connection because of "busy circuits." The design of the communications system may ignore these facts, yielding an "as-is" service, or it may try to remedy them, as does a *value-added network*. In most cases, the overall computer system works better and more efficiently if these problems are solved within the communications system, as close to their source as possible. Solving the problems costs in terms of capacity and delay, so by making this trade close to the source of the problems, the solution can be closely tailored to the specifics of the problem and have the least cost.

Error Control

All practical communications channels expose the signal to corruption by noise. Computer communications must prevent these errors from entering the data stream undetected, or better yet, must identify and correct the errors as they happen. Among the most effective and widely used techniques for error control are the so-called "block codes." In a block coding system, such as shown in Figure 3-5, data bits are grouped into a sequence (usually around 1,000 bits), algebraically encoded, and the resulting block then treated as a unit for communications purposes.

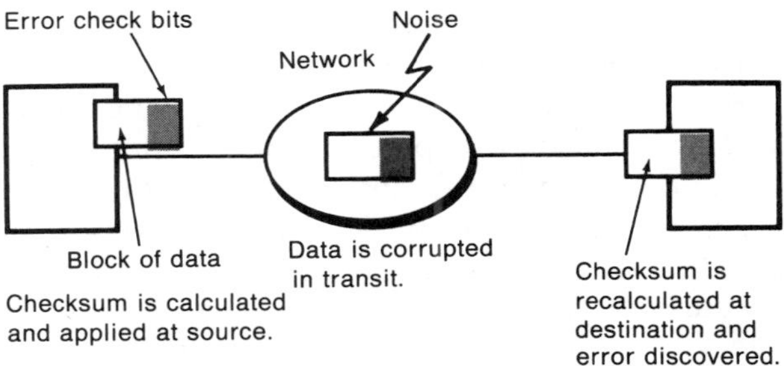

Figure 3-5. Block error control.

Overload Control (Flow Control)

Overload is the name of the situation that occurs when the users of the communication system try to submit more traffic to the net than there is traffic-handling capacity. As with error control, there are two basic strategies that can be employed. The situation can be ignored as in Figure 3-6 or the system design may incorporate techniques for combatting overload. One of the best ways to prevent overload is to restrict rates of flow into the network by monitoring both ends of a connection and observing the rate at which the destination is able to accept traffic. The source must not be allowed to exceed this rate.

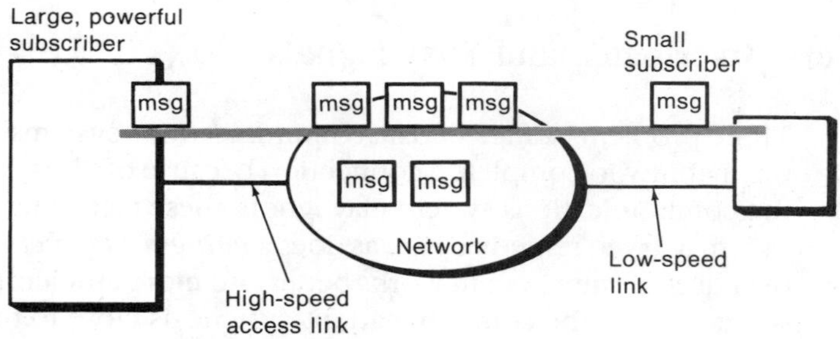

Figure 3-6. Flow control.

Without flow control, the high-performance host can send faster than the low-performance host can receive. The excess traffic either piles up in the network or must be discarded, neither of which is desirable. The solution is to match the input rate to the output rate. Source-destination, or "end-to-end" flow control is not always possible, however. It requires that there be a control mechanism and a means to send the control information, in timely fashion, from the destination back to the source.

Busy Signals

Nearly all useful communications systems connect many different users. Some communications systems are *single-threaded* in that a single connection to a destination will monopolize that system's access link. While a connection is active, all other attempts by other users will fail, as shown in Figure 3-7. This is a serious flaw in data communications systems and is a principal cause of unsatisfactory behavior. Computer communications typically involve short bursts of communications with many different destinations in rapid succession. If a connection attempt is blocked, the originating computer process will be suspended. This can disrupt the flow of other processes. The resulting systemwide lockups can reduce overall performance to a low level. In a nonmultiplexed, or blocking system, a single connection will monopolize the destination. Additional connection attempts will fail, and receive a busy indication. The telephone system works this way.

Communications systems which are built on block communications, such as message and packet switching, can overcome this problem by multiplexing the data streams from different sources as in Figure 3-8. In this way, multiple connections can coexist, sharing a single physical link. In the worst case, each connection may have less capacity than it would obtain alone, but normally,

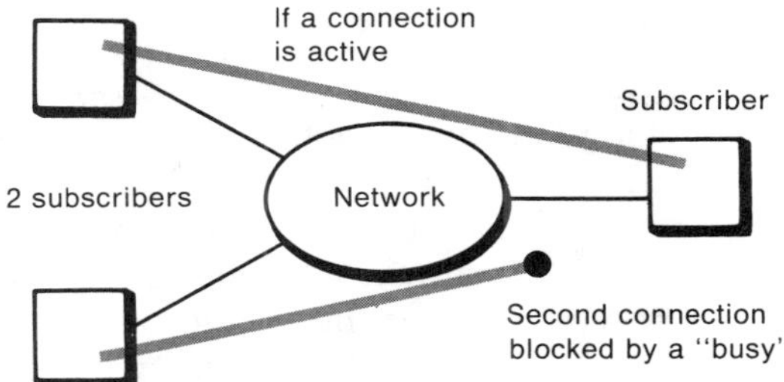

Figure 3-7. A "busy" destination.

one connection will find adequate capacity in the "gaps" left by the others. Two converging streams of data can be merged and the otherwise wasted time reclaimed. Neither stream is made to wait, but each stream may encounter additional delay.

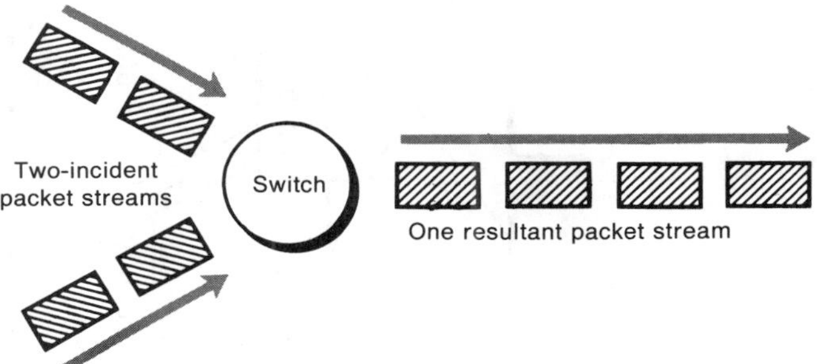

Figure 3-8. Multiplexing in a packet system.

Circuit, Message, and Packet Switching

If it were possible, all users of data communications systems would prefer to have a dedicated, point-to-point link to every destination with which they need to communicate. Since giving everyone a wire to everyone else is impractical, *switching systems* are employed to allow a set of communications gear to be shared among a group of users. Data-switching systems may be considered to be one of three basic types: circuit, message, or packet.

The first electrical communications systems were data-oriented. The telegraph system preceded the telephone system. Mechanical teletypewriters were introduced at about the same time as the voice telephone system. The telegraph system and teletypewriters for special purposes were the extent of data communications technology until the Second World War when communications technology was greatly advanced and the foundations for modern communications systems were established. Most of the concepts and operating principles of modern message-oriented communications can be traced to that period.

Circuit Switching

Circuit-switching systems, which share the technology of the telephone system, are the antecedents of most present communications systems. A circuit-switching system consists of a number of switching centers interconnected by trunks. The switches shown in Figure 3-9 are composed of two parts: the switch matrix which carries the data to be switched, and a switch controller which manages the operation. Circuit-switched communications, whether voice or data, are conducted as a three-phase process:

- circuit establishment
- data exchange
- circuit clearing

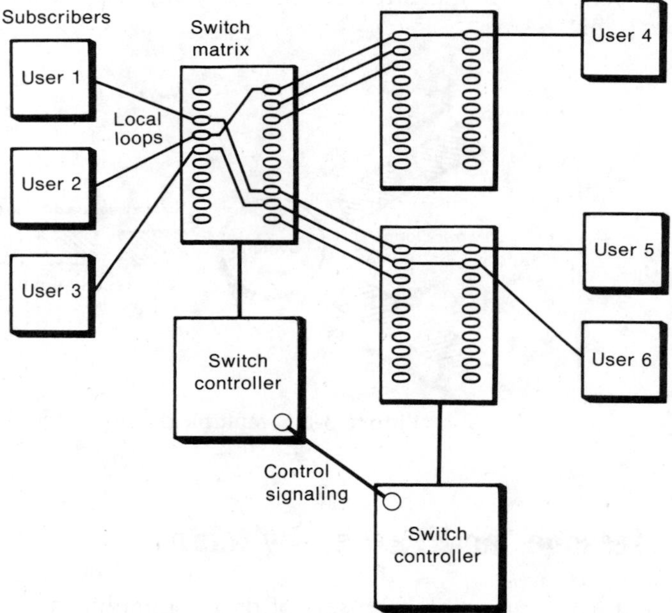

Figure 3-9. Circuit switching.

Circuit Setup

Before communications can begin, the sender must establish a data path to the receiver of a message. Figure 3-10 shows the phase of "dialing the call," in which the sender tells the network the address and other control information about the call. The network then must find a path to the destination and reserve switching capacity along the route to handle the subsequent data. To do this, the switches along the required route of connection pass the request for connection in relay fashion from one to the next, making the necessary matrix switch closures as they go. In practical systems, this process takes from 5 to 30 seconds. If the desired destination is already engaged (connected to something), the connection attempt fails.

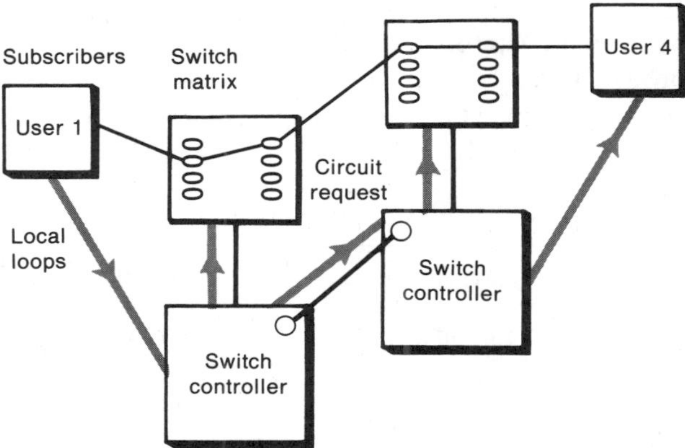

Figure 3-10. Circuit setup.

Data Exchange

If the circuit is established as in Figure 3-11, it appears to the users as a direct connection joining the pair of them. The users may send whatever data they please, generally without regard to protocols or other restrictions. They seem to be connected by a dedicated, direct-wire link with constant delay and constant capacity. In some respects, this is good—it imposes few restrictions which are not inherent in the underlying communications links. On the other hand, the network provides no help with managing the flow of data, nor does it help when errors are introduced into the data by communications problems. Furthermore, bceause there is no reason to adopt standard protocols to use the network, most systems built around circuit switching have no particular standardization of interfaces or operations and are often rigidly specialized in function.

Circuit Clearing

When data exchange is complete, the users must "hang up." They must break their connection and free the resources so that (presumably) other calls may be

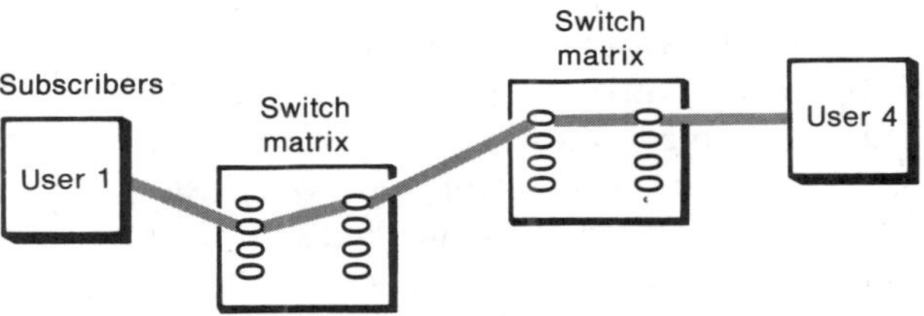

Figure 3-11. Data exchange.

conducted by other users and they may themselves call or be called by other users.

One advantage of circuit switching is familiarity—it's the basis of most traditional communications. A second advantage is transparency. Once the connection is established, it behaves like a dedicated link, without need for protocols. So long as the two ends agree on how to exchange data, they may communicate. The disadvantages are long connection setup delays and the exclusive nature of the connection (see Table 3-1).

Table 3-1. Circuit Switching

Advantages	Disadvantages
Simplicity	Long circuit setup delays
Familiarity	No error correction
Constant delay	Single User/Busy Signal
Constant capacity	No incentive for standards

Two of the problems with circuit switching—single-threaded connections and long circuit setup delay—are severe limitations for modern data systems. The practical effect of these limitations is that circuit-switching systems fail under load because modern computers must run multiple processes simultaneously and must be able to communicate with multiple destinations at the same time. When overall system load is heavy, it is likely that a desired destination will be engaged at any time. Therefore, in a single-threaded system under heavy load, the likelihood is great that a connection attempt will fail by encountering a busy signal, which further exacerbates the situation by preventing the system from disposing of its load. The second difficulty arises from the length of time needed to establish a connection. An average size for a computer message is about 1,000 characters (about half a display screen) which takes about one second to transmit. If it requires up to thirty seconds just to establish the connection, the utilization of the communications system will be poor. Circuit switching works well for voice communications where the call duration is long, but much less well for computer-generated traffic, which may require rapidly changing connections in communications with many destinations in rapid succession.

Message Switching

The message-switching system in Figure 3-12 offers some improvements for computers, compared with circuit switching, by relieving the problems of circuit setup time and the single circuit connection. With message switching, no physical circuits are set up within the switches. Instead, the information is grouped into blocks, or messages, and these messages are passed into and across the communications system sequentially. The switching operation consists of deciding, on each message individually, what is to be done to move nearer the message's destination. The military AUTODIN system is a message-switching system. Commercial TELEX networks allow the sender to choose between circuit switching (basic TELEX service, which connects the sending terminal directly to the receiving machine) and an enhanced service which accepts and stores the message for delivery.

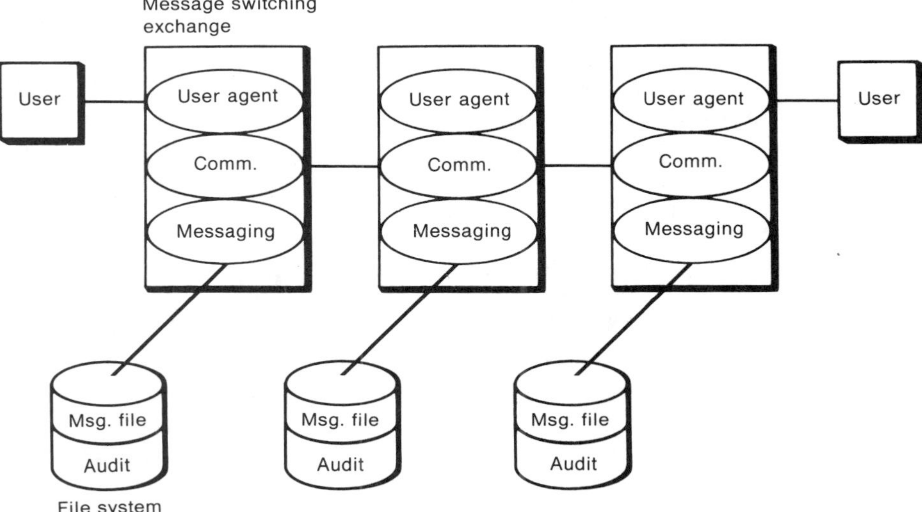

Figure 3-12. Message switching.

There are two principal parts of the message system: one within the user's computer, and the other which constitutes the switching system. The user of a message system must format information into a standard form (which depends on the message system) before submitting it to the network. The network is composed of a series of switching exchanges which pass the message along a chain as it approaches the destination. An exchange has three parts:

- user interface
- communications handler
- message processor with filing system

The user interface admits new messages to the system and disposes of deliveries. The communications handler manages communications among the exchanges, and the message processor files and routes transmissions with the other exchanges. Each exchange is responsible for the messages it holds, and therefore keeps an audit trail (list of messages it has processed) which shows what happened to each transit message. The process of sending a message involves three steps: submission, transmission, and delivery.

Submission

The user composes a message in the proper format using whatever means his system provides, and then submits it to the message delivery system as in Figure

3-13. The message format is described by a *protocol* which defines the structure of the header and contents of the body. The header must contain the destination (where the message is to be sent) and the source (who sent it) as well as other control and status information like the time of posting, the importance (priority), and any other special handling information (such as security classification). This header information remains attached to the message until it is finally delivered so that any switch along its route may have the full information needed for routing and delivering the message. The standard for message formatting must be implemented by all users in order to be understood by the message system. This is a limitation on the freedom of the users, but it makes possible the interoperation of various types of users. It also establishes rules of behavior, which can simplify the operation of the message system and make it more efficient.

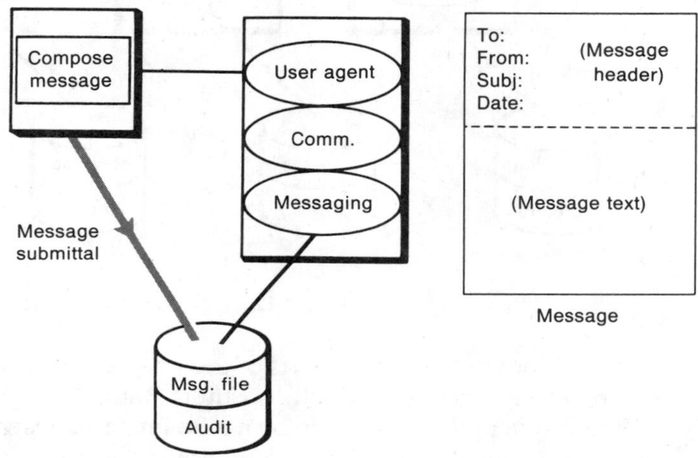

Figure 3-13. Message submission.

In the submission process, the message system accepts responsibility for the message and must thereafter either correctly deliver it or notify the originator of failure. Some systems, like financial message systems, have financial liability during their ownership of the message and so go to great lengths to assure accountability.

Transmission

After receiving a message, the switching system proceeds to find a path to the destination. There are many different technologies, but most rely on a store-and-forward technique. The message is transmitted step by step, as in Figure 3-14, from one switch to the next, with each step coming closer to the destination. When a switch receives the message, it immediately makes a copy and stores it in a *message buffer*. It then examines the destination address and decides on the best disposition, which will usually be to forward the message on to the next switch on the route. The next step in the path must acknowledge receipt of the message and thereby take responsibility before the current switch is absolved of responsibility. In this way, there is always some clearly identifiable point of responsibility. When a message is finally delivered to its destination, all switches along the route may delete their buffered copy. Some systems retain a copy of the message in each switch, along with its time of receipt, time of forwarding, and other accounting information. This audit trail may be retraced later if there is a question about the contents or ultimate delivery of the message.

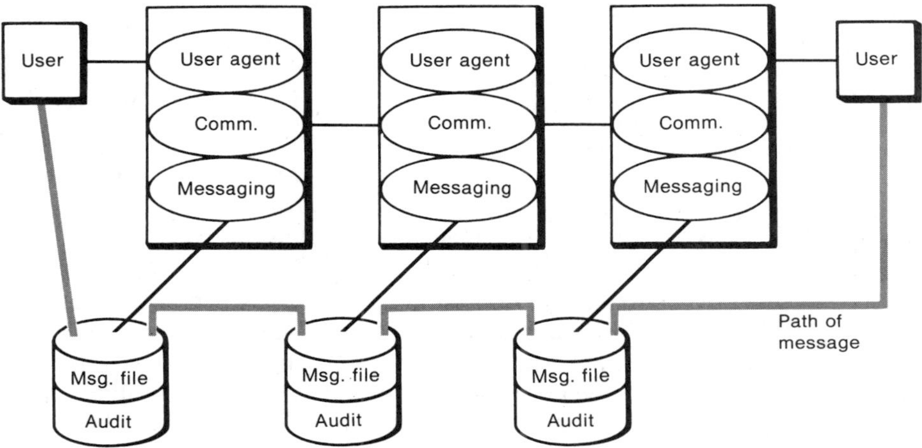

Figure 3-14. Message transmission.

During transmission, the message is handled by whatever means are convenient for the switches. Since the internal store-and-forward mechanisms of the message system do not concern the users, the switches can optimize the internal mechanisms to yield the best performance and reliability, without regard to external standards.

Delivery

The final message switch in the chain will take on the duty of message delivery, shown in Figure 3-15. The message is converted into some external format and arranged in sequence with other messages. It may be that the destination is not available, in which case the message must be retained, or *queued*. It may be that other messages have arrived simultaneously and their orderly flow must be managed so that none is lost or corrupted. In the best case, the destination will accept messages in timely fashion so that they do not accumulate and congest the switch, but nothing requires that this always be so.

Because message systems take formal responsibility for the message, they must do considerable work to assure that messages are not lost, forged, or corrupted. The price of this accountability is that the message switches are usually large and complex because they must process and keep a copy of each message. In addition, message delivery times can be long (minutes or hours). (See Table 3-2)

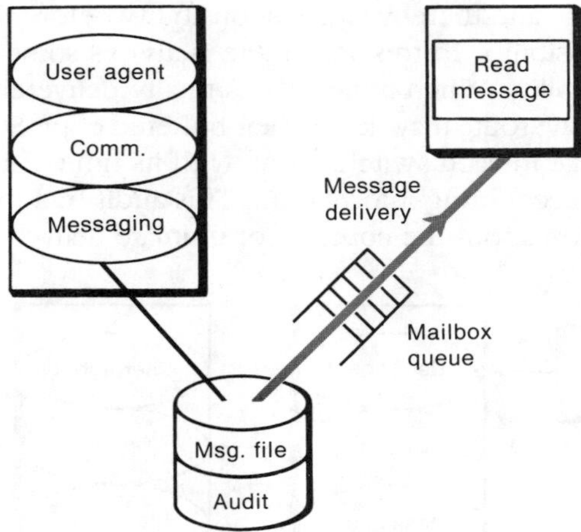

Figure 3-15. Message delivery.

Compared to circuit switching, message switching has the considerable advantage of being designed for data transmission, and of allowing a sender to post a message without the delays of circuit setup or busy signals. Message switching can be implemented entirely with logical switches. No actual circuits are established, and this promotes efficient use of the internal links and switches. However, even though the data is transmitted in blocks (the messages), most practical systems have very loose rules, or none at all, about how long a message can be. The rules are too loose for really efficient handling by computers.

Table 3-2. Message Switching

Advantages	**Disadvantages**
Message accountability	Large and complex switches
Interoperability	Variable time in transit
Switches can average peaks and valleys in traffic	Network can "fill up" and block
Switches can hold traffic for destinations	

Packet Switching

As we have seen, both circuit-switching and message-switching systems have attractive features. Circuit switching provides simplicity: set up the channel and then forget about it. Message switching is particularly attractive for computer-based systems and for efficient data transmission systems. Packet switching was developed to incorporate some of the useful qualities of each, while providing services like data error control and data flow control. From the beginning, packet switching was designed specifically for the needs of computers, as opposed to voice telephony or telegraphy. The result is a technique that takes advantage of the peculiarities of modern data systems. Computers make special needs of communications by

- using data in bursts, or blocks
- requiring low-delay channels
- being intolerant of errors
- needing interoperability
- multiprocessing

Packet switching was invented with the advantages and limitations of both circuit and message switching very much in mind, and practical systems can be designed to look more like one or the other. To present a more circuit-switched appearance, a packet system can provide a *virtual-circuit interface*. A virtual circuit provides a channel between a pair of hosts over which they may exchange information nearly transparently. Alternatively, a packet system can be designed to present a *datagram interface*, which is similar to that of a message system. A datagram is a block of user data plus a header and trailer that contains all the requisite control and addressing information needed to instruct the communications system on processing and delivering the datagram (see Figure 3-16).

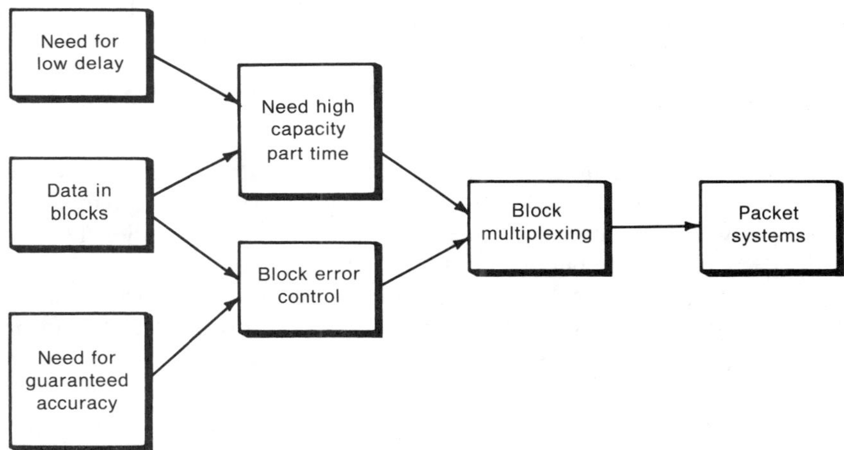

Figure 3-16. Block-oriented computer communications.

Packetizing the Data

All computer systems deal with information internally in blocks, and usually, a host system has some natural internal message size in which communications are conducted. Before a message may be passed into the packet-switching network, it must be formed into packets according to the specifications of the packet-switching system. Figure 3-17 shows how a host can divide a message into a sequence of packets, and pass them, one at a time, into the network. Each packet has three parts: *header, body*, and *trailer*. The header contains control information such as the destination address, flow control information, and perhaps the type of delivery service desired. The body contains the user's data which may be text data, program images, or other information unrestricted in form. The trailer usually contains error detection information in a checksum.

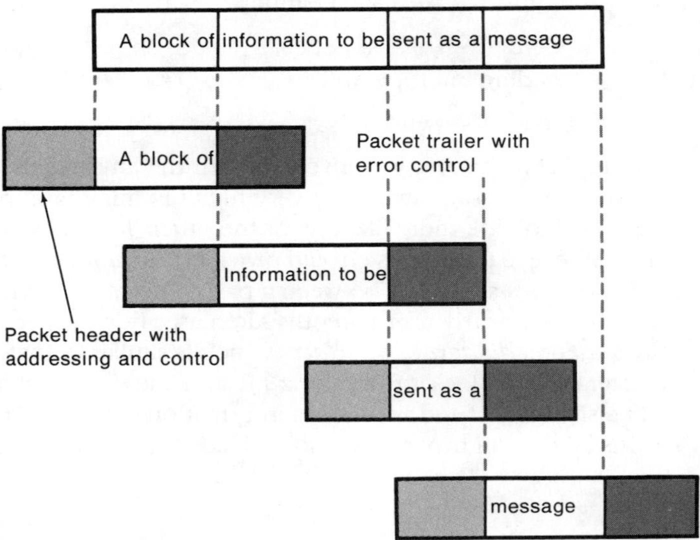

Figure 3-17. Packetizing the data.

The structure of a data packet is analogous to a postal letter as shown in Figure 3-18. In a letter, the message enclosure is contained inside an envelope which represents the packet control header and trailer. The envelope has all the information needed for transporting and delivering the letter. The information transported is never seen and is of no concern to the postal system. This division allows the network to concentrate on moving the information, without restricting the user data to something that the network understands.

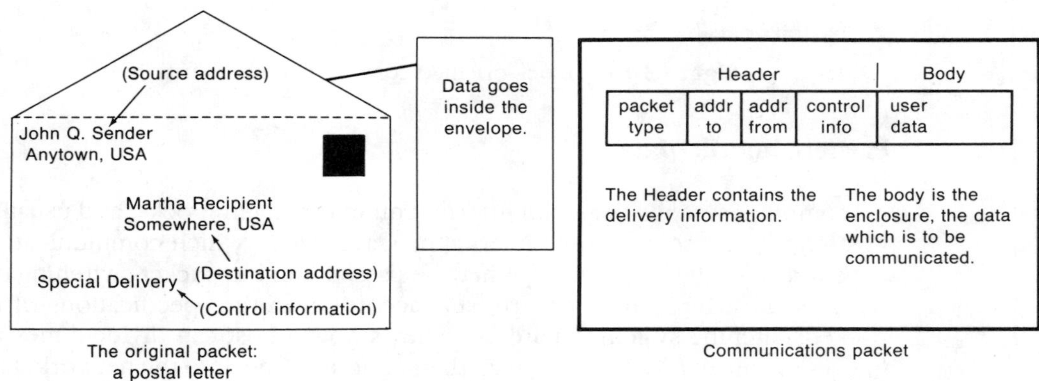

Figure 3-18. The postal packet analogy.

Packet-Switch System Overview

Figure 3-19 shows the elements of a typical packet network. The users of the network are the hosts, which connect into the net via the host interface. The host interface is usually built to a well-defined standard which does not change, even if the underlying network changes. A principal objective of the host interface is to conceal as much detail as possible, and present the host with an idealized view of the network as a system which makes no errors and always delivers messages with minimum delay. As with the basic communications system shown in Figure 3-1, the subnetwork is composed of trunks and switches arranged to make best use of the (presumably) scarce transmission resources. The trunk circuit

- manages user data flow into and out of subnet
- corrects interswitch data errors
- coordinates net management and troubleshooting
- yields an improved communications medium to users

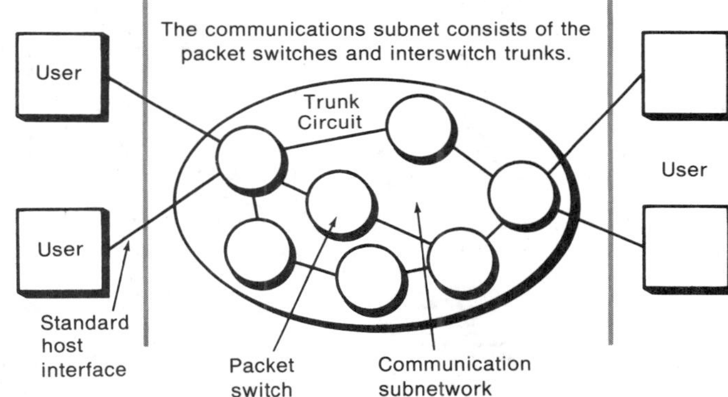

Figure 3-19. A packet-switching system.

Packet switching is used in networks of different size and technology. Most large, commercial data networks use packet switching, but so do smaller private networks. Even small-scale systems for local distribution, such as Ethernet or Token-Bus networks, are based on packet switching. A set of informal terms has evolved to distinguish several classes of network: WAN, MAN, and LAN.

The WAN, Wide Area Network, is typically national or global in scope and serves many different users, often as a common carrier. The MAN, Metropolitan Area Network, sometimes called a Campus Area Net, is similar to the WAN, often using the same technology, but over a smaller area and often for a restricted set of users. A MAN can be tailored for the needs of a single private subscriber, a university, or a business that covers an area larger than a kilometer in some dimension. LANs, Local Area Networks, are employed when the distance spanned by the network is small (less than a kilometer) and when it is possible to manage the network informally among a small set of related users. In any of these cases, the data network is a separate subsystem which serves the hosts as a common user utility and which can be optimized to give the best service at reasonable cost, without unduly burdening the hosts.

Hosts

Figure 3-20 shows the two parts of a host: the applications programs and the network interface. The applications programs implement whatever function the host is intended to perform. The host computer

- lets local users access network resources as easily as local
- lets remote users access local resources
- removes networking details from application programs

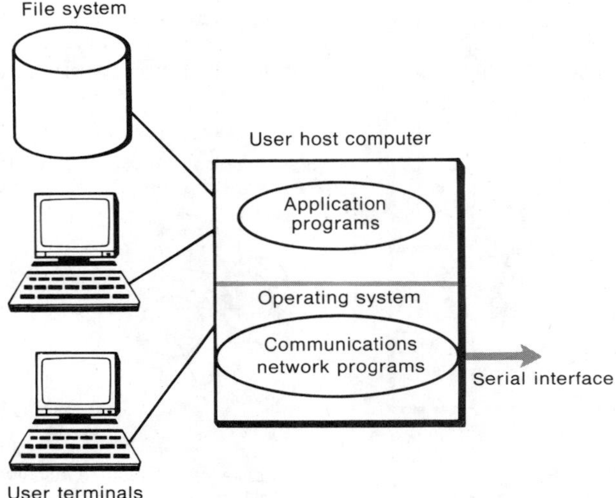

Figure 3-20. Structure of a host.

Usually, the applications programs have been developed without much attention to communications, and it is important to shield them from networking details. The network interface, therefore, is implemented by separate programs, usually within the operating system. The applications programs using the network can access the networking software via idealized software interfaces, much as they access the systems terminal services or file system. Within the network software there is a further division into *network driver*, which deals with the network, and *protocol software*, which deals with the remote host. The network driver incorporates the specialized programs needed to operate the interface hardware. There are great differences in the details of X.25, Ethernet, or Token-Bus and the network driver must cope with and isolate these details from the applications. The protocol software implements the standards needed for effective end-to-end or host-to-host communications, such as IBM's System Network Architecture (SNA), Government OSI Profile (GOSIP), or the Department of Defense's TCP/IP.

Structure

The structure of a packet switch is shown in Figure 3-21. Switches have two primary functions. First, they provide the access ports to which the hosts connect. The host access portion of the switch implements the network side of the network access protocol and manages the flow of packets into and out of the network. Host access also provides additional services such as access control (to prevent unauthorized use of the port) and a variety of management tools such as accounting records (the base data from which to prepare bills) and various statistical information to help with measuring network performance. Inside the switch, the host access mechanism is connected to the store-and-forward mechanism. Store-and-forward is responsible for the internal operation of the network, such as managing the interswitch trunks, and the routing of packets flowing through the network.

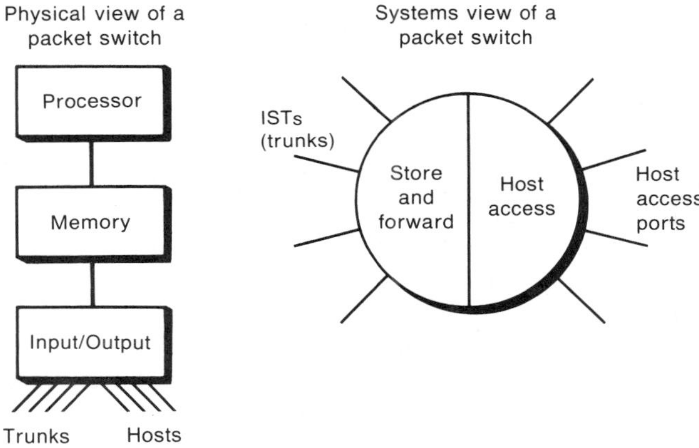

Figure 3-21. Structure of a packet switch.

Although a packet switch performs the function of communications switching, its hardware layout is more like a modern computer than a telephone switch. In a telephone switch, the switch matrix is a self-contained unit managed by a separate control processor. The communications paths being switched remain within the matrix, never entering the control processor. In most current packet switches, the communications switch is tightly integrated with the control processor and there is no separate external switch matrix. All communications paths flow through the switch main memory, which serves as both an intermediate data buffer and as storage for the switch control program. The reason for this tight coupling is in the nature of packet switching. Each packet that arrives either from a host port or from a trunk must be individually processed. Although the packet switch does not examine the user data field, it must individually process the control header of each packet. For example, the destination address must be examined as part of the routing calculation. Other control information is contained in the header as well, depending on the detailed switch architecture.

Typical packet switches handle approximately 500 to 2,000 packets per second, and at these rates, it is most efficient for the control program in the switch to have direct access to the packets as they rest in the intermediate data buffers during the switching process. Figure 3-21 shows the hardware structure of a switch in which the serial data channels of the host and trunk ports have direct access to the switch main memory. Packets are transferred into memory under control of the hardware. As each packet transfer completes, the processor is notified, and a packet process is scheduled at high priority so that the input channel can be immediately reused. The packet input processing requires 100 to 300 microseconds of processor time on a typical switch.

After the packet has been placed in memory by the hardware, control and routing calculations are done. For a typical packet switch, the internal processing requires from 1 to 5 milliseconds before the packet can be transmitted onto a neighbor switch or to a local destination host (provided that the output channel is not busy with another packet). As a packet is transmitted across the network, it will encounter this set of processing steps at each switch. To minimize overall delay, this tandem processing must be optimized.

Interswitch Trunk (IST)

The Interswitch Trunks (IST) are the communications circuits that link the packet switches. Figure 3-22 shows several types of ISTs, which can be provided by many different technologies. Simplest and most common are landline circuits based on telephone technology. These ubiquitous links are in the majority, and as the new high-capacity fiber technology becomes more widely available, these will dominate. However, other technology is available (e.g., radio circuits) to fill specialized needs. Radio circuits often have much poorer performance: lower bandwidth due to limited radio spectrum, and higher error rate due to environmental effects. Packet switching is a good way to deal with such problems. Radio channels are scarce and sometimes contain irreplaceable links that are hard to use because of errors. Packet switching allows the troublesome details to be concealed from the user. IST error control mechanisms can correct data errors without involving the hosts at all, and the automatic routing inherent in packet switching can reduce the effect of radio fading. This permits a medium to be used effectively when it otherwise would be completely unsuitable for data communications. Another example is a satellite channel. Satellite links have extremely long delay because of the propagation delay to and from the orbital height of synchronous satellites. Often too, the ground station equipment is very expensive. Without a way to multiplex the use of satellite channels among a number of users, it cannot be used effectively. Packet switching multiplexes ISTs among the data packets from all subscribers using a path without making them aware of the fact. It provides a good way to use a medium which otherwise would not be used efficiently.

An IST is inherently an analog system. Pulses on a wire or radio signal transmissions are analog and require processing to support data transmission. For this reason, all ISTs have a modem at each end for analog transmission links, or a *digital interface (DSU)* for digital or fiber transmission. The combination of the transmission link and the modem or DSU is the IST.

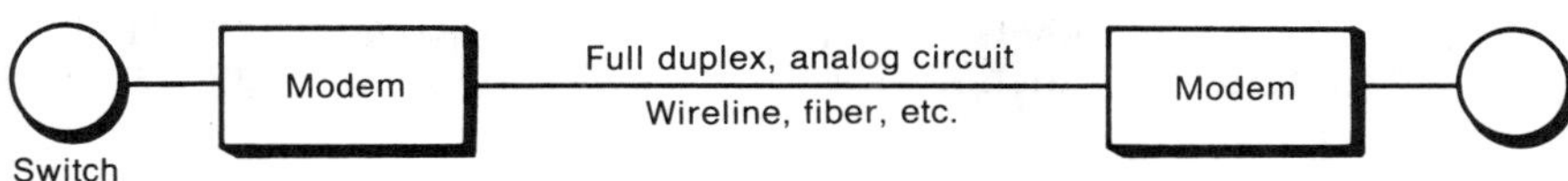

A. A terrestrial wireline interswitch trunk.

B. A radio channel interswitch trunk.

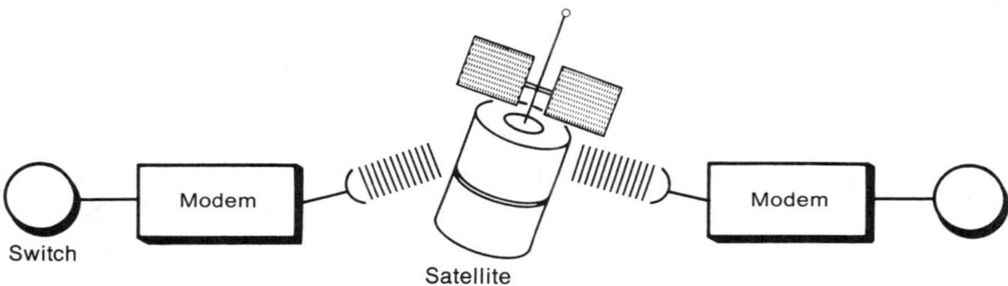

C. A satellite channel interswitch trunk.

Figure 3-22. Interswitch trunks.

Operation

The operation of a packet-switching system can be considered in the same three phases as that of a message-switching system: submission, transmission, and delivery. The subscriber is involved in the submission and delivery phase, and here is where the process of building and decomposing packets takes place. Packet networks go to considerable lengths to remove the involvement of the user in the transmission process.

Submission

Figure 3-23 outlines the process that takes place when a packet is formed. There are three principal elements: the host, the access link and the packet switch. An application program generates messages in the host, and uses the communications interface software to packetize the messages. The host connects directly to the access link (b), which is the physical transmission channel joining the host to the packet switch. The access link is a communications channel; it is a scarce resource that must be managed and which causes errors. The third element is the network access packet switch (a). This switch performs all the initial interfacing functions for the packets submitted by the user host.

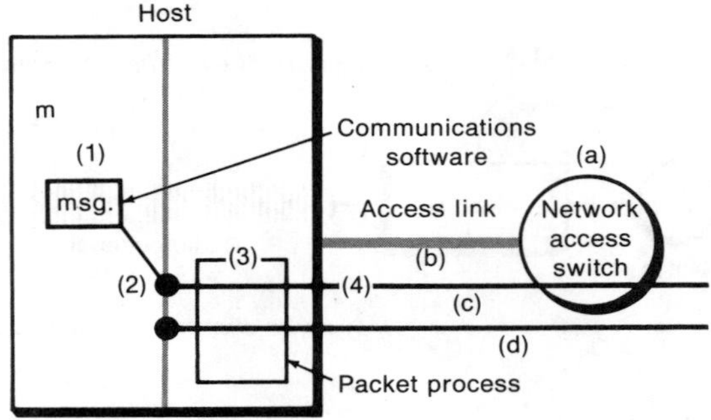

Figure 3-23. Packet submission.

The submission process in Figure 3-23 has several steps. First, a user process creates a message to send (1), and presents it to the communications software within the host. The packet process examines the message and derives the destination address. If there is a path open to the destination, it might be used, perhaps shared, with other users. If there is no path, one must be established and this is when the virtual circuit is established (2). At any time, there may be many communicating processes, and so there may be a number of paths open (c, d), all sharing the physical resources of the single access link. When the path is established, the packet process breaks the user's message into packets (3) and sends them into the network. The network's reliable transmission mechanism is then responsible for managing the packets at all points on their way to where they are turned over to the destination (4).

Transmission

The elements involved in transmitting the packets to the destination are the source packet switch, the ISTs, the collection of intermediate tandem or store-and-forward switches, and the destination switch. Figure 3-24 shows a simple network with five nodes and several alternate paths from source to destination.

The goal of the network is to find the shortest, least congested path from the entry point to the exit point where the packet can be delivered to the destination. In the figure, the packet enters the network (1) via the host access port and is passed to the store-and-forward process (2), which determines that at that instant, trunk (b) is the best route. The packet is transmitted (3) toward an intermediate node (c) where it is received and where transit processing is performed (4). The transit node cannot immediately forward the packet because the best available output trunk (e) is busy, so the packet is placed in a queue (d) to await its turn on the trunk. Eventually the trunk is free, and the packet is forwarded (5) across trunk (e) to the destination switch (f). Destination processing is performed (6) and the packet is passed to the host delivery portion of the destination switch. A number of mechanisms are at work within the network to solve typical problems.

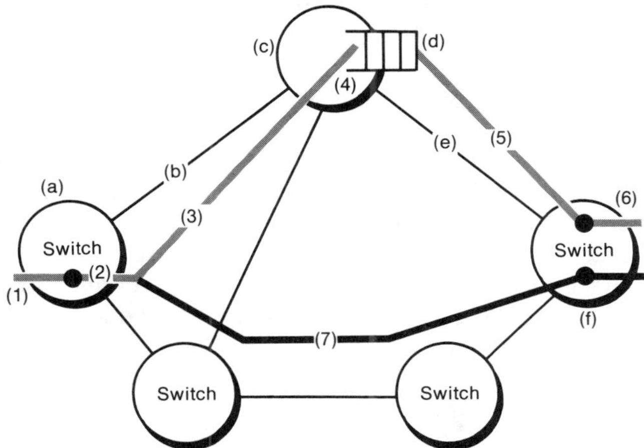

Figure 3-24. Packet transmission.

Alternate Routing

If all elements are working, the best path across the network is from (a) through (c) to (f). But suppose IST (e) fails. Then there is no point sending traffic destined for (f) via (c). Rather, a totally different path (7) is optimum, and should be used. The packet network should be able to find such alternates automatically without any outside influence and with complete independence from the hosts. In fact, the host should be able to continue to submit traffic and use the network as the failure is identified and the routing readjusted. Fully automatic networks such as the Arpanet work in this way.

Error Control

Suppose link (e) has not failed, but instead occasionally introduces a bit error by changing a data bit from a 1 to a 0. The efficient solution is to manage each link individually, and in this case, switches (c) and (f) are responsible for detecting and correcting the data errors on link (e). To do so, they might employ a block error detection scheme based on a packet checksum as discussed earlier. The checksum of packets arriving at (f) is calculated and failing packets are discarded. When (f) discards a packet, it also withholds its acknowledgment. After a timeout period, switch (c) will transmit a new copy of the packet, which is expected to arrive in good order. This localized error control is efficient because data errors are never forwarded, and it promotes low-delay transmission because the retransmission timeout may be set to a very "tight" value tuned to the properties of a specific IST.

Flow Control

When the sending host is much more powerful than the receiving host (can send traffic faster than the receiver can accept), it is necessary to restrict the flow into the network to less than or equal to the value that the destination can accept. Otherwise, traffic will "pile up" within the destination node. Such a pile-up is a serious failure and must be avoided because it can exhaust the resources of the destination switch. When this happens, no traffic can flow and throughput drops to a low level. Because all source-destination pairs will have some imbalance, it is necessary for all packet networks to cope with such overloads. One of the best mechanisms is based on a quota system. When a path is first established, the sender is allocated a certain number of packets to send into the net. The destination monitors the acceptance rate into the destination host. For each packet accepted, the source is allocated one more; for each packet sent in, the allocation is reduced by one. The destination switch sends control messages back to the source indicating allocation increments. All packet networks which work well have such a mechanism.

Delivery

The process of delivering the packets from the network to the destination host involves the elements shown in Figure 3-25: the destination switch (a), the destination host, and an access link (b).

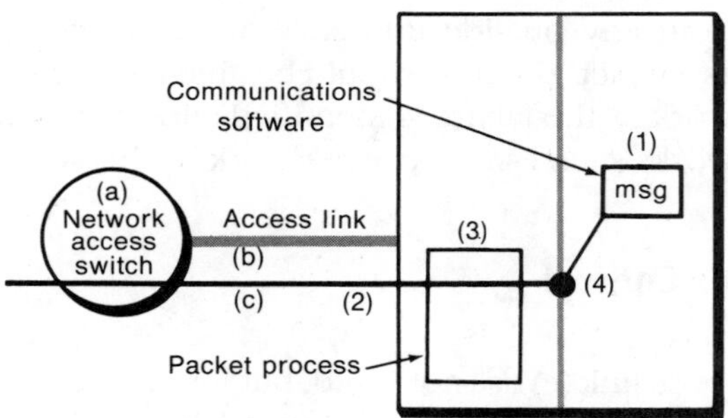

Figure 3-25. Packet delivery.

The delivery process begins in the destination node (a). First, the packets must be received from the network store-and-forward transmission process. Next, the sequence numbers applied at the source are checked and the packets are reordered so they may be delivered in the same order as received by the net. Packets are then sent one at a time (2) into the host where the packet-receiving process (3) manages local flow and error control and rebuilds (4) the original native protocol host messages (1).

Summary

All significant families of computer equipment have packet-switching network interfaces available. In some cases, computer vendors have developed a proprietary packet architecture, such as SNA or Digital's DECNet. Almost all vendors support TCP/IP architecture and associated Arpanet protocols. Packet switching provides a practical set of solutions to many present-day communications problems.

The performance of packet switching systems varies considerably as does computer central processor performance, and it is difficult to describe packet switching with a few numbers. However, it is possible to outline the performance of typical systems. Any type of computer, from a PC to a large mainframe, can be a packet-switching host. The host software burden is in two parts: program storage for the network driver and protocol software, and memory buffer storage allocation. The program size is about 50,000 bytes regardless of the computer.

Buffer storage for a small machine is another 50,000 bytes, but in a large system supporting many simultaneous conversations, it can be up to a megabyte. Present-day hosts can send or receive up to 50 packets per second and can sustain, at best, about 50,000 bits per second throughput.

The network host access links are usually based on standard common carrier circuit offerings, which range from 1,200 to over a million bits per second, but 9,600 and 56,000 are most common. Usually, average link loading, the percentage of capacity used by user data rather than resting idle, is 20 percent or less.

Network trunk circuits use the same basic transmission links as the access links and again, the most common rates are 9,600 and 56,000 bits per second. The busiest trunks in a network may approach average loads of 50 to 75 percent of bit rate, but if a net is designed to these levels, it will have inadequate peak-handling capacity. Typical values are 20 percent or less.

The capacity of a packet switch has numerous dimensions and it is difficult to give simple figures for throughput. However, a small end-office switch suitable for a private customer premises installation might have a capacity of 100 packets per second distributed among several hundred simultaneously active virtual circuits, whereas a large central office tandem switch would have several thousand packets per second capacity and potentially several thousand virtual circuits.

The Future

A considerable body of packet-switching technology is well established in both network equipment and host interfacing. The Ethernet specification is clearly preferred for LANs, while X.25 dominates WANs. In the future, some new, much higher performance interfaces will emerge. Of these, the Fiber Digital Data Interface (FDDI) interface looks the most promising, offering bit rates of

Table 3-3. Packet Switching

Benefits	**Costs**
Desirable interface; flow- and error-controlled	Host interface and protocol software required
Multiplexed	Unpredictable network delay and capacity
Efficient sharing of links	Protocol overhead
Low cross-net delay	Packet-switch equipment needed at network nodes

100 megabits per second. An entirely new generation of software and hardware interfaces will be required to effectively use this network technology.

The world's major communications carriers and telephone companies are behind the second major technology thrust, ISDN. The ISDN is an attempt to unify voice and data switching so that a single set of specifications and even switching machinery can define and serve all users of communications media. In ISDN, as shown in Figure 3-26, there is a single type of subscriber connection to the network which may be used for voice, data, video image, facsimile, and so forth. The access link and the entire switching system is based on digital switches. Subscriber equipment must convert traffic into the standardized digital form before it is sent over the network access link.

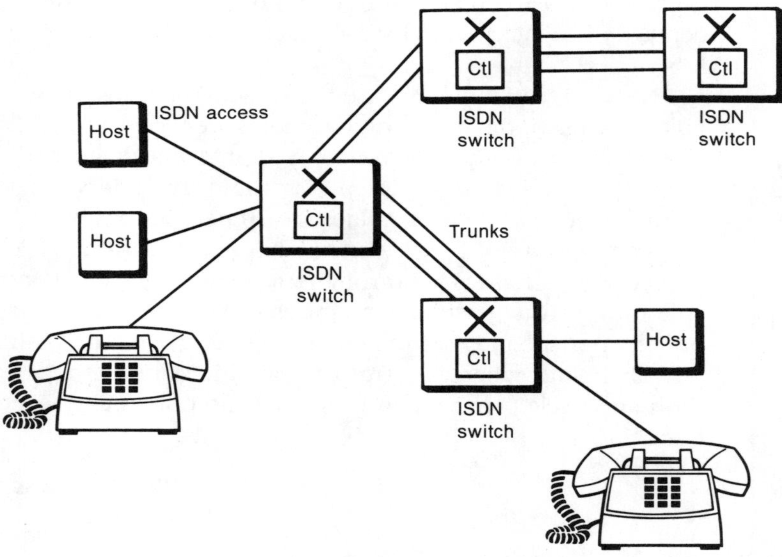

Figure 3-26. ISDN overview.

One of the options included in the ISDN specification for the AT&T 5ESS switch is a packet service included within the central office switching equipment as shown in Figure 3-27. To use this service, one of the two B-channels may be preconfigured as an X.25 access link. The central switch would then be equipped with one or more *packet processors*, which manage the network end of the access link exactly according to the X.25 specification. This option is offered in the 5ESS switch release 4 and later.

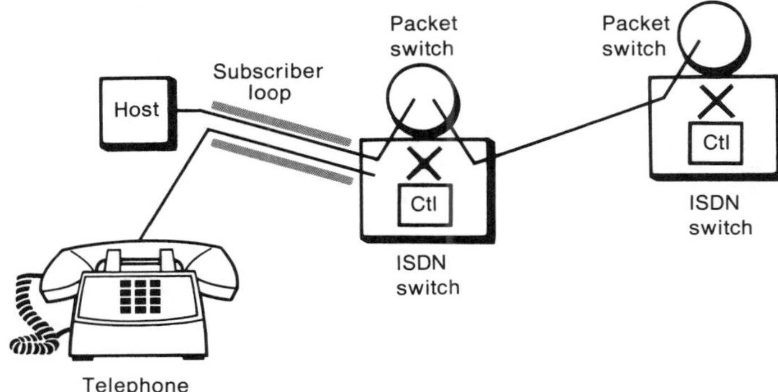

Figure 3-27. The ISDN Packet Service.

A second possibility is shown in Figure 3-28, which illustrates the option of supporting a local private packet-switching facility in conjunction with an ISDN wide area service. In this case, the packet switch is colocated with the user premises hardware, and contained within what is called the Network Termination apparatus. No intrasite (local) traffic need enter the public switch (where it would accrue charges). Only traffic to an off-premise address need leave the LAN switch.

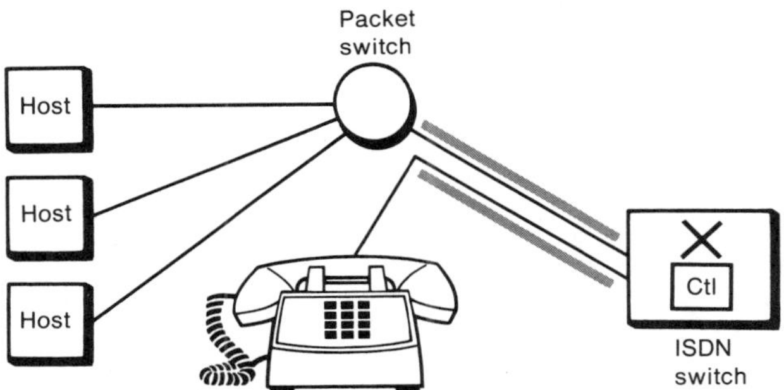

Figure 3-28. ISDN user-supplied packet.

In the future, it is clear that packet services will be an indispensable part of the communications planner's options. Host systems will offer a broader range of standard features as both public and private communications systems converge on a set of high-performance standard technologies such as ISDN and FDDI. The ultimate beneficiary should be the data communications user.

Chapter 4

Packet Network Standards

Donald V. Glen

Chapter 4

A SERIES OF PACKET MODE STANDARDS HAS BEEN developed through the International Telegraph and Telephone Consultative Committee (CCITT), the International Organization for Standardization (ISO), and the American National Standards Institute (ANSI) with the cooperation of other standard bodies and governments around the world. Through these efforts, packet mode data transmission recommendations such as CCITT X.25 and X.75 are achieving a state of maturity. [A reference list of standards discussed is provided at the end of this chapter.] The original 1976 version of X.25 has evolved to the 1988 version. Significant changes and enhancements were approved for 1980 and 1984, but the revisions that took place between 1984 and 1988 are considered to be relatively minor. Based on the evolution since 1976, CCITT X.25 (1988) is a mature standard. However, one can expect more fine tuning to be performed with X.25 as with other recommendations and standards.

Some of the fine tuning can be seen in the process that takes place in the United States. After each adoption of the latest version of X.25 by the CCITT, ANSI and the federal government have subsequently approved the standard for commercial use in the United States and by government agencies, respectively. During 1984, an ANSI task group undertook the task of defining specific requirements for the use of CCITT Recommendation X.25, International Standard (IS) 7776 [high-level data link control (HDLC) procedures] (ISO 1985a) and IS 8208 [X.25 packet layer procedure (PLP)] (ISO 1988a). As a result of this work, the Board of Standards Review of ANSI has recently approved publication of American National Standard X3.100 "Interface between Data Terminal Equipment (DTE) and Data Circuit-Terminating Equipment (DCE) for Operation with Packet-Switched Data Networks (PSDN), or between two DTEs by Dedicated Circuit."

ANS X3.100 will subsequently be adopted as a joint Federal Information Processing Standard (FIPS) and Federal (Telecommunication) Standard (FED STD). The ANS X3.100 is known then as FIPS PUB (Publication) 100 and FED STD 1041 (Figure 4-1). It is unlikely any changes will be necessary to ANSI X3.100 before it is adopted by the federal government.

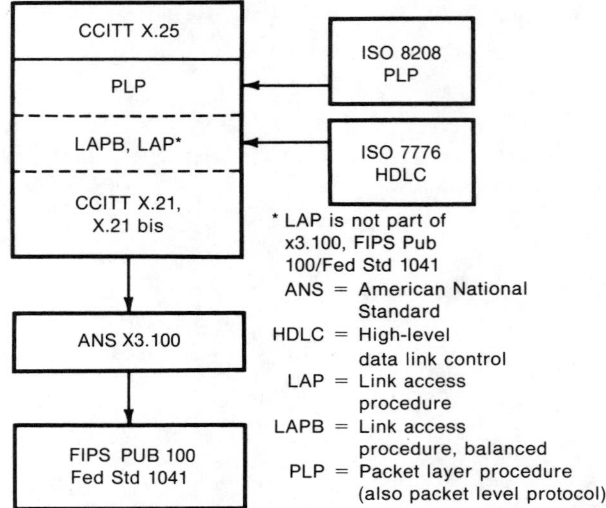

Figure 4-1. Related packet-switching standards.

This chapter provides an overview of packet mode switching, recommendations CCITT X.25, X.32, X.31, and X.75, and standards such as ISO 7776, ISO 8208 and ANS X3.100.

CCITT X.25 (1988) describes a user-network interface between data terminal equipment (DTE) and data circuit-terminating equipment (DCE) operating in the packet mode. Two DTEs that wish to communicate are connected to DCEs in an intervening packet-switched public data network (PSPDN) via a dedicated circuit. CCITT X.25 is written so that it views the interface from the perspective of the DCE.

ISO 7776 and ISO 8208 can be equated to the X.25 data link and packet layers. They specify a DTE/DTE interface and the DTE side of a DTE/DCE interface. Although ISO 7776 and ISO 8208 are compatible with X.25, they provide additional guidelines describing

- a DTE/DTE interface that allows two DTEs to directly exchange data without an intervening network
- a circuit-switched connection
- the interconnection of a public and private packet-switched network

ISO 7776 is a standard that is literally ubiquitous. Data link layer recommendations and standards that utilize the HDLC class of procedures include X.25 LAPB, X.75 single-link procedure (SLP), ISDN Q.921(I.441)LAPD, and for LAN, ISO 8802-2 logical link control types 1 and 2.

American National Standard X3.100 (1988a) is based on CCITT X.25, ISO 7776, and ISO 8208. It adopts the three standards and covers both the DTE/DCE and DTE/DTE interfaces.

CCITT X.32 modifies X.25 procedures so that access to a PSPDN can be across a nondedicated circuit. X.32 has been called a "dial-in, dial-out" X.25

because it allows the use of a public switched telephone network (PSTN), an ISDN, or a circuit-switched public data network (CSPDN) to access the PSPDN.

Two cases for the support of packet mode terminals by ISDN are defined in CCITT X.31. Case A provides support as a transparent circuit connection to PSPDNs. Case B provides support via the ISDN virtual circuit service.

The characteristics and operation of a signaling system between public data networks providing data transmission services are described by CCITT X.75. It bears a strong, but not total, resemblance to X.25 by adopting many of the same procedures. Each of these standards is discussed in more detail later in this chapter.

Packet-Switched Networks

The complete title for CCITT Recommendation X.25 is "Interface Between Data Terminal Equipment (DTE) and Data Circuit-Terminating Equipment (DCE) for Terminals Operating in the Packet Mode and Connected to Public Data Networks by Dedicated Circuit." It is a standard for the connection of computer and terminal equipment to packet-switched public data networks.

Concepts

Three concepts require introduction for the discussion of X.25 and the other packet standards. The first is the traditional view of DTEs and DCEs connected to a communications network as shown in Figure 4-2. The figure shows the DTE/DCE interface between the computer/terminal equipment (DTE) and interfacing equipment (DCE) required to couple with transmission circuits in a communications network. An example of the DCE is the modem that converts digital signals into quasi-analog signals for transmission. It also converts the quasi-analog signals into digital signals for acceptance by the DTE. This is not quite the way the DCE is considered within a packet network.

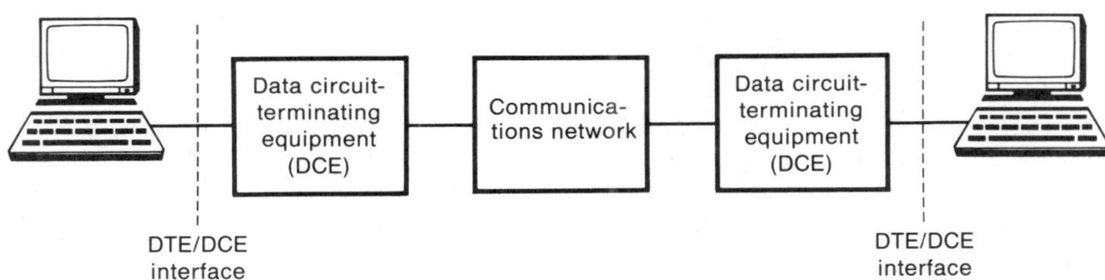

Figure 4-2. Connection of DTE/DCE equipment to communications network.

The second concept, that of virtual circuits, is not limited to packet operation. A virtual-circuit service provides a communication arrangement between users over various real equipment during a period of communication. A virtual-circuit service, when related to packet operation, has certain attributes for the transfer of data. A *logical channel* is established between two user locations before data packet transmission is started. The establishment of logical channels permits the sharing, through multiplexing, of a single physical link by up to 4,095 DTE pairs. There can be two types of X.25 virtual-circuit services on the same link: virtual calls (VCs) and permanent virtual circuits (PVCs) (Figure 4-3). The VC is dynamically set up and cleared each time the service is needed. It is analogous to the use of a dial-up telephone call in a circuit-switched service. The PVC does not require call setup or clearing because the circuit is permanently assigned by the network. This is analogous to a dedicated leased line. Each of the services can provide simultaneous multiple communications over the multiplexed link and all packets follow the same route once the path is established. Although the logical channel may be dedicated for the duration of the call as in a VC, or permanently assigned as with a PVC, the link is not—it is shared throughout.

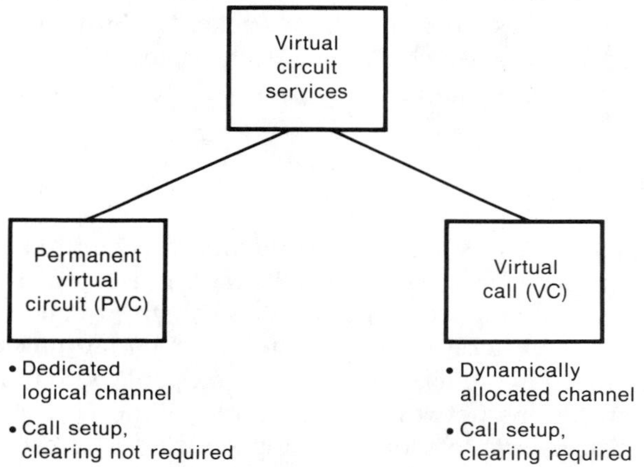

Figure 4-3. Two types of virtual-circuit services.

A third concept applicable to considering packet networks is the illusion of transparency between users when communicating through the respective terminals and/or host computers. In reality, the data terminal is communicating with the network, which contains nodes that are communicating with each other and then finally with the destination user.

Other concepts exist that could be considered in a discussion of packet-switching networks and X.25. Those just described suffice for introductory purposes.

Implementation

The three concepts can now be considered relative to the implementation of packet-switched, virtual-circuit services (Figure 4-4). An example of virtual-circuit service that can provide PVC and VC service, Figure 4-4A has a DTE consisting of an intelligent data terminal, with X.25 protocols, and a modem that are located at user A. A host computer and a front-end processor (FEP) with an X.25 interface are located at user B's premises. An X.25 node, consisting of a modem, data switching exchange (DSE), and data service unit (DSU) in combination with a channel service unit (CSU) is located between the two users. The function of a DSE is defined as "equipment installed at a single location to switch data traffic" (NCS 1985). In the case of a packet network, the DSE can also be considered the DCE containing embedded X.25 network intelligence. Hence, in this example, the DCE is not located at the user premises as it would be in the usual circuit-switched network.

User A is connected to the X.25 node via an analog line that, for example, has a signaling rate of 4.8 or 9.6 kb/s between modems. An X.25 network interface exists between the terminal and modem according to CCITT Recommendation X.21 or X.21 bis (e.g., EIA-232-D) for data rates of less than 20 kb/s. User B is connected via a digital line and DSU/CSU at a signaling rate of 56 kb/s. The X.25 network interface here could be according to CCITT Recommendations V.35, V.28, and V.24, which collectively are for data rates greater than 20 kb/s. The analog and digital lines are both leased for shared use according to logical channel number assignments corresponding to PVC or VC service.

A circuit configuration that is most appropriate for VC service is illustrated in Figure 4-4B. This configuration consists of an asynchronous (start-stop) terminal and modem at user C. The X.25 node consists of a packet assembly/disassembly (PAD) unit, data switch, and two modems that are used on analog lines to users C and D. User D also has an asynchronous terminal, a modem, and an X.25 PAD. The function of the PAD associated with each user is to allow a simple asynchronous terminal to communicate through a packet network to other devices. The PAD is defined by three CCITT Recommendations (X.3, X.28, and X.29). It provides the intelligence that permits the "dumb" terminal to communicate using the X.25 protocol. In this example, user C can initiate a call setup to user D, but user D cannot establish a link to user C. The use of X.3/X.28/X.29 protocols permits simple asynchronous terminals to access an X.25 packet network. On the other hand, intelligent terminals that have more capability become limited due to a lack of flexibility in the PAD approach. A standard to allow dial-in or dial-out operation between DTEs and PSPDNs via a public-switched telephone network (PSTN) or circuit-switched public data networks (CSPDN) is within the realm of CCITT Recommendation X.32.

An example of interconnected DSEs and packet networks is shown in Figure 4-5. The two simple configurations from Figure 4-4 can now be connected through the nodes that are part of a PSPDN. User E is connected to the PSPDN via a PSTN and is similar to user D. A PAD with multiple inputs is shown as part of the implementation at the user premises. This is a more common type of PAD than a unit with only one input as shown in Figure 4-4. A connection to a second PSPDN shows that virtual-circuit service can be established through a number of X.25 networks. The CCITT Recommendation X.75 "Packet-Switched Signalling System Between Public Networks Providing Data Transmission Services" allocates gateway responsibilities between signal terminal equipment (STE) in different public networks for internetworking over links between ISDNs and PSPDNs.

Users A, B, and D have the potential to initiate data packet exchange with each others' data terminals and the host computer. Users C and E can initiate calls to A, B, and D, but not to each other. The others cannot call in to C or E.

In one routing scenario, assume that user D has a message to send to user B, the host computer. The message will have to be distributed among several packets because of its length. A virtual circuit has to be established before the first data packet is sent. First, a connection to user B is requested by sending a Call Request packet to DSE 2. The DSE 2 has the options of routing to DSE 1 or to DSE 3. For this case, it decides to route to DSE 3 because of heavily loaded trunks between DSEs 1 and 2. DSE 3 sends the request to DSE 1, which then routes the Call Request to the host computer at user B. If the host computer accepts the request, it returns a Call Accepted packet to DSE 1. This packet is then relayed to DSE 3, to DSE 2, and finally to user D's PAD. The asynchronous terminal then gets a "connect indication" from the PAD. The route that was established with the Call Request will be used to exchange all data packets in a duplex mode between users D and B. All routing decisions have been made so that an established route now exists between users. Each packet that is transmitted between the two users contains data and virtual-circuit identification. At the end of a data exchange, a Clear Request packet is sent by one of the users when the virtual-circuit connection is to be broken. This is an example where the virtual-circuit service is a VC since a call-setup and call-clearing phase was performed. A PVC does not require the call setup or subsequent clearing. Any of the users depicted within Figure 4-5 can have one or more virtual circuits estab-

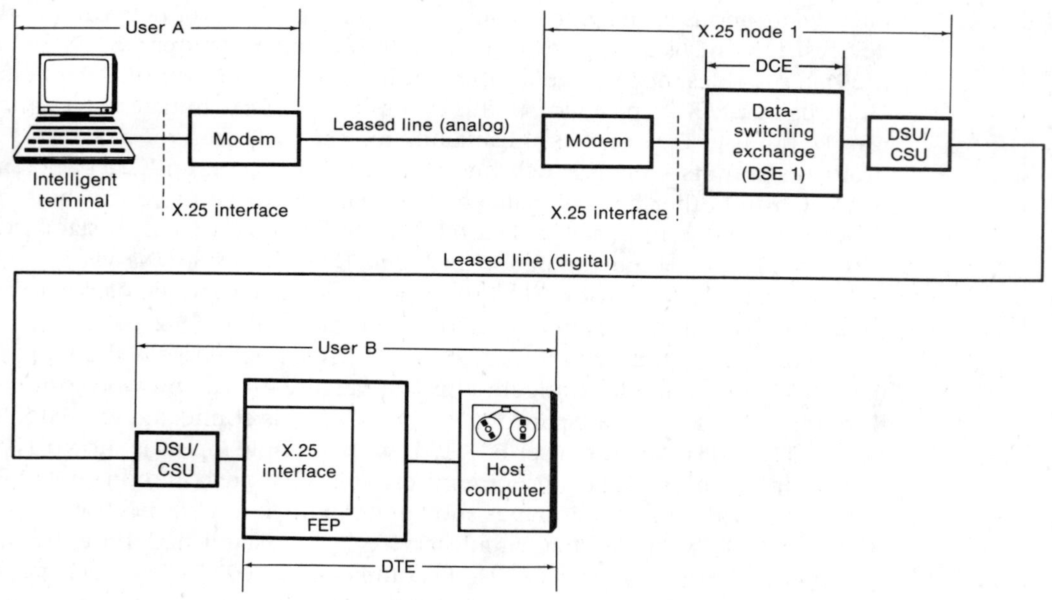

A. Using an intelligent terminal and host computer.

Figure 4-4. Packet-switched virtual-circuit services.

lished within the constraints for call establishment between terminals given above.

Users C and E have to initiate call setup to the other users. However, to access an X.25 node they are required to dial in a telephone number, either manually or automatically, along with appropriate identification, passwords, and connection codes.

The call-setup, data-transfer, and call-clearing phases that have been described are depicted in Figure 4-6 with a time-sequence diagram relative to open systems interconnection (CCITT 1988b, ISO 1985b). The last packet shown in the call-clearing state is Clear Confirmation. It is only of "local significance" between the DTE and DCE. These packet types are described in succeeding sections.

The DTE data exchange between users D and B is also shown as packets that traverse an OSI configuration that includes relay nodes in Figure 4-6. Data units from upper OSI layers have header information added at the packet and data link layers. This X.25 frame structure is presented at the physical layer and transmitted through the communication media to the first relay node DSE 2. The header information is removed and subsequently replaced as the data unit moves through DSE 2. The same procedure is followed at DSE 3 and DSE 1. At

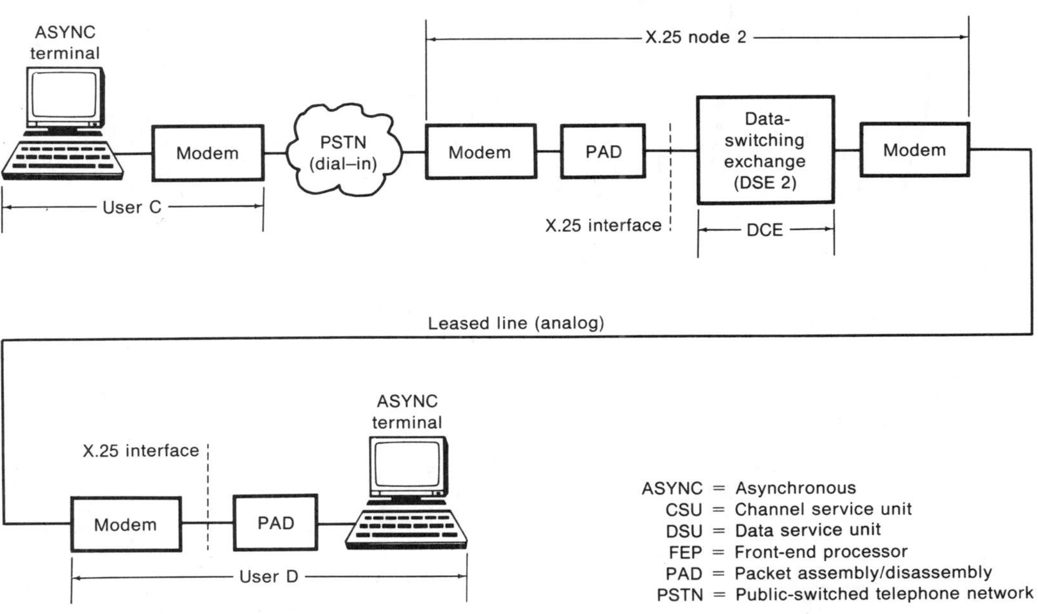

B. Using asynchronous terminals.

Figure 4-4. (cont.)

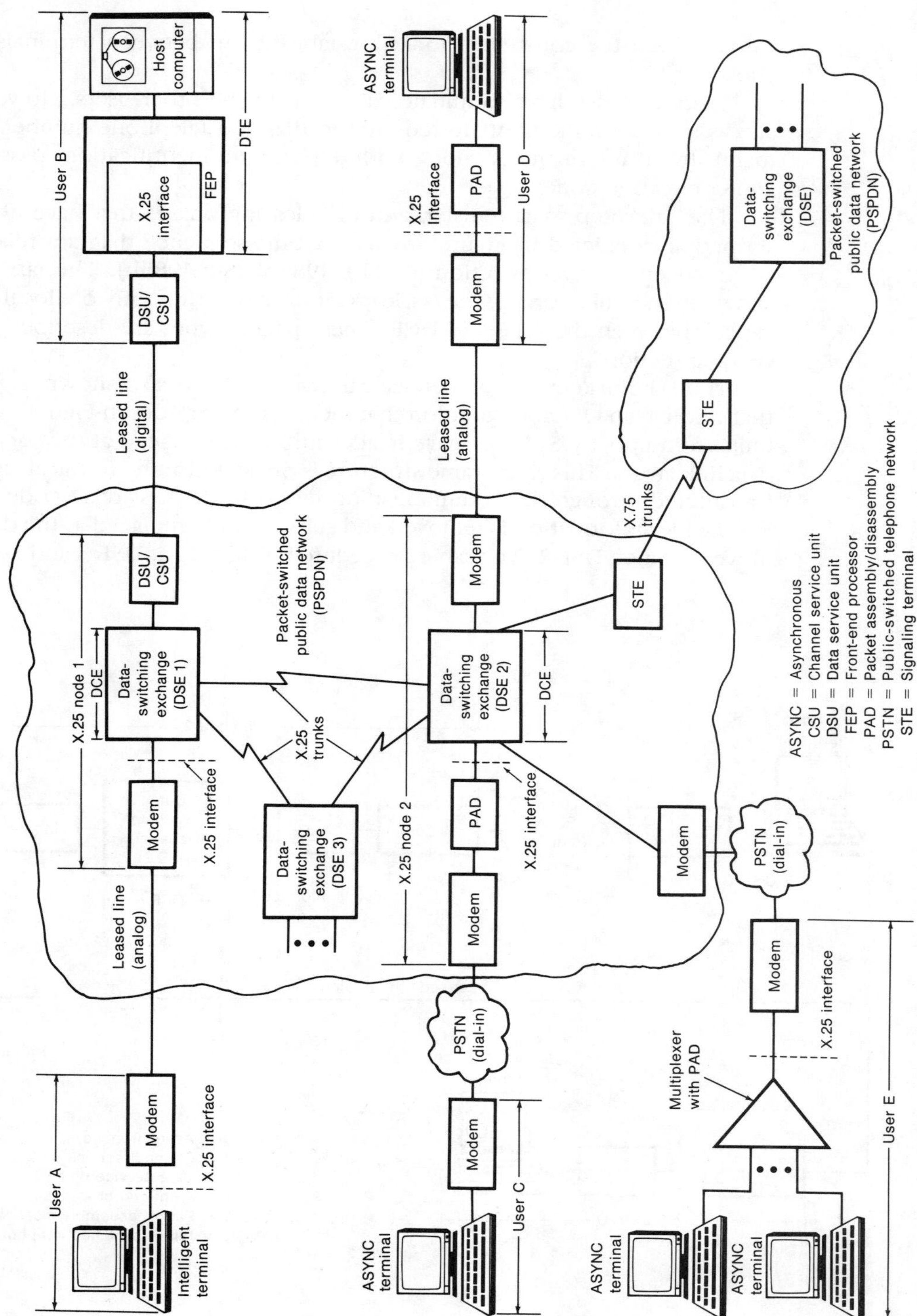

Figure 4-5. Terminals interconnected through a packet-switched network.

user B's DTE, header information is removed at each OSI layer until applications data is presented as the terminal output. The pertinent X.25 recommendations for layers 1, 2, and 3 are also shown in Figure 4-6.

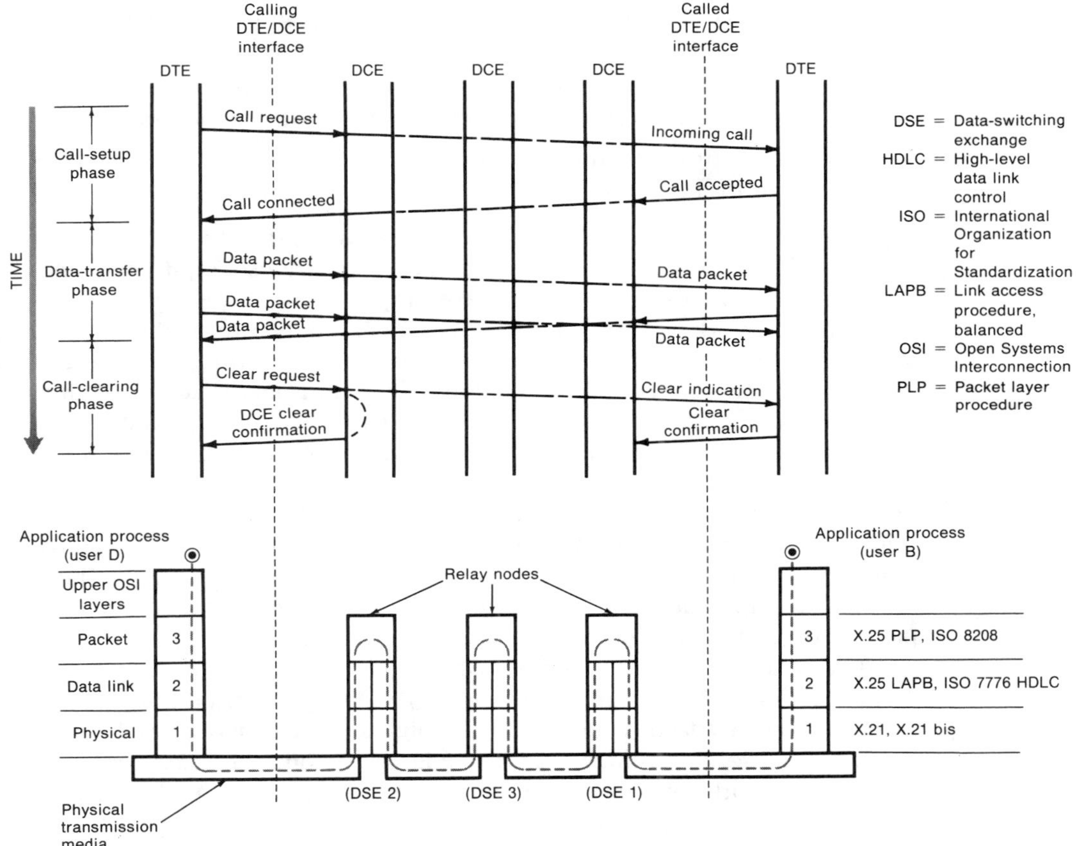

Figure 4-6. DTE packet exchange and relation to open systems interconnection.

CCITT X.25 and Related Standards

Procedures have been defined for CCITT Recommendation X.25 relative to the first three layers of the OSI reference model. At the physical layer, CCITT X.21 (1988c) specifies mechanical, electrical, functional, and procedural characteristics. It is applicable to circuit- and packet-switched operation. CCITT X.21 has not been widely accepted in the United States for two reasons. The first is the wide acceptance of EIA-232-C, which is superceded by EIA-232-D. Second, X.21 requires more intelligence at the interface since characters are interpreted for call-control purposes. Both reasons translate into a cost of changeover. For an "interim period," X.21 bis (CCITT 1988d) which encompasses EIA-232-D (EIA 1985) and EIA-449 (EIA 1977) is acceptable.

At the data link layer, the protocol is intended to provide three basic functions:

- link initialization, which is necessary to begin communication in a known state
- flow control between user systems, which is necessary to ensure that data frames are not sent more quickly than they can be received
- error control, which is necessary to detect mutilated frames and ensure against losing entire frames

In general, the intent of CCITT X.25 LAPB (and LAP) and ISO 7776 (HDLC) is to control errors on the transmission lines between: user equipment and the PSPDN, or two DTEs without an intervening network, respectively.

At the network layer (i.e., packet layer for X.25) the protocol function is to access a public (or private) packet-switched network through a dedicated or circuit-switched connection. When communications take place through a circuit-switched network, including a public data network, a public telephone network, or a circuit-switched ISDN, the connection is according to ISO 8208 with identification procedures, when required, defined in CCITT X.32. The packet layer procedures deal with addressing, call setup and clearing, data transfer and delivery confirmation, and flow and error control related to the communications network, and provide a reset and restart capability. The reset and restart capability enables the reinitializing of communication network paths should error(s) occur at the packet layer.

Three supplemental standards related to CCITT X.25 define a PAD facility. These are CCITT Recommendations X.3 (1988e), X.28 (1988f), and X.29 (1988g). The PAD facility allows nonintelligent asynchronous DTEs (without the capability to incorporate X.25 procedures) to communicate over a packet-switched network with a host computer or terminal that uses X.25. The PAD is a separate box containing hardware and software that is attached to the terminal. The standards define the facility as follows:

- X.3 describes the PAD functions and parameters that are used to control the unintelligent start-stop terminal.
- X.28 describes the protocol between a terminal and PAD.
- X.29 describes the protocol between two PADs or between a PAD and a packet mode DTE.

Physical Layer

This section describes the functions and operation of CCITT X.21 and EIA-232-D. The first is described because of its embedded relationship within X.25, the second because of its dominant position in the United States as a DTE/DCE interface standard.

X.21 Interface

CCITT Recommendation X.21, "Interface Between Data Terminal Equipment (DTE) and Data Circuit-Terminating Equipment (DCE) for Synchronous Operation on Public Data Networks," is applicable for use with both circuit- and packet-switched networks.

Earlier, an X.25 DCE was described as being different than the normally understood definition of a DCE. Differences will now be described concerning CCITT X.21, which may, in error, be considered only as a physical layer interface standard. The misconception arises from two factors: X.21 specifies physical characteristics of the interface and call-control procedures for data connection in a circuit-switched network that are analogous to data transfer in a physical circuit. Considering call-control procedures as being within the OSI physical layer is incorrect because circuit- and packet-switched call establishment has similar functionality—that is, to establish network connections (Pense 1984).

There is, however, a difference in functionality between call-setup and data-transfer states for circuit- and packet-switched networks. In circuit-switched networks, the first three layers of the OSI reference model are involved during call establishment. For example, the network layer is involved in switching and routing between end users. Once the connections between users are made, only the physical layer is involved in the data transfer phase.

In packet-switched networks, the functionality of the first three layers of the OSI reference model is involved not only during the call-setup state, but also during the data-transfer state through the use of LAPB and packet-level procedures. The critical point is that X.21 is literally a two-part standard. In the first part, the physical elements of X.21 apply to circuit- and packet-switched public data networks. In the second part, the recommendation describes the control procedures for connections in a circuit-switched network. Ordinarily, only the physical elements of the first part will apply to X.25.

At layer 1 of the OSI reference model, X.21 provides for data signaling rates that apply to circuit- and packet-switching.

Layer 2, the data link layer of the OSI reference model, provides for synchronization, error detection, error recovery, and flow control functions. These functions are specified within X.21 for circuit-switched applications using a character-oriented protocol. For packet-switched networks, these same functions are performed by bit-oriented protocols such as X.25 LAPB and ISO 7776 HDLC.

Layer 3, the network layer of the OSI reference model, provides for connection control, multiplexing, and network-dependent error and flow control. For circuit switching, X.21 specifies only connection establishment and release, i.e., connection control. Connection control and other layer 3 functions for packet switching are according to X.25 and ISO 8208 packet-layer procedures.

Description: X.21

The electrical characteristics of X.21 comply with CCITT Recommendations X.26 (1988h) and X.27 (1988i). A 15-pin, D-type connector is defined by ISO 4903. The connector carries eight DTE/DCE interchange circuits that are defined according to procedural definitions in CCITT X.24 (1988j). The DTE/DCE physical interface lines are depicted according to conventional understanding in Figure 4-7. According to X.24, the interface between the DTE and DCE is located at a connector that is the interchange point between the equipment. As explained earlier, this DTE/DCE physical interface is not necessarily the X.25 interface. This depiction is best suited to a circuit-switched network. It illustrates one of the many anomalies that exist in standards work.

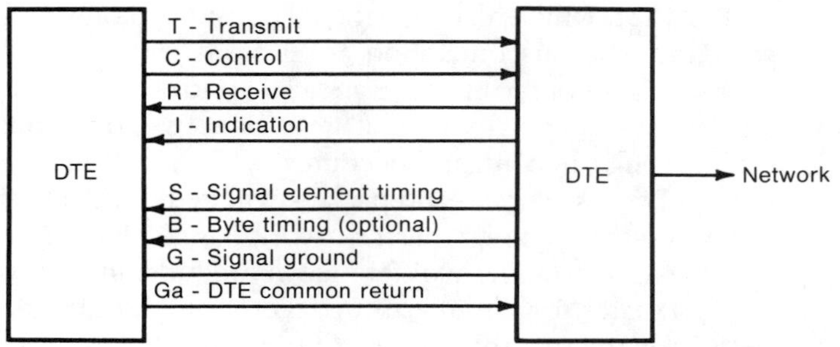

Figure 4-7. X.21 signal interchange lines.

The functions of the interchange circuits are as follows:

Circuit T: Transmit (to DCE)—carries control signals during call-control phases and data during data-transfer phase

Circuit C: Control (to DCE)—provides control information (on-hook, off-hook) in conjunction with the T circuit

Circuit R: Receive (to DTE)—similar to T, but in opposite direction

Circuit I: Indication (to DTE)—works in conjunction with circuit R by providing indicators that R has data or control signaling from the distant DTE

Circuit S: Signal element timing (to DTE)—provides bit timing for synchronous operation

Circuit B: Byte timing (to DTE)—provides signals that are used for grouping bits into octets (optional)

Circuit G: Signal ground or common return

Circuit Ga: DTE common return

Extensive information is contained in figures and tables of X.21 describing transition states for call control and data transfer during circuit-switched service. There are two basic phases of the interface to consider: quiescent and operational (see Table 4-1). There are two states in the quiescent phase: ready and not ready. All characters for call-control purposes are selected from International Alphabet No. 5 (IA5) according to CCITT Recommendation T.50 [equivalent to ISO 646, ANSI X3.4 (American Standard Code for Information Interchange-ASCII), and FIPS PUB 15]. During call control when information is exchanged between the DTE and DCE, correct alignment of characters is necessary. Two or more "SYN" characters precede each sequence of call-control characters to establish alignment.

Table 4-1. X.21 Phases of Interface Signals

Phase	Result
Quiescent	
Ready state: DTE T = 1, C = OFF; DCE R = 1, I = OFF	DTE or DCE can enter operational phase
Not ready state: DTE T = 0, C = OFF; DCE R = 0, I = OFF	DTE or DCE is inoperative
Operational	
DTE T = DATA, C = ON; DCE R = DATA, I = ON	States needed during circuit- and packet-switched data transfer

An example of transitions between states is given in Table 4-2. Based on work by Tannenbaum (1981), this illustration of a circuit-switched connection between DTEs illustrates some features of X.21. An originating DTE places a call to a remote DTE, data bits are exchanged, and then the connection is cleared by the originating DTE. The transitions are described in two parts according to X.21 terminology (state) and as an analogy with the telephone system.

Table 4-2. Some X.21 Transitions for Call Placement, Data Transfer, and Call Clearing

Step	State	DTE T (Transmit)	DTE C (Control)	DCE R (Receive)	DCE I (Indication)	Telephone Analogy
1	Ready	1	OFF	1	OFF	No connection, idle (on-hook)
2	Call Request	0	ON	1	OFF	DTE picks up phone
3	Proceed to Select	0	ON	+	OFF	DCE gives dial tone
4	Selection Signal	IA5	ON	+	OFF	DTE dials phone number
5	Call Progress Signal (X.96)	1	ON	IA5	OFF	Remote phone rings
6	Call Accepted	1	ON	1	ON	Remote phone picked up
7	Data Transfer	Data	ON	Data	ON	Conversation
8	DTE Clear Request	0	OFF	Data	ON	DTE says goodbye
9	DCE Clear Indication	0	OFF	0	OFF	DCE says goodbye
10	DCE Clear Confirmation	0	OFF	1	OFF	DCE hangs up
11	Ready	1	OFF	1	OFF	DTE hangs up (on-hook)

According to CCITT convention, 1 is OFF and 0 is ON. In the READY (on-hook) state, the four signaling lines are all 1s (step 1 in Table 4-2). To place a call, a DTE sets T = 0 and C = ON (step 2). This is similar to a person picking up the handset to place a telephone call. The DCE begins sending an IA5 (ASCII) + character on the R line (a digital dial tone) signaling the DTE that address dialing can begin (step 3). The remote DTE is dialed by IA5 characters being sent on the T line (step 4). Call-progress signals are now sent by the DCE to inform the DTE of call status such as call completed (phone rings) or try again (number busy) and others according to CCITT Recommendation X.96 (step 5). If the call is accepted, the DCE sets the I line to ON (step 6) and, in a full-duplex connection, data exchange can begin (step 7). Either the originating or remote DTE can begin call termination by setting the C line to OFF. With this action, a DTE cannot send more data, but it must accept data from the other DTE until the transfer is completed (step 8). The originating DCE now sets the I line to OFF (step 9). After the remote DTE sets its C line to OFF, the DCE at the originating DTE will set R = 1 (step 10). The originating DTE then sets T = 1 as an acknowledgment to the DCE and the interface is again in a READY (on-hook) state.

In the event of call collision, when outgoing and incoming calls arrive simultaneously, the incoming call is canceled and the outgoing call is placed.

The data link and packet layer procedures of X.25 function when the C and I lines are ON (steps 6 and 7).

Description: EIA-232-D

Interface standard EIA-232-D (EIA 1985) is a revision of EIA-232-C (EIA 1969), one of the four options in X.21 bis. The revisions bring the standard into compliance with CCITT and ISO standards. Electrical characteristics comply with CCITT Recommendation V.28 (CCITT 1988l) and functional characteristics with V.24 (CCITT 1988m). A 25-pin, D-type connector is defined by ISO 2110. Specific revisions reflect the addition of a specification for the 25-pin interface connector, inclusion of the Local Loopback, Remote Loopback and Test Mode interchange circuits, redefinition of Protective Ground, and the addition of Shield. Terminology changes are Driver to Generator and Terminator to Receiver (EIA 1985).

The electrical characteristics specify digital signaling parameters for the interchange circuits between the DTE and DCE. For timing and control circuits, the function is considered ON when the voltage is more positive than +3 V with respect to signal ground (circuit AB) and OFF when the voltage is more negative than −3 V with respect to signal ground (Table 4-3). The signaling rate is to be 20 kb/s, or less, when the effective shunt capacitance of the load is 2,500 pf, or less. A distance is not specified for the signaling rate in EIA-232-D. However, EIA-232-C specified 15 m for 20 kb/s.

The interchange circuits between DTEs and DCEs fall into four categories:

- ground or common return
- data circuits
- control circuits
- timing circuits

Table 4-3. EIA-232-D Interchange Voltage Interpretations

Interpretation	**<−3 V**	**>+3 V**
Binary state	1	0
Signal condition	Marking	Spacing
Function	OFF	ON

Table 4-4 provides a list of equivalent interchange circuits for EIA-232-D, CCITT V.24, and EIA-449. Footnote 1 for Table 4-4 identifies those circuits that are specified for leased circuits and packet-switched service (X.25, Layer 1). Those 13 circuits are defined as follows (Circuit CE (Ring Indicator) is defined to specifically show it is not needed for packet-switched services):

Circuit AB (CCITT 102): Signal Ground or Common Return—common ground reference for all interchange circuits

Circuit BA (CCITT 103): Transmitted Data—data generated by the DTE for transmission

Circuit BB (CCITT 104): Received Data—data received by the DTE from a remote DTE

Circuit CA (CCITT 105): Request to Send—conditions the local DCE for data transmission

Circuit CB (CCITT 106): Clear to Send—indicates to the DTE whether the DCE is ready to send data in response to Request to Send

Circuit CC (CCITT 107): DCE Ready—signals on this circuit indicate status of the local DCE (e.g., off-hook condition)

Circuit CD (CCITT 108/2): DTE Ready—signals on this circuit control switching of the DCE to the communication channel (CCITT 108/1, Connect Data Set to Line, when implemented, is an alternative to 108/2 for packet-switched service)

Circuit CE (CCITT 125): Ring Indicator—the DCE indicates to the DTE through an ON condition that a ringing signal is being received (not needed for leased or packet-switched services)

Circuit CF (CCITT 109): Received Line Signal Indicator—indicates to the DTE that a carrier signal is being received by the DCE

Circuit DB (CCITT 114): Transmitter Signal Element Timing—the DCE provides clocking signals to the DTE so that data on Circuit BA (Transmitted Data) is timed according to Circuit DB

Circuit DD (CCITT 115): Receiver Signal Element Timing—clocking signal for Circuit BB (Received Data)

Circuit RL (CCITT 140): Remote Loopback—the DTE provides control signals to the DCE to activate a loopback at the remote DCE while isolating the remote DTE during the test

Table 4-4. Nearest Equivalent Interchange Circuits

EIA-232-D	CCITT V.24	EIA-449	Description	Gnd	Data from DCE	Data to DCE	Control from DCE	Control to DCE	Timing from DCE	Timing to DCE
AB	102[1]	SG	Signal Ground/ Common Return	X						
BA	103[1]	SD	Transmitted Data			X				
BB	104[1]	RD	Received Data		X					
CA	105[1]	RS	Request to Send					X		
CB	106[1]	CS	Clear to Send				X			
CC	107[1]	DM	DCE Ready				X			
CD	108/2[1]	TR	DTE Ready					X		
CE	125[2]	IC	Ring Indicator				X			
CF	109[1]	RR	Received Line Signal Detector				X			
CG	110	SQ	Signal Quality Detector				X			
CH	111	SR	Data Signal Rate Selector (DTE)					X		
CI	112	SI	Data Signal Rate Selector (DCE)				X			
DA	113	TT	Transmitter Signal Element Timing (DTE)							X
DB	114[1]	ST	Transmitter Signal Element Timing (DCE)						X	
DD	115[1]	RT	Receiver Signal Element Timing (DCE)						X	
SBA	118	SSD	Secondary Transmitted Data			X				
SBB	119	SRD	Secondary Received Data		X					
SCA	120	SRS	Secondary Request to Send					X		
SCB	121	SCS	Secondary Clear to Send				X			
SCF	122	SRR	Secondary Received Line Signal Detector				X			
RL	140[1]	RL	Remote Loopback					X		
LL	141[1]	LL	Local Loopback					X		
TM	142[1]	TM	Test Mode				X			

[1]These interchange circuits are listed in X.21 bis for synchronous transmission using leased circuit service, and packet-switched service (X.25, layer 1).
[2]Add for use with direct call or address call facilities.

Circuit LL (CCITT 141): Local Loopback—the DTE initiates action so that signals are used to control the LL test condition in the local DCE (determines whether the DCE and local interface are working properly)

Circuit TM (CCITT 142): Test Mode—signals indicate whether the local DCE is in a test condition

A subset of the control circuits is usually implemented to control data transmission and reception. There are five control circuits, (CA, CB, CC, CD, CF) that must be in the ON condition for this implementation of the OSI physical layer to allow data to be sent (Circuit BA) and received (Circuit BB).

Table 4-4 shows equivalency for EIA-449 (EIA 1977) circuits that can operate to 100 kb/s for 12 m using EIA 423-A (unbalanced configuration) and 100 kb/s for 1,200 m using EIA-422-A (balanced configuration). This distance will decrease to 12 m at 10 Mb/s. These signaling rates are transmitted on 24 AWG twisted-pair copper conductors. Despite better performance characteristics of EIA-449, the implementation has not matched EIA-232-D (and preceding versions) due to higher cost and the entrenchment of the latter.

CCITT V.35, V.28, and V.24

Another option within X.21 bis is the combination of CCITT Recommendations V.35, V.28, and V.24. Appendix II of V.35 (CCITT 1988k) specifies electrical characteristics for *balanced*, double-current interchange circuits that are used for data and timing. CCITT V.28 (1988l) applies to electrical characteristics for *unbalanced*, double-current control circuits (Table 4-5). The functions of the interchange circuits for V.35 and V.28 are defined in V.24 (CCITT 1988m).

Table 4-5. V.35/V.28/V.24 Circuits

Double Current Circuit	Interchange Circuit (V.24)	Function
Data and timing (V.35)	103	Transmitted Data
	104	Received Data
	114	Transmitter Signal Element Timing (DTE)
	115	Receiver Signal Element Timing (DCE)
	102	Signal Ground or Common Return
Control (V.28)	105	Request to Send
	106	Ready for Sending
	107	Data Set Ready
	109	Data Channel Received Line Signal Detector

Voltage levels for V.35 operation are as shown in Table 4-3. This X.21 bis option is intended for 48 or 56 kb/s operation. Further study has been proposed to perform a test of cable length corresponding to actual operation.

Data Signaling Rates

CCITT X.25 operates in user classes of service 8 to 11 as defined in CCITT X.1. User classes of service are data signaling rates of 2.4, 4.8, 9.6, and 48 kb/s for DTEs operating in the synchronous mode using the X.25 interface. Since 56 kb/s is a standard signaling rate in North America according to ANS X3.1, it is recommended in place of 48 kb/s. The use of 64 kb/s (also part of X.1) is for ISDN service. Packet mode operation is not defined for operation in excess of 64 kb/s.

Data Link Layer

Data link access procedures that are used for data interchange between a DCE and a DTE or between two DTEs are described in this section. One of these procedures, the HDLC, is a bit-oriented protocol. Other procedures that are based on HDLC, but incompatible, are ANS X3.66, Advanced Data Communications Control Procedures (ADCCP), Burroughs Data Link Control (BDLC), IBM Synchronous Data Link Control (SDLC), and Sperry Universal Data Link Control (UDLC).

The HDLC, X.25 LAPB, and other procedures satisfy the basic functions of the OSI data link layer, which provides for

- link initialization, which allows the DTE to begin operation in a known state
- flow control, which ensures that frames are sent at a rate that does not create an overflow between DTEs or a DTE and a DCE
- error control (at the data link layer) to detect errors in frames through a cyclic redundancy check (CRC) and sequence numbers to protect against the loss of entire frames

Both LAPB and LAP are described in the data link layer element (Section 2) of CCITT Recommendation X.25. Both procedures can operate over a single physical circuit. In this instance, data interchange between a DTE and DCE is described as an SLP. An optional multilink operation is available with LAPB. With this option, an SLP is used independently on each physical circuit, but an added multilink procedure (MLP) is used on the same multiple parallel LAPB data links. The MLP is seen as an added sublayer of the data link layer, between the packet layer and multiple SLPs in the lower portion of the data link layer. An MLP performs the functions of accepting packets from the packet layer and distributing the packets across multiple SLPs for transmission across the DTE/DCE interface. Packets received from the DTE or DCE SLPs are sequenced for delivery to the DCE or DTE packet layer, respectively.

The LAP procedure was originally developed for X.25 (1980). It is not part of ANS X3.100 nor FIPS PUB 100/FED STD 1041. The LAP procedure, while still part of X.25 (1988) exists in support of existing systems. LAPB is the preferred procedure and is readily available from manufacturers of, for example, PADs and packet switches.

Basic Characteristics

There are three types of stations, three types of link configurations, and three data transfer modes defined in the HDLC and related standards (see Figure 4-8).

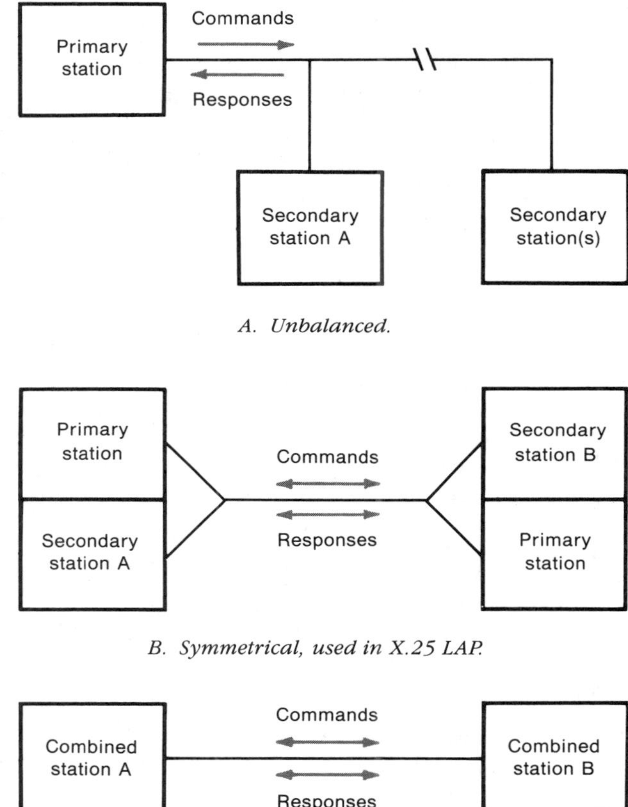

Figure 4-8. Link configurations.

The station types are

- *Primary*. This station has the responsibility of controlling the operation of a link. A primary station sends commands and receives responses from the secondary station(s) on the link.
- *Secondary*. This station operates under the control of the primary station. A secondary station receives commands from, and sends responses to, the primary station.
- *Combined*. This station is used where equal control is required at both ends of a link by combining the features of primary and secondary sta-

tions. A combined station sends and receives both commands and responses.

The link configurations are

- *Unbalanced*. This configuration has one primary station and one or more secondary stations, and is used in point-to-point and multipoint operation with half-duplex and duplex transmission (Figure 4-8A).
- *Symmetrical*. This configuration has two independent, point-to-point, unbalanced logical station configurations multiplexed on a single data line (Figure 4-8B). There are two primary-to-secondary station logical channels with the primary stations having overall responsibility for mode setting. Half-duplex and duplex operation is supported. This configuration is used in the original LAP, which is still part of X.25 (1988). It is not supported in ISO 7776 HDLC procedures.
- *Balanced*. This configuration consists of two combined stations that are connected only for point-to-point operation. Half-duplex and duplex operation are supported (Figure 4-8C). This configuration is used in X.25 LAPB with duplex transmission.

Communication between two stations is conducted in three logical states: *information transfer, initialization*, or *logically disconnected*. There are three modes of operation for information transfer:

- *Normal Response Mode (NRM)*. This mode is an unbalanced configuration where the secondary station may transmit information only as the result of responding to a primary station (i.e., polling). This mode is on multidrop lines and point-to-point links although not efficient on the latter due to polling overhead.
- *Asynchronous Response Mode (ARM)*. This mode is an unbalanced configuration in which the secondary station may initiate transmission without receiving explicit permission from the primary station. This mode is used infrequently.
- *Asynchronous Balanced Mode (ABM)*. This is a balanced configuration where transmission can be initiated without receiving permission from the other combined station.

There is one mode during the initialization state. During the Initialization Mode (IM), a secondary or combined station may be initialized by a primary or combined state when it appears, for example, that the secondary or other station is not operating normally.

There are two modes during the logically disconnected state (LDS). In the Normally Disconnected Mode (NDM), the secondary station is logically disconnected from the unbalanced data link configuration and cannot receive or initiate information transfer. The Asynchronous Disconnected Mode (ADM) applies to balanced or unbalanced link configurations. In ADM, a secondary or combined station is logically disconnected from the link and is not permitted to initiate or receive information. However, a single frame indicating station status can be sent by the secondary/combined station without explicit permission.

From the definitions for stations, link configurations, and modes of operation during logical states, one can determine which apply to X.25 LAPB (Table 4-6).

Table 4-6. HDLC Characteristics Applicable to X.25 LAPB

Characteristic	Operation
Station	Combined
Link configuration	Balanced
Modes	Asynchronous Balanced Mode (ABM), Asynchronous Disconnected Mode (ADM), Initialization Mode (IM)
Transmission	Duplex, synchronous

Many of the procedures that have been defined are unnecessary for packet network operation. The following sections will concentrate on the applicable requirements for X.25 LAPB operation.

Frame Structure

There are two frame structures, one for basic (modulo 8) and one for extended (modulo 128) operation. The LAPB modulo 8 procedure is available on all networks whereas the LAPB modulo 128 is optional according to CCITT X.25. The modulo 128 provides an extended frame sequence numbering where more packets need to be outstanding (without acknowledgment) between stations, as in a satellite transmission where delays are longer. The initial descriptions herein of the frame structure adhere to modulo 8 and SLP. The modulo 128 and MLP are mentioned when appropriate.

The frame structure is shown in Figure 4-9. Also shown is the relationship of packet layer data within the information field. The packet layer descriptions are given in the next section.

Flag Sequence (8 bits). All frames start and end with the sequence 01111110. Synchronization is achieved as the DTE hunts continuously for this sequence. Only one flag is needed as both the closing flag for one frame and the opening flag for the next frame. "Bit stuffing" is used to avoid the loss of synchronization. A transmitter inserts a zero bit in any field within a frame (between flags) after the occurrence of five consecutive ones. The receiver continuously examines the bit stream to determine the appearance of five 1s. If the sixth bit is a 0, that bit is deleted and the five 1s are passed as data. If the sixth bit is a 1, the receiver inspects the seventh bit. If the seventh bit is a 0, a flag sequence has been received; if it is a 1, an abort has been received. An abort is performed by the transmitter when at least seven, but less than fifteen, contiguous 1s are sent without a 0 insertion. (Note that this discussion could be interpreted to relate to the second through eighth bits in a flag field.)

Address Field (one octet). The address field identifies the intended receiver of a command frame or the transmitter (combined station) of a response frame.

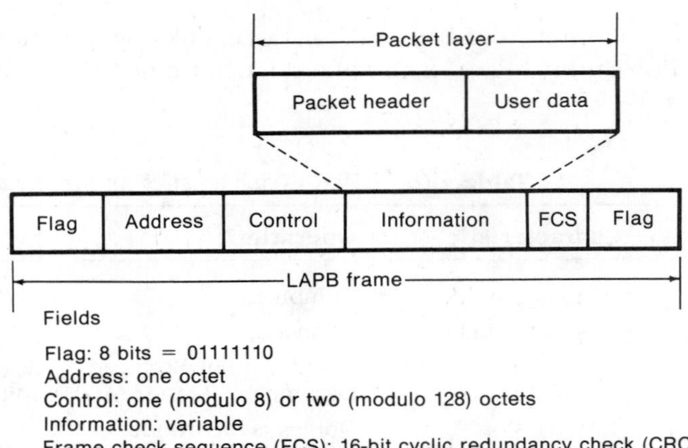

Figure 4-9. Frame structure and packet layer relationship.

The address field also allows for differentiation between SLP or the optional MLP through bit encoding.

Control Field (one or two octets). The control field consists of one octet for modulo 8 (basic) operation and one or two octets for modulo 128 (extended operation)—one octet for frame formats that do not contain sequence numbers and two octets for those that do.

There are three types of control field formats. A frame can contain an information (I), supervisory (S), or unnumbered (U) control field (Figure 4-10). The I format is used to transfer data across a data link. Only I frames have the send sequence number N(S), the number of the transmitted frame. Variable S acts as a frame counter and takes on the value of the modulo (8 or 128) minus one. For modulo 8 operation, the maximum value of outstanding (unacknowledged) frames would be 7 (k = 7). The variable S is incremented by one each time there is a completed I frame transmission.

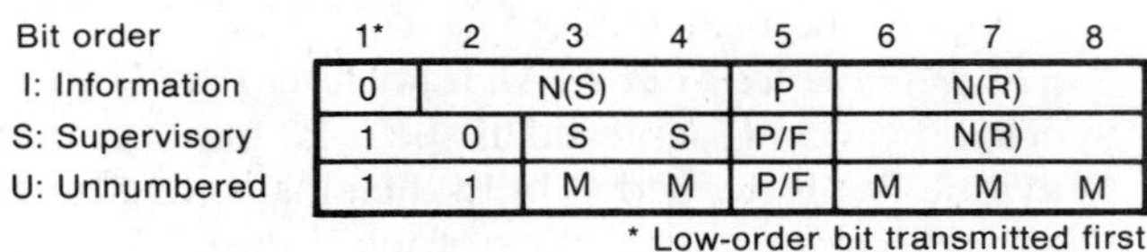

Bit order	1*	2	3	4	5	6	7	8
I: Information	0		N(S)		P		N(R)	
S: Supervisory	1	0	S	S	P/F		N(R)	
U: Unnumbered	1	1	M	M	P/F	M	M	M

* Low-order bit transmitted first

M = Modifier function bits
N(S) = Send sequence number
N(R) = Receive sequence number

P/F = Poll/Final bit
P = Poll bit (Poll = 1)
S = Supervisory function bit

Figure 4-10. LAPB control field formats for basic modulo 8 operation.

The I frames (and S frames) also contain N(R) which is the expected sequence number of the next received I frame. The variable R is equal to the expected N(S) contained in the next I frame received. The use of N(S) and N(R) is for flow and error control between the DTE and DCE. N(R) serves as an acknowledgment for frames received.

The poll (P) bit set to one is used by the DCE or DTE to solicit a response from the DTE or DCE, respectively.

The S format is used by the DTE to perform data link supervisory control functions such as acknowledge or request retransmission, or to request the temporary suspension of transmission of I frames. In a response frame, the P/F bit is known as the final (F) bit. When set to one by the DCE or DTE, it indicates that the response frame sent by the DTE or DCE, respectively, is the result of a poll command. The supervisory (S) function bits in the format are encoded for commands and responses to indicate receive ready (RR), reject (REJ), and receive not ready (RNR).

RR is a supervisory frame used by the DCE or DTE to indicate command or response such as

- readiness to receive an I frame
- acknowledgment of previously received I frames
- clearance of a busy condition due to RNR
- status request (P = 1) of the DTE or DCE, respectively

RNR indicates a busy condition where, for example, the receive buffer is full or to request DTE or DCE status with P = 1. REJ is used to request retransmission of I frames starting with N(R). Lower numbered frames [N(R)−1] are acknowledged. REJ is used also to indicate clearance of a busy condition due to RNR and request for DTE or DCE status with P = 1.

The three supervisory and five unnumbered commands that are used in X.25 LAPB and ISO 7776 are a subset of the complete HDLC/ADCCP command/response repertoire.

The U format is used by the DTE to provide additional data link control functions. This format is unnumbered because it carries no sequence numbers, but it does include a P/F bit that may be set to 0 or 1. The five modifier (M) bits can be encoded for commands to indicate set asynchronous balanced mode (SABM) and disconnect (DISC). The M bits can also be encoded to indicate unnumbered acknowledgment (UA), disconnected mode (DM), and frame reject (FRMR). These are defined as follows:

- SABM—an unnumbered command that is used to place the addressed DCE or DTE in an ABM information transfer phase where all command/response fields will be one octet in length (SABME applies to extended, modulo 128, operation)
- DISC—an unnumbered command that terminates the mode (e.g., ABM) previously set by the DCE or DTE
- UA—an unnumbered response by the DCE or DTE that acknowledges mode-setting commands such as SABM, SABME, DISC (indicates the clearance of a busy condition that was reported earlier by the same DCE or DTE through an RNR frame)
- DM—an unnumbered response that reports a status where a DTE or DCE is logically disconnected from the link and is in the disconnected phase

- FRMR—an unnumbered response by the DCE and DTE that reports an error condition not recoverable by retransmission of the identical frame (e.g., receipt of a command or response control field that is undefined or receipt of an I frame where the information field exceeds the maximum permitted length)

Commands and responses within the supervisory and control field formats will be supported by DCEs and DTEs for basic and extended operation.

Frame Check Sequence Field (16 bits). The FCS field shall be a 16-bit sequence. The notation used to describe the FCS is based on the property of cyclic codes that enables a code vector to be represented by a polynomial.

The order of bit transmission is such that addresses, commands, responses, and sequence numbers shall be transmitted with the low-order bit first.

Data Link Operation

The text in this section is adapted from "Examples of the Operation of Bit-Oriented Data Link Control Protocols," by J. W. Conard. It is part of a data communications tutorial series called OSI Data Transfer that is available from Omnicom, Incorporated, 501 Church Street NE, Suite 206, Vienna, VA 22180. This text has been specifically edited to reflect LAPB operation.

The conventions that are used for illustrations in this section are shown in Figure 4-11. Each heavily marked arrow represents a single frame transiting a data link between two stations. The two stations involved are the DTE on the left, whose hypothetical link address is "A" (DTE A), and the DCE or remote DTE equipment on the right, whose link address is assumed to be "B" (DXE B).

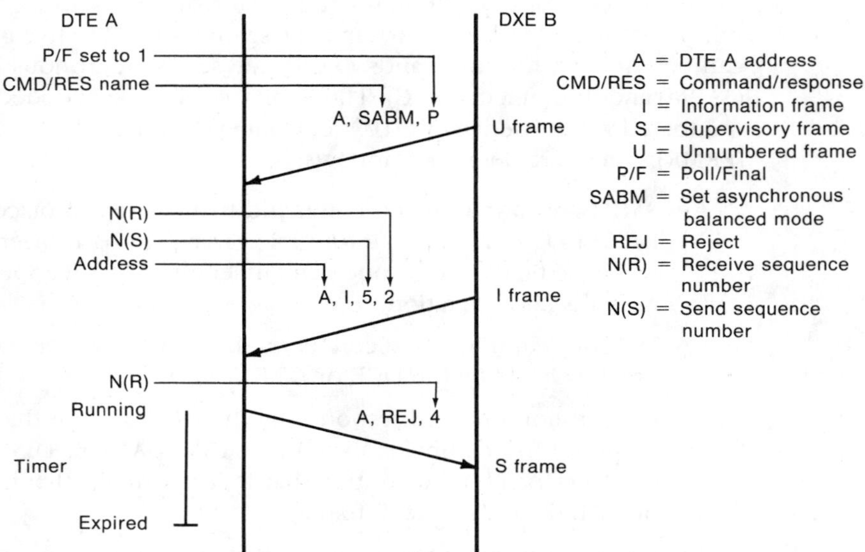

Figure 4-11. Conventions used in balanced procedure examples.

Each heavy arrow includes a legend that describes the content and meaning of that particular frame. The legend includes: the address carried in the address field of the frame; the command or response type coded in the control field of the frame; the setting of the P/F bit, bit five of the control field; and, where appropriate, sequence numbers. As is explained later, some examples do not include the address designator. P/F is only indicated where bit five is set to 1. A "P" indicates that bit five of a command frame is set to 1. An "F" indicates that bit five of a response frame is set to 1. The absence of a P or F indicates that bit five is set to 0 and has no meaning.

Frames may be any of three types, each of which is illustrated in Figure 4-11. The U frame is an unnumbered command or response used to convey data link control information. It is unnumbered because it carries no sequence numbers. The designation "A,SABM,P" in the figure indicates that this frame is an SABM command addressed to station A and that it has the P-bit set to 1 to force a response.

The I frame is the information frame. It is used to carry user data across the data link. The information frames are sequentially numbered. Each I frame carries both send and receive sequence numbers. The send sequence number, N(S), is the number of each frame. The receive sequence number, N(R), is the acknowledgment number. It indicates that all frames up to and including N(R)-1 have been successfully received. The N(R) is the next in-sequence frame expected to be received. In Figure 11, the designation "A,I,5,2" indicates that this is a command information frame sequence numbered 5 addressed to station A. It also indicates that the sender, station B, is expected to receive frame number 2 next. It therefore acknowledges the correct receipt of frames numbered 1 and below.

The third frame shown in the figure, the S frame, is a supervisory frame. There are three types of LAPB basic or extended supervisory commands and responses: RR, RNR, and REJ. The example "A,REJ,4" illustrates a REJ frame carrying the link address A. Supervisory frames carry an N(R) indicating the next frame expected by the sender. In this case, the sender next expects to receive frame number 4 and therefore acknowledges frames numbered 3 and below.

Data Link Addresses in Balanced Operation

There are some unique differences in the way the data link address is used in balanced operation as contrasted with the unbalanced operation. In unbalanced configurations, a unique address is assigned to each secondary station on the link. This address is contained in the address field of every frame transmitted by the primary to a secondary station. This same address is also used by the secondary in every response frame that it sends to the primary. As a result, in unbalanced operation, the frame address field always identifies the secondary.

In balanced operation, a unique address is assigned to each of the two stations. Since the stations combine the attributes of both primary and secondary stations, they send both commands and responses to the other station so that each station also receives both commands and responses from the other station. The address field is the mechanism used to tell the difference between a command and response. To separate the two logically independent data streams sharing the link there is a simple rule that may be applied to sort out the combined station address convention. According to LAPB and ISO 7776, commands always carry the destination address and responses always carry the source address. But there is a difference in address assignment in the two standards.

The address field in LAPB differentiates between commands and responses. Address A(SLP) or C(MLP) is assigned to the DTE and address B(SLP) or D(MLP) is assigned to the DCE.

In DTE/DTE operation (ISO 7776), address assignment is determined through bilateral agreement of the network system managers.

Figure 4-12 illustrates addressing for modulo 8 single link operation from the perspective of station A as follows:

1. If the address of the incoming frame is A, the frame is a command.
2. If the address of the incoming frame is B, the frame is a response.
3. If the address is other than A or B, discard the frame.

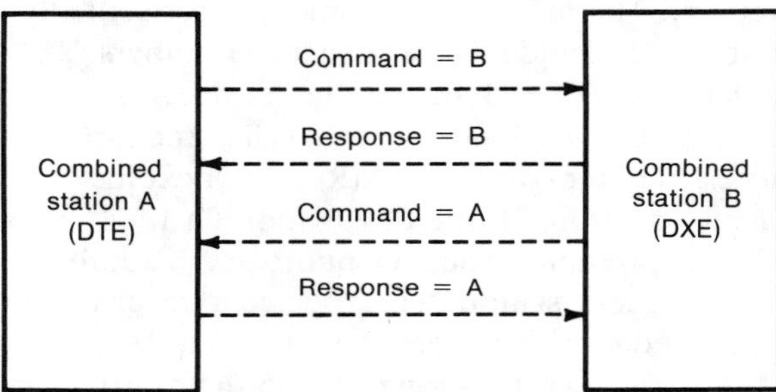

Figure 4-12. Balanced procedure address convention.

The example of balanced procedure that follows will make use of these conventions. In the figures, station B on the right is identified as a DXE, designating it as either a DCE or a DTE. Frame nomenclature includes the address. Data link setup, information transfer, data link disconnection, and error recovery examples are shown.

Establishing the Balanced Data Link

Normal Data Link Setup. Balanced stations usually indicate that they are active by sending continuous flags over the data link. As illustrated in Figure 4-13, many also go through a disconnect procedure prior to initializing the data link. This, suggested by the rules, has the advantage of making sure the station is alive and ready to start up the data link.

A station wishing to set up the data link transmits an SABM command with the P-bit set and starts the response timer. The other station, upon receiving the SABM, returns UA response with the F-bit set and initializes the local variables and counters. The initiating station receives the UA response, resets its send and receive variables, and stops the timer. The data link is now active and either station may begin sending information frames.

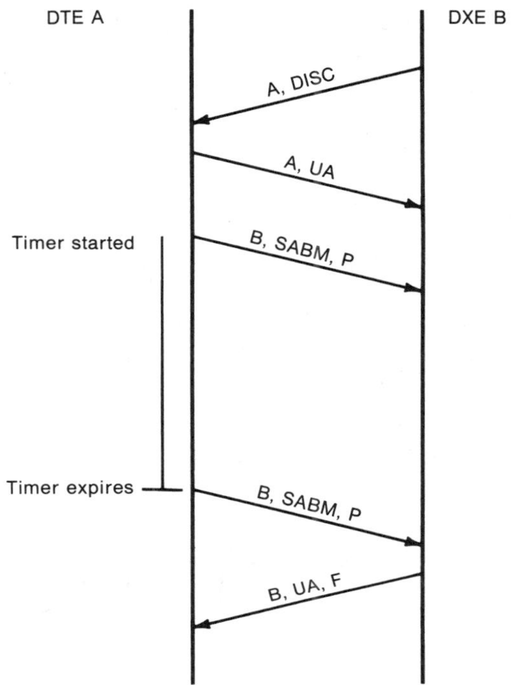

Figure 4-13. Balanced data link setup, no contention.

Should the timeout expire without a UA response from the other station, the originator will repeat the SABM, as shown in the figure. This would be repeated until a UA is received or until, after N tries, the link is declared nonoperational. In this case, higher-level intervention will be necessary.

Timers are used at the DTE or DXE to detect whether a required action or response has taken place within a predetermined interval—for example, an unnumbered response to a command. Error recovery or the reissuance of the P-bit occurs when the timer expires, as shown in Figure 4-13.

Contention During Data Link Setup. Since both stations on a balanced data link have equal status, it is possible that they will both attempt to initialize simultaneously. This is called mode-setting contention and is resolved by giving a station the choice of when to start the operational mode. Figure 4-14 illustrates this procedure.

Assuming that the sent and received unnumbered commands are identical (e.g., SABM) each station sends a UA response. The stations then may enter the indicated phase either upon sending the UA response to the incoming command [(1) in the figure], or upon receipt of the UA response to their mode-setting command [(2) in the figure]. If the UA response is not received, the station can enter the mode after the timer expires or it may reissue the command.

If the colliding commands are different, the stations should go to the disconnected phase and transmit a DM response before retrying.

Examples of a simple one-way and a more complicated two-way simulta-

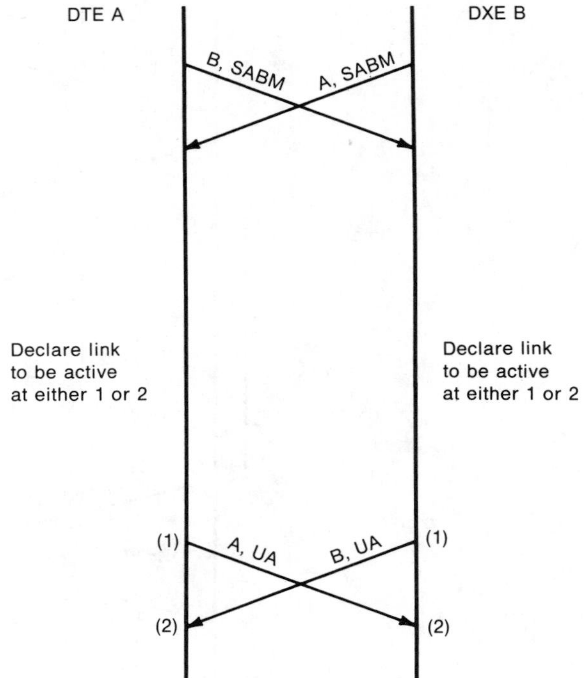

Figure 4-14. Balanced data link setup with contention.

neous information transfer are given next. These are followed by illustrations of some error recovery situations.

Simple One-Way Information Transfer

Figure 4-15 illustrates a case of simple one-way transfer of user information between the DTE and DXE. Remember that in the case of X.25, the DXE represents the network node.

After the data link has been activated (Figure 4-13), either station can begin sending I frames. In this case, the DTE has been sending, and as Figure 4-15 begins, the DTE is sending an I frame carrying sequence number 5. Since the DTE has received no information frames from the DXE, frame 5 carries an N(R) of 0, indicating that the DTE is expecting frame 0. The DXE acknowledges frame 5 by sending an RR with an N(R) of 6. The RR is used because the DXE has no information frames to send.

The DTE continues to transmit I frames sequentially numbered 6, 7, and 0. (Remember that the modulo of sequence numbers is 8. An option for a modulo of 128 exists but is not used in these examples.) The DXE confirms receipt of frames 6, 7, and 0 with RR 1. The DTE then sends frame 1, which is acknowledged by the RR 2. Information transfer continues in this manner as long as the link is active.

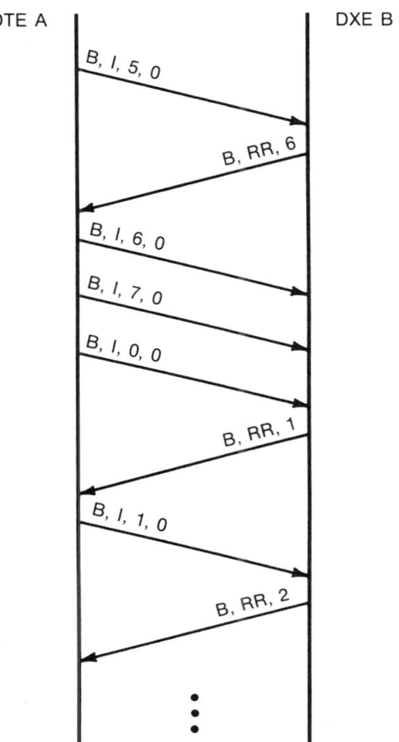

Figure 4-15. Simple one-way information transfer.

Two-Way Simultaneous Information Transfer

Figure 4-16 illustrates the exchange of I frames in both directions simultaneously. Although it seems much more complicated, careful study will show that it can be broken down quite simply. The apparent complexity arises primarily from the fact that acknowledgments of incoming frames are "piggy-backed" on outgoing frames.

In the figure, DXE B is sending information frames sequentially numbered 0 through 5 to DTE A. Simultaneously, DTE A is sending information frames 0 through 3 to the DXE. Note that at the instant DTE A sends frame 1 (B,I,1,1), it has received frame 0 from the DXE but has not received frame 1. The N(R) of outbound frame 1 is therefore 1 acknowledging frame 0.

Continuing with the fourth information frame from DTE A to DXE B, the frame is marked B,I,3,3. This acknowledges the receipt of three frames from DXE B. Further information frames are not sent from DTE A to DXE B, but three more frames arrive at DTE A that were received after B,I,3,3 was sent. The last frame sent from DTE A to DXE B is supervisory and acknowledges the receipt of six frames from DXE B. Note that N(S) is incremented with the transmission of each I frame.

As you study the example, remember that a send sequence variable, called

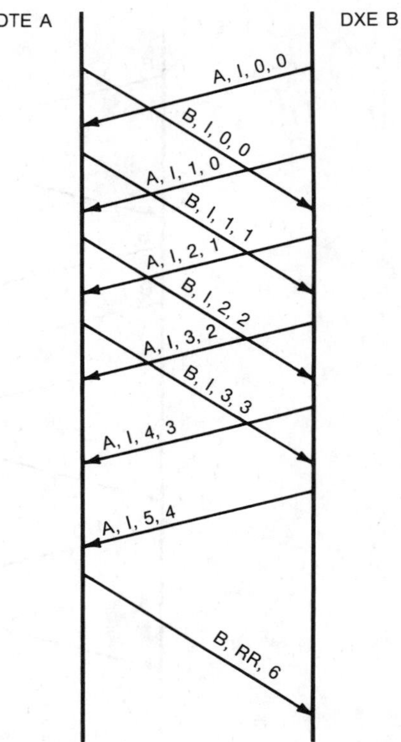

Figure 4-16. Two-way simultaneous information transfer.

V(S) and manifested as the N(S) in the frame, and a receive sequence variable, called V(R) and manifested as the N(R) in the frame, exists for each direction of data flow. An information frame being transmitted carries, as the N(S), the current value of the station's V(S)—that is the sequence number of this frame. The frame also carries, as the N(R), the current value of this station's V(R)—this is the implicit piggy-backed acknowledgment of information frames numbered N(R)-1 and below.

Busy Condition and Flow Control

A "station busy" condition may arise whenever the station is temporarily unable to accept incoming information frames. This situation can be caused by some internal constraint, such as the receive buffers being exhausted or the station being engaged in some higher-priority task. Whenever the busy condition arises, the station must "throttle down" the input to avoid being overwhelmed by the incoming data. This process is called flow control. An example of flow control is given in Figure 4-17.

In the figure, station A is receiving incoming information frames. For some system-dependent reason, it cannot accept additional frames. It indicates this to the other station by transmitting an RNR supervisory frame. Under the protocol rules, the station receiving the RNR, in this case DXE B, is to stop transmitting

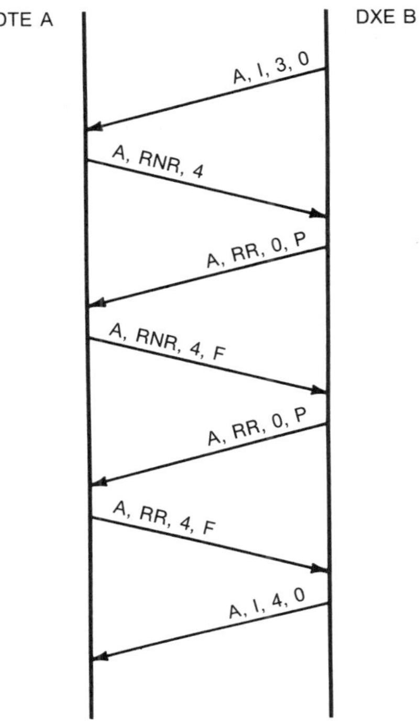

Figure 4-17. Busy condition and flow control.

information frames immediately. The busy station is permitted to discard any information frames arriving after it sends the RNR.

The station receiving the RNR will usually poll the busy station at some periodic interval looking for a "not busy" response in the form of an RR. When the condition that caused the busy is cleared, the station sends an RR and data transfer can resume, beginning with the frame indicated by the N(R) in the "not busy" RR frame. As shown, the P or F is set.

Disconnecting a Balanced Data Link

It is important that all outstanding information frames be accounted for before an exchange is completed or before an active data link is disconnected. This procedure is illustrated in Figure 4-18.

DTE A, wishing to close out operations with DXE B, sends an RNR command with the P-bit set to one. This supervisory command acknowledges all outstanding information frames from DXE B. DXE B responds with an RR and F-bit. The response confirms that DXE B has received all DTE A transmissions. If DTE A wishes DXE B to remain in an active phase, the sequence ends at this point. If, however, DTE A wishes to logically disconnect from DXE B, it will transmit a DISC command. DXE B will respond with a UA response and assume a disconnected phase awaiting a subsequent mode-setting command.

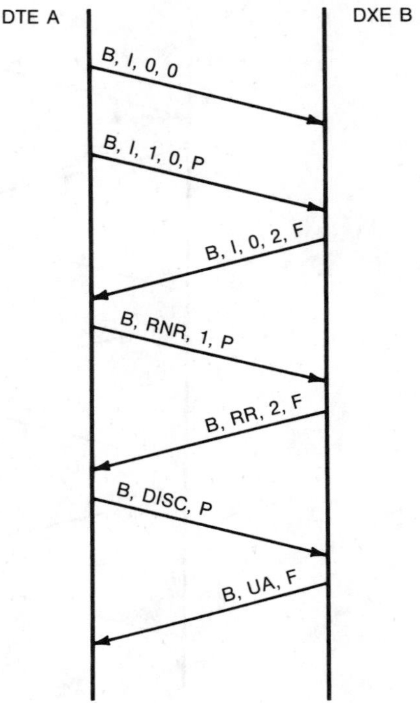

Figure 4-18. Closeout and disconnection.

Error Recovery in Balanced Operation

The final group of examples illustrates the basic error recovery procedures used in balanced operation.

Timeout Recovery. Timeout functions are used to detect that the expected acknowledgment to a previously transmitted frame has not been received. Expiration of the response timeout causes recovery to be initiated.

Figure 4-19 illustrates the need for timer recovery. In this case, the last frame in a sequence of information frames (frame 3 here) was errored during transmission. Because it was the last frame, the receiver, DXE B, cannot know, by receiving a subsequent out-of-sequence frame, that the error occurred. The transmitter DTE A, however, started a response timer as the frame was transmitted. This timer expires and the station initiates recovery action. This is usually done by polling the other station with an RR status request with the P-bit set. Since the poll demands a response, the station will receive the current value of the V(R) at the other station as an N(R). In the case of the example, this will indicate that frame 3 is still expected and was, therefore, never received. With this information, the lost frame can be retransmitted.

Reject Recovery. Bit-oriented protocols provide a recovery mechanism (REJ) which must be implemented by both stations. With REJ, the station detecting an N(S) sequence error can inform the sender immediately instead of waiting for the sender to detect the missing response through a P/F exchange. This makes operation on duplex links more efficient.

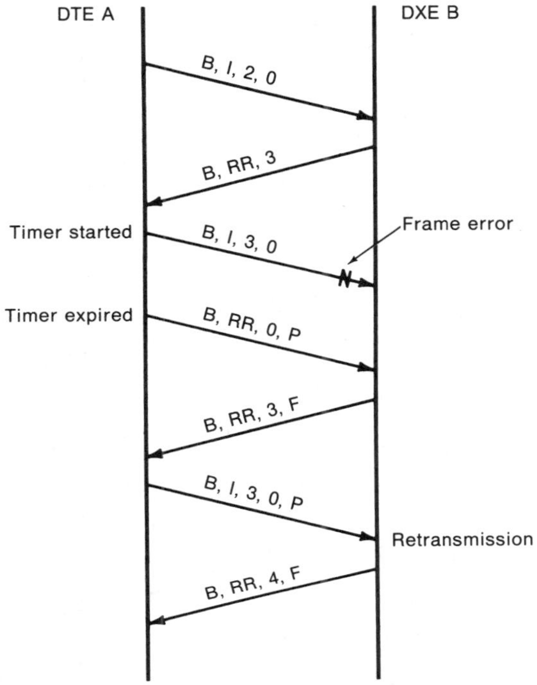

Figure 4-19. Timeout recovery.

In Figure 4-20, the DXE becomes aware of the missing (discarded due to error) frame 4 as soon as it receives frame 5. At this point, it transmits a REJ with an N(R) of 4. This cues the DTE to initiate retransmission of all frames sent, beginning with frame 4. It may continue to send additional frames after the retransmitted frames.

Only one REJ may be outstanding at any instant because of the implicit acknowledgment carried in the N(R) of the REJ. To send another REJ before recovering the first would be to acknowledge receipt of the frame that the station just said it was missing. The REJ condition is cleared upon receipt of an information frame with a sequence number equal to the N(R) of the reject frame.

Frame Rejection and Data Link Reset. Occasionally an abnormal condition occurs that is not recoverable by the normal recovery procedures. These situations call for the use of the FRMR response. Such conditions also will usually result in the resetting of the data link and all variables and sequence numbers. Conditions that result in the transmission of an FRMR include the receipt of undefined or not implemented commands, receipt of an incorrectly constructed frame, receipt of an information field that is too long, or receipt of an invalid N(R), i.e., N(R) that acknowledges a frame that has not been sent. This last example is illustrated in Figure 4-21.

The FRMR includes a LAPB or ISO 7776 information field that is intended to aid the other station in diagnosing the problem. This information field includes a copy of the control field of the defective frame, the current values of

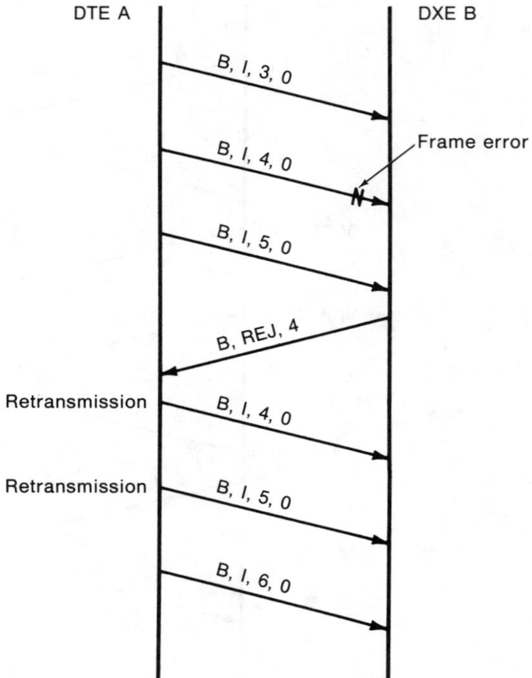

Figure 4-20. Reject recovery.

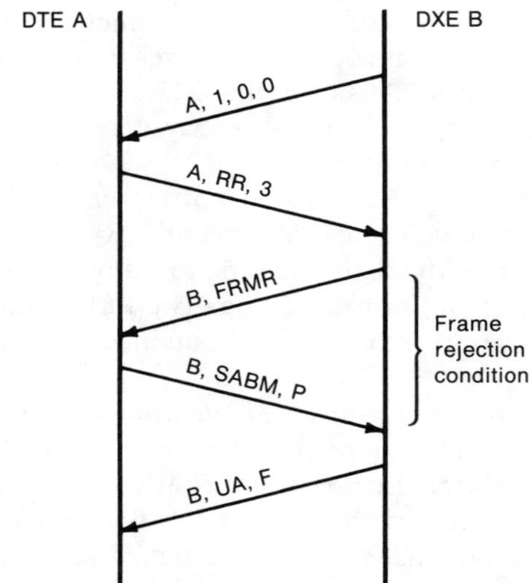

Figure 4-21. Frame rejection and link reset.

the sender's sequence variables, and a group of four bits indicating the nature of the problem.

In the figure, the DXE sends information frame 0 to the DTE and receives an RR, 3 in response. The RR, 3 confirms receipt of frame 2, a frame that has not been sent. In response, the DXE sends an FRMR frame that indicates "invalid N(R)" as a reason code. Since it now becomes obvious to the DTE that sequence number control has been lost, it sends an SABM command. In addition to the SABM command, a DISC command, an FRMR response, or a DM response *received* by the DXE will clear the frame rejection condition. The DXE can also clear the condition by *sending* the same commands and responses.

As shown in Figure 4-21, if the DXE can continue in the information transfer phase, it returns a UA response back to the DTE and resets its send and receive state variable to zero. If the DXE cannot continue, a DM response is returned to the DTE and the disconnected phase is entered.

Unacknowledged frames that are outstanding at the instant of a data link reset remain unacknowledged and must be recovered, perhaps at a higher level.

Packet Layer

The packet layer governs the transfer of packets at a DTE/DCE or DTE/DTE interface. The packet layer in a sending DTE performs the function of packetizing messages delivered from a higher level and then delivering the information to a data link layer protocol for transmission to a DXE (i.e., DTE or DCE). At the receiving DTE, the packet layer receives packets from the data link layer, checks packets for correctness, removes packet layer headers, and formulates messages from the packetized user data before transfer to a higher level. The packet layer provides the following capabilities:

- multiplexing—sharing of communication facilities
- data transfer—sending and receiving data
- flow control—controlling data transfer rates
- interrupt transfer—transfer of information independent of the data stream
- error control—packet layer error detection
- reset and restart—reinitializing communication paths should packet layer errors occur

Through these capabilities the packet layer provides for the two types of virtual circuits mentioned at the beginning of this chapter: VC, which is similar to a telephone dial-up connection for information transfer between DTEs, and the PVC, which is similar to a leased line between DTEs.

The previous section described the envelopment of packet layer information at the data link layer. The link access procedure, LAPB, a subset of the asynchronous balanced mode of HDLC, serves to provide negligible bit-error rates and minimizes lost, duplicated, or out-of-sequence packets. Each packet to be transferred across the DTE/DXE interface is contained within the information field of the LAPB frame. The following section describes the packet types within the information field.

Packet Formats and Types

Both CCITT X.25 and ISO 8208 begin the description of packet formats with a potential for incorrect interpretation. Each document starts by describing the general format identifier (GFI) field. This might cause one to believe that the GFI follows the control field in an LAPB frame. Not true. In an actual transmission, the logical channel group number (LCGN) subfield follows the control field of the data link layer. The reason for this apparent misunderstanding is the depiction of the packet format (Figure 4-22). Normally not noted by the reader is a clarification found in X.25 and 8208: "Bits of an octet are numbered 8 to 1, where bit 1 is the low-order bit and is transmitted first. Octets of a packet are consecutively numbered starting from 1 and are transmitted in this order." Many packet formats are described in X.25 and 8208, but all use the same basic format starting with the same three octets that contain the LCGN, GFI, logical channel number (LCN), and packet type identifier.

The LCGN and the LCN comprise the logical channel identifier (LCI) field within ISO 8208. This field is binary-coded for all packets but consists of all zeros in restart, diagnostic, and registration packets.

Logical Channel Group Number Field (4 bits). The LCGN combines with the eight bits of the second octet (LCN) to potentially identify 4096 logical channels. The LCGN has local significance only and is not part of the network channel numbering. The significance can be, for example, to identify a group of channels that are to be used for VCs, PVCs, and whether duplex or half-duplex transmission is used.

General Formal Identifier Field (4 bits). The GFI indicates sequence number modulo 8 or 128 and the type of packet that will follow. These include call-setup, clearing, flow control, interrupt, and data packets. The GFI bits are as follows:

When bit 8 is set to 1, it is the Qualifier-bit (Q-bit) in data packets and when set to 0, it indicates all other packets. This convention exists within X.25 (CCITT 1988a) and ISO 8208 (ISO 1988a). However, an additional use has been defined for bit 8 in both standards. When the GFI is part of call-setup and call-

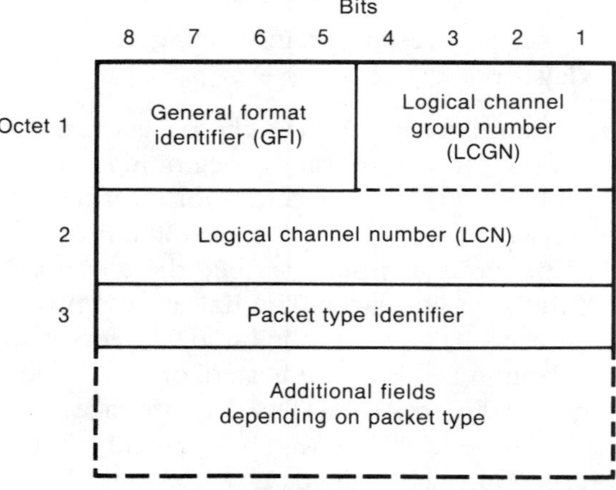

Figure 4-22. General packet format.

clearing packets it defines a short or long address and is called the A-bit. When the A-bit is set to 0, the "short" address format is supported by all networks. When the A-bit is set to 1, a "long" address format may be supported by some network, particularly ISDNs. A short, 12-digit address format is defined in CCITT Recommendation E.164 for use prior to 1997. A long, 15-digit address format is defined in CCITT E.164 for use after 1996.

Bit 7 is the delivery confirmation bit (D-bit). When D is set to one in the data and call-setup (i.e., call-accepted, call-connected) packets, delivery confirmation of user data is requested from the remote DTE.

Bits 6 and 5 are used to distinguish between modulo 8 (when bit 5 = 1 and bit 6 = 0) or modulo 128 (when bit 5 = 0 and bit 6 = 1) sequence numbering.

This field is binary-coded.

Logical Channel Number Field (8 bits). The LCN combined with the LCGN provides 12 bits that are used to identify channels 0 to 4095 (Figure 4-23). Channel 0 is only for diagnostic or restart packets and not for a VC or PVC.

The assignment of the number of VC or PVC logical channels is made arbitrarily so that there is flexibility in the number of channels assigned. If there are no PVCs, the VC can start with logical channel 1. For incoming calls from the

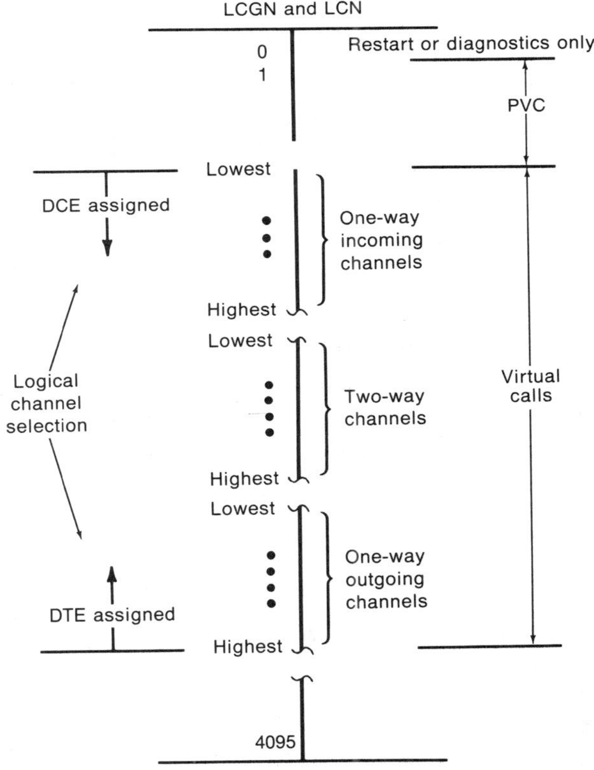

Figure 4-23. LCI assignment for VCs and PVCs.

network to a DTE, the DCE will assign the lowest numbered logical channel that is available. To minimize collision, outgoing calls are assigned the highest numbered available channel number by the DTE.

Packet Type Identifier Field (8 bits). The packets in X.25 are divided into six groups, as shown in Table 4-7. All packets apply to VC service. Call-setup and call-clearing packets are not used for PVC service. Some of these packet types, such as those used for call setup, data transfer, and call clearing are depicted in Figure 4-6. Within the context of ISO 8208, the packet types are also for DTE/DTE operation. Coding for the packet type identifier occupies the eight bits of the third octet of the packet. Flow control and reset packet types (RR, RNR, and REJ) are coded for modulo 8 or 128 operation.

Table 4-7. X.25 Packet Types

From DCE to DTE	From DTE to DCE
Call Setup and Call Clearing	
Incoming Call	Call Request
Call Connected	Call Accepted
Clear Indication	Clear Request
DCE Clear Confirmation	DTE Clear Confirmation
Data and Interrupt	
DCE Data	DTE Data
DCE Interrupt	DTE Interrupt
DCE Interrupt Confirmation	DTE Interrupt Confirmation
Flow Control and Reset	
DCE RR	DTE RR
DCE RNR	DTE RNR
	DTE REJ
Reset Indication	Reset Request
DCE Reset Confirmation	DTE Reset Confirmation
Restart	
Restart Indication	Restart Request
DCE Restart Confirmation	DTE Restart Confirmation
Diagnostic	
Diagnostic	
Registration	
Registration Confirmation	Registration Request

Call Request and Incoming Calls

The Call Request and Incoming Call frame and packet sequence as it would be transmitted, low-order bit first, is shown in Figure 4-24. As shown, the frame and packet structure would be applicable to VC service. The relation of CCITT

X.25 LAPB and ISO 7776 HDLC to the OSI data link layer is shown at each end of the frame. The packet layer fields of X.25 and 8208 are shown relative to the OSI network layer. The packet is part of the data link frame as it is transmitted across the physical layer and transmission media between users (Figure 4-6). There is a similar format for the Call Accepted and Call Connected frame and packet structure.

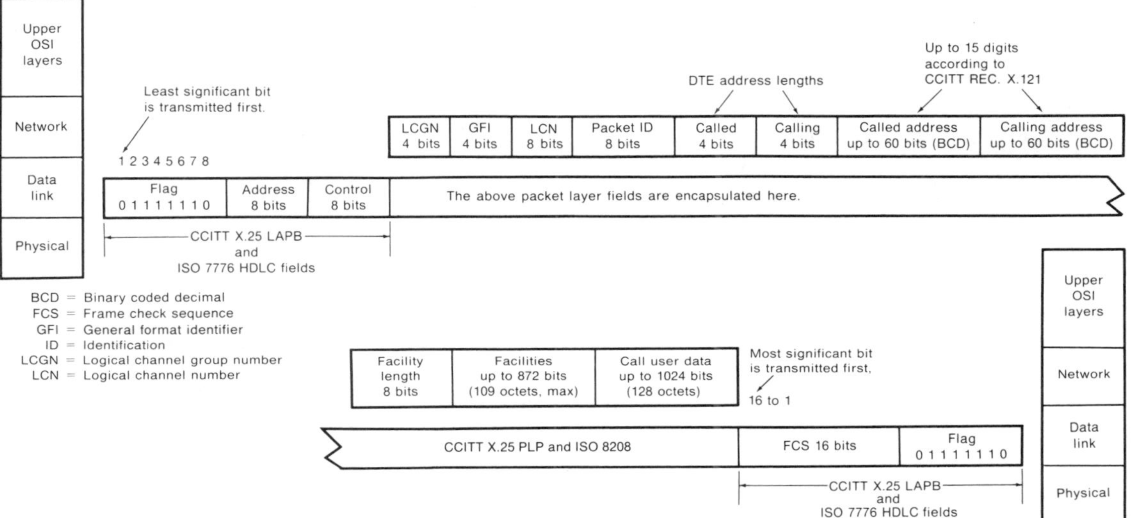

Figure 4-24. Call Request and Incoming Call frame and packet format.

According to ISO 8208, the Call Request and Incoming Call packets are the same between two DTEs, but are two different "physical" packets between a DTE and DCE because of the intervening network (see Figure 4-5).

The flag, address, and control fields were described previously in the section entitled "Frame Structure." These fields are followed by the LCGN, GFI, LCN, and packet type identifier fields which are common to all packets. These are followed by four address fields, two facility fields, and the call-user data field.

Address length fields. The low-order bits (1, 2, 3, 4) in this octet indicate the length of the called-DTE address. The high-order bits (5, 6, 7) indicate the length of the calling-DTE address. This semioctet format is used when the A-bit is set to 0. When the A-bit is set to 1, the address length field will be one octet in length and the maximum value is 17. The address-length indicators are binary coded.

Address field. The called address and the following calling address are based at CCITT Recommendations X.121 or E.164. Each address is allowed up to 60 bits. Binary-coded decimal (BCD) is used for encoding. Using four bits per digit, this translates to a maximum of 15 digits. CCITT X.121 has a maximum of 14 digits and E.164 has a maximum of 15 digits. Note that this field is BCD while the other fields are binary coded.

Facility length field. This octet following the address field indicates the length of the facility field in binary code.

Facility field. This field provides for optional network facilities such as closed user groups (CUGs), fast select, and recognized private operating agency (RPOA) selection, which will be described later. The maximum length of the field does not exceed 109 octets although the actual length depends on the facilities that are available from the network.

Call-user data field. This field, when used, has 16 octets in all cases except when used with the fast-select facility. When used with fast select, it has a maximum of 128 octets. Call-user data may consist of a user password at the destination DTE.

The FCS and flag fields of the data link layer complete this frame. The FCS coefficient of the highest term which is found in bit position 16 of the FCS field is transmitted first.

Call Accepted and Call Connected

The Call Accepted and Call Connected frame and packet structure is similar to the Call Request and Incoming Call structure. However, only the first three octets are mandatory. These packets are used, for example, with the D-bit set to 1 in the GFI to indicate that D-bit procedures can be used in the call.

Data Packets and Flow Control

The same flag, address, control and FCS fields that were shown for the Call Request and Incoming Call frame and packet structure also apply for Data packets (Figure 4-25). The LCGN, GFI, and LCN were described previously in the section entitled "Packet Formats and Types." The uniqueness of the Data packet fields lies in the use of techniques that can control the rate of packet transmission through the acknowledgment of packet delivery. This is accomplished through the use of send and receive sequence numbers and the D-bit confirmation. Also, there is a similarity of flow control procedures between the data link and packet layers. At both layers, there is a procedure of counter incrementation to keep track of frames or packets.

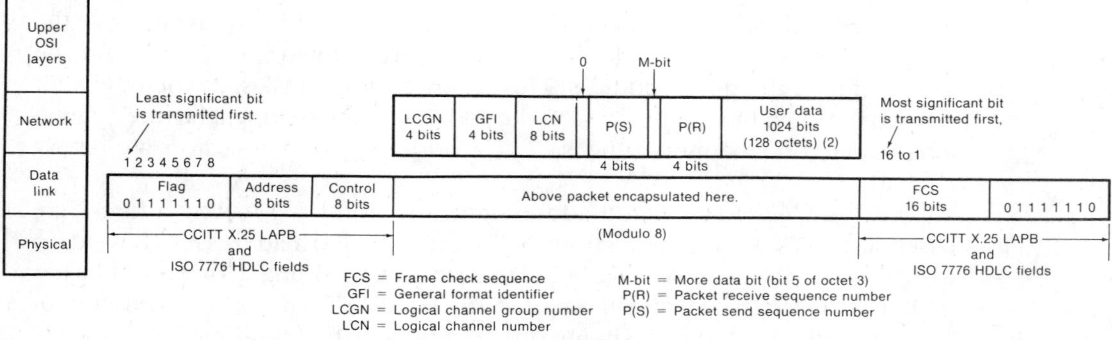

Figure 4-25. DTE and DCE Data frame and packet format.

The following description of flow control procedures for Data packets applies to VC or PVC logical channels. The basic premise is that the transmission of Data packets across a DTE/DXE interface is controlled separately for each direction by authorizations from the receiver (ISO 1988a).

Data packets in each direction of transmission are sequentially numbered 0 through 7 (modulo 8) or 0 through 127 (modulo 128). The modulo, 8 or 128, is the same in both directions or transmission. This sequential packet send sequence number, P(S), is contained only in the Data packet (Figure 4-25).

The first Data packet in a sequence is numbered P(S) =0. Next, a window (W) through which packets can be sent is defined. The window defines the consecutively numbered packets that can cross a DTE/DXE interface according to the P(S). The default value W = 2 is demonstrated in Figure 4-26 where P(S) = 0 and P(S) = 1 are authorized. The "lower window edge" has the P(S) = 0 for the first packet authorized to be sent. The "upper window edge" is P(S) = 1 for the second packet authorized to be sent. In this example, only these two packets can be sent by A before a packet receive sequence number, P(R), acknowledgment is sent by the receiver. The P(R) sent by the receiver (B) identifies the next packet sequence number that is expected. Upon acknowledgment of the first packet, P(S) = 0, through P(R) = 1, the window (W = 2) can slide up so that P(S) = 2 can be sent. For modulo 8, the P(S) and P(R) numbers rotate 0 through 7 as the packets are sent. Sending the P(R) implies acceptance of the Data packets up to and including P(R)-1. Incrementation of P(R) can be greater than 1. In this example, P(R) can equal 2 if both packets have been received.

The use of P(R) as a flow control technique is based on changing the rate at which the value of P(R) is incremented. If necessary, this allows a slowing of packets across the DTE/DXE interface so that network capacity is not exceeded. The P(R) is conveyed in Data, RR, and RNR packets.

The delivery-confirmation bit (GFI, bit 7) has the following significance for data packets:

1. When D = 1 in a data packet, the returned P(R) indicates receiving that packet by a remote DTE.

2. When D = 0, a local update takes place. This is *not* an acknowledgment of receipt from a remote DTE.

The standard user data field in the data packet is 128 octets. Other data fields that can be offered by the network are 16, 32, 64, 256, 512, 1,024, 2,048, or 4,096 octets.

The M-bit (bit 5 of the third octet), when set to 1 in the Data packet, indicates that a DTE or DCE will be sending more data in subsequent packets. The M-bit procedure works in combination with the D-bit procedure.

Call Clearing and Diagnostics

A call or call request may be cleared across the DTE/DXE interface of a logical channel by any party at any time. A VC can be terminated by a called or calling

Assume window size W = 2

A: LET ME SEND AS MANY SEQUENTIALLY NUMBERED DATA PACKETS AS I'M PERMITTED TO BY W—THAT'S PACKETS 0 AND 1

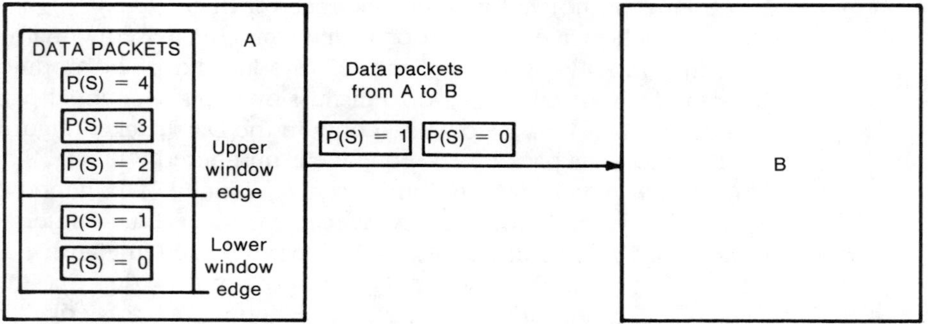

B: A, HERE'S SOME DATA FOR YOU. BY THE WAY, I HAVE RECEIVED ALL DATA PACKETS UP THROUGH 0 SO THE NEXT PACKET I'M EXPECTING TO RECEIVE FROM YOU IS PACKET 1

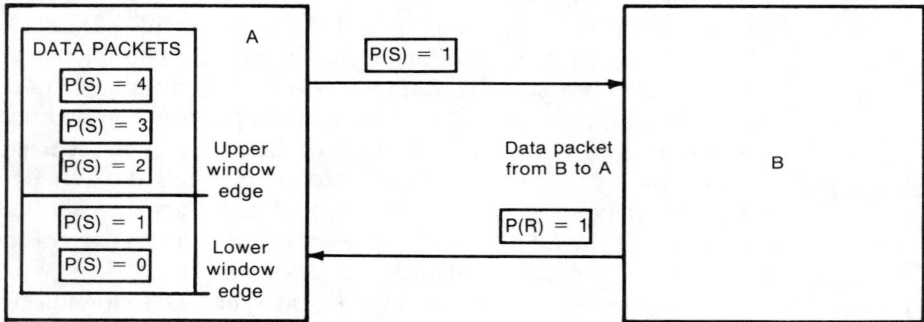

A: SO YOU GOT MY PACKET 0 AND EXPECT 1 NEXT. WELL, THAT'S ALREADY IN MY WINDOW (AND WAS SENT). I'LL MOVE MY WINDOW EDGES SO THAT PACKET 1 IS AT THE LOWER EDGE AND PACKET 2 IS AT THE UPPER EDGE. NOW I CAN SEND PACKET 2

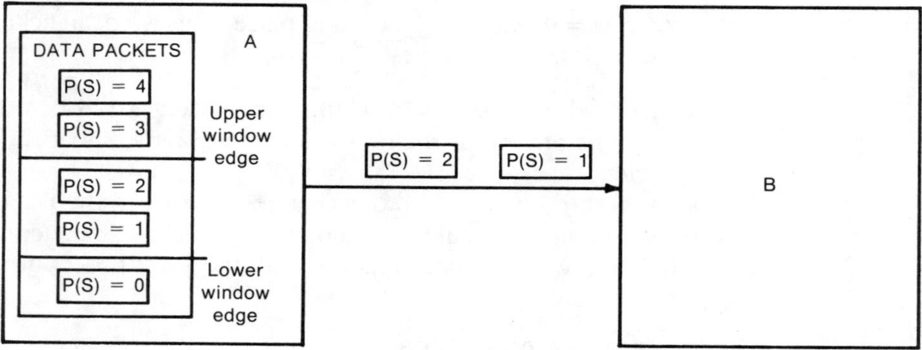

Figure 4-26. Flow control schematic *(ISO 1988a).*

DTE because of call completion or error detection. (In Figure 4-6, the clear request is generated by user D.)

The Clear Request and Clear Indication frame and packet structure is shown in Figure 4-27. The LAPB/HDLC flag, address, and control fields are the same as described previously in the section entitled "Frame Structure." The packet layer fields, LCGN, GFI, LCN, and packet type identifier were described previously in the section entitled "Packet Formats and Types." The cause field (octet 4) and diagnostic code (octet 5) are shown in the packet layer of Figure 4-27. Other fields follow these when the extended format (modulo 128) is used. For modulo 8, only the frame check sequence and concluding flag follow the diagnostic code field.

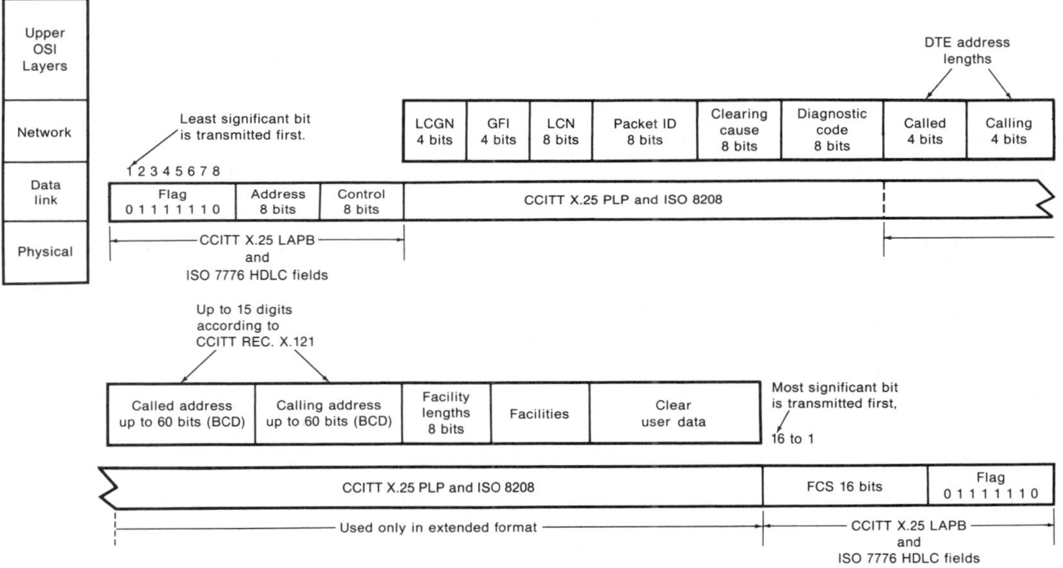

Figure 4-27. Clear Request and Clear Indication frame and packet format.

The Clearing Cause Field (octet 4) contains the reason for clearing the call. The definition of each clearing cause is given in CCITT Recommendation X.96, "Call Progress Signals in Public Data Networks." The coding is given in CCITT X.25 and ISO 8208. Some reasons for clearing a call or call request are applicable to both VCs and PVCs. Other reasons apply to either VCs or PVCs.

The Clearing Cause Field in a Clear Request packet is set to "DTE Originated" by a DTE when the remote DTE has initiated a clear, reset, or restart procedure. The reasons for coding the Clearing Cause Field in a Clear Indication packet are more extensive. Some of these are number busy, remote number out of order, incompatible destination, network out of order, network congestion, RPOA (Recognized Private Operating Agency) out of order, and fast select acceptance not subscribed.

The diagnostic code field contains additional information concerning the reason that a call is cleared. The diagnostic code is optional in a Clear Request packet. The coding of X.25 network-generated diagnostic fields is given in both CCITT X.25 and ISO 8208. Some reasons for not allowing a packet are that it is unidentifiable, too short, too long, unauthorized, or that the GFI is invalid.

Clear Confirmation

The clear confirmation is sent by a DCE (for local significance) or remote DTE in response to a clear request (Figure 4-6).

The DTE and DCE Clear Confirmation frame and packet format is shown in Figure 4-28. The basic (modulo 8) packet format within the frame contains only three octets consisting of the LCGN, GFI, LCN, and packet-type identification. The extended format that is shown in the figure is used for DCE Clear Confirmation only in conjunction with charging information which is an optional user facility.

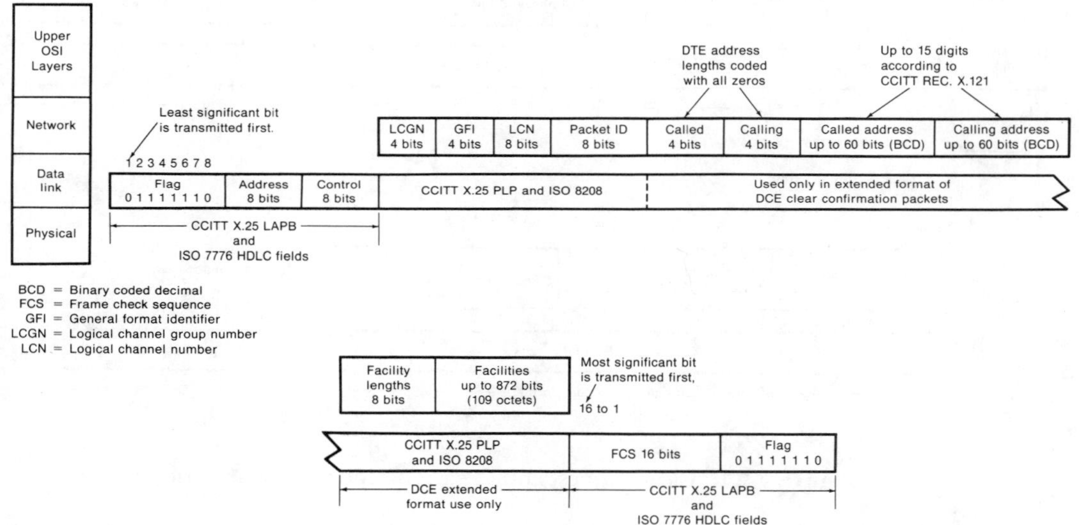

Figure 4-28. DTE and DCE Clear Confirmation frame and packet format.

Optional User Facilities

Optional user facilities are added packet layer capabilities for use between a DTE or DXE. The following is a description of some of the facilities that are in Sections 6 (descriptions) and 7 (formats) of CCITT X.25 and Sections 13 (descriptions) and 15 (formats) of ISO 8208. Each facility that is described applies only to VC service.

Flow Control Parameter Negotiation. Flow control parameters are the packet and window sizes at the DTE/DXE interface for each direction of data transmission. Negotiation through this facility allows changes to be made in packet and window default values. "Packet size" refers to the maximum user data field lengths in Data packets.

When this facility is subscribed, a calling DTE may separately request, in the Call Request packet, window and packet sizes for both directions of data transmission in a virtual call. Window and packet sizes can be different at each end of the virtual call. Default values of packet and window sizes are assumed for both directions of data transmission by the DXE when packet and window sizes are not specified in the Call Request packet. Default packet sizes are 128 octets and the default window size is 2. The called DTE accepts the call if the flow control parameters can be supported.

Packet sizes that can be negotiated are 16, 32, 64, 256, 512, 1,024, 2,048, and 4,096 octets. The window sizes can be 1 through 7 for normal numbering and 1 through 127 for extended sequence numbering. A value of zero is not allowed.

Throughput Class Negotiation. The throughput class refers to the signaling rate that can be used for data transmission. The negotiation can be coded in the Call Request/Incoming Call and Call Accepted/Call Connected packets (Figure 4-6). The values of throughput classes are 75, 150, 300, 600, 1,200, 2,400, 4,800, 9,600, 19,200, 48,000 and 64,000 bits per second. However, it is appropriate to use 56 kb/s rather than 48 kb/s since the former is available in North America.

Throughput classes can be different for each direction of data transmission. When throughput classes are not requested by the DTE, the DXE will assume that default values of throughput are applicable in each direction.

Closed User Groups (CUGs). This optional user facility enables users to form groups of DTEs to and/or from which access is restricted in a DTE/DCE environment. Other DTEs that are not members of a CUG are not permitted access, so a CUG is the equivalent of a private network. However, a DTE can be a member of one or more CUGs. The complexity of CUG restrictions that can be achieved is illustrated in Figure 4-29 and listed in Table 4-8.

Table 4-8. CUG Information for Figure 4-29

DTE	Subscription	Make Calls To	Receive Calls From
A	CUG with outgoing access (CUG1)	B, D, E	B
B	CUG with incoming access (CUG1; CUG2 with outgoing calls barred)	A	A, C, D, E
C	CUG (basic) (CUG2)	B	D
D	CUG with incoming access (CUG2 with incoming calls barred)	B, C	A, E
E	No CUG subscription	B, D	A

There are seven CUG facilities:

- *Closed User Group*. This is the basic facility that permits a DTE to belong to one or more CUGs. Communication between DTEs is permitted only to those belonging to the CUG(s). (DTE C, Figure 4-29.)

- *Closed User Group with Outgoing Access.* This facility allows a DTE that belongs to a CUG(s) to originate VCs to a DTE that does not belong to any CUG or to a DTE that belongs to a CUG with incoming access. (DTE A, Figure 4-29.)
- *Closed User Group with Incoming Access.* This facility allows a DTE that belongs to a CUG(s) to receive VCs from a DTE not belonging to a CUG or from DTEs belonging to CUGs with outgoing access. (DTEs B and D, Figure 4-29.)

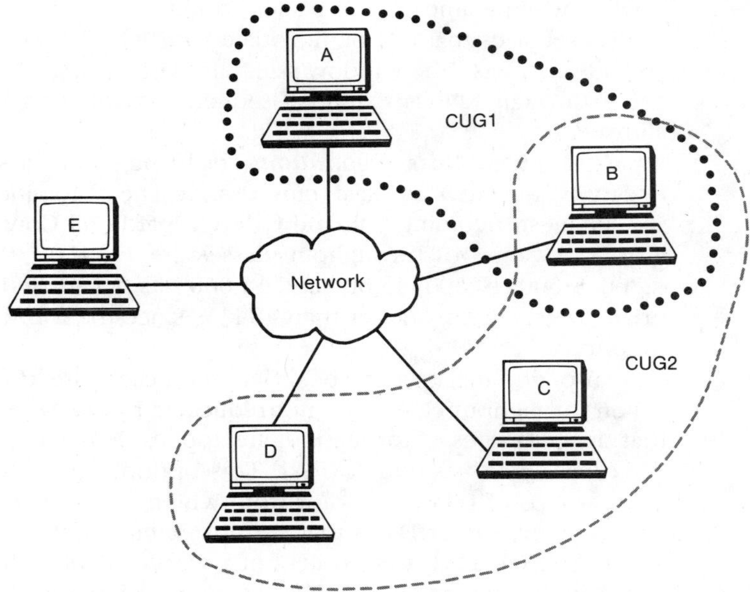

Figure 4-29. Allowable connections in a hypothetical CUG environment *(ISO 1988a).*

- *Incoming Calls Barred within a Closed User Group.* A DTE within a CUG can originate VCs to other DTEs within the same CUG but incoming calls from DTEs in the same CUG are not permitted. (DTE D, Figure 4-29.)
- *Outgoing Calls Barred within a Closed User Group.* A DTE can receive VCs from other DTEs in the CUG but outgoing calls to DTEs in some CUGs are not permitted. (DTE B, Figure 4-29.)
- *Closed User Group Selection.* This facility enables a calling DTE to specify in the Call Request packet which CUG has been selected for a VC. The Incoming Call packet indicates to the called DTE the CUG that has been selected. A basic format of the CUG selection facility is used to allow a DTE to belong to 99 or fewer CUGs. An extended format of the CUG selection facility is required for membership in 100 to 9,999 CUGs.
- *Closed User Group with Outgoing Access Selection.* This facility can be used if a DTE does not belong to a preferential CUG. This facility can be

used if the network supports it and if the DTEs subscribe to a CUG with outgoing access or to a CUG with incoming access or both. Up to 9,999 CUGs are permitted.

A second category of CUGs is that of bilateral closed user group (BCUG) facilities. This facility permits pairs of DTEs to form bilateral relations allowing free access between each other while limiting access to or from other DTEs. There are three BCUG related facilities:

- *Bilateral Closed User Group*. This is a basic facility that enables a DTE to belong to one or more BCUGs.
- *Bilateral Closed User Group with Outgoing Access*. This facility allows the DTE that belongs to a BCUG to make outgoing VCs to DTEs not belonging to any BCUG.
- *Bilateral Closed User Group Selection*. This facility allows the calling DTE to specify the BCUG selected for a VC in a Call Request packet. The number of BCUGs to which a DTE can belong is network-dependent.

Fast Select. This optional user facility applies only to VC service for a particular call (per-call basis). Fast Select allows the exchange of 128 octets of user data during call setup and call clearing. If there is no restriction on response, the Fast Select facility allows the Call Request packet to contain 128 octets of user data in the call-user data field. (See Figure 4-6 to clarify packet transmission.) During call establishment, the DXE is authorized to send 128 octets via a Call Connected packet (call user data field) or a Clear Indication packet (clear user data field). During call clearing, Fast Select allows the calling DTE and DXE to send 128 octets of information in the clear user data field of the Clear Request or Clear Indication packet. If there is restriction on response, the DCE is not authorized to transmit a Call Connected packet.

The importance of Fast Select is the ability to exchange user data during short duration calls. This facility also acts as a partial datagram service. According to FED STD 1037A (NCS 1985), a datagram is a self-contained, independent unit of data routed between DTEs without prior communication being required between the DTEs or the network. In other words, a virtual circuit does not have to be established prior to data transmission. Necessary addressing and routing information exists within each packet, thus creating a high overhead factor for each packet.

Fast Select Acceptance. This optional user facility applies only to VC service for a period of time agreed to by the DTE and DCE. When this user facility is subscribed to, the network DCE is authorized to transmit to the DTE incoming Fast Select packets. If the Fast Select Acceptance is not subscribed to, the DCE will block incoming Fast Select calls to the DTE.

RPOA Selection. This user facility allows a user to specify one or more specific RPOA networks through which a VC is to be routed. The facility field of a Call Request packet in basic format contains the identification of one RPOA. The extended format is used for a Call Request packet that identifies the multiple RPOAs that are selected. The RPOAs are identified according to the network identification codes for PSPDNs and ISDNs. The identification codes should appear in the facilities field in the order that the subscriber wishes the RPOA transit networks to be traversed. The last RPOA selected could be an international record carrier for calls to a foreign country.

The value of RPOA selection is that it is very possible that more than one packet network may be required to permit two DTEs to communicate within a country. This allows the calling DTE to define the required networks. The selection could also allow a user to take advantage of security features that may exist on particular networks. Another advantage could be in performance by selecting networks that match user throughput requirements.

Within the United States, the RPOA selection can be important in meeting regulatory requirements that relate to the competitive nature of the communications industry.

Characteristics of ANS X3.100

ANS X3.100 is the domestic version of CCITT X.25, ISO 7776, and ISO 8208. A summary of some of the required elements of the standard is given in Table 4-9. Each element is listed under physical, data link, and packet layers. This description can also apply to FIPS PUB 100/FED STD 1041.

Table 4-9. Typical Requirements of ANS X3.100

Element	Requirement
Physical Layer	
Data signaling rates	4.8, 9.6 kb/s
Interfaces	EIA-232-D, EIA-449, EIA-530, V.35/V.28/V.24
Data Link Layer	
Procedure	LAPB/ISO 7776 HDLC
Configuration	Point-to-point
Operation	Duplex
Frame Check Sequence (FCS)	16-bit
Single link addresses: DCE	10000000
Single link addresses: DTE	11000000
Smallest NI supported: DCE	263 Octets
Smallest NI supported: DTE	135 Octets
Outstanding information frames	k = 7
Packet Layer	
Procedure	X.25 PLP/ISO 8208
Services	VC and PVC
Packet sequence numbering	Modulo 8
User data field	Octet aligned
Diagnostic packets	Optional support by networks
Diagnostic code	Standard/nonstandard

Table 4-9. (cont.)

Element	Requirement
Retransmission request	Environment-dependent
D-bit procedure	Supported by all DTEs
Interrupt Packet user data field	1 to 32 octets
RPOA selection	Basic and extended
Address extension facilities	40 digits (20 octets)

Physical Layer

Only two data signaling rates are required: 4.8 and 9.6 kb/s. Other transmission rates are permissible as long as they comply with those defined by CCITT Recommendation X.1 (CCITT 1988n) and ANS X3.1. For example, according to these standards, asynchronous operation can be at 300 or 1,200 b/s while synchronous operation might be at 2.4 or 4.8 kb/s. However, 56 kb/s is a standard rate in North America so it is preferred over 48 kb/s. A transmission rate of 64 kb/s is recognized because it is planned for the user's DTE through the ISDN.

There is a choice among physical interface standards that are appropriate at the DTE/DCE interface. The choice is dependent on the data signaling rate that will be used. For signaling rates of 19.2 kb/s or less, EIA-232-D is the choice. It supercedes EIA-232-C, which is acceptable until the new standard is implemented by equipment manufacturers. There are three choices for the interface standard when the signaling rate exceeds 19.2 kb/s:

- CCITT V.35 in combination with V.28 and V.24
- EIA-449
- EIA-530

Electrical characteristics for EIA-449 may be according to EIA-422-A for balanced voltage circuits or EIA-423-A for unbalanced circuits. EIA-530 combines the mechanical characteristics of the popular 25-pin connector of EIA-232-D with the electrical characteristics of EIA-422-A. This permits data signaling to take place at up to 10 Mb/s for a distance of 3 meters. EIA-423-A can also be used in conjunction with EIA-530 (EIA 1987).

Note that the EIA physical layer interface standards come under CCITT X.21 bis within X.25. CCITT X.21 bis, as part of X.25, also covers V.35 (for data and timing circuits), V.28 (for control circuits), and V.24 for interchange circuits.

Data Link Layer

ANS X3.100 contains specific data link layer requirements that are to be used in the United States and by the U.S. government. Otherwise, the data link layer procedures are according to X.25 LAPB and ISO 7776 HDLC. The LAP procedures in X.25 are *not* part of the domestic packet mode standards.

Provisions are made for the operation of two combined stations that are connected in a point-to-point, single-link operation or as an option in a multilink configuration. An address field identifies a frame as a command or a response. The address field also allows for recognizing a single-link or the optional multilink operation by different address-pair encoding. This is done by assigning codes to DCEs (10000000) and DTEs (11000000) for single-link operation. Another pair of codes is assigned to DCEs (11100000) and DTEs (11110000) for multilink operation. For direct DTE/DTE operation, when there is no intervening packet network between DTEs and dedicated paths are used, one of the DTEs uses a DCE address, e.g., DTE 1 (10000000) and DTE 2 (11000000).

For purposes of universal operation, there are specific requirements for the maximum number of bits (N1) that are to be supported in an information frame. There may be two different values that a DCE will accept from a DTE or that a DTE will accept from a DCE. In the first case, the DCE must accept from the DTE frames containing up to and including 2,104 bits (263 octets). This is known as DCE N1 and does not include flags and zero bits that are inserted for transparency. In the second case, the DTE will accept from the DCE frames containing up to and including 1,080 bits (135 octets). This is the value of DTE N1 and again excludes flags and transparency bits.

Three types of control field formats were described earlier in this chapter. They are information, supervisory, and unnumbered frames. The information frames contain send sequence numbers, N(S), and receive sequence numbers N(R). The supervisory frame contains only N(R) and the unnumbered frames contain neither. The value of k relates to N(S) and N(R) and indicates the maximum number of sequentially numbered I frames that may be unacknowledged by a DTE or DCE. For modulo 8 operation, k = 7; for modulo 128 operation, k = 127. These values are adopted by X3.100 from X.25 without change.

Packet Layer

The provisions of CCITT X.25 and ISO 8208 apply to packet layer operation. These, however, are subject to particular clauses that are contained in ANS X3.100.

The services for packet-switched data networks are from CCITT Recommendation X.2 which states that VC service and PVC service are essential to packet data transmission.

Packet layer operation requires that packet sequence numbering will be modulo 8 or modulo 128. A description of data packets and the use of packet sequence numbering and flow control is given earlier.

The first three octets of the packet consist of the LCGN and the GFI in the first octet, the LCN in the second octet, and packet identification in the third octet. After that, an integral number of octets is required. Receipt of a packet with a nonoctet-aligned field is considered an error. If the data link layer does not provide error recovery, appropriate procedures are invoked at the packet layer.

There are provisions for dealing with error conditions in the various packet types through the use of diagnostic codes. Diagnostic codes are useful because they allow a DTE to take recovery actions after an error procedure has occurred. In the event a virtual call is cleared with a diagnostic code indicating network congestion, the DTE may wish to wait an interim period before attempting another call. However, if the diagnostic code indicates a procedural error (i.e., local procedure error), maintenance may be required to correct a problem at the DTE/DCE interface. To facilitate recovery action, standard diagnostic codes are preferred in the Clear Request, Reset Request, and Restart Request packets. Nonstandard diagnostics can be used by DTEs through bilateral or multilateral agreements.

Diagnostics for error conditions in the packets, actions to be taken, and diagnostic encoding are part of X.25 and 8208. These also are adopted by X3.100. According to X.25 and ISO 8208, "The first diagnostic in each grouping is a generic diagnostic and can be used in place of the more specific diagnostics within the grouping." However, ANS X3.100 has a specific clause that requires that, "A generic diagnostic code shall not be used when a more specific diagnostic code is known to be applicable."

Optional user facilities are also available through X3.100. Described in X.25 and 8208, the facilities are available for an agreed period (as for PVCs) while others are available on a per-call basis (as for VCs). Examples of optional user facilities are extended frame sequence numbering (modulo 128), multilink procedures, D-bit confirmation, nonstandard default packet sizes (i.e., 16, 32, 64, 256, etc.), closed user groups, RPOA selection, and others. Most of the facilities do not apply for PVCs because the channels are already connected. Classifications such as E (essential) or A (additional) indicate whether the facility must be provided or that it may be available in some of the networks, respectively.

CCITT X.25 (and X3.100) has a list of applicable call progress signals adopted from CCITT Recommendation X.96. These signals are encoded in Clear Indication, Reset Indication, Restart Indication, and Registration Confirmation packets. Some of the call progress signals are mandatory in all networks (e.g., local procedure error). Other call progress signals are mandatory when an optional user facility is provided. Examples of matchups between user facilities and call progress signals are RPOA selection and RPOA out of order, reverse charging acceptance and reverse charging acceptance not subscribed, and fast-selection acceptance and fast-select acceptance not subscribed.

ANS X3.100 and FIPS Pub 100/Fed STD 1041 differ very little from CCITT X.25, ISO 7776 and ISO 8208. One might ask, "If this is true, why bother to have something such as X3.100?" The value of such a standard is that it helps to clarify the interpretation and implementation of the international standards for use in the United States by agreement among providers and users of the service.

CCITT X.32: Dial-In, Dial-Out Packet Mode

The CCITT has recognized the need for a DTE/DCE interface that would allow access to a PSPDN through a PSN, such as a PSTN, an ISDN, or a CSPDN. CCITT Recommendation X.32 (1988o) allows a dial-in, dial-out access capability between a DTE and a PSPDN when a dedicated circuit is not economical nor obtainable.

Basically, X.32 allows for a PSN between a DTE and the packet network. The DCE remains defined as it was in Section 2 (i.e., a data-switching exchange with X.25 intelligence in a PSPDN). One of the more significant aspects of X.32 is the emphasis that is placed on DTE and DCE identification, including the optional use of encryption, before a VC is placed. Another part of X.32 specifies the CCITT V-Series modem characteristics for the physical level interface when a DTE accesses a PSPDN via a PSTN. While using a CSPDN access, the X.32 DTE/DCE interface recommendation is CCITT X.21 or X.21 bis. As can be expected, X.25 LAPB access and packet-level procedures, with some additions, are used for the VC. PVCs are not appropriate in X.32.

In addition, CCITT X.31 provides details for access to a PSPDN by way of an ISDN. However, a distinction is needed as to the relative position in using X.31 and X.32. The X.32 interface coincides with the R reference point while X.31 coincides with the S reference point of the ISDN reference configuration (Figure 4-30). The two are separated by the terminal adaptor (TA) that adapts non-ISDN equipment interfaces to be served by an ISDN user-network interface (also see Scace 1986).

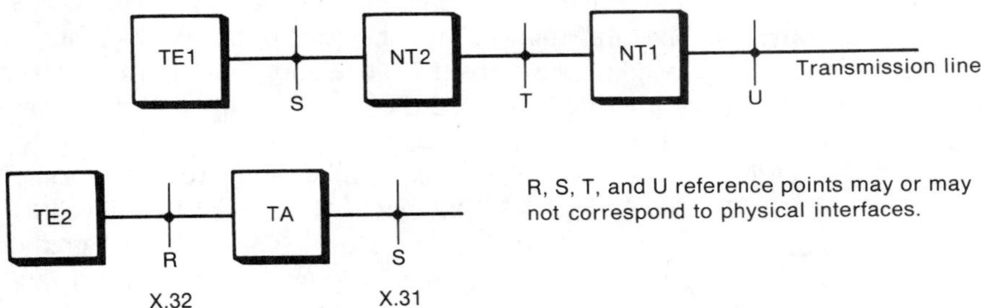

Figure 4-30. Location of CCITT X.32 and X.31 at ISDN reference points.

In Figure 4-30, TE1 represents terminal equipment, such as an ISDN telephone or ISDN terminal with an ISDN-compatible interface. NT2, network termination 2, provides OSI reference model layer 1, 2, and 3 functions found in PBXs, LANs, and terminal controllers. NT1, network termination 1, provides OSI reference model layer 1 functions such as physical and electromagnetic termination of the network. TE2 represents terminal equipment, such as an X.25 DTE that has an ISDN-incompatible interface. TA is the terminal adaptor and it allows a TE2 to be served by an ISDN user-network interface. (This allows TE2 + TA = TE1.)

A dial-in operation for accessing a PSPDN (Figure 4-31) can take place using an automatic or manual call procedure (Figure 4-31A). Another operation allows a dial-out access from a PSPDN to a DTE (Figure 4-31B). In this case, an automatic answering procedure is recommended, but manual answering is permitted. Following "dial-in-by-the-DTE" or "dial-out-by-the-PSPDN" procedures, a packet mode DTE may then initiate or receive VCs. The VCs are independent of the dial-in and dial-out.

According to X.25 procedures, a DTE accesses a PSPDN via a leased-line,

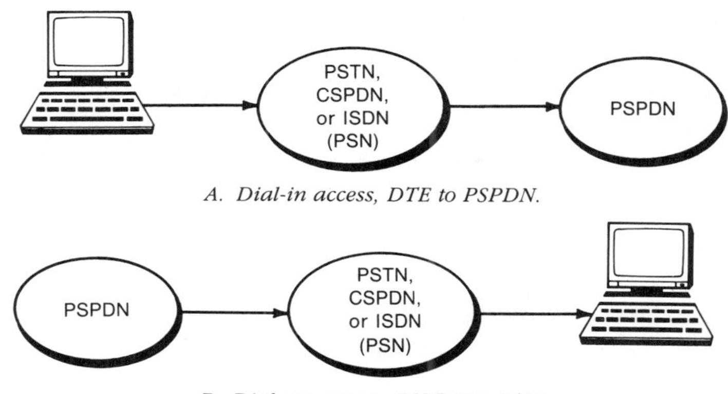

B. Dial-out access, PSPDN to DTE.

CSPDN = Circuit-switched public data network
ISDN = Integrated services digital network
PSN = Public-switched network
PSPDN = Packet-switched public data network
PSTN = Public–switched telephone network

Figure 4-31. CCITT X.32 dial-in, dial-out access.

dedicated circuit. Another DTE attached to the packet network is then accessed through another dedicated circuit. This takes place according to X.25 intelligence in the DTEs and the DCE. A DTE without X.25 capability can access a PSPDN via a PAD based on CCITT X.3, X.28, and X.29 procedures and a switched-circuit network. Other DTEs on the network cannot reach a DTE that does not have X.25 intelligence. In contrast, CCITT X.32 procedures allow DTEs to communicate following dial-in, or dial-out, and after establishing the VC.

Services

There are three types of DTE services defined in X.32. The switched access available to a DTE depends on whether the DTE is nonidentified (i.e., unidentified according to X.32), identified, or customized. All three service types support dial-in, dial-out operation. Switched access capabilities, called attributes, are offered to each service in varying degrees and set each service apart (Table 4-10).

For nonidentified service, the attributes are either not provided, or a network default is in effect. The identified services are somewhat similar to the nonidentified services with an important exception: charges can be handled by an identified DTE. A nonidentified service does not allow paid calls to be made, nor reverse charges to be received, by a DTE. There are other nonidentified service parameters, including the following:

- DTEs are allowed to operate with different networks without subscribing to them.
- Optional user facilities (i.e., incoming and outgoing calls barred; one-way logical channel outgoing and incoming) are not generally available except those that govern the direction of VC placement.

Customized DTE service requires a registered address prior to VC placement. The attributes are user-selectable according to network-provided options.

The range of optional user facilities available to the three services is according to CCITT X.25. The facilities available to custom services are

- On-line facility registration
- Extended packet sequence numbering
- D-bit modification
- Packet retransmission
- Incoming calls barred
- Outgoing calls barred
- One-way logical channel outgoing
- One-way logical channel incoming
- Nonstandard default packet sizes
- Nonstandard default window sizes
- Default throughput classes assignment
- Flow control parameter negotiation
- Throughput class negotiation
- Closed user group related facilities (CUG, CUG with outgoing access, CUG with incoming access, incoming calls barred within a CUG, outgoing calls barred within a CUG)
- Bilateral closed user group related facilities (BCUG, BCUG with outgoing access)
- Fast-select acceptance
- Reverse charging acceptance
- Local charging prevention
- Network User Identification (NUI) subscription
- NUI override
- Charging information subscription
- RPOA subscription
- Hunt group
- Call redirection
- Call deflection subscription

Many of these services are unavailable to nonidentified and identified service. Examples are Closed User Groups, Bilateral Closed User Groups, and the last seven facilities in the list, starting with Network User Identification (NUI) Subscription. Other facilities are available to the nonidentified and identified services on a dial-in-by-the-DTE or dial-out-by-the-PSPDN basis. Therefore, as in all standards described in this chapter, the documents themselves should be consulted. For facilities available in nonidentified and identified services, refer to CCITT X.32.

Table 4-10. Summary of X.32 DTE Services and Attributes

Attributes	Nonidentified Services	Identified Services	Customized Services
DTE identity	No	Yes	Yes
DTE identification method	No	Yes (ND)[1]	Yes (ND)
DTE address	No	Yes[2]	Yes
Registered address	No	Yes[2]	Yes
Registered PSN number	No	No	Yes[3]
X.25 subscription set	Yes (ND)	Yes[4]	Yes [3]
Logical channel assignment	Yes (ND)	Yes (ND)	Yes[3]
Dial-out-by-the PSPDN Availability	Yes (ND)	Yes[2]	Yes[3]
Dial-out access type	Yes (ND)	Yes (ND)	Yes[3]
X.32 optional user facilities	No	No	Yes[3]
DCE identity presentation	Yes (ND)	Yes (ND)	Yes (ND)
Link layer address assignment	Yes (ND)	Yes (ND)	Yes[3]

[1]Network Default
[2]A network option or by network default
[3]Selected by user when desired
[4]A network default or, if a NUI override permission is in effect, the user selects this X.25 packet layer facility

DTE and DCE Identification

The DTE identification is used for billing and accounting purposes. Identification may also be used to provide a calling DTE address to a called DTE, or to allow a DTE to obtain a service not available to DTEs that have not established an identity.

Identification of a PSPDN is of value to the DTE. Identification allows

- the exchange of encrypted keys and passwords between the DTE and DCE
- DTE selection of network parameters or procedures
- PSPDN identification that has been accessed by the PSN so that the proper CUG operation can take place

The DCE (the network) identity consists of the Data Network Identification Code (DNIC) from CCITT X.121 and an optional designator.

The registered address of a DTE may be

- an X.121 number from the PSPDN numbering plan [DNIC + Network Terminal Number (NTN)]
- an X.121 number from the PSN numbering plan for CSPDNs and PSTNs, or CCITT E.164 for ISDNs

A DTE is considered identified when two components, administrative or procedural, are fulfilled. Administrative registration can be explicit or nonexplicit. An explicit registration is a direct arrangement between the DTE and the

PSPDN. A nonexplicit registration is a prearrangement between a DTE and a PSN, after the PSN has reached an agreement with the PSPDN, or through an arrangement with another authority. The procedural component is fulfilled when the identity of the DTE is given to the DCE by one of the following four methods. Three of the methods can be fulfilled prior to VC establishment while one of the methods is used per VC. A DTE that is identified prior to VC establishment can obtain either identified or customized service.

Prior to VC establishment, DTE identification can be provided by the PSN, through a data link layer Exchange Identification (XID) procedure, or packet layer registration. Per VC, DTE identification is through a NUI facility.

PSN-Provided DTE Identification

For dial-in, a DTE that is a subscriber to a PSN can have its identity signaled by the PSN (PSTN, ISDN, or CSPDN) to the PSPDN during the connection establishment stage. For dial-out, the DTE identity can become known to the PSPDN through information at the PSN that has been registered for dial-out operation.

XID Procedure for DTE Identification

The XID frames are data link layer commands and responses occurring before the logical link for a VC is established (disconnected phase of CCITT X.25). The XID may be used by the DCE and DTE, for DTE and DCE identification, authentication, or selection of X.32 optional user facilities. An unnumbered control field format is used in the XID procedure.

Registration Procedure for DTE Identification

A Registration Request packet can be sent by the DTE to the DCE during packet layer procedures for DTE identification and to possibly specify X.32 optional user facilities. A Registration Confirmation packet must be returned to the DTE by the DCE to complete the registration procedure. This procedure is always initiated by the DTE.

NUI Facility for DTE Identification

The NUI is an optional facility that can be offered by the PSPDN on a per-VC basis at the packet layer. It is also optional for the DTE to use it. When used, the DTE identification occurs during call setup and is contained in the facility field of the Call Request packet.

Identification of the DCE can be provided by the PSN, XID procedure, or packet layer registration, but everything is not the same as it is for DTE identification. For dial-out by the PSPDN, the PSN number identifying the DCE may be provided by the PSN to the DTE. DCE identification can also be optionally provided by the XID, and packet layer registration procedures, according to the identification protocol that is used to guard against inaccurate DCE identification. "The identification protocol consists of exchanges between the 'challenged' party and the 'questioning' party. The 'challenged' party provides and, optionally, certifies its identity and the 'questioning' party checks and authenticates this identity" (CCITT 1988o).

Physical Layer

For a switched access between a DTE and a PSPDN across a CSPDN, the DTE/DCE interface is according to CCITT X.21 or X.21 bis. For a switched access path between a DTE and a PSPDN via a PSTN, the physical layer interface is according to the CCITT V-Series characteristics and interfaces for modems. Duplex or half-duplex operations can be available across the PSTN when the modem characteristics are used (Table 4-11). Table 4-11 also indicates the primary and fall-back signaling rates and other requirements for modem operation with the PSTN.

Table 4-11. V-Series Modem Characteristics

Transmission	Signaling Rate (b/s)	CCITT Recommendation
Duplex	1,200	V.22, alternatives A, B, or C mode (i)[2]
	2,400/1,200[1]	V.22 bis, modes (i) or (iii);
		V.26 ter, modes (i) or (iii)[3]
	9,600/4,800[1]	V.32
Half-duplex	2,400	V.26 bis, alternative b[4]
	4,800/2,400[1]	V.27 ter

[1]These are primary and fall-back signaling rates.
[2]Alternatives A, B, or C, mode i, refers to 1,200 b/s synchronous operation over the DTE/DCE interface with particular circuit, scrambling, and encoding requirements.
[3]Modes (i) or (iii) refers to 2,400 or 1,200 b/s synchronous operation.
[4]Alternative b refers to the phase encoding of the line signal.

Data Link Layer

Data link layer requirements in X.32 are based on the ISO HDLC balanced classes of procedure and are met through the use of X.25 LAPB. Duplex transmission is recommended and half-duplex is optional. The address assignment to the DTE and DCE depends on the direction of the switched access call, whether dial-in, or dial-out. The balanced station address convention is used where commands always carry the destination address and responses always carry the source address.

This data link layer operation allows for the additional use of the unnumbered control field format XID command and response. The XID frames can be used for identification, authentication, and selection of X.32 optional user facilities. Following successful completion of these procedures, the data link is then established under normal LAPB procedure.

A half-duplex transmission module (HDTM) extends LAPB operation over a PSTN where half-duplex circuits are used. The HDTM is located between the physical layer and the LAPB (Figure 4-32). Together, the HDTM and LAPB compose the data link layer. The use of LAPB in this way is called LAPX—link access procedure, half-duplex (or extended).

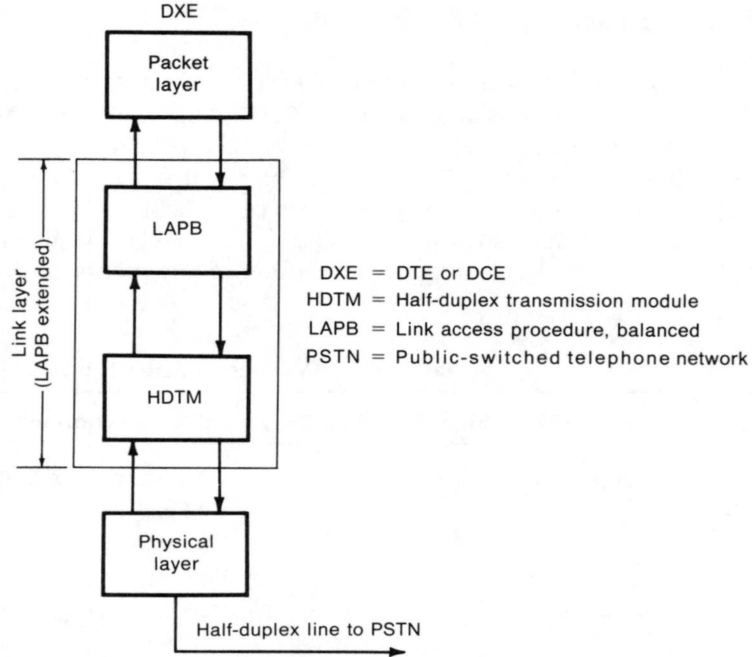

Figure 4-32. Layer relationships at a DTE or DCE with LAPB and HDTM for PSTN access.

The purpose of the HDTM is to convert the LAPB duplex operation to half-duplex operation by coordinating the use of the half-duplex line in the PSTN between the DTE and DCE. Coordination is accomplished by exchanging signals with the remote HDTM and interacting with the physical layer and LAPB. A physical circuit through the PSTN must be established by call control procedures before the HDTM can begin operation.

Packet Layer

According to X.32, the identification and authentication of DTEs and DCEs can also take place at the packet layer. If a failure takes place at the physical and/or the data link layers, the packet layer identification and authentication of the DTE and DCE are no longer valid.

For DTE and DCE registration, the DTE must first send a Registration Request packet to the DCE. For DTE or DCE identification to be completed, it is necessary for a Registration Confirmation packet to be sent from the DCE to the DTE. For DCE identification, the DTE initiates action by sending a Registration

Request packet so that the DCE has an opportunity to identify itself. Again, for the registration procedures to be complete, a confirmation packet must be sent by the DCE after the identification protocol is concluded.

The identification protocol allows exchanging one or more pairs of messages between a "questioning" and the "challenged" party. There are two security options that can be used for exchanging identification and authentication information between a DTE and the DCE. The basic option is security grade 1; the enhanced option is security grade 2. Security grade 1 provides for one exchange of protocol elements between the challenged parties (i.e., one pair of messages is exchanged). Security grade 2 allows the exchange of an additional pair of protocol elements if the first exchange is valid. The first exchange provides identification; the second provides authentication for greater security. "Are you really who you say you are?" can be ascertained.

An additional option in security grade 2 provides for the use of encryption to prevent unauthorized access to the PSPDN. A public key encryption technique that is endorsed by X.32 is the Rivest, Shamir, Adleman (RSA) algorithm. It is described in Appendix II of the document.

The identification protocol elements in security grades 1 and 2 are transmitted between the parties in either a sequence of XID frames or registration packets. Both methods may be offered by a network, but the identification and authentication must be done entirely with one method.

Optional Facilities

Secure dial-back and temporary location are two X.32-exclusive optional user facilities. Secure dial-back offers still more security as part of the customized DTE service. A DTE dials in to the PSPDN, identifies itself, and then disconnects. The PSPDN then dials out to the DTE, using the DTE's registered PSN number, and identifies itself. Then the DTE identifies itself again. Elements of the identification protocol are used in this procedure.

The temporary location facility applies to DTEs with registered PSN numbers that accept dial-out calls from the PSPDN. If a DTE is moved to another location, the DCE can reach it by using a number that is different from the registered PSN number. The alternate access number is an X.121 number from the PSN numbering plan. By using a temporary location facility, a DTE may specify when it can be reached through the alternate access number. Upon expiration of time, the number to reach the DTE reverts to the registered PSN number at the initial location.

CCITT X.31: ISDN Support of Packet Mode Terminals

Two cases of support of packet terminal equipment by an ISDN are described in CCITT X.31 (1988o). Case A, access to PSPDN service, and Case B, ISDN virtual-circuit service provide access for two types of packet mode terminal equipment. The first type of terminal equipment consists of X.25 DTEs, known as

TE2s, supported on ISDNs by TAs. The second type of packet mode ISDN terminal is called a TE1 (Figure 4-33). Therefore, TE2 + TA = TE1, but the capability of a TE1 may exceed that of the TE2.

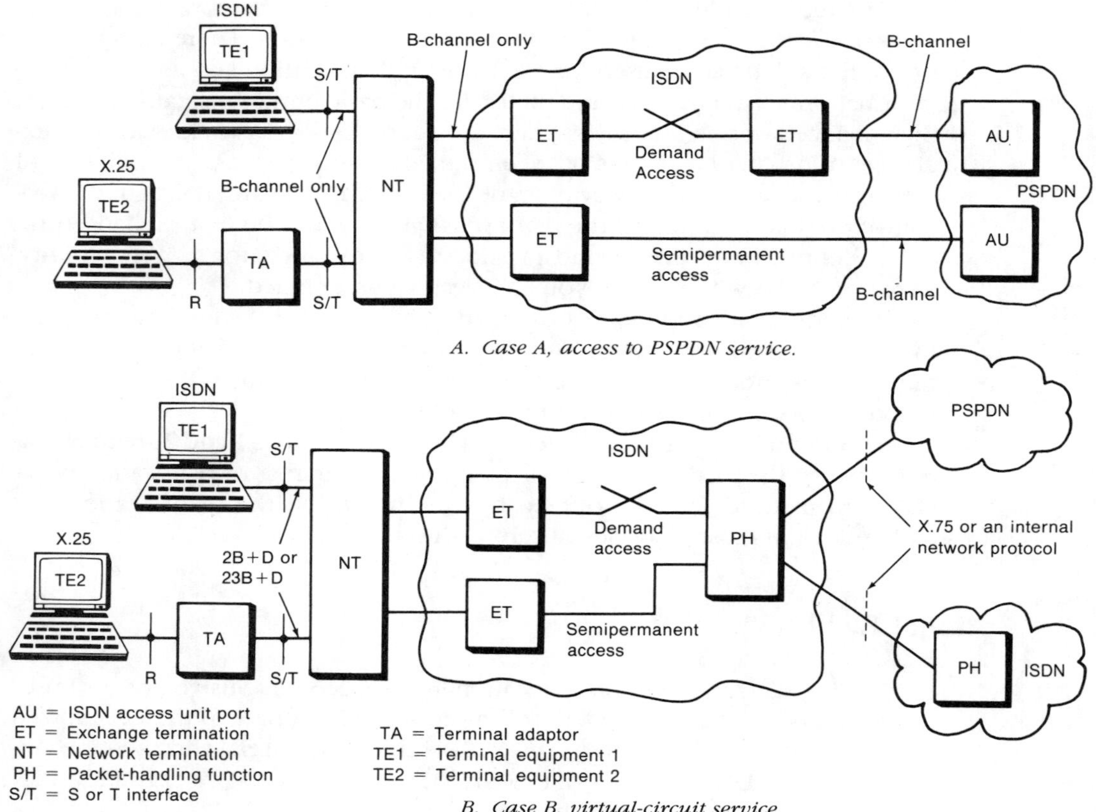

Figure 4-33. ISDN access cases defined by CCITT X.31.

Packet mode TE1s and TE2/TAs connect to an ISDN at either the S or T reference point. Figure 4-33 denotes this by indicating S/T which serves as a user-network interface.

There are two types of access scenarios shown for Case A and Case B; semipermanent (nonswitched) and demand (switched) access. In Case A, only ISDN B-channels can be used to access the PSPDN at the user-network interface, while in Case B, both B- and D-channels can be used. (A general knowledge of ISDN is anticipated in this description of CCITT X.31. For those unfamiliar with ISDN, a description by Scace (1986) is recommended.)

An ISDN basic rate interface (BRI) of 2B+D and a primary rate interface (PRI) of 23B+D are available for ISDN access as defined by X.31. However, X.31 only applies to a packet mode operation involving a single ISDN network connection on either a B- or D-channel.

For Case A (Figure 4-33A), the ISDN provides a transparent handling of packet messages. The only support that is provided is a 64 kb/s circuit-switched or semipermanent connection between the TE1 or TE2/TA and the PSPDN port. The access unit (AU) at the PSPDN port provides an interworking function which transfers and translates signaling information between two signaling networks in such a way that the significance of the information is the same in both networks. Complete ISDN signaling procedures are not needed to establish the semipermanent connection on the B-channel. Q.931 messages on the ISDN D-channel are not used. The procedures for Case A, demand access, for a connection-oriented network service (CONS) are described in the next section. The connection mode network service requires that a virtual circuit is established before data units are exchanged. CONS is the basis for X.25 operation—the establishment of data links before information is transmitted.

For Case B (Figure 4-33B), the ISDN provides a packet-handling (PH) function to the TE1 or TE2/TA and the PSPDN. The PH function carries out complete processing of X.25 data link and packet layer procedures. A PH function logically belonging to the ISDN may be physically located in a PSPDN node. This service is still defined as an ISDN virtual-circuit service. B-channel and D-channel access procedures are described in the following sections. A summary of several X.31 characteristics is given in Table 4-12.

Table 4-12. Characteristics for Case A and Case B

Characteristic	Case A: Access to PSPDN	Case B: Virtual-circuit service
Operation	Circuit mode	Packet mode
Type of access	Semipermanent (nonswitched) Demand (circuit-switched)	Semipermanent (nonswitched) Demand (circuit-switched)
Access channels	ISDN B-channels only	ISDN B- and D-channels (2B+D, 23B+D)
User rate	64 kb/s on B-channel	64 kb/s on B-channel 16 kb/s on D-channel, multiplex (for 2B+D)
Packet-handling function (PH/AU)	Outside ISDN in PSPDN	Within ISDN
Signaling at S/T interface	For semipermanent access via B-channel (see Figure 34) For demand access via B-channel (see Figure 34)	For semipermanent access via B-channel (see Figure 34) For demand access via B-channel (see Figure 34) For demand access via D-channel (see Figure 35)
Addressing	ISDN numbering plan (E.164) and PSPDN number assignments (X.121)	ISDN numbering plan (E.164) only
Internetworking	Semipermanent, ISDN signaling procedures (only Q.921) prior to X.25 LAPB and PLP Demand access, ISDN signaling procedures (Q.921 and Q.931) prior to X.25 LAPB and PLP	X.75 or internal network protocol

B-Channel Access at the S/T Interface

In both Case A and Case B, TE1 and TE2/TA terminals that support packet operation on the B-channel implement the same stacks of protocols shown in Figure 4-34. The stack on the left, which may be unavailable in some systems, is used for signaling on the D-channel. Implemented at the S or T interface, it establishes circuit-switched access to the packet-handling function—the PH in the ISDN or the AU in PSPDN. The protocols on the right are used to support packet-switched signaling and information transfer on the B-channel. Essentially, the stack on the left sets up the connection through a D-channel for information transfer on the B-channel.

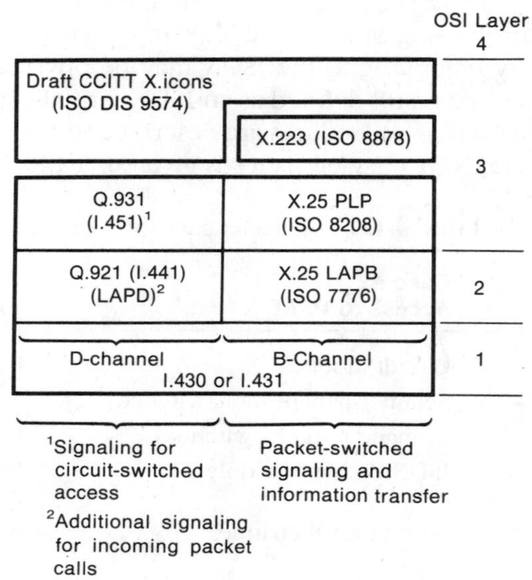

Figure 4-34. Protocol layers at S and T reference points when B-channel is used in ISDN.

At the top of Figure 4-34, CCITT X.223 (ISO 8878) defines the mapping of X.25 packet layer procedures to the elements of the connection mode network service. In addition, ISO DIS 9574 (ISO 1988b) and draft CCITT X.icons (CCITT 1988r) specify the method of providing the CONS by ISDN TE1s (at the S or T reference point) or TE2s (at the R reference point).

At the physical layer, Recommendation I.430 is to be used if the ISDN access is a BRI and I.431 is to be used if the ISDN is a primary rate interface PRI. At the data link layer, Q.921 (LAPD) is to be used over the D-channel (signaling) and X.25 LAPB (ISO 7776) on the B-channel (information). At the network layer, Recommendation Q.931 (equivalent to I.451) is to be used on the D-channel and X.25 PLP (ISO 8208) on the B-channel.

For semipermanent connections on the B-channel, no additional procedures are needed. Demand access requires additional procedures. These are being developed in the draft versions of CCITT and ISO DIS 9574 (1988b) documents that deal with providing connection mode network service by packet mode terminal equipment to an ISDN. The additional procedures are to be used if a B-channel is not already established or if an additional B-channel is needed to support additional information transfer between DTEs.

According to CCITT X.31, there are three classes of service to notify the user of incoming calls. One or more of these classes are to be provided by the network on a subscription basis:

- no notification
- conditional notification
- unconditional notification

With the no notification class, the ISDN allocates incoming calls to a D- or B-channel using a network algorithm. Q.931 is not used to notify the user of incoming calls. Two subclasses of no notification are recognized:

- semipermanent connections to the PH where an Incoming Call packet will be directly delivered over the connection
- user-initiated demand connections at the called side, in which the user is responsible for initiating calls to the PH using Q.931 procedures

With the conditional notification class, Q.931 procedures are used by the ISDN to activate a channel for delivery of an incoming call when there is no available channel in an active state. Whether a state is active is determined by Q.931 procedures.

With the unconditional notification class, Q.931 procedures are used by the network to notify the user of each X.25 incoming call. All information that can be copied from the X.25 Incoming Call packet to the Q.931 SETUP message is copied.

When demand access on the B-channel is *originated by* the TE1 or TE2/TA, a Q.931 connection request causes the ISDN D-channel signaling procedure to establish a B-channel. When demand access on the B-channel is *originated toward* the TE1 or TE2/TA, a call offering procedure *will* be used if the "unconditional notification class of service" has been subscribed. The call offering procedure *may* be used if the subscriber has the "conditional notification class of service."

The call-offering procedure determines which DTE (TE1s and/or TE2/TAs) is to receive the call and which B-channel is to be used. In both instances of originating access (by or to the DTE), X.25 LAPB and X.25 PLP procedures are followed after the B-channel connection is made.

D-Channel Access at the S/T Interface

Packet operation across the D-channel applies only in Case B, virtual-circuit service. The D-channel provides a semipermanent connection which enables the ISDN user terminals to access a PH function within the ISDN or vice versa.

The protocol stacks shown in Figure 4-35 are implemented by the TE1s and TE2/TAs at the S or T interface. At the physical layer, I.430 is used if the ISDN access is a BRI and I.431 is used for the PRI. At the data link layer, Q.921 (LAPD) is used on both sides of the protocol stacks. At the network layer, Q.931 (I.451) is used to provide the call-offering procedure which precedes the Incoming Call packet according to X.25 PLP (ISO 8208). Message exchanges according to Q.931 enable the identification of user terminals and on which channel (B or D) an Incoming Call packet is sent.

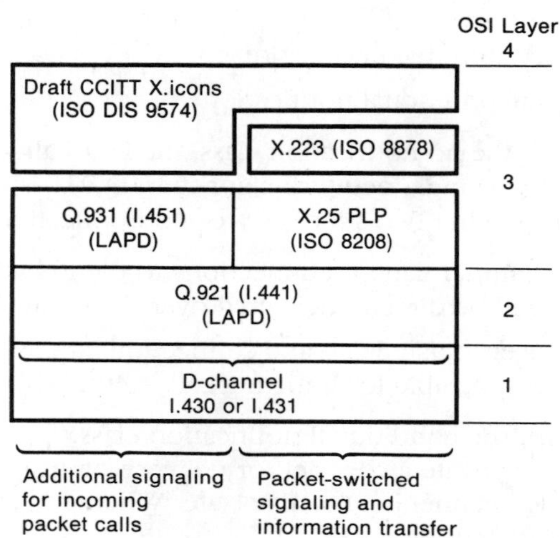

Figure 4-35. Protocol layers at S and T reference points when the D-channel is used in ISDN.

On the D-channel, the maximum length of user data allowed is 256 octets and the throughput cannot exceed 16 kb/s at a basic interface.

The use of LAPD in ISDNs adds unique capabilities because of the ability "to interleave multiple data links, each from a different source" (Scace 1986). This multiple capability distinguishes LAPD from LAPB with other differences being relatively minor. LAPB does not multiplex and operates only on a "clear-channel" at a user rate of 64 kb/s. Another difference is that LAPD operates only at modulo 128.

To achieve multiplex capability, the LAPD address field occupies two octets instead of one in LAPB. The address consists of a terminal endpoint identifier (TEI) and a service access point identifier (SAPI). Each TE1 or TE2/TA at a particular interface is assigned a specific TEI. The assignment of a standardized SAPI value specifies a particular LAPD capability. The designation of SAPI = 0 indicates the transport of signaling information across an interface. The designation of SAPI = 16 indicates the transport of packet data across an interface.

Recommendation X.31 defines the use of SAPI = 16. According to X.31, a single SAPI = 16 LAPD link, as viewed by the network, must support multiplexing of logical channels at layer 3. Multiple SAPI = 16 LAPD logical links operating simultaneously must also be supported because the user may have multipoint access and the TE1 or TE2/TA is allowed to operate with more than one TEI. Based on this operating requirement, the ISDN must be able to support simultaneous multiplexing at layer 2 and layer 3 for D-channel packet mode operation.

Further, all X.25 packets, including Call Request packets and Incoming Call packets, must be sent to and from the terminal equipment in numbered information frames (I-frames) in a SAPI = 16 LAPD link.

For outgoing calls, the TE1 or TE2/TA conform to X.25 procedures operating over the ISDN layer 2 using SAPI = 16. For incoming calls without a call-offering procedure, the TE1 and TE2/TA also conform to X.25 procedures over the ISDN layer 2 using SAPI = 16 LAPD. There are two conditions that apply. The X.25 procedures are followed when the interface on which the TE1 or TE2/TA is connected has subscribed to the no-notification or conditional class of service, and the ISDN decides not to use the call offering procedure.

For incoming calls with the call offering procedure in effect, X.25 protocol procedures are used over ISDN layer 2 using SAPI = 16 LAPD as before. However, the ISDN call-offering procedures can also be operated over ISDN layer 2 with SAPI = 0 or for an interim period on some networks with SAPI = 16. Using SAPI = 0 allows B- or D-channel selection for user information transfer. Using SAPI = 16 negates channel negotiation and all calls will only be on the D-channel.

The protocol stacks in Figures 4-34 and 4-35 apply at the S or T interfaces. The stack shown in Figure 4-36 summarizes the protocol layers that apply at the R reference point. It also allows us to ascertain the importance of the terminal adaptor (Figure 4-30) between the R and S/T interfaces. A number of functions are performed by the TA for B-channel access:

- rate adaption—adapting terminals operating at data signaling rates lower than 64 kb/s to 64 kb/s through HDLC interframe flag stuffing
- signaling—mapping signaling information between the S/T and the R interfaces
- synchronization—coordinating D- and B-channel activities and synchronizing the TA with PH/AU through the exchange of sync patterns
- maintenance—communicating information over test loops about performance and fault management, configurations, and other network characteristics

A specific function of the TA is to perform LAPB-LAPD mapping when access to the ISDN virtual-circuit service takes place through the D-channel. Address field mapping converts an LAPB address length of one octet to an LAPD address length of two octets and vice versa. Control field mapping for information frames (I-frame) accounts for LAPB sequence numbering (usually modulo 8) and LAPD sequence numbering (N(S) and N(R)) which always is modulo 128. Also, the frame check sequence (FCS) values on the LAPB and LAPD link are independent so that the FCS has to be recalculated for each I-frame.

An interesting proposal employs LAPD (Q.921), rather than LAPB (X.25), as the layer 2 protocol over the B-channels (Unsoy 1988). Multiplexing at layer 2 over B-channels would be possible. At layer 3, X.25 packet layer procedures would remain. Some benefits would ensue—the 64 kb/s user channel would be used more efficiently and TAs would have to support only LAPD rather than

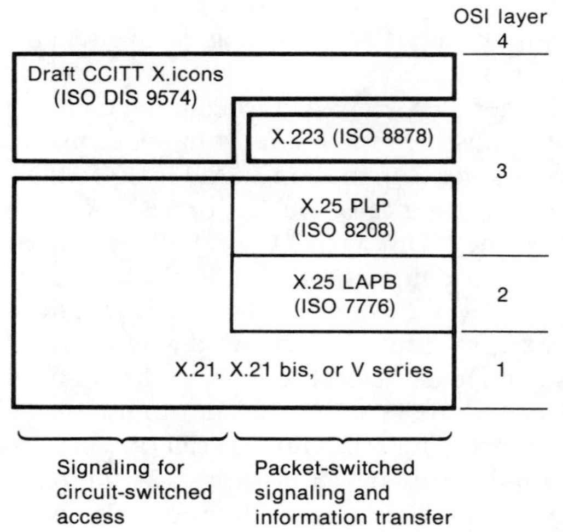

Figure 4-36. Protocol layers at the R reference point.

LAPD and LAPB. The disadvantage is that only new ISDN terminals would be able to take advantage of this service; existing packet mode terminals could not.

CCITT X.75: Signaling Between PSPDNs

The basic difference between CCITT X.25 and CCITT X.75 is that the former defines the interface for packet mode DTEs connected to PSPDNs while the latter defines an interface for a signaling system between PSPDNs, between ISDNs and PSPDNs, and between ISDNs that provide packet-switched data transmission according to X.31 (Case B, virtual-circuit service).

Internetwork links consist of one or more circuits between two directly connected signaling terminals (STEs). Each STE is part of an exchange within a public network (see Figure 4-5). The basic system structure (Figure 4-37) consists of transmission facilities, the exchange interfaces (X or Y), link and packet layer procedures within the STE, and higher layer functions. STE-X/STE-Y (X/Y) refers to the interface of the two STEs. Although there is a close relationship between X.25 and X.75 procedures, differences do exist.

Physical Layer

At the physical layer, the characteristics of the signaling terminal/physical circuit interface are defined by CCITT Recommendation G.703, physical/electrical characteristics of hierarchical digital interfaces, for data signaling rates of 64 kb/s, and optionally, 2.048 Mb/s or 1.544 Mb/s.

In the United States, the V.35/V.28/V.24 combination applies with 56 kb/s duplex transmission being supported. As an added option, circuits operating at

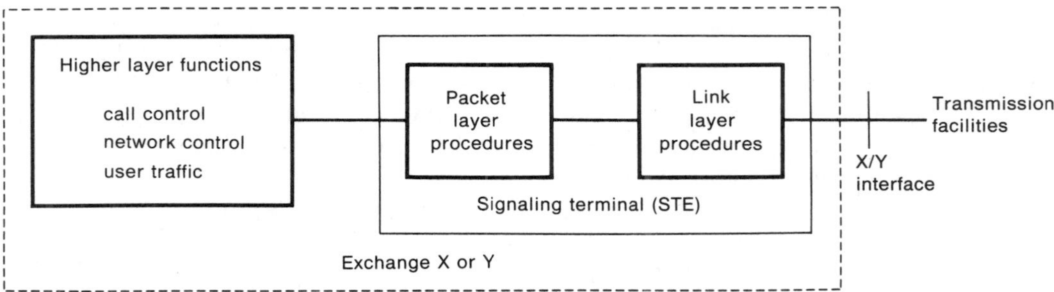

Figure 4-37. Basic structure of X.75 signaling procedures *(CCITT 1988r).*

a data rate greater than 19.2 kb/s may use EIA-530, which is recommended rather than EIA-449. STE interfaces operating at data signaling rates of 19.2 kb/s, or less, can use EIA-232-D (ANSI 1988b).

Data Link Layer

At the link layer, X.75 uses X.25 procedures on duplex links between STEs. SLPs are based on X.25 LAPB. MLPs are also similar and apply when multiple physical circuits in parallel use the SLP on each link. The MLP is then used for data interchange over the multiple parallel links. The description of LAPB procedures for the two recommendations is quite similar except that the terminology is related to STEs rather than DTEs and DCEs.

The link layer frame structure is similar in X.25 and X.75 (Figure 4-9). Modulo 8 and modulo 128 sequence numbering is supported. The address field is one octet and the control field is 2 in both recommendations. The control field formats for numbered information transfer (I format), numbered supervisory functions (S format), and unnumbered control functions (U formats) conform to LAPB, but there is a two-octet alternate U format for modulo 128 in X.75. The alternate U format provides additional link control procedures.

The addressing commands and responses (RR, RNR, REJ, SABM, SABME, DISC, UA), N(S) and N(R) numbers, and P/F bits all apply in the procedures. The use of timers in X.75 is also defined and based on the need for the transmission of commands, responses, or retransmissions occurring within a given period. Both X.25 and X.75 define the MLP as an added upper sublayer of the data link layer between the packet layer and multiple SLPs in the data link layer.

There is no provision for LAP in X.75.

Packet Layer

At the packet layer, X.75 resembles X.25, but it is not the same. CCITT X.75 relates to the transfer of packets at STE-X/STE-Y interface. The packets are contained within the data link layer information field but with additional octets (compared to X.25) for network utilities.

Logical channels are used for simultaneous VCs and/or PVCs (see Figure

4-23). Each VC and PVC is assigned an LCGN (0 to 15) and an LCN (0 to 255). Both are assigned during the call-setup phase. The range of logical channels and logical channel groups available for assignment to VCs is agreed to bilaterally for a period of time between the networks. An LCGN and an LCN are assigned to the PVC at the time of establishment. The combination of LCN = 0 and LCGN =0 is not used for VCs or PVCs.

The VCs can be distributed over the available STEs when multiple STE X/Y interfaces are used between the networks. Selection of a particular STE can be performed once by the originating network and by each transit network for a call request. The selection of a specific X/Y interface is network-dependent. During a particular VC, each packet related to the call uses the STEs selected at call setup.

Packets transmitted over PVCs use the STEs selected at the time of circuit establishment. When multiple X/Y interfaces are used by the networks, a bilateral agreement assigns the STE X/Y interface to the circuit. Network utilities (transit network identification) can be used where multiple STE X/Y interfaces are available at the networks.

A slightly different set of packets is used to set up VCs in X.75. Incoming Call, Call Accepted, and Clear Indication packets are not required (see Figure 4-6). Table 4-7 showed the packet requirements across DTE/DCE and DCE/DTE interfaces. The following are packet types that cross the STE-X/STE-Y interface.

For Call Setup and Clearing:

- Call Request
- Call Connected
- Clear Request
- Clear Confirmation

For Data and Interrupt:

- Data
- Interrupt
- Interrupt Confirmation

For Flow Control and Reset:

- Receive Ready (RR)
- Receive Not Ready (RNR)
- Reset Request
- Reset Confirmation

For Restart:

- Restart Request
- Restart Confirmation

As in X.25, there is no need for Call Setup and Call Clearing packet types for PVCs. A PVC is continually in a data-transfer state except during restart procedures. Data, Interrupt, Flow Control, and Reset packets may be transferred on

PVCs. Sequential numbering of the packets transmitted in each direction takes place for VCs and PVCs. The sequence numbering is performed modulo 8 or 128, cycling 0 to 7 or 0 to 127, respectively. The standard maximum data field is 128 octets. Optional values are 16, 32, 64, 256, and 1,024 octets. This differs from X.25 because maximum data field lengths of 2,048 and 4,096 are available, in X.25, but are for "further study" in X.75.

Delivery confirmation (D-bits), More data (M-bits), and Qualifier bits (Q-bits) are also used for similar purposes in X.75. Flow control principles described for X.25 are also used. At the X/Y interface of each VC or PVC logical channel, the transmission of data packets is controlled separately for each direction. The window size is modulo 8 or 128 with W = 2 being the default. The packet send, P(S), and receive P(R) are also modulo 8 or 128.

The formats of X.75 packets are based on the general structure of packets in X.25. The most significant difference between X.25 and X.75 packets is the addition of the network utility field (63 octets, maximum). The actual length of the field depends on the utilities that are available and requested by the user. These additional octets are part of the Call Request and Call Connected packets, and may be added to the Clear Request packet. The network utility field complements the user facility field and serves to separate user service signaling from network administrative signaling. All STEs are required to transparently pass X.25 user facilities across X.75 interfaces. The network utility fields are added between the called and calling DTE addresses and the user facility fields (Figure 4-38). In the figure, the general format identifier is coded 0D01 (modulo 8) or 0D10 (modulo 128). D is the delivery confirmation bit. More than 18 octets of call user data will be present only when the fast select optional user facility is requested.

In order to identify the DTE addresses, two numbering plans are used. The numbering plan for an X.75 interface between two PSPDNs or between a PSPDN and an ISDN will be X.121. When X.75 is used between two ISDNs, the numbering plan will be E.164. Escape digits apply to both numbering plans where required.

There are three categories of network utilities. The *International Mandatory Network Utilities* must be supported by all international X.75 interworkings, and include

- Transit network identification
- Call identifier
- Throughput class indication
- Window size indication
- Packet size indication
- Fast select indication
- Closed user group indication
- Closed user group with outgoing access indication
- Called line address modified notification
- Transit delay indication

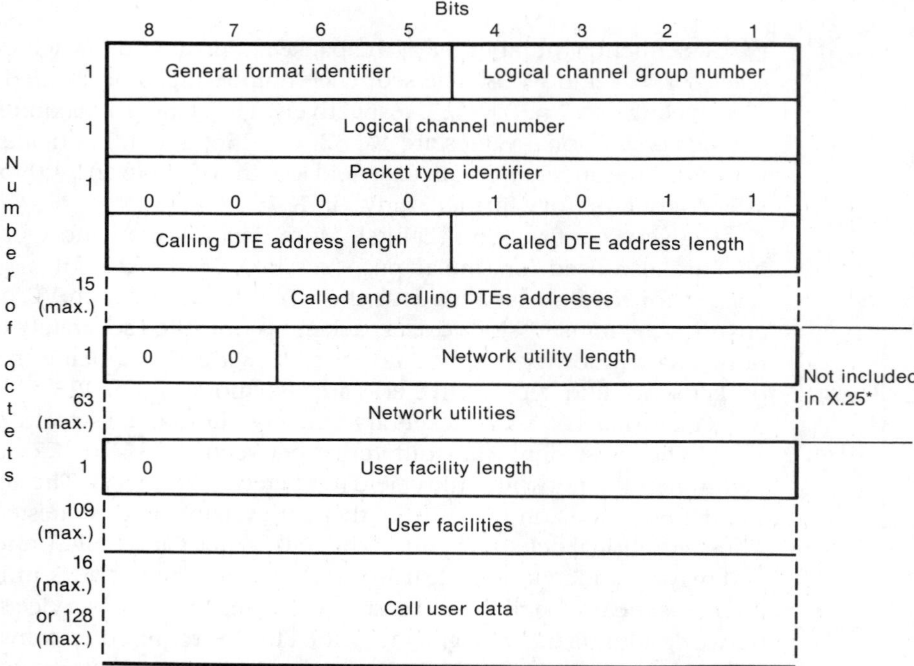

Figure 4-38. X.75 Call Request packet format *(CCITT 1988r).*

The *International Optional Network Utilities* must be supported by all international X.75 interworkings, subject to bilateral agreement, and include

- Reverse charging indication
- Clearing network identification code
- Transit delay selection
- Tariffs
- Network user identification
- Utility marker

The *National Network Utilities* may only be supported on links between networks in the same countries, and include RPOA selection.

All three categories are supported in the U.S. version of X.75 which will be called ANS X3.178.

A *transit network identification utility* is used to identify a network controlling part of the virtual circuit. If the transit network is a PSPDN, it is identified by a four-digit DNIC. An ISDN is identified by a four-digit ISDN Network Identification Code (INIC) that is composed of: 0 + E.164 Country Code + National Network Digit(s). Some countries can also use 9 instead of 0 to identify additional ISDNs. The E.164 Country Code is 1 for the United States. National Network Digit(s) consist of values agreed to within a given country. Some DNICs are shared by more than one network. In that case there are additional requirements specified by the FCC (ANSI 1988b).

The network identification just described is also used for CUG identification, CUG outgoing access indication, clearing network identification and RPOA selection utilities.

The *call identifier utility* is always present in the Call Request packet. This parameter is established by the originating network and serves as an identifying name for each virtual circuit that is established. A VC is uniquely identified when the call identifier is used in conjunction with the calling DTE address.

The *throughput class indication utility* can be used by an STE to specify a throughput class value for a particular call as selected at the calling DTE/DCE interface. Any transit STE can also request a value in the Call Request packet. An agreed upon default value is assigned if a throughput class is not requested. The value of the throughput class can be 75, 150, 300, 600, 1,200, 2,400, 4,800, 9,600, 19,200, 48,000, 56,000 (in the U.S.), and 64,000 bits per second.

The *closed user group indication utility* is used to establish VCs by DTEs which are members of international CUGs.

The *transit delay indication utility* is used in satellite and cable links. This utility signals the anticipated cumulative transit delay of a virtual circuit in the Call Request and Call Connected packets when requested by the calling DTE. The transit delay is a mean value based on characteristics of the originating network that is signaled by the STE. An STE in the transit network will add the value of the transit network with which it is associated. A final value is returned in the Call Connected packet.

The *tariffs utility* passes information among networks participating in the VC so that billing and call-accounting can take place.

The *network user identification utility* provides supplementary network user identification for billing, security, or network management purposes.

Summary

This chapter has provided an overview of CCITT X.25 and related packet mode standards that have been developed through international cooperation and are being implemented in the United States and overseas.

ANS X3.100 is the domestic version of X.25, ISO 7776, and ISO 8208 describing provisions that are recommended in the United States.

CCITT X.32 is a dial-in, dial-out packet mode recommendation that defines methods of accessing a packet-switched public data network across the public-switched telephone network, a circuit-switched data network, or an ISDN. CCITT X.31 provides the basis for supporting packet mode terminal equipment by ISDNs.

CCITT X.75 defines the interface for packet-switched signaling between public data transmission networks, including PSPDNs and ISDNs.

The thrust of this chapter has been to provide a reference for packet mode standards. The descriptions are not complete because all possible material and explanations cannot be given and the standards are continuously evolving through the efforts of standards committees. For additional information, consult the most recent drafts of the CCITT recommendations, ISO standards, American National Standards, and network specifications. A detailed analysis of the technical differences between X.25 and ISO standards 7776 and 8208 is given by Kessler (1988).

References

ANSI. 1988a. dpANS X3.100. American National Standard for information systems—interface between data terminal equipment (DTE) and data circuit-terminating equipment (DCE) for operation with packet-switched data networks (PSPDN), or between two DTEs, by dedicated circuit.

———. 1988b. dpANS X3.178. American National Standard for information systems—packet switched signaling system between networks providing data transmission services.

CCITT. 1988a. CCITT Recommendation X.25. Interface between date terminal equipment (DTE) and data circuit-terminating equipment (DCE) for terminals operating in the packet mode and connected to public data networks by dedicated circuits.

———. 1988b. CCITT Recommendation X.200. Reference model of open systems interconnection for CCITT applications.

———. 1988c. CCITT Recommendation X.21. Interface between data terminal equipment (DTE) and data circuit-terminating equipment (DCE) for synchronous operation on public data networks.

———. 1988d. CCITT Recommendation X.21 bis. Use on public data networks of data terminal equipment (DTE) which is designed for interfacing to synchronous V-Series modems.

———. 1988e. CCITT Recommendation X.3. Packet assembly/disassembly facility (PAD) in a public data network.

———. 1988f. CCITT Recommendation X.28. DTE/DCE interface for a start-stop mode data terminal equipment accessing the packet assembly/disassembly facility (PAD) in a public data network situated in the same country.

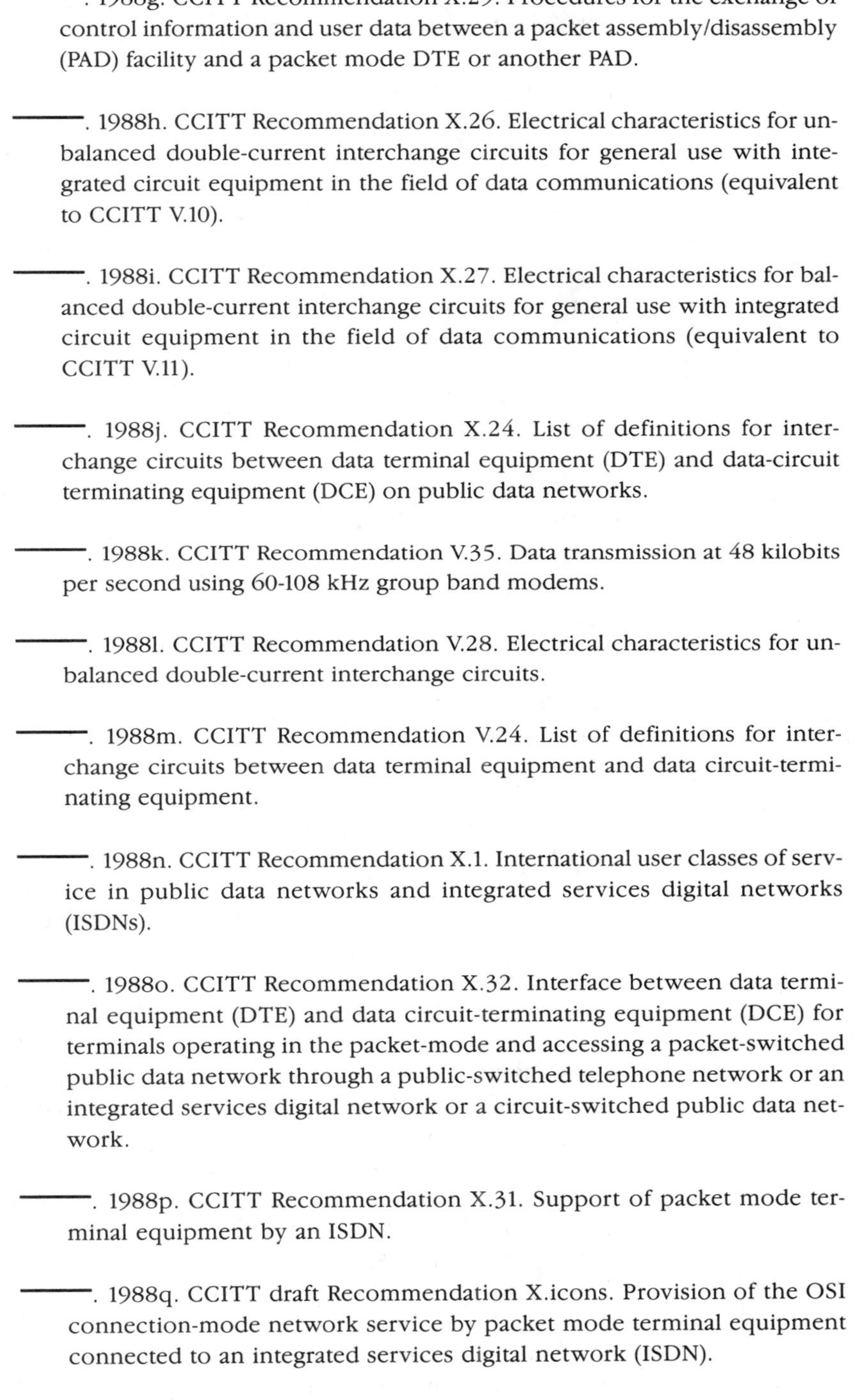

———. 1988g. CCITT Recommendation X.29. Procedures for the exchange of control information and user data between a packet assembly/disassembly (PAD) facility and a packet mode DTE or another PAD.

———. 1988h. CCITT Recommendation X.26. Electrical characteristics for unbalanced double-current interchange circuits for general use with integrated circuit equipment in the field of data communications (equivalent to CCITT V.10).

———. 1988i. CCITT Recommendation X.27. Electrical characteristics for balanced double-current interchange circuits for general use with integrated circuit equipment in the field of data communications (equivalent to CCITT V.11).

———. 1988j. CCITT Recommendation X.24. List of definitions for interchange circuits between data terminal equipment (DTE) and data-circuit terminating equipment (DCE) on public data networks.

———. 1988k. CCITT Recommendation V.35. Data transmission at 48 kilobits per second using 60-108 kHz group band modems.

———. 1988l. CCITT Recommendation V.28. Electrical characteristics for unbalanced double-current interchange circuits.

———. 1988m. CCITT Recommendation V.24. List of definitions for interchange circuits between data terminal equipment and data circuit-terminating equipment.

———. 1988n. CCITT Recommendation X.1. International user classes of service in public data networks and integrated services digital networks (ISDNs).

———. 1988o. CCITT Recommendation X.32. Interface between data terminal equipment (DTE) and data circuit-terminating equipment (DCE) for terminals operating in the packet-mode and accessing a packet-switched public data network through a public-switched telephone network or an integrated services digital network or a circuit-switched public data network.

———. 1988p. CCITT Recommendation X.31. Support of packet mode terminal equipment by an ISDN.

———. 1988q. CCITT draft Recommendation X.icons. Provision of the OSI connection-mode network service by packet mode terminal equipment connected to an integrated services digital network (ISDN).

———. 1988r. CCITT Recommendation X.75. Packet-switched signaling system between public networks providing data transmission services.

Dally, K. L. 1986. *CCITT Recommendation X.25, Open Systems Data Transfer, Transmission No. 23*. Available from Omnicom, Inc.; 501 Church Street, NE; Suite 302; Vienna, VA 22180; (703) 281-1135.

EIA. 1969. EIA-232-C. Interface between data terminal equipment and data communication equipment employing serial binary data interchange (October).

———. 1977. EIA-449. General purpose 37-position and 9-position interface for data terminal equipment and data circuit-terminating equipment employing serial binary data interchange (November).

———. 1985. EIA-232-D. Interface between data terminal equipment and data circuit-terminating equipment employing serial binary data interchange (final draft, December).

———. 1987. EIA-530. High speed 25-position interface for data terminal equipment and data circuit-terminating equipment.

ISO. 1985a. ISO 7776. Information processing systems—Data communications—High-level data link control procedures—Description of the X.25 LAPB-compatible DTE data link procedures.

———. 1985b. ISO 7498. Information processing systems—Open systems interconnection—Basic reference model.

———. 1988a. ISO 8208. Information processing systems—Data communications—X.25 packet level protocol for data terminal equipment (working draft of second edition of ISO 8208).

———. 1988b. ISO DIS 9574. Information processing systems—Data communications—Provision of the OSI connection-mode network service by packet mode terminal equipment connected to an integrated services digital network (ISDN) (revised draft proposal).

Kessler, G. C. 1988. A comparison between CCITT Recommendation X.25 and International Standards 8208 and 7776. *IEEE Transactions on Communications* 36, no. 4 (April).

NCS. 1985. *Glossary of Telecommunication Terms, Federal Standard 1037A*. October 1985. Available at GSA Business Service Centers across the country, or from GSA; Specification Branch (WFSIS); Room 6039; 7th and D Streets, SW; Washington, DC 20407.

Pense, E. 1984. X.21 circuit-switching protocol in the open systems interconnection environment. *Open Systems Data Transfer, Transmission No. 11* (August). Available from Omnicom Information Service; 501 Church Street, NE; Suite 206, Vienna, VA 22180.

Scace, E. 1986. Integrated services digital networks (ISDN). *Digital Communications*. Indianapolis: Howard W. Sams & Company.

Tannenbaum, A. 1981. *Computer Networks*. Englewood Cliffs, New Jersey: Prentice-Hall, Inc.

Unsoy, M. 1988. How packet-mode transmission services will evolve in ISDN. *Data Communications* 17, no. 4 (April).

Chapter 5

Future ISDN Planning

C. Anthony Cooper

Chapter 5

THE ISDN HAS BECOME A KEY FOCUS OF NETWORK PLANNING efforts throughout the telecommunications industry and is likely to influence the introduction of new network technology throughout the remainder of this century. This chapter begins with a review of ISDN planning efforts during the past decade and gives a current perspective on ISDN architecture.

Origins of ISDN

ISDN originated during the late 1970s as a national and international concept for future telecommunications with the major goal of defining digital interfaces, both customer-to-network and network-to-network. It now constitutes the target architecture for the evolution of today's public telephone networks toward ubiquitous, end-to-end digital telecommunications networks. ISDN offers a framework in which both voice and nonvoice services can be efficiently and economically provided with the new technology being deployed throughout modern telecommunications networks.

The major principles embodied in the ISDN architecture have been adopted as recommendations by CCITT. As part of its early efforts in this area, CCITT defined ISDN as

> A network evolved from the telephone Integrated Digital Network that provides end-to-end digital connectivity to support a wide range of services, including voice and nonvoice services, to which users have access by a limited set of standard, multipurpose, user-network interfaces.

The use of a few, standard, user-network interfaces to support a large variety of services implies that the telecommunications service (or mix of services) provided at a particular location can generally be changed without having to alter that interface.

ISDN is to the telecommunications network of the 1990s what the stored program controlled (SPC) network was to the telecommunications network of the 1960s. ISDN is a natural extension of the SPC network concept, providing digital connections in place of analog connections, while building on the same concept of using network intelligence for expanded functionality and control. To provide an ISDN user with ready and flexible access to this network intelligence, out-of-band signaling is used over ISDN access links. To strengthen the network's internal signaling capabilities for efficiently using this network intelligence, ISDN's interoffice signaling is carried over a separate, message-oriented common channel signaling (CCS) network.

Due in part to the emphasis in the United States on standardizing a transmission-level interface for ISDN, some perceive ISDN as a standardized access mechanism for a digital network. As the complement to ISDN access considerations, those network aspects pertaining mainly to interoffice signaling and the further development of network intelligence are sometimes referred to as the Intelligent Network. Indeed, it is often useful to partition the complex consideration of a modern telecommunications network in this manner.

Motivations for ISDN

For about the past thirty years, beginning with the introduction of T1-carrier systems in the interoffice plant during 1962, new telecommunications technology has evolved based largely on the use of digital signals for transmitting and switching customer information and for controlling and operating the network. Digital technology is now used to provide stored program control and time-division switching fabric in switching machines, for implementing CCS in the interoffice portion of the network, for fiber and some radio transmission systems, and for the more recently available types of digital loop carrier systems. A natural extension of such applications of digital technology in telecommunications networks is the use of digital technology in all portions of the loop plant, thereby extending digital telecommunications all the way to the customer. Such customer-to-customer, or end-to-end, digital connectivity is a key attribute of ISDN.

Economy

The principal driving force behind all phases of this introduction of digital technology (or indeed the introduction of any new technology) into a telecommunications network is the economic advantage to be gained by such introduction. While extensive work has been performed on ISDN's deployment economics, as well as on the technical requirements needed to achieve them, the fundamental idea behind the economic advantages of ISDN is fairly simple to illustrate.

Suppose that a customer who receives one network service over one loop costing about $500 wishes to obtain a second network service. That second service could be provided by either using a second loop or by adding digital loop electronics, which can create more channels, to the existing loop. Projecting the use of large-scale integrated circuitry and high-volume production for such ISDN-based digital loop electronics places their component cost at roughly $50, which compares favorably with the $500 cost of a hypothesized second loop.

To provide a more complete picture of ISDN economics from the perspective of a network provider, operations expense as well as equipment costs must be considered. Operations considerations motivate the incorporation of features in ISDN's digital loop electronics to help automate troubleshooting aspects of the maintenance process; they also impose a minimum range requirement on ISDN's digital loop electronics in order to simplify the installation of an ISDN-equipped loop. A major objective of ISDN is to provide support for all network services in an integrated manner, meaning that the same type of network equipment can be used for many different types of service. This minimizes the need to deploy service-specific network equipment or to engage in service-specific network operations. The overall result of ISDN economic studies is generally attractive with respect to a network provider's operations expenses and equipment costs.

A network provider should also consider the revenue potential from the realization of new network services that exploit ISDN's capabilities. This largely depends upon the perspective of network users concerning both current and potential new services provided through ISDN.

Efficiency

Network users as well as network providers have a sound motivation for using digital technology in telecommunications equipment. Motivated initially by the need for communications with and between digital computers, a significant number of customers have been employing for many years a variety of modems to adapt digital signals from their computer host and terminal devices for transmission over telecommunications networks that provide an analog customer-network interface. The Digital Data System (DDS) was introduced in 1976 to meet the needs of such customers more efficiently by providing private line communications through a digital customer-network interface. Since then, various network providers have offered other types of services, such as digital circuit-switched and packet-switched communications.

The extension of digital telecommunications all the way to the customer allows network providers and the makers of digital terminal devices to exploit new technology—both for supporting current services in a more efficient manner and for creating new services. In addition to the classic support of data communications for computer-related applications, newer types of digital terminal devices connected to an end-to-end digital telecommunications network have the potential for communicating higher quality voice with encoding techniques which no longer need to work through a large number of analog-to-digital conversions contained within a telecommunications network. End-to-end digital connectivity offers the potential for using low bit-rate voice encoding techniques to realize point-to-point bundles of more economical voice channels and for providing a range of video services from improved facsimile to full-motion video. Furthermore, combining ISDN's end-to-end digital connectivity with its out-of-band signaling feature creates significant potential for establishing new services that give network management and control features to the ISDN user.

Planning Principles and Key Attributes

In general, ISDN architecture planning efforts have proceeded in accordance with several guiding principles. Perhaps the fundamental principle is that ISDN plans must be flexible. Other guidelines include the following:

1. ISDN should build to the greatest extent feasible upon currently deployed network facilities. The existing loop plant and digital transmission facilities, as well as the time-division switches and the CCS systems* currently being deployed, will be used by ISDN.
2. ISDN must be able to interwork with an operating company's existing network without requiring major changes to those portions that are not initially upgraded to ISDN.
3. ISDN should be consistent with both national and international standards.
4. ISDN should provide building-block capabilities which constitute foundations for both existing and new service features.
5. ISDN architecture should be modular in design, thereby encouraging mutually compatible, multiple-vendor implementations of all ISDN piece-parts, and avoiding total reliance on a single vendor's equipment.
6. The operations functionality designed into the ISDN architecture should be consistent with the plans for operations systems.

The key attributes possessed by any ISDN implementation and distinguishing it from non-ISDN implementations include

- end-to-end digital connectivity
- integrated services access
- standardized customer-network interfaces
- out-of-band signaling
- customer control

End-to-end digital connectivity offers economies associated with new technology as exploited by digital equipment. Both capital costs and operating expenses are reduced, as compared to older, analog equipment. Digital networks provide inherently zero loss transmission.

Integrated services access enables a customer to access a wide variety of

*The CCS systems used by ISDN are those based on CCITT's Signaling System Number 7 protocol.

network services over a single access link. This permits the sharing of network equipment and operations over many services.

ISDN uses a small family of standardized customer-network interfaces to provide all network services. This is corollary to integrated services access and provides a significant advantage to the customer of network services because it promotes portability of customers' terminal equipment.

ISDN provides the customer with out-of-band signaling. One advantage of this attribute is that the customer has a communications channel with the network at all times, not just during call setup. Out-of-band signaling, as provided on ISDN's access links, uses a message-oriented approach and is easily adaptable to accommodate new service features.

Building upon the message-oriented, out-of-band signaling provided by ISDN's access links makes it possible to give the customer control over the mix of services and service features.

Particularly in the United States, public policy decisions have had a strong influence on ISDN planning. One example illustrates this influence. To meet the requirements of an FCC order, the user-network interface for ISDN within the United States was designated as being within the transmission system used to provide ISDN access—unlike the CCITT recommendation which identifies reference points for possible interfaces between distinct telecommunications systems. The T1 committee accredited by ANSI initiated a project in 1985 to develop such a standard interface for ISDN's Digital Subscriber Line (DSL). At the present time, this sizable effort has resulted in a draft American national standard for this interface.

The attractiveness of ISDN to large customers with national scopes of operation is likely to depend on the attainment of nationwide compatibility for ISDN interfaces and service control procedures. Hence a key market-based challenge for the evolving ISDN is maximizing such compatibility.

Considerable technological development will continue to take place in the telecommunications field. These developments will, together with each network provider's business and market considerations and the public policy decisions provided by governmental agencies, drive the evolution of ISDN. Technology-based challenges posed to the evolving ISDN include the effective incorporation of fiber transmission and fast packet-switching technologies and the more effective use of software-based technology for meeting customer demands in new and more attractive ways. These new technologies influence the realization of ISDN attributes.

Architecture for Current Implementations

Within the United States, trials and initial implementations of ISDN by various BOCs have been serving customers since 1986. These implementations are, for the most part, based upon the target ISDN architecture surveyed here. The ISDN architecture characterizes the fundamental aspects of ISDN's transmission and switching functions, together with the relevant features of ISDN's signaling, protocols, services, performance, operations, and considerations for interworking between the ISDN and non-ISDN portions of a public telecommunications network. Major elements of the ISDN architecture have been incorporated into standards by CCITT and ANSI's T1 Committee. Technical requirements for ISDN equipment are also needed to support ISDN implementations.

A succinct overview of the ISDN architecture is provided by Figure 5-1. The access portion of the ISDN architecture supports a small number of standard interfaces for providing network services to any type of customer. Two types of ISDN customers are shown here: an end user of a telecommunications-based service, and an "enhanced service vendor" which creates the information being accessed by the end user. Because public policy at this time imposes restrictions on the provision of "enhanced services" by the BOCs, it is pertinent to plan for the telecommunications service needs of this type of ISDN customer.

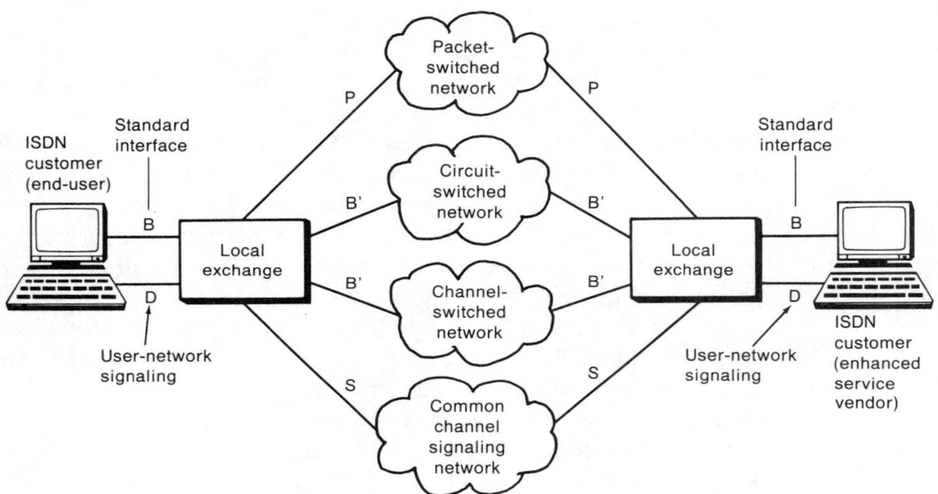

Figure 5-1. Overview of the ISDN architecture.

In ISDN, the local exchange can use any combination of transport and control resources to meet a customer's service needs. These resources include circuit-switched, packet-switched, and channel-switched (essentially private line) forms of transport and also message-oriented CCS for control. This is illustrated in Figure 5-1, where S denotes signaling information moved between network nodes by means of CCS, P denotes users' packet information and B′denotes users' circuit-switched or channel-switched information.

Access

ISDN initially provides two standard customer-network interfaces for the delivery of all network services: basic access or the basic rate interface (BRI) which provides the customer with up to 144 kb/s of information, and primary access or the primary rate interface (PRI) which provides the customer with up to

1.536 Mb/s of information. Both of these interfaces operate in a synchronous, full-duplex mode. This approach provides a single ISDN interface for each of the two most popular, currently deployed network access technologies.

BRI is intended for delivery over most existing two-wire, nonloaded loops. To enhance the quality of analog voice service on certain long loops, series inductors called load coils have been inserted at regularly spaced intervals. Such loading reduces the attenuation of a loop in the voice frequency band, but because it simultaneously causes a substantial increase in attenuation for frequencies in excess of 4,000 Hertz, loaded loops cannot effectively transmit the high frequencies used by digital loop electronics.

PRI is intended for delivery over T1 carrier systems which use four-wire transmission and digital repeaters spaced about one mile apart. As customer-network interfaces based upon fiber and digital radio become technologically attractive, the standardization of additional ISDN interfaces can be anticipated.

Some or all of the information-carrying capacity of a basic or primary access is provided to an ISDN user as various combinations of ISDN channels, illustrated in Figure 1 as B and D. The ISDN channels now defined and applicable in the United States are the B-channel (bearer) delivering 64 kb/s, the D-channel (delta, implying an incremental nature) delivering 16 kb/s for BRI and 64 kb/s for PRI, the H_0-channel (high-speed bearer) delivering 384 kb/s, and the H_{11}-channel delivering 1.536 Mb/s. The D-channel is used to carry signaling for the B-, H_0-, and H_{11}-channels, and is nearly always required by any ISDN user. The D-channel can also carry users' information in a message-oriented format.

Observe, with reference to Figure 5-1, that B-channels are able to carry the types of user information illustrated as B′ (that is, circuit-switched or channel-switched information) and as P (that is, packet-switched information). Similarly, a D-channel is able to carry user-network signaling information and the packet-switched user information illustrated as P. For the near term, the H_0- and H_{11}-channels would carry user information on a channel-switched basis.

Standards Recommendations

CCITT has provided standards recommendations for the customer-network interfaces that deliver basic or primary access. As shown in Figure 5-2, reference points labeled T, S, and R separate various functional groupings which either may represent distinct equipment units or be suitably combined into a single equipment unit. These reference points permit the use of both ISDN terminals (TE1) and, by means of a TA function, non-ISDN terminals (TE2). A PBX or LAN may or may not be present in a particular application. To facilitate the movement of a TE1 between T and S reference points of the same rate, CCITT recommendations for the physical, link, and network layers (which are layers 1, 2, and 3 of the OSI reference model) are the same for both the T and S reference points.

Let's summarize some significant CCITT recommendations for interfaces at the T and S reference points. Recommendation I.430, which defines the layer 1 protocol (essentially the physical and electrical characteristics) for basic access, specifies four-wire transmission operating at 192 kb/s in each direction. Of this

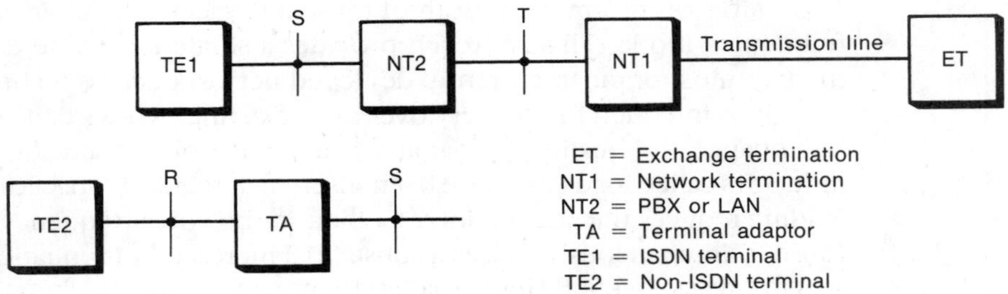

Figure 5-2. CCITT-defined reference points for a customer-network interface.

192 kb/s, 144 kb/s support two B-channels and one D-channel and the remaining 48 kb/s are available locally as overhead for functions such as framing and support of a passive bus. Recommendation I.431 defines layer 1 for primary access.

Recommendations Q.920 and Q.921 of CCITT's 1988 *Blue Book* (which update Recommendations I.440 and I.441 of CCITT's 1984 *Red Book*) define the layer 2 protocol for the D-channel of both basic and primary accesses. This layer 2 protocol, which is formally named the link access procedure on the D-channel (LAPD), resembles the high-level data link control (HDLC) protocol. Recommendations Q.930, Q.931 and Q.932 of CCITT's 1988 *Blue Book* (which update and expand upon Recommendations I.450 and I.451 of CCITT's 1984 *Red Book*) define the layer 3 protocol for the D-channel of both basic and primary accesses. This layer 3 protocol contains a number of messages for use in the control of calls and supplementary services. In CCITT's 1988 *Blue Book*, Recommendation Q.931 treats basic call control, and Recommendation Q.932 treats supplementary services.

The network termination (NT1), transmission line and portions of the exchange termination (ET) make up the transmission system that supports ISDN access. Particularly in the case of basic access, the technology for supporting full-duplex digital transmission at the required rate is quite new. Indeed the 144 kb/s rate of basic access is not a theoretical upper limit for rates achievable over a typical loop plant. Rather, this rate reflects a compromise between sufficient capacity to meet anticipated services needs and what was anticipated to be developable within a reasonable amount of time. In order to encourage innovation and independent development, CCITT has left unspecified the interface between the NT1 and ET.

There are some additional challenges concerning the realization of these interfaces in the United States. Figure 5-3 depicts the customer-network interface in terms of the previously mentioned functional groupings TE1, NT1 and ET, and introduces the reference point U. The NT1 provides functions associated with layer 1 of the OSI reference model including transmission line termination, line maintenance, timing, and powering, as well as those functions which are required to map the loop transmission format into the standard customer interface. Because many of the functions associated with the NT1 are layer 1 functions, they must occur within a limited distance from the customer's terminal equipment, and hence, must be incorporated in network channel terminating equipment (NCTE). However, the FCC has treated NCTE for ISDN as customer premises equipment (CPE). This implies that an interface standard must be established at this U reference point.

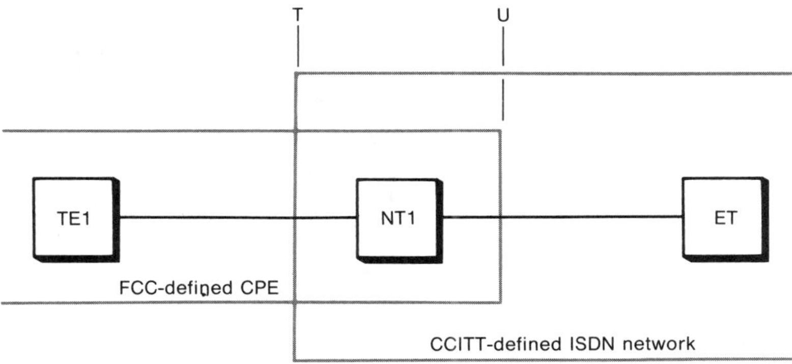

Figure 5-3. Reference points in the United States.

For basic access, the technology needed to provide digital transmission over two-wire loops is currently emerging. A substantial effort was begun during 1985 by the T1 committee accredited by ANSI to develop a U interface standard, and this effort produced a draft American national standard. Key elements of the advanced technology selected for this draft standard include an adaptive digital echo canceler, a 2B1Q line code, and overhead bits used for certain maintenance functions such as in-service performance monitoring. The result of studies made in support of this standards effort indicated that a wide-band hybrid working in conjunction with an adaptive digital echo canceler provided advantages over time-compression multiplexing, another digital line transmission technique that was considered. The 2B1Q line code designation means that two binary bits are encoded onto one quaternary or four-level symbol. This 2B1Q line code reduces by half the symbol rate on the transmission line, thereby lessening the attenuation which the signal must overcome.

Basic Access Architecture

The physical architecture for providing basic access is illustrated in Figure 5-4. For customers beyond the range of nonloaded loops, and potentially in other economical applications, digital loop carrier (DLC) will be used to deliver basic access. DLC applications are intended to support loops that conform to the present Carrier Serving Area (CSA) design rules. The use of deployed and future versions of DLC to support basic access appears technically feasible, and a number of choices are available concerning the relation between DLC bandwidth efficiency and DLC functionality for such applications.

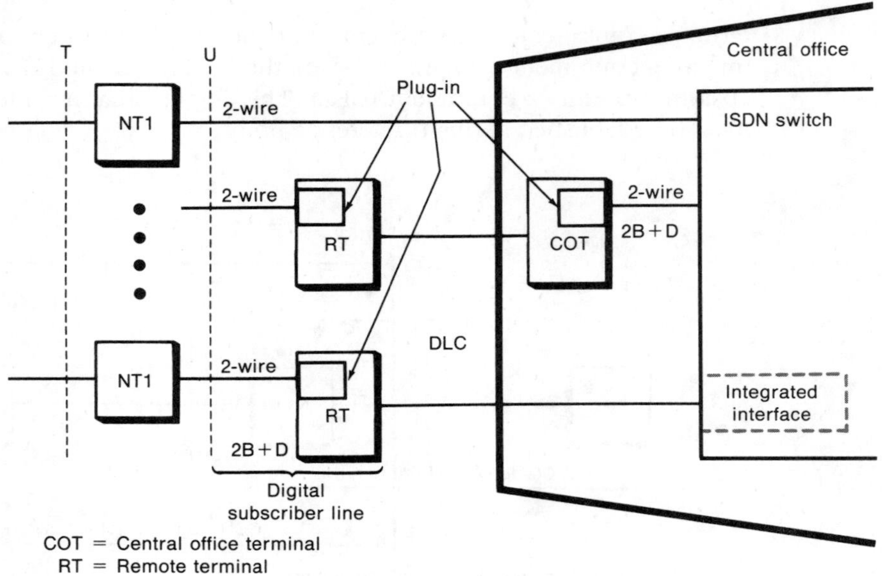

Figure 5-4. Architecture for ISDN basic access.

Switch and Interoffice

A focal point of the ISDN network architecture is the ISDN central office, which provides interfaces to the access network that delivers basic and primary access, and to the circuit-switched, packet-switched, channel-switched (dedicated line), interoffice signaling, and operations support networks. Figure 5-5 provides a view of the ISDN switch architecture. The ISDN central office contains an ISDN ET, which separates the channels provided by the basic and primary access lines and provides a D-Channel processing function to separate LAPD (layer 2 protocol) frames containing signaling information from those containing customer data.

LAPD frames, which can contain either user-network signaling information or customer data, are distinguished with respect to such content by means of a subfield in the layer 2 address of the LAPD protocol. This subfield is called the service access point identifier (SAPI) and has a length of 6 bits. (The total address consists of two bytes which contain this 6-bit SAPI, a 7-bit TEI subfield, a command/response bit, and one address-extension bit in each of the two bytes.) A SAPI value of 0 designates frames with signaling information, and a SAPI value of 16 designates frames with customer data information that is processed at layer 3 as packet data in accordance with the X.25 protocol.

Switched Networks

The ISDN ET provides control functions to

- process signaling information from each D channel

- exert control upon certain elements of the circuit-switched, packet-switched and channel-switched networks located within that ISDN central office
- pass information for network control and operations over the interoffice signaling and operations systems networks, respectively

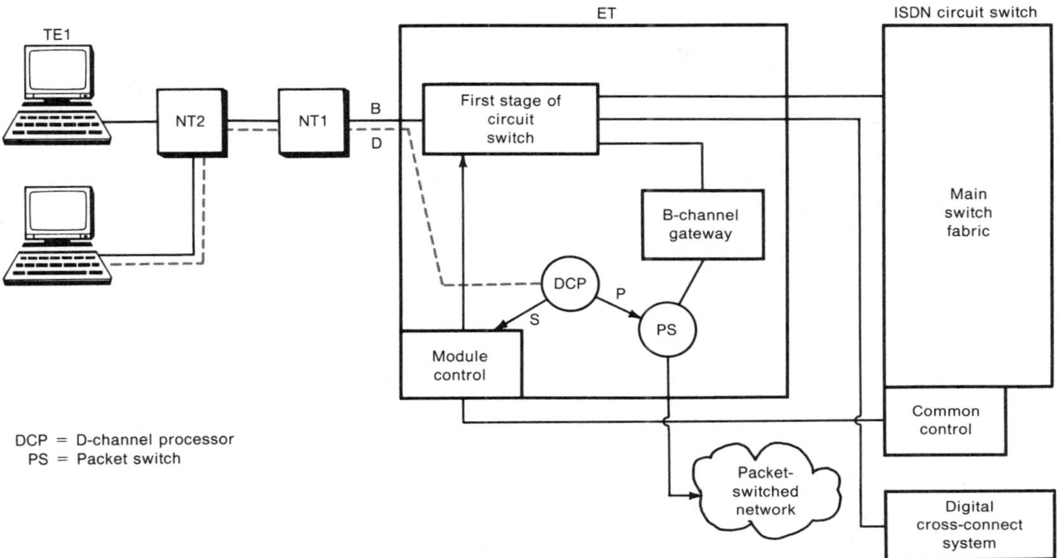

Figure 5-5. ISDN switch architecture.

The ISDN ET generally contains time-division switching fabric for supporting circuit-switched services and, through some form of "nail-up" arrangement, access to channel-switched services. In Figure 5-4, a Digital Cross-Connect System is shown as a means for mechanizing the establishment of cross-connects for private line services—referred to here as channel-switched services. The ET also contains or provides access to functions needed for packet-switched services such as packet assemble, packet routing, and interfacing with external packet switches.

The synchronization required to support the ET will be provided by every ISDN central office through its Building Integrated Timing Supply, which receives a reference for interoffice synchronization in accordance with one of the alternatives provided by the ISDN synchronization plan. This plan is essentially an extension of the plan now used to synchronize time-division switches.

Interoffice Signaling Transmission

For interoffice signaling, ISDN uses the CCS network currently being deployed. This CCS network uses the Signaling System Number 7 protocol recommended by CCITT. This protocol provides a very high degree of reliability and accuracy, and it also possesses considerable flexibility for the subsequent addition of new features to support future network and service needs.

CCITT Recommendation I.211 suggests that 64 kb/s clear channel capability (64 CCC) be available through ISDN's circuit-switched and channel-switched networks and also recognizes the 64 kb/s restricted capability, in which a customer is restricted from sending an all-zeros byte. The ISDN access network can initially support 64 CCC. The draft American national standard for the DSL's U interface incorporates this feature.

Existing T1 carrier systems that are used to provide primary access or interoffice transmission for ISDN may require modification of their terminal equipment in order to deal with long strings of zeros*. A recommended method is Binary 8 Zero Substitution (B8ZS). With this method, a string of eight consecutive zeros is replaced by a distinctive pattern that includes bipolar violations (variations from the normal pattern of alternating voltage polarities for adjacent 1 bits normally used in T1 carrier's bipolar signal) so that the substitution may be detected at the far end where the original signal is to be recovered. Such attention to the needs of 64 CCC is required for both the distribution and interoffice plant. Since most of the fiber-based transmission systems now used extensively for interoffice transmission employ some form of BnZS or equivalent technique, they meet the needs of 64 CCC.

The numbering plan developed for ISDNs in North America is consistent with CCITT Recommendation E.164, and is intended to be incorporated into the current North American Numbering Plan. A ten-digit format will be retained for ISDN subscriber numbers assigned by network providers now using the North American Numbering Plan.

Service

Perhaps the single most important point relating to services and ISDN is that ISDN is not a service. ISDN provides a network which supports a wide range of services. The basic and primary accesses of ISDN permit the simultaneous provision of a wide range of network services, both existing and new, and network features internal to ISDN also permit easy changes to the service mix so provided.

For large business customers, the bearer channels of ISDN can initially support improved Centrex-based services, dedicated line and switched special services, and improved PBX-based services. These services include both the existing services offered today and integrated voice, data and (initially slow speed) video services. In addition, the out-of-band signaling feature of ISDN's access network, together with the use of service systems internal to ISDN, can support improved custom local area signaling services and customer-controlled circuit reconfiguration services.

An extended need of the large business customer is the ability to permit employees to "work anywhere," that is, to access from the home or temporary

*To maintain the proper timing of its line repeaters, T1 carrier systems generally have a requirement that no more than 15 consecutive zeros be transmitted. This requirement is easily met by the properties of PCM voice, but it can be violated by an arbitrary data stream. Some newer types of T1 repeaters may have greater tolerance to strings of consecutive zeros.

office those same telecommunications services which are available in the regular workplace. This need can be expected to accelerate the introduction of ISDN access for small business and residence customers.

It has generally been necessary for any new network capability to interwork with the existing network capabilities. Existing services provided to a customer with ISDN access must interwork with those same services provided to a customer with non-ISDN access. The impact of such interworking on each customer's perception of service should be minimal. ISDN must interwork with the existing network capabilities that support circuit-switched and private line voice services, as well as packet-switched, circuit-switched and private line data services. This planned interworking will be realized through use of the functionality provided within ISDN, with minimal modification of the existing network other than that required by deployment of ISDN equipment.

Performance

Network performance plans consider the impact on service quality of various network impairments, establish an end-to-end performance objective for each impairment, and allocate those objectives to appropriate network segments. Current work on ISDN performance focuses on two broad categories of ISDN services, namely those using circuit-switched or channel-switched capabilities, and those using packet-switched capabilities. The integration of circuit-switched and packet-switched capabilities, made possible with a subsequent generation of switching technology, requires a new perspective on ISDN performance. Also, performance issues associated with signaling-based services may need consideration as operating experience with those services accumulates.

For services based on ISDN's circuit-switched and channel-switched capabilities, the pertinent performance parameters are transmission impairments of several types, call-setup and call-clearing delays, blocking, availability and cut-off calls. The impairments affecting digital transmission performance are digital (or bit) errors, slips, misframes, phase jitter and propagation delay. The previously cited transmission impairments also influence packet-switched service performance, though the manner of impact is somewhat different. Use of the error-detecting and packet-retransmitting features available in most packet-oriented protocols will effectively translate digital errors into additional time delay, due to retransmission of packets in which errors have been detected. Additional performance parameters that influence the perceived quality of these services include packet-queueing delay and accuracy of packets delivered.

The impact of a particular performance parameter on customer perceptions of service quality can depend to a great extent upon the type of service, e.g., voice or nonvoice. Hence, one of the larger challenges in ISDN performance planning is defining acceptable performance requirements for the ISDN integrated access facility.

The functionality provided in ISDN has the potential for supporting multiple grades of performance parameters, thereby making multiple grades of service with multiple pricing levels technically possible. As one example, a customer may request that a bearer channel be maintained to different levels of a digital error measure, depending on whether the customer uses that channel to carry voice, data, or video information, or otherwise depending on customer choice. Another example would be different levels of availability selected by customer choice. The in-service performance monitoring functions planned for maintenance of the access and interoffice transmission portions of ISDN, together with certain other functions provided by operations systems and service systems, can support multiple grades of service. The out-of-band signaling feature of ISDN's access network allows the customer to request different grades of performance without intervention by operating company personnel.

Operations

Just as the challenge to the ISDN architecture planners is to evolve the network in an upward compatible fashion toward an integrated network capability, the challenge to the operations planners is to evolve the operations systems toward a more integrated structure. A 1990's view of operations for a mature ISDN serving area has been developed at Bellcore and is serving as a target for operations planning in support of the initial ISDN implementations of various BOCs.

With early ISDN implementations, service provisioning to initially establish ISDN's basic access requires a determination of whether a customer is served by a qualified distribution facility. If so, the service order can be completed without special loop conditioning. The draft American national standard for the basic access U interface is intended to operate over nearly all nonloaded loops up to a maximum range of 18 kilofeet so that a preponderant majority of nonloaded loops becomes qualified. This will substantially simplify the provisioning process for basic access. For primary access, provisioning will require a distribution facility, such as a T1 carrier system, which is capable of handling a DS-1 (digital signal number one).

Augmenting or changing the service mix provided through an established basic or primary access is significantly less labor-intensive than for like changes to services provided through non-ISDN access. Appropriate bearer channels for a customer's desired service mix are enabled (or disabled) at the ISDN switch under software control, and linkages to appropriate service systems are also established (or disestablished) under software control. While operating company personnel may generally be involved in applying these software controls during the initial deployment of ISDN, the out-of-band signaling feature of ISDN's access can allow the customer to exert such controls without intervention by operating company personnel. Spare capacity of bearer channels in DLC systems and remote access arrangements would have to be traffic-engineered to support such operation. Also, tariff issues related to such operation would require attention.

ISDN will support in a standardized manner many services, such as various private line services, off-premises stations and remote exchange lines, which are now considered special services.

Network maintenance in ISDN makes use of new, in-service performance monitoring and surveillance functions, which are made economically attractive by emerging technology and should significantly reduce operating expense. Performance monitoring, based upon CRC techniques, will be used on transmission facilities in both the access and interoffice portions of ISDN, and, together with appropriate memory and processing functions, can indicate any problem that exists or has existed during a previous time period. The draft American national standard for the basic access U interface incorporates such CRC-based, in-service performance monitoring. T1 carrier systems used for primary access and for interoffice transmission employ a similar CRC-based, in-service performance monitoring feature based upon the extended superframe format, which extends the superframe structure from the current 12 to a new value of 24 193-bit frames (containing 4,632 bits). It divides the 8 kb/s channel derived from the 193rd bit position into subchannels used for framing, for a CRC, and for the communication of various alarm and performance data. Maintenance with the help of in-service performance monitoring should significantly reduce the need for demand and periodic testing and, in cases where an operating company so desires, can also identify performance degradations before they affect service.

A Look at the Future

ISDN provides a strong telecommunications infrastructure for public telecommunications networks, guiding the coherent introduction of new technology and supporting all network services. Because of its public network orientation, the benefits of ISDN will reach out to all members of society with a cost-effective, state-of-the-art telecommunications capability.

During the near and intermediate term, it is reasonable to anticipate that the functions and features of the initial ISDN implementations will expand to include all of the key items described so far. Digital loop electronics to implement the standard U interface will be deployed when they become available. Connectionless services may have customer appeal, and procedures could be defined to implement them over ISDN's D-channel.

In the longer term, two fundamental trends in telecommunications network technology are significant. First, the technologies of synchronous multiplexing, single-mode fiber transmission, and improved capabilities for the processing of high-rate bit streams together have the potential for some dramatic innovations. The planning focus for using such technologies can be called broadband ISDN. Second, the increased use of processing functionality throughout a modern telecommunications network will be used to automate operations more fully and also to provide new services based on improved network management and control. The planning focus for using such technologies will be the Intelligent Network.

Synchronous multiplexing of high-rate digital signals is a promising technology with significant implications for both transmission and switching systems. This technology provides substantial advantages in terms of simplicity and flexibility over the earlier asynchronous multiplexing methods which, for rates above the 1.544 Mb/s of T1 carrier systems, rely upon bit-stuffing techniques to maintain proper timing relations between transmission line signals and multiplex equipment.

The low-loss feature of single-mode fiber permits the repeaterless transmission of very high rates over most loop distances. For such distances, rates in the order of 600 Mb/s now appear quite feasible, and, pending further study, rates in excess of 2 Gb/s may also be attractive. Serial bit-stream processing technology is quite significant for the equipment at network nodes that must handle the high-rate bit-streams delivered by single-mode fiber. Observe that serial processing at high rates generally tends to favor simple operations, while more complex processing is done after parallel conversion to lower rates. Hence, some examination of the protocols supported by such processing techniques appears to be needed.

ISDN today can be characterized as providing integrated access, that is, a standardized access which supports all services. With the next generations of technologies, it may become feasible to characterize the future broadband ISDN as providing an integrated network. Observe in Figure 5-1 that behind ISDN's integrated access, there are a number of specialized subnetworks—packet-switched, circuit-switched, channel-switched and signaling. The replacement of these specialized subnetworks with a unified technology would constitute an integrated network. Considerable work remains in developing a better understanding of the technical feasibility and economic desirability of this concept.

ISDN is an architecture which supports varied implementation strategies, based upon the specific needs of a particular operating company. In response to existing and emerging services, as well as to rapid advances in technology, ISDN offers an economical network architecture for serving both voice and nonvoice traffic. With its strong reliance on standards, the ISDN will take maximum advantage of the benefits deriving from standardized interfaces for integrated services access. ISDN will provide a network which meets current and future needs by providing a flexible, multiservice capability. It will minimize costs by utilizing state-of-the-art technology, while at the same time building upon the strengths of currently deployed network equipment.

References

Bell Communications Research. 1986. ISDN System Planning Considerations. Science and Technology Series, ST-NPL-000002.

CCITT. 1985. Integrated Services Digital Network (ISDN). Recommendations of the Series I. *Red Book III*. Fascicle III.5, Geneva.

———. 1989. Digital access signalling system. Recommendations of the Series Q. *Blue Book*. To appear.

Chapter 6

Transmission in ISDN

Syed V. Ahamed
Victor B. Lawrence

Chapter 6

DIGITAL SWITCHING AND DIGITAL TRANSMISSION ARE TWO important technologies that laid the foundation for the IDN in the late 1970s to mid-1980s. Analog voice or voice band data signals from customer premises transported over the local loop are digitized at the central office (as shown in Figure 6-1) using either PCM at 64 kb/s or adaptive differential pulse code modulation (ADPCM) at 32 kb/s. The digitized signals are time-division multiplexed to form 1.544 Mb/s data (conforming to the standard T1 carrier signal in the U.S.) or 2.048 Mb/s (conforming to the European CEPT hierarchy). Digital switching and transmission at the higher multiplexed rate occurs throughout the network. Analog-to-digital and digital-to-analog decoding occurs at the edges of the network so that analog signals can be used for voice communication.

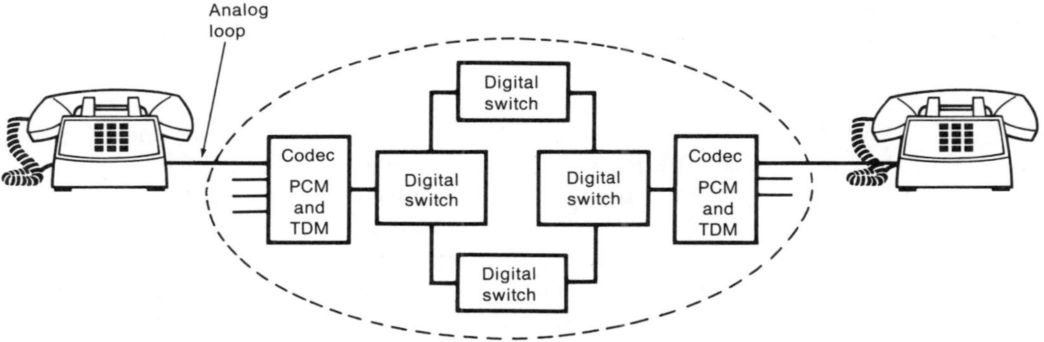

Figure 6-1. Integrated digital network.

The next important technically challenging step is to extend the digitization to the local loop to provide varieties of new digital services to the customer. The ISDN (Figure 6-2) offers end-to-end digital connectivity between customers. Telephones and other data terminals are connected to the network through the digital subscriber line and to the central office where signals are demultiplexed and switched. The digitization of the local subscriber loop provides full-duplex digital transmission at speeds of 192 kb/s over the two-wire twisted pair that was traditionally used to provide band-limited 4 kHz analog voice or voice band data.

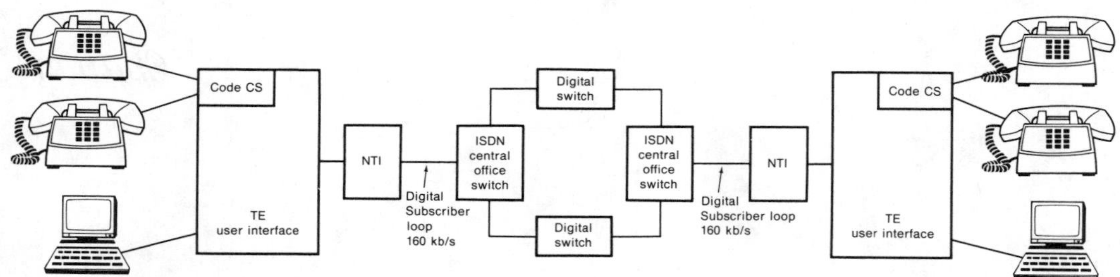

Figure 6-2. ISDN network.

The Subscriber Loop Plant

Figures 6-3 to 6-6 show different variations of the subscriber network. Figure 6-3 shows the physical configuration of the subscriber loop. A star-tree topology of several types of copper wires with different lengths and diameters in cables is installed overhead on poles or buried underground in ducts. The wires taper off gradually as they progress radially from the central office to the customer premises. The wires are taped to form carrier serving areas as shown. The size of the cables from the central office tapers because of the branching in both the feeder and the distribution. The distance from the customer premises to the central office ranges from a few hundred meters to about 40 kM.

Figure 6-4 shows the star-tree transmission media and electronic apparatus (repeaters and multiplexers) that interface between the feeders and distribution and the interconnections between drops in the distribution cable to the individual customer's premises. This figure also shows the role of the main distribution frame at the central office that connects customers' loops to various services within and out of the central office. From the pedestal to the customer, the pairs are dedicated and relatively inexpensive. Generally, enough pairs are installed to meet future needs. From the distribution to the feeder, the number of pairs per customer is fewer. The tapping of the wires produces *bridged taps* which allow parallel connections. In certain cases, there may be bridged taps on branches that have already been bridged. Bridged taps increase the flexibility of customer connections, because they allow the same line to be connected to customers in different geographical areas. However, when subscribers are connected, the other parallel paths remain open-circuited except for party lines. Figure 6-5 shows the architecture and use of fiber in the feeder and Figure 6-6 shows the transition to fiber in the distribution.

Characteristics

The subscriber loops in the predivestiture Bell System have been surveyed three times for their important physical and electrical characteristics. The first survey

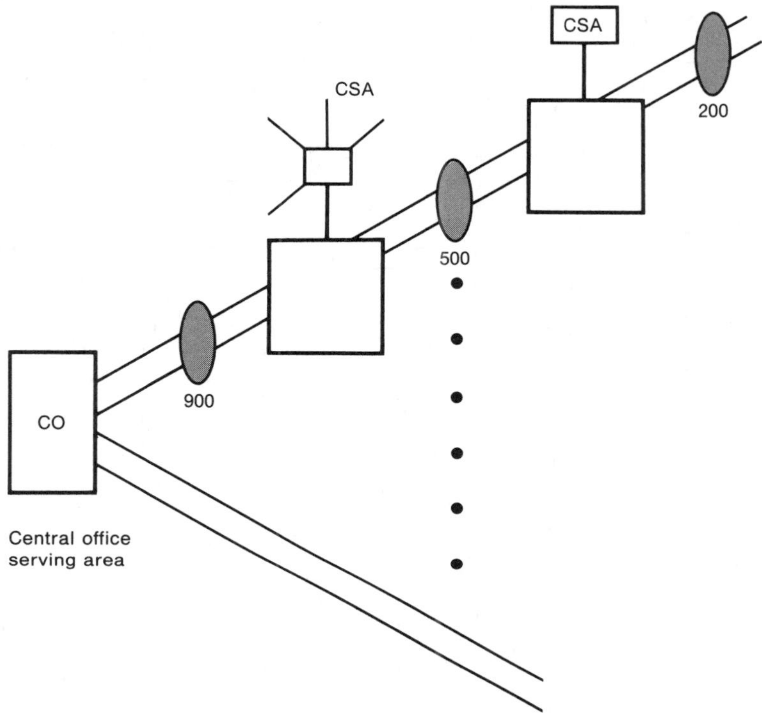

Figure 6-3. Subscriber network star-tree topology.

(Gresh 1969), focusing on the physical and audio frequency characteristics, was undertaken in 1964. The initial intent of the second survey (Manhire 1978), undertaken in 1973, was to update the earlier results and report any major changes. However, during the late seventies, the study of the loop plant in view of the high-speed subscriber digital lines became essential. The primary object of this investigation was to evaluate the potential of the plant to carry data in the range of 64 to 384 kb/s. The results (Ahamed 1982a), published in 1982, established the high-speed digital capabilities and the limitations of the American loop plant.

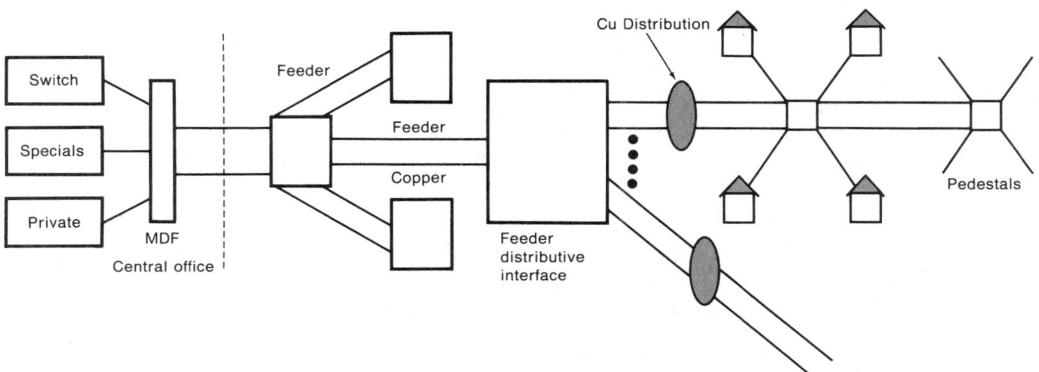

Figure 6-4. Subscriber network star-tree transmission media.

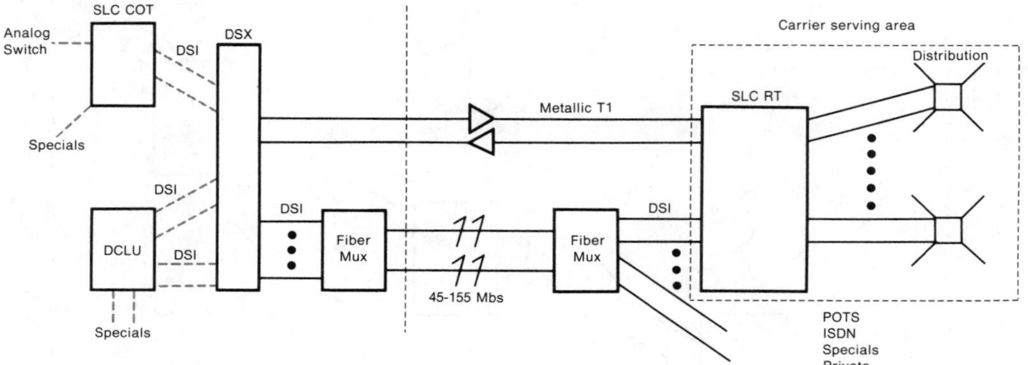

Figure 6-5. Fiber feeder and carrier.

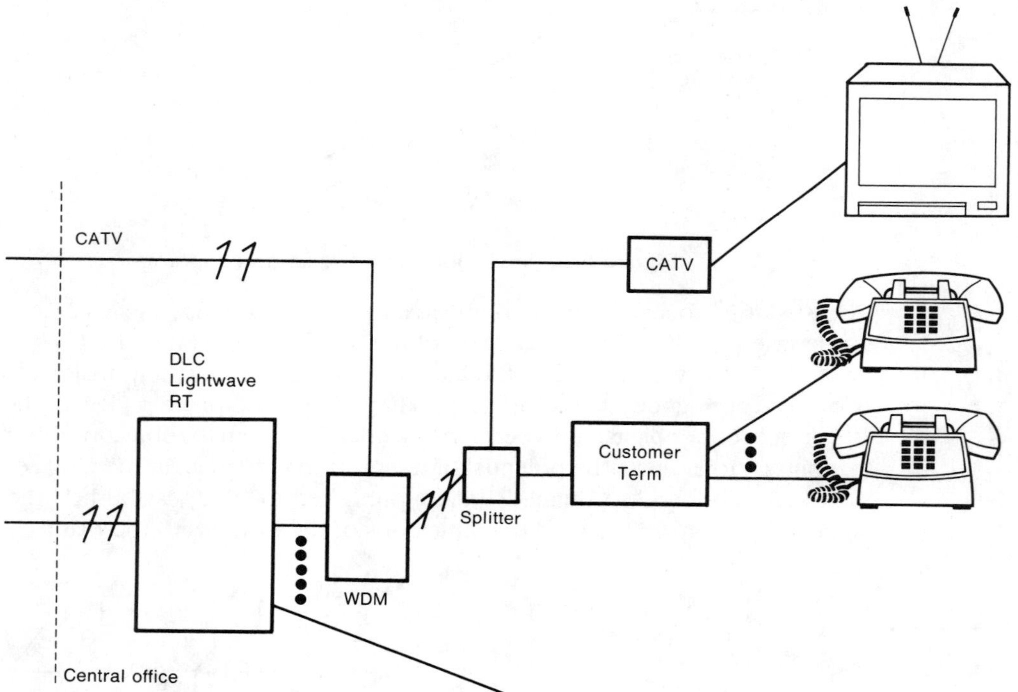

Figure 6-6. Fiber distribution.

The third survey (Bell Communications Research 1987) was undertaken in 1983 with the intent of updating the earlier results and also characterizing the American loop plant with respect to the Basic-rate ISDN services and high-speed data communication from central office to the carrier serving centers. In the next two sections, we explore the results (Ahamed and Singh 1986, Lechlieder and McDonald 1986) from this last and perhaps most exhaustive survey of the predivestiture Bell System.

Physical Characteristics

The 1983 Loop Survey presents a cross section of all the loops that may be expected to carry the data traffic. The mean length of the loops surveyed is about 3.29 km and the mean bridged tap length is 0.57 km. The presence of loading coils beyond 5.48 km (18,000′) makes the longer loops unsuitable for Basic-rate repeaterless ISDN data transmission.

Out of the 2,290 loops investigated in this survey, about 34 percent have loading coils, are longer than 18,000 ft (5.486 km), have nonstandard cable sections, or are otherwise unsuitable for ISDN data transmission. After eliminating those loops, about 66 percent (1,520) of the entire loop population surveyed constitutes the truncated data base over which the digital data transmission is readily feasible. Twenty-four percent of the 2,290 loops surveyed had load coils to selectively strengthen the audio frequency signal in the voice frequency applications, thus rendering them unsuitable for the ISDN considerations. Only 10 percent of these nonloaded loops were longer than 4.57 km (15,000′), and only 10 percent had bridged taps longer than 0.91 km (3,000′). About 50 percent of the loaded loops were shorter than 5.48 km (18,000′), partially because of voice special services and/or errors caused when the working length was reduced from over 5.48 km while rearranging the cable sections for new customers.

Four dominant wire sizes are used. The finest diameter wire generally encountered is #26 American Wire gauge (AWG) and is roughly equivalent to the 0.4039 mm wire used in European countries. The coarse wire is #19 AWG with a diameter of 0.9119 mm. The two intermediate wire sizes used in the loop plant are #24 (0.5105 mm) and #22 (0.6426 mm) AWG.

About 45 percent of the ISDN loops under 5.48 km (18,000′) in the 1983 survey have a working length less than 1.83 km (6,000′); 65 percent of the loops have a working length less than 2.74 km (9,000′); 82 percent are less than 3.65 km (12,000′); and 95 percent are under 4.57 km (15,000′). Shorter loops have the finer #26 AWG PVC cable. Longer loops tend to have more sections of the cable with coarser wire sizes (#24, #22, and #19). The #19 AWG has an insignificant proportion in the ISDN loops, even though the #24 and #22 AWG cables tend to have equal proportions at about 43 percent in the loops at 5.33 km (17,500′). At this loop length, the #26 and #19 AWG cable share the remaining 14 percent equally.

Electrical Characteristics

Enhanced transmission rates envisioned for the Basic-rate ISDN services can range from 144 kb/s to 400 kb/s. The mode of transmission (TCM or AEC) influences line rate. The line code influences the actual symbol rate. Thus, the range of frequencies at which loop plant characteristics become significant depends upon the mode and the code chosen for this application. In the U.S., where the RBOCs have chosen the 2B1Q code for the Basic-rate access, the range of spectral interest falls between dc (direct current) to about 80 kHz. The loop plant has to be investigated in view of the national and need characteristics of the particular environment. Codes, rates, and access methodologies have to be individually tailored to the specific region (or country) under consideration.

In the U.S., subscriber loop system studies have been undertaken and a summary of results presented here are derived from the data of the predivestiture Bell System. Three frequencies chosen to span the spectral band are 40, 60, and 80 kHz. Ninety percent of the loops display signal attenuation under 33, 37, and 40 db loss at the respective frequencies. Ninety-five percent of the loops have signal attenuations less than 35, 40, and 43 db at 40, 60, and 80 kHz. The mean loss of the 45 percent (i.e., <1.83 km), 65 percent (i.e., <2.74 km), 82 percent (i.e., <3.65 km), 95 percent (i.e., <4.57 km) and 100 percent of the nonloaded ISDN loops is about 11.4, 15.1, 18.6, 21.1, and 22.2 db at 80 kHz, respectively. Ninety percent of the ISDN loops under 1.83 km, under 2.74 km, under 3.65 km, under 4.57 km, and under 5.49 km, display a loss of 18, 25, 33, 37, and 40 db at 80 kHz, respectively.

These losses indicate the dynamic range for the line equalization device required of the line termination equipment at the U interface (discussed later in this chapter in the section entitled "Transmission Requirements"). They also indicate the loss in the signal strength as it travels to and from the ISDN customers. These losses have to be interpreted in conjunction with the *crosstalk* and *impulse noise* characteristics inherent in the loop plant. Highly attenuated signals resulting from longer loops and higher bit rates become prone to inaccurate and noisy signal transmission.

Impairments in the Digital Subscriber Loops

The sources of impairments for the transmission of data in the digital subscriber loops arise from the electrical and physical nature of the subscriber network. First, consider the electrical nature. The grouping and collection of twisted wire pairs causes two major impairments; crosstalk and impulse noise. The imperfection of the signal recovery at the receiver is caused by echoes and *intersymbol interference (ISI)*. Next, the physical nature of the network, i.e., the presence of cable discontinuities, bridged taps, imperfect line conditions, etc., discussed in the last section causes severe *attenuation, dispersion*, and echo conditions. Data recovery from the highly variable and nonideal loop plant becomes a major limitation for the range and the rate at which ISDN data can be accurately transmitted. Each of these limitations is discussed next.

Crosstalk

Crosstalk is perhaps the most significant limitation in the digital subscriber loop. Caused by the capacitive coupling of the signal of one wire pair to another, the amplitude distribution of crosstalk noise is modeled with a Gaussian (normal) distribution when the number of crosstalk interferences is large. In this case, the power spectral density is not flat and is dependent on the power transfer function of the crosstalk coupling and the transmitted signal power spectrum.

There are two kinds of crosstalk: *near-end crosstalk (NEXT)* and *far-end crosstalk (FEXT)*. They are shown in Figure 6-7. FEXT (Figure 6-7B) suffers the same channel loss as the signal but NEXT (Figure 6-7A) does not. Therefore, in the situation where the signals are traveling in both directions within the same cable, such as DSL, NEXT will be much greater than FEXT. As has been reported, NEXT increases at a rate of 4.5 db/octave ($f^{3/2}$) while FEXT increased by 6 db/octave (f^2) (AT&T Bell Laboratories 1982).

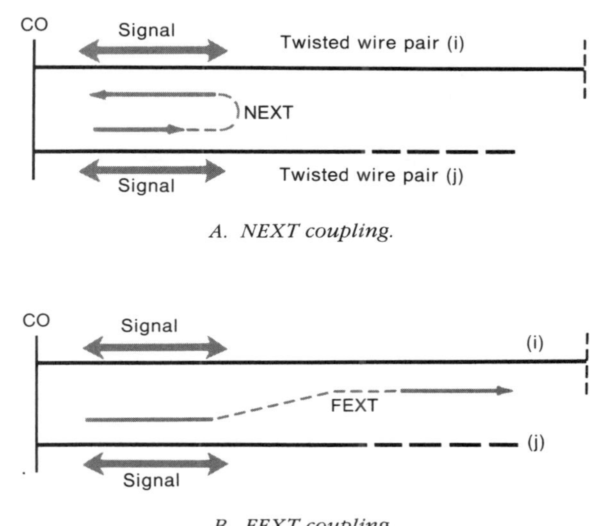

A. NEXT coupling.

B. FEXT coupling.

Figure 6-7. NEXT and FEXT crosstalk paths in cables.

It has also been shown that, with linear equalization, the NEXT power is the integral of the received signal power spectrum weighted by the function $f^{3/2}/|C(f)|^2$, whose gain increases with frequency at a rate higher than $f^{3/2}$ due to the low-pass nature of the channel frequency response C(f). Therefore, to reduce NEXT, one must design the system so that the received signal has as little power at high frequencies as possible.

Impulse Noise

Impulse noise is characterized by infrequent high amplitude bursts of noise and is generally evaluated by the number of events per unit time instead of its statistical distribution. Most of the time, it is caused by central office switching, transients, and lightning. Impulse noise can corrupt the signal beyond recognition. Interleaved block error correction code (Ahamed 1984) can prevent noise interruption in reception. Accurate characterization of the noise may be used in designing error-correcting codes.

Echoes

Figure 6-8 shows a simplified model of a hybrid transformer. If Z_b is matched to the channel impedance Z_L, the receiver will be isolated from the transmitter. However, the complete isolation of the receiver from the transmitter requires that Z_b be matched to the channel impedance Z_L at all frequencies, which is not possible. In practical situations, variations in cable impedances with frequency are strongest at lower frequencies and the impedance matching is better at higher frequencies. A hybrid transformer normally provides better echo attenuation at higher frequencies than at lower frequencies, resulting in relatively large echo power at low frequencies. This explains why echo pulses tend to have long tails. An *echo canceler (EC)* is used to cancel unwanted echo. The hybrid transormer will normally provide about 10 db loss. For example, the desired far-end signal-to-echo noise ratio (SNR) at the receiver is −30 db for a 40 db channel attenuation. To provide 25 db SNR, 55 db echo cancellation is required.

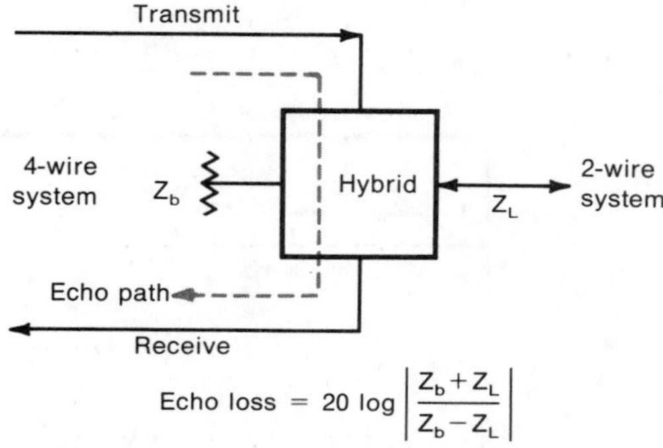

$$\text{Echo loss} = 20 \log \left| \frac{Z_b + Z_L}{Z_b - Z_L} \right|$$

Figure 6-8. A simplified hybrid model.

Since echo power is high at low frequencies, a high-pass filter can be added into the echo path. This will improve SNR if the 3 db frequency of the high-pass filter is well chosen. An optimum filter that minimizes the mean-square error can also be found if the channel response is known. The improvement in SNR can reduce the requirements on the EC and a high-pass filter can also reduce the length of the echo path impulse response. This is beneficial because the number of EC taps required depends directly on the length of echo path impulse response.

Bridged Taps

As we discussed at the beginning of this chapter, some subscriber loops have bridged taps, open-circuited wire pairs tapped onto the main wire pairs. The presence of the bridged taps affects the frequency response of the cable, and, as a result, distorts the pulses. The effect of bridged taps is discussed in more detail in later sections.

Intersymbol Interference

For band-limited linear channels with frequency dependent attenuation and delay, pulses are dispersed and span several baud periods, which interferes with other pulses. This effect is known as intersymbol interference (ISI). One useful graphical representation of a data signal that allows immediate evaluation of the amount of ISI is an eye diagram (see Figure 6-9). A large vertical open eye implies a small ISI, which corresponds to a large noise margin for the receiver decision device.

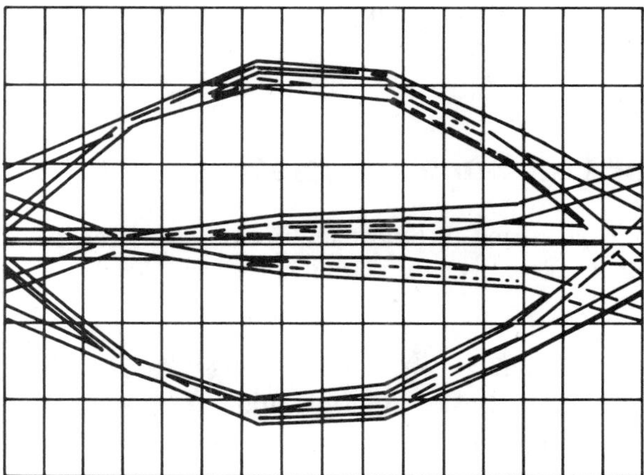

Figure 6-9. An eye diagram in the presence of ISI.

Important information also obtained from an eye diagram is the sensitivity of error probability of the system to timing jitter. This is related to the horizontal eye opening. The wider the horizontal eye opening, the better immunity the system will have to sampling phase and timing jitter.

The criterion for zero ISI is called the *Nyquist criterion*. The minimum bandwidth required to meet the Nyquist criterion is one half the baudrate. In practical designs, excess bandwidth is required. The larger the excess bandwidth, the wider the horizontal eye opening. In fact, as the excess bandwidth increases, the impulse response decays more rapidly, resulting in less ISI. Two factors must be considered to determine the amount of excess bandwidth required for a particular system: the effects of excess bandwidth on the design of the timing recovery circuit and noise penetration. First, it is clear that the timing recovery is more critical for narrow horizontal eye openings than for wide openings. The excess bandwidth has to be large enough to give a sufficiently wide horizontal eye opening so the system can achieve the required performance in error probability. The following factors should be considered when adjusting excess bandwidth:

- timing recovery technique
- steady-state sampling phase (may not be at the maximum of the eye)
- timing jitter variance

For a given excess bandwidth, the sampling phase has to fall within a certain range to achieve the required SNR. This gives the restriction to the steady-state sampling phase as well as the maximum allowable timing jitter. Secondly, wider excess bandwidth generally implies more noise penetration into the system. Recall that the NEXT, one of the dominant impairments, has a power spectrum that increases rapidly as frequency increases. An increase in the excess of bandwidth thus increases the noise power rapidly.

Up to this point, we have concentrated on the design of systems which give zero ISI. If we allow a controlled amount of ISI, *partial response signaling* (another class of signaling) may be considered. This extra degree of freedom will be useful in designing more efficient systems and the controlled ISI can still be removed eventually.

Provision for Full-Duplex Operation

There are four different techniques that can be used to achieve full-duplex transmission over the digital subscriber loop:

- space division multiplexing
- frequency-division multiplexing
- time-division multiplexing
- echo cancellation

The space division multiplexing approach uses four wires (AT&T Bell Laboratories 1982). Different physical wires are used for the two directions of transmission, and this mode of operation is overly wasteful of cable resources already invested in the network.

The frequency division multiplexing (FDM) approach is a well-understood technique. The loop bandwidth is split into two bands of frequency for the two directions of transmission, as shown in Figure 6-10. The directional isolation is achieved by spectral filtering.

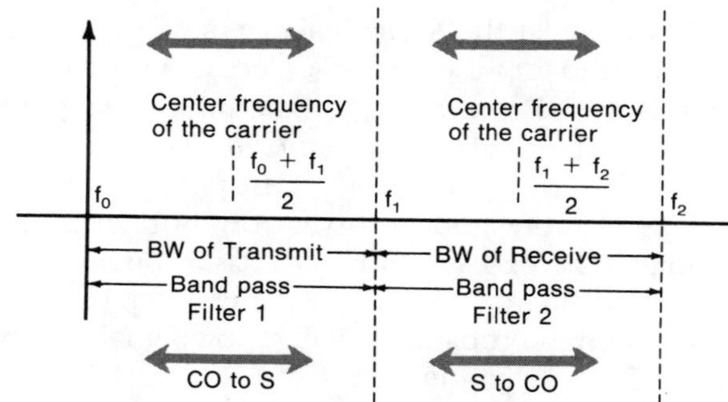

Figure 6-10. An FDM technique for separation of the transmit and receive signals.

An advantage of the FDM approach is that the effect of near-end crosstalk is minimized because the transmitted and received signal spectra are separated.

However, in practical systems, the available bandwidth is less than half the loop bandwidth and consequently restricts the rate at which signal elements can be transmitted. The lower signaling rate requires, for a given bit rate, an increase in the number of bits per signal element. This increase reduces immunity of the line signal to noise and other impairments.

In the burst mode or Time Compression Multiplexing System (TCM) (Ahamed, Bohn, and Gottfried 1981; Bosik and Kartalopoulos 1982), the intervals of transmission and reception are isolated in time as shown in Figure 6-11. The information is stored in the form of blocks of bits and sent alternately in each direction in the time interval allocated (Figure 6-11A). The transmit and receive signals do not overlap and are distinguished at each end. A time diagram for the burst-mode time compression system is shown in Figure 6-11B. A uniform rate of information from the source is stored in buffers in the transmitter and transmitted in a bursty form at a rate higher than twice the information rate. At the receiving end, bursty data from the line is received into buffers and then emptied out uniformly. Pipelining is introduced (Ahamed 1982b) so that the first bit does not delay waiting for the last bit before transmission on the line. Due to the propagation delay present in the loop, a guard time is provided between bursts and therefore the line rate during bursts is higher than twice the data rate. For Basic-rate access, a practical burst rate is 384 kb/s. The number of bits per burst depends on two factors. Very long blocks require fewer alternations and hence reduce the overall effect of propagation delay. However, very long blocks are undesirable for voice traffic because this introduces longer signal delays which produce degradation in speech quality. If all the transmitted signals emanating from the central office over all pairs in a cable bundle are synchronized, near-end crosstalk is eliminated because the received signals occur in a different distinct time interval.

The fourth method is the echo cancellation technique (Agazzi, Hodges, and Messerschmidt 1982; Werner 1984; Miller and Ahamed 1987). In Figure 6-12, we show a typical subscriber loop connection using echo cancellation with emphasis on the four-wire to two-wire conversion. Remember, the four-wire to two-wire conversion within the subscriber terminal and at the central office is provided by a hybrid circuit. Ideally, the hybrid circuit should uncouple the transmission paths of the transmitted and received signals. Unfortunately, because of various impedance mismatches, hybrids are generally not properly balanced. As a result, a part of the transmitted signal will leak into its own receiver. The power of this leakage can be several orders of magnitude larger than the desired received signal. Similarly, at bridged taps, some of the signals will be reflected back and will appear as a far echo which will generally be smaller.

The echoes appear as interference at the receiver's input. To achieve reliable full-duplex two-wire transmission, the echo(s) and the desired signals must, in some manner, be isolated from each other. This is achieved by using echo cancellation while permitting the use of the full bandwidth of the loop.

Echo Cancellation

Echos are a part of the transmitted signal being returned to the sender. The effect of any discontinuity is a reflection. Remember, the subscriber loop plant

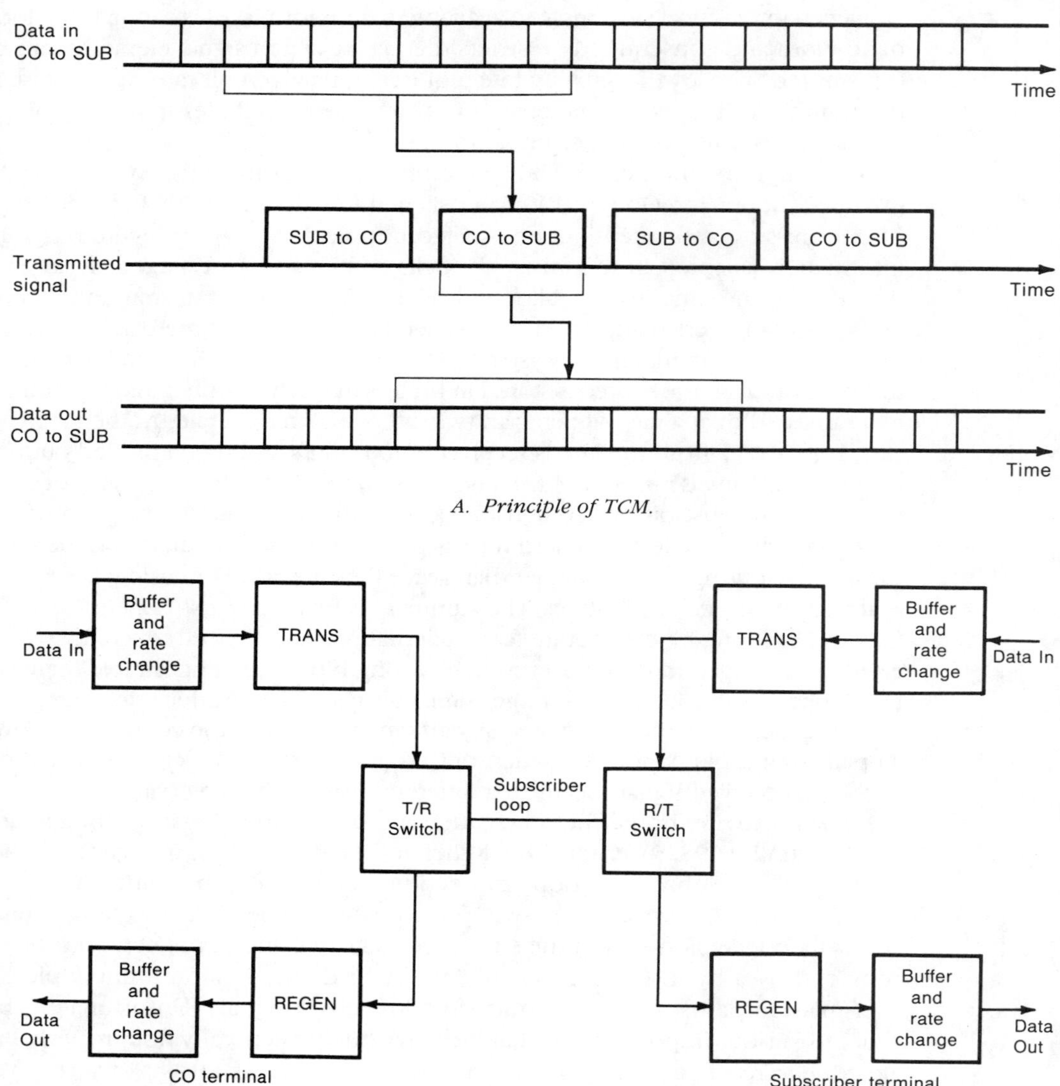

A. Principle of TCM.

B. Implementation of the TCM principle.

Figure 6-11. TCM for the transmission of bidirectional ISDN data.

is an extremely nonhomogeneous environment for the echo-free transmission of any signal. Numerous discontinuities exist in the flow of the data signal from the transmitter to the receiver. First, consider the loop interface as data enters the twisted wire pair. The source impedance of the transmitter is different from the line impedance, causing a discontinuity and reflection point. Second, wire gauge discontinuities offer an impedance mismatch resulting in another reflection point. Third, the bridged tap points make a third reflection point. The transition between cables (e.g., PVC to pulp, buried to overhead, one tempera-

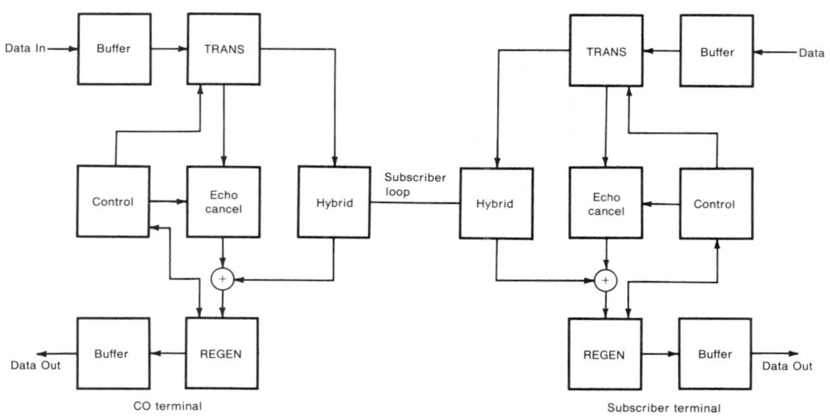

Figure 6-12. Hybrid duplex for the transmission of bidirectional ISDN data.

ture to another, etc.) are all sources of discontinuities and are potential reflection points. Finally, at the receiver, the network termination impedance is not identical to the loop impedance.

To prevent these reflections from totally obliterating the received signal, the functioning of the EC becomes highly critical and cancellations in the region of 60 db become mandatory to meet the ISDN bit-error-rate (BER) requirement. Longer loops need more cancellation since the echo signal strength remains relatively steady as the received signal becomes more and more attenuated (and dispersed).

The limitations of analog signal processing prevents these devices from being serious contenders for ECs. The digital devices incorporated in tapped delay line filters hold enormous promise, provided the data-transmission rates are consistently lower than the digital multipliers and adders in the tapped delay lines. The crucial question in most echo cancellation devices is the amount of time they have to completely cancel the echo of the previously arrived sequence of pulses from the present pulse before the next pulse arrives. The bottleneck is generally the arithmetic processing ability of the digital devices used with the tapped delay line. These devices generate the signals equal to and opposite to the combined echoes of all the discontinuities in the loop at finite instants of time within any pulse period.

The performance of the EC is generally one of the most crucial requirements enabling data transmission at the physical layer to satisfy the BER specified in the network. The Basic-rate ISDN channel units at the U interface incorporate the ECs. Numerous vendors such as Siemens, Erricson Northern Telecom, and AT&T are in close competition to mass produce these interface cards and devices with suitable adaptive ECs to meet the requirements of a vast majority of the loops in the loop plant. In most of these devices, the ECs constitute the critical component because of the stringent demands on its capacity to subtract the echo signal to within 0.1 percent or 60 db of the initial value.

Echo Cancellation Requirement

The amount of echo cancellation that is required for various conditions of signal levels is important because unreasonable echo cancellation requirements could make the terminal unfeasible. Experimental results showing 50–54 db can be achieved with present technology. The amount of echo cancellation that can be achieved is limited by the nonlinear impairments present in the system.

A general formula for the required amount of echo cancellation or Echo-Return-Loss Enhancement (ERLE) (AT&T Bell Laboratories 1982) can be derived using Figure 6-13. The transmitted and received power levels in dbm are designated by X and R, respectively. The echo experiences a loss, L1, when passing through the hybrid. Similarly, the received signal experiences a loss, L2, when passing through the same hybrid. Thus, the power levels of the echo and the received signal, at point A, are equal to X-L1 and R-L2, respectively. If ERLE is the amount of echo cancellation achieved by the ER, the residual echo, after subtraction, is equal to X-L1-ERLE, and the amount of SNR achieved at the input of the receiver is given by

$$\text{SNR} = R - L2 - (X - L1 - \text{ERLE})$$

Solving for ERLE:

$$\text{ERLE} = \text{SNR} - R + X - L1 + L2$$

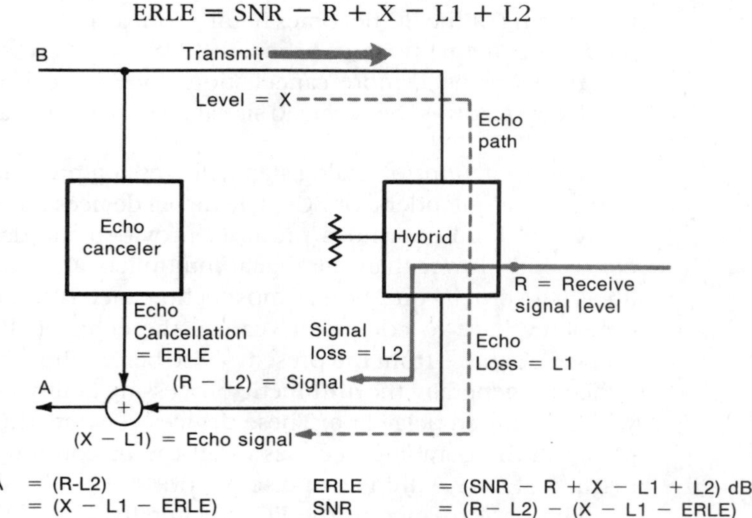

Figure 6-13. Echo cancellation requirement in db.

Several values for ERLE have been computed. With requirements of L1 = −3 db and L2 = 3 db, an SNR of 9 db gives ERLE of 65 db. With the same requirements, an SNR of 13 db gives ERLE of 69 db. With requirements of L1 = 8 db and L2 = 3 db, an SNR of 9 db gives ERLE of 54 db. With the same requirements, an SNR of 13 db gives ERLE of 58 db.

Parameters of L1 = −3 db and L2 = 3 db assume that the worst-case transhybrid loss, L1, is actually a gain. As mentioned previously, with modern technology it is possible to build hybrids which guarantee worst-case transhybrid losses of at least 8 db.

The echo cancellation requirements of L1 = −3 db and L2 = 3 db are quite stringent. They are at the limit of what present technology can achieve.

A simplified block diagram of an echo cancellation system is shown in Figure 6-14. The purpose of the echo canceler (EC) is to synthesize a replica of the channel traversed by the echo(s) from a point in the transmitter to the input of the receiver. Under ideal conditions, the EC and the echo channel have the same inputs and outputs, and the signal, after subtraction, consists of only the desired signal.

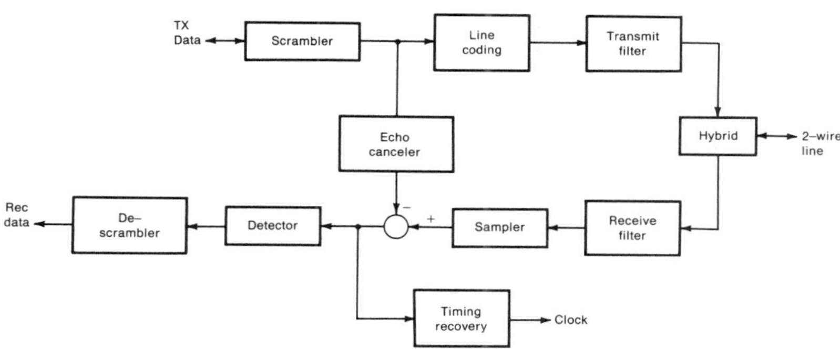

Figure 6-14. An echo canceler hybrid duplex system.

Echoes also arise because of impedance mismatches in the hybrid couplers throughout the network. Such couplers become essential whenever transitions between two-wire and four-wire circuits occur. The leakage signal at the local hybrid is called the near echo. Similarly, the echo at any bridged taps also generates a certain amount of signal leakage. Both these echoes contaminate the received signal, causing error in the recovery of the far-end transmitted signal.

Under ideal conditions, the echo canceler generates to cancel both of the echoes, leading to a pure transmitted signal after it has undergone the deterministic amount of channel attenuation and dispersion. The characteristics of the near echo and bridged taps echo may differ dramatically, thus leading to a duality of requirements in their performance. Typically, the upper range of near-echo canceler attenuation requirement can become 55 to 60 db, whereas the bridged-tap canceler requirement may be quite modest at 15 to 20 db. The delay of the two echoes also differs considerably because of the differences traversed by these two echo paths.

The in-band echo cancelers (or the Nyquist or interpolating type) are particularly attractive in the implementation. The synchronous type of echo cancelers operates at the symbol rate and any timing jitters can adversely affect the performance. Synchronization problems can be quite severe in the later type of cancelers.

Echo cancelers for the baseband channel can be configured two ways as shown in Figure 6-15. When the transmitted data y(t) is formulated as

$$y(t) = \sum_{m=-\infty}^{\infty} a_m g(t - mT)$$

a_m is the transmitted data symbols, g(t) is the pulse shape of the transmitted data, and T is the symbol rate. Similarly, the echo response can be formulated as

$$t(t) = \sum_{m_z -\infty}^{\infty} a_m h(t - mT)$$

where h(t) is represented as

$$h(t) = g(t) \times f(t)$$

The echo path has a time domain response of f(t) or a transfer function of F(jw) in the spectral domain.

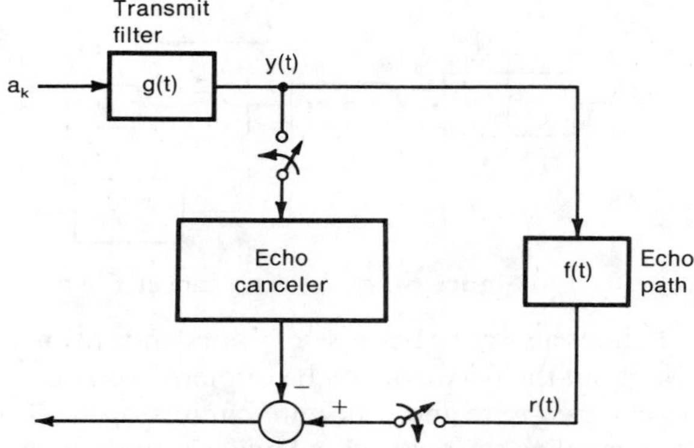

A. Baseband channel EC with sampled transmitted data.

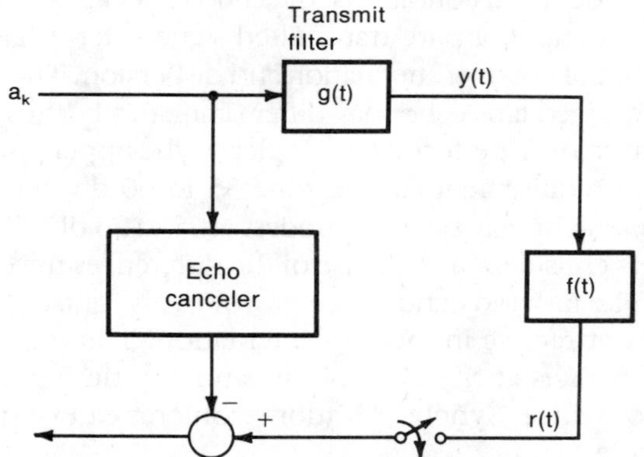

B. Baseband channel EC with transmitted data symbols.

Figure 6-15. Configurations for baseband channel ECs.

In Figure 6-15A, the transmitted data waveform y(t) is sampled at input to the echo canceler. This signal is passed through a transversal filter (see Figure 6-16). When the filter tap weights are properly matched, a signal that is a close replica of the echo signal may be generated. When this signal is subtracted from the received signal, which is also sampled at the same rate, the echo cancellation is complete.

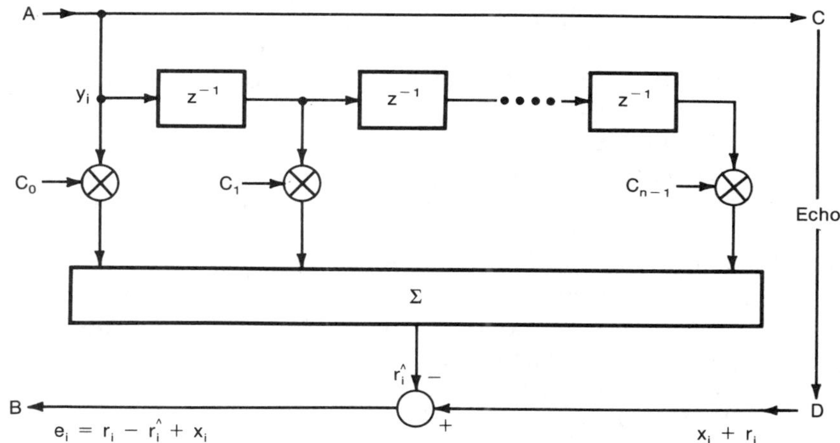

Figure 6-16. A transversal filter echo canceler.

In Figure 6-15B, the transmitted data symbols are applied directly to the canceler. Here, the transmit filter is in the echo path and becomes an integral part of the canceler and of the transmission path. It is the combined response of the transmit filter, and the echo paths are replicated by the transversal filter in the canceler.

The bandwidth of the transmitted (and echo) signals can approach the baud rate. The sampling rate at the input of the echo canceler in Figure 6-15B has to be at least twice the baudrate. Whereas the sampling rate in Figure 6-16 is the same as the baudrate, the sampling rate at the canceler output becomes greater than the input-sampling rate. The problem of incompatibility in the sampling rates thus prevails.

Interleaved echo cancellation is an approach generally taken to solve the problems of incompatible sampling rates. It is based upon the fact that the transmit clock is readily available. Integer multiples of this rate are used for sampling, and the tracking of the echo signals can accurately be done at discrete instants during the integer fractions of the baud interval. When the received signal is also sampled at this higher rate and echo signals are canceled at appropriate instants within the baud interval, echo cancellation is complete and accurate.

Line Codes

The line codes significantly influence the system's performance. They affect the range and susceptibility to errors arising from the digital subscriber line impairments we've discussed. Numerous line codes exist. The choice of a particular code for the ISDN application depends upon the bit rate and the characteristics of the loop plant. At the 80 kb/s (B+D) access, the subscriber loop environment displays features different from those at the 144 kb/s (2B+D) access. For the intermediate rates ranging between 384 kb/s (5B+D) through the Primary rate or 1.544 Mb/s (23B+D), the subscriber loop plant offers diversely varying spectral impulse noise and crosstalk characteristics. The line code at each of these projected ISDN rates for the future has to be appropriately chosen.

The widely prevalent code in the trunk and loop plant is the alternate mark inversion (AMI) code (AT&T Bell Laboratories 1982; Miller and Ahamed 1987) as it is commonly used with the T1 carrier systems. For Basic rate access ISDN, the 2B1Q code recently chosen by the BOCs in the U.S. will also dominate the digital subscriber loop applications. AMI is accepted for easy coding and decoding and for average zero frequency spectral component. However, it is criticized for inefficient utilization of the bandwidth, which causes increased susceptibility to crosstalk and impulse noise. In the loop plant, where there is ample opportunity to pick up low-power frequency and its harmonics, the average zero frequency signal content of the AMI code provides some immunity at low frequencies. This feature also protects the transceiver against low frequency drifts during signal recovery at the receiver. These features of the AMI code made it a favored choice in some of the digital carrier applications, predominantly the T1 carrier system (AT&T Bell Laboratories 1982).

However, the frequent repeatering of the T1 systems cannot be duplicated in the digital subscriber environment for ISDN. This consideration has prompted the deployment of the more efficient block codes. In this environment, the average frequency loss of the typical loops at the ISDN rates is too large in relation to the crosstalk and impulse noise power that prevails in the spectral band to carry the digital signal.

Perhaps the simplest of the block codes is the 2B1Q code where two binary bits are coded at one of the four quaternary levels. This code offers the desirable feature of the AMI code of having no zero frequency spectral energy, but also reduces the bandwidth requirement to about half that of the AMI code. However, since there is no zero state in this code, the peak energy content is skewed toward the higher end of the frequency rather than at one-half frequency. This consideration prevents the 2B1Q code from offering the full 6 db noise advantage over the AMI code.

There are two other penalties associated with the 2B1Q code. First, the encoders and decoders (codecs) are slightly more complicated. Second, the eye openings are proportionally reduced due to the presence of four levels at +3, +1, −1, and −3 (or three eye openings) as compared to the three levels at +1, 0, and −1 (or two eye openings). This is not seen as a major disadvantage since the signal processing components for data recovery are becoming more and more sophisticated. For the sake of comparison, the AMI and the 2B1Q eye diagrams (Ahamed and Lawrence 1987) are depicted in Figures 6-17 and 6-18, respectively.

The 2B1Q code is only one of the many tens of block codes that appear viable for ISDN. An entire family of the quadrature amplitude modulation (QAM) coding techniques (thus leading to different QAM codes) is also available. The factors that have led to the choice of the 2B1Q code from the more

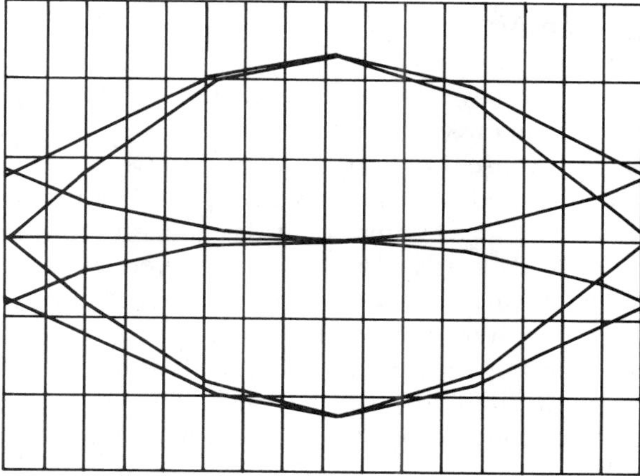

Figure 6-17. An ideal AMI eye diagram.

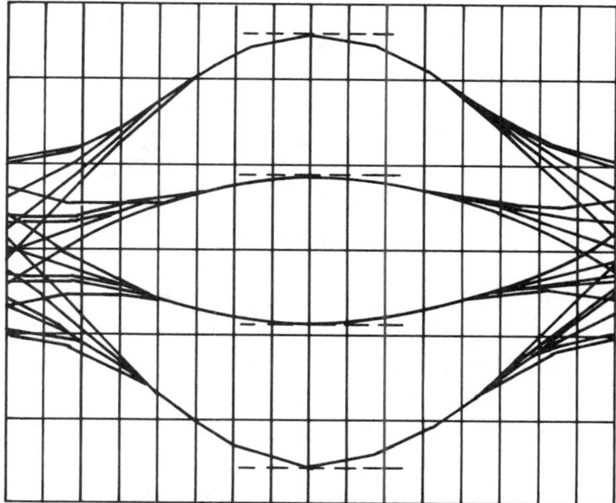

Figure 6-18. An ideal 2B1Q eye diagram.

commonly used AMI code may thus be extended to other types of QAM codes. The bandwidth may be reduced at the expense of component and circuit complexity, or the data rate may be raised (to almost the T1 rate without repeaters) in the subscriber loops. It is important to remember that the actual feasibility of such codes for ISDN applications is not established even though there is ample promise.

The competing strategies in the fiber optic networks (Elrefaie and Romeiser 1986; Ahamed 1987) for very high rates of data transmission are multilevel codes and wave-division multiplexing. We will not elaborate on this topic because fiber networks offer ample bandwidth. In this environment, the system components (e.g., sources, pin diodes, and detectors) limit the range (Ahamed 1987, 1988) rather than the fiber.

Spectral Shaping

Data signals have spectral energy. The subscriber loop plant unwittingly offers an excellent environment for exchanges of the spectral energies of various signals. In a sense, the signals suffer both degradation and contamination as they are propagated, switched, and processed. For this reason, it is essential for the ISDN system and component designers to contain the signal energies of any particular data stream within an allocated and well-chosen spectral band. The choice of bandwidth has to meet two conflicting objectives. First, it should be wide enough to contain the signals to communicate the data effectively. Second, it has to be narrow enough so that it does not contaminate other signals flowing in the loop plant and also is not contaminated by other signals. The choice of codes, discussed in the previous section, also plays a role in the compatible coexistence of the many carriers and data signals in the subscriber plant. The study of these objectives and the associated techniques leads to spectrum management in the loop plant.

By appropriate choice of spectral shaping, certain regions may be emphasized or deemphasized to serve this duality of requirements. Spectral shaping is a powerful technique practiced by ISDN systems designers to bound and contain spectral energies of various signals. The basic principle behind this technique lies in evaluating the segment of the spectral band that is most effective in signal transmission and then comparing it with the bands where it may crosstalk, contaminate, or otherwise influence the other signal carriers.

Signals flow from one circuit into another by stray capacitances, leakage currents through the conductance of copper wires, improper shielding, and even by stray electromagnetic coupling. The coupling parameters are generally frequency-dependent, as are the signals that crosstalk into each other. Hence, a set of spectral shaping rules suitable for one carrier system becomes inapplicable to another environment. The designers generally must tailor the spectral shaping individually to a particular application.

At the implementation level, spectral shaping can be accomplished by appropriate filters—analog or digital devices. The eventual objective for ISDN is to limit and contain the signal energies in the various subscriber circuits and ISDN central offices. It is imperative that the ISDN bearer service meets the bit-error-rate (BER) error tolerance for the data services. It is also essential that the SNR and delay requirement (as they are both influenced by the filtering) for the voice and video services is within the range of tolerance.

One of the examples of spectral shaping exists in the circuit-switched digital capability (CSDC) introduced by predivestiture Bell System (Bosik and Kartalopoulos 1982). When this service was introduced, there was a finite probability that the TCM mode at 144 kb/s, used by CSDC in the loop plant, would adversely affect the analog carrier systems especially prevalent in the U.S. (Rao 1976) by contaminating the lower end of the spectral band. For the CSDC system, the code selected was the AMI code, and very little signal energy prevails at the lower end of the spectrum where contamination of the analog subscriber carriers (such as SLC-1 or SLC-8) is likely. For this reason, AMI signals transmitted into the loop plant were incorporated into the system. The crosstalk gain for the coexisting carriers was quite large compared to the penalty for the CSDC system.

Equalization

Over the next few years, ISDN will be realized by deploying the existing telephone lines to reach the customers. Newer networks of communication, such as fibernets, LANs, cable TV networks, etc., designed to reach subscribers with more elaborate services, are being introduced gradually. However, any form of communication between the ISDN central office and the subscriber is accompanied by two distinct effects upon the signal: attenuation and dispersion.

Attenuation leads to the loss of signal level. Dispersion leads to the redistribution of the signal energy from one spectral band to another. When the data is recomposed from the received signal without any form of signal processing, the recovery of the original data is error-prone. Equalization of the channel attenuation and dispersion is an attempt to undo the degradation that the signal suffers as it travels the subscriber on any given communication channel. In the loop plant, a perfect equalizer totally undoes the subscriber line attenuation and dispersion. However, the implementation of this subscriber line inversion device is nontrivial. Subscriber lines can display a wide range of characteristics. They can offer spectral singularities, reflection or echoes of the transmitted signal, temperature-dependent loss, dispersion, and more.

In order to make dependable data recovery in the ISDN environment, line effects are tackled by two distinct strategies: equalization and echo cancellation. With equalization, the signal degradation in line for the forward transmission of the signal is restored. With echo cancellation, the effects of systemic reflections of the transmitted signal adding to the received signal are accurately subtracted out.

There are two aspects to the line equalization problem. We have already mentioned bridged taps, the open-circuited line stubs of variable length offering a branch point in the forward transmission of signal. One component is received at the receiver. The other component travels up the open tap, gets reflected, and arrives a little more attenuated, distorted, and delayed at the receiver. During continuous transmission of data, the delay causes serious concern because the reflected and delayed pulse can occupy the duration in which the succeeding pulses are to arrive. Hence, the line equalizers address the two major aspects of signal restoration. First, they overcome the line effects. Second, the undo the effects of bridged tap reflections. Both these functions of the equalizers have to be adaptive since the ISDN subscriber loop length and configuration are extremely variable.

Equalization can be accomplished in the analog or digital domain. Analog equalizers have been successfully built and deployed, especially for the T1, T1C (Davis, Graczyk, and Griffen 1979), and CSDC systems. However, adaptive analog equalization (using distributed poles and zeros) can be limited, at best, because the digital signal-processing features are absent.

Decision feedback equalizers (which are coarse digital type of devices) can offer reasonable adaptability against bridged taps even if their topology is complex. These devices use tapped delay lines with appropriate tap weights to inject a signal equal to and opposite to the delayed signal. During the training sequence, these weights are adjusted so that the delays from the taps and/or discontinuities are completely canceled. Any residual effects are continuously monitored so that the average reflections are as close to zero as possible. In Figure 6-19, we depict a single transmitted pulse, the received eye diagram and the received eye diagram after equalization in a typical subscriber loop. In this example, the reflections are due to a single bridged tap of about 0.366 km of #22 AWG located at 2.834 km from the central office within a 3.84 km loop made up entirely of #22 AWG cable (Figure 6-19A). The performance of the equalizer in reconstructing the received pulse to a discrete binary one is evident by comparing Figures 6-19B and 6-19C, respectively.

Effective equalization requires basic strategy. In a loop plant where bridged taps prevail, reflections from these open-ended wire pairs is inevitable. However, if the reflection from an average bridged tap can be statistically computed in the particular loop environment, the basic equalizer can be designed to undo the tail of the reflected pulse. Thus, the extent to which any particular loop deviates from the average loop with an average bridged tap causes an error in the residual tail of the received pulse. The process of total equalization can thus be reduced from that of total tail cancellation to that of the cancellation of the residual tail in the residual pulse. If an elegant algorithm in the adaptation of the equalizer is included, a startup and equalization procedure can be significantly simplified. Such a strategy calls for the detailed simulation of the loop environment.

Adaptive digital equalizers are generally realized as finite transversal filters. The basic premise of these equalizers is to adapt the tap weights to minimize the noise and ISI. The receiver decisions are utilized to generate the error signal. A simplified form of an adaptive equalizer is shown in Figure 6-20. With no ISI, the input to the slicer matches the transmitted data symbols. The receive filter generally rejects out-of-band noise even though it may be sometimes matched to enhance the signal content in view of frequency-dependent attenuation of the digital subscriber line. When the sampled signal is applied to the adaptive transversal line (or tapped delay line) equalizer with a finite number of taps, the line equalization can be effectively accomplished, provided the taps of the delay line are appropriately adapted.

The adaptation process is based upon the error signal, which is used in the feedback loop adjusting the tap weights (i.e., increasing or decreasing their values) so that the slicer input exactly matches the data symbols. In steady state, the receiver decisions generate the error signals. In the ideal condition, when there is no ISI and noise, the input to the slicer will be exactly equal to the transmitted data symbols and the slicer input and output will be the same, thus requiring no further adjustment of the tap weights. Noise alone causes a slight oscillation of the tap weights around their optimum values. Because ISI is deterministic and signal-dependent, however, it forces the weights to cancel themselves out. Slow variations of the channel response are also tracked by decision-directed equalizers.

It is possible to conceive that the untrained equalizer (i.e., an equalizer whose tap weights are totally different from their optimal values), will have such severe ISI that the data symbols may never be recovered. For this reason, the initial tap settings are done by going through a training sequence in which the transmitter is generating a sequence of data symbols known to the receiver. This

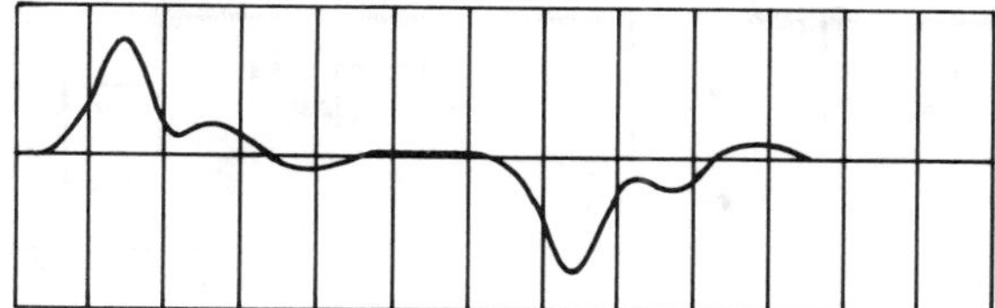

A. Reflections due to single bridged tap.

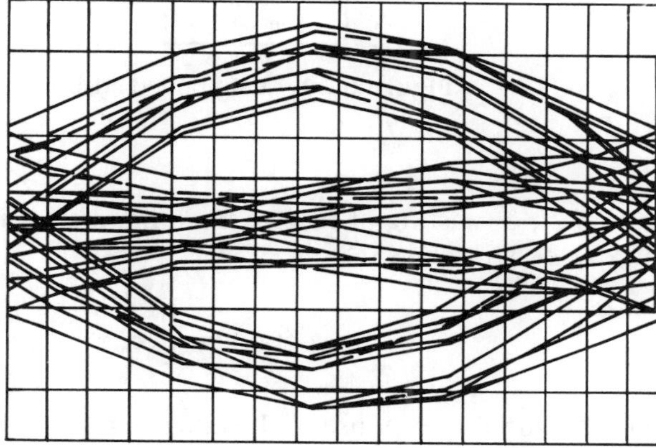

B. Eye diagram with no equalization.

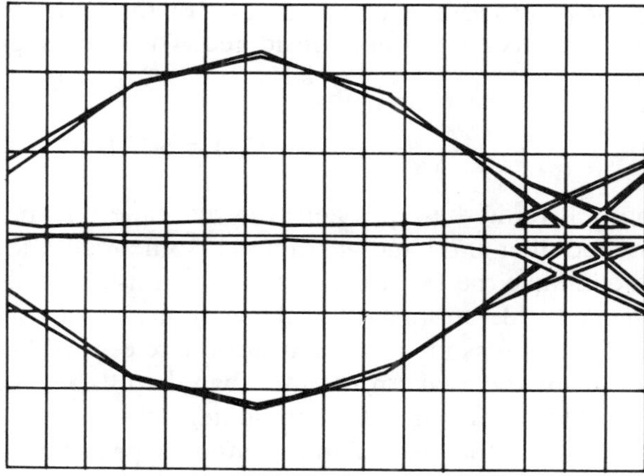

C. Eye diagram after equalization.

Figure 6-19. A single transmitted pulse and its reception.

sequence is used in place of the slicer output as the equalizer adjusts its tap weights. Once the preset training time is completed, the transmitter starts to transmit real data and the slicer output is used to check the error signal.

In a general sense, two types of equalizers are feasible. The linear equalizer

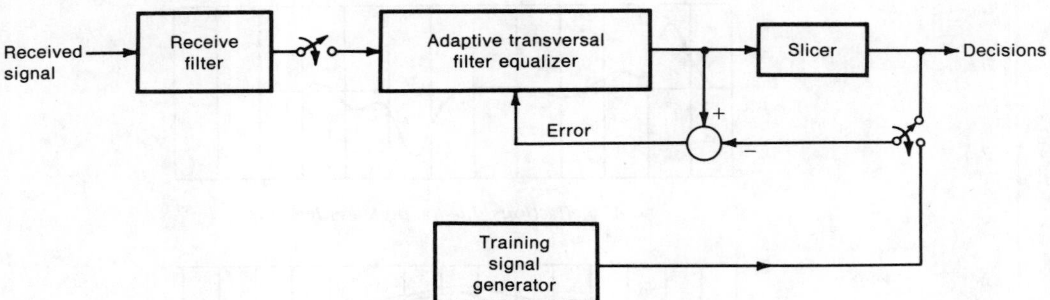

Figure 6-20. A simplified adaptive equalizer.

(Figure 6-21, consisting of receive filter, baudrate sampler, and a discrete time filter) can be written as

$$C(z) = \sum_k c_k z^{-k}$$

where the impulse response of the equalizer is c_k. This type of equalizer tends to reduce the ISI by enhancing the gain where the channel has inherent loss. A certain amount of noise enhancement takes place because of the equalizer gain. Two criteria for the linear equalizers are zero forcing and mean-square error. In the linear zero forcing equalizer (LE-ZF), the ISI is completely removed and the noise enhancement is not considered. The filter is realized with a transfer function

$$C(z) = S_h^{-1}(z)$$

where $S_h(z)$ is the equivalent discrete-time channel transfer function after a matched filter and baudrate sampler. Some realizations of the LE-ZF equalizers can eliminate the ISI at the expense of noise power. However, from an overall design consideration, it offers the least probability of error in the symbol recovery. For this reason, a linear mean-square error (LE-MSE) can be attempted by minimizing the total error (rather than the ISI) between the slicer input and the transmitted data symbols. This strategy does not minimize the probability of error because the residual intersymbol error does not have a Gaussian distribution. Still, this approach is considered as a fair approximation for minimized probability of error in symbol recovery.

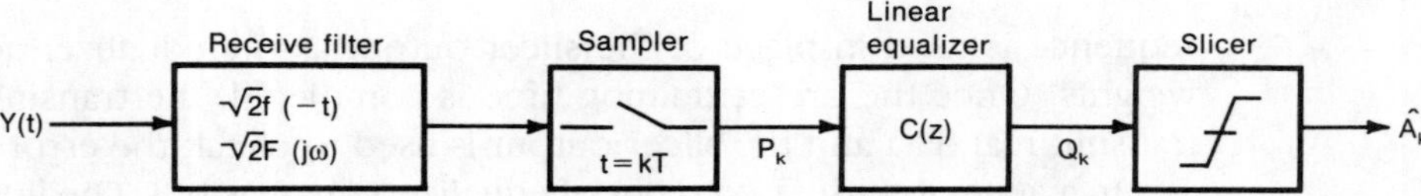

Figure 6-21. A general structure of a linear equalizer.

In practice, the approximations to the LE-ZF and LE-MSE can be realized as finite impulse response (FIR) and infinite impulse response (IIR) filters. The implementational problems of IIRs make the FIRs a viable choice. Channels carrying data rarely have an exactly rational transfer function, which makes it impossible to completely cancel out its effects. For the realization of the FIR filters in the digital communication field, only causal effects are considered. That is, the symbols already transmitted can affect the current symbol, rather than the symbols that are already transmitted and still to be transmitted both going to affect the current symbol. Hence, the general form of the FIR filters which is written as

$$C(z) = \sum_{k=-N}^{N} c_k z^{-k}$$

where C(z) is the output from the FIR filter, $c_k$is the tap weights, (2N + 1) is the number of shift register position on the transversal filter, becomes

$$z^{-N} C(z) = \sum_{k_{20}}^{zN} c_{k-N} z^{-k}$$

This representation has only negative powers of z and can be viewed as being causal. In these representations, the degrees of freedom to adjust the transversal filter are (2N + 1) and represent the tap weight setting on the filter. The concept of zero forcing is meaningless in transversal filter implementation because the degrees of freedom are restricted. The concept applicable here is peak distortion criterion, which forces to minimum the peak eye closure for the 2N samples within the length of the equalizer. The second criterion used with FIR transversal filter tap weights is the minimization of mean-square error. Both criteria can be implemented.

Another structure competing with the sampled matched filter is called the fractionally spaced equalizer (Figure 6-22). This later type of equalizer serves as a matched filter and a transversal filter. In the design of the fractionally spaced equalizer, the receiver phase is not accurately known in relation to the baud interval and the filter has constrained complexity. Both cause a slight degradation in the performance and both have advantages against aliasing in frequency and time domain. The variations in the sampling phase do not cause noise enhancements. In fact, this type of transversal equalizer can adapt automatically for sampling phase. It performs substantially better than the baudrate transversal filters operating with channels with noticeable band-edge delay distortion.

Decision feedback equalizers (DFE) can offer considerable noise reduction when severe ISI is present. They are easier to implement than the linear equalizer but suffer from the possibility of error propagation. Hence, with certain caution DFEs may become attractive alternatives to linear equalizers. The DFE (Figure 6-23) can be separated into a forward filter C(z), which can be implemented as a fractionally spaced equalizer, and a feedback filter. The latter serves to filter the detected data symbols at the output of the slicer and subtracts the

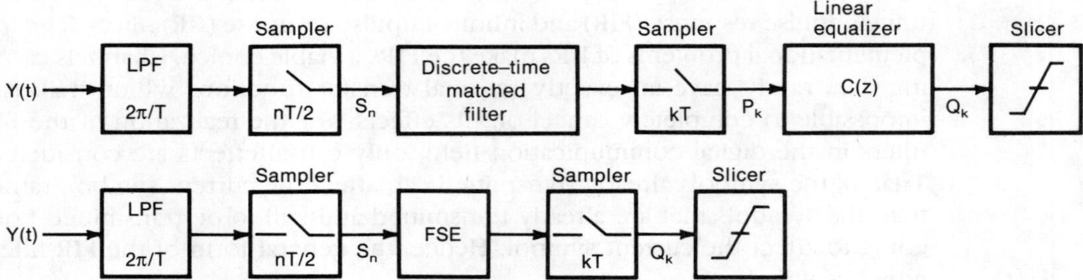

Figure 6-22. Two realizations of fractionally spaced equalizers.

resulting estimate from the forward filter output to give the slicer input. The feedback filter sits in the feedback path and hence is strictly causal. The delay terms are strictly positive and can be represented as

$$D(z) = \sum_{k=1}^{\infty} d_k z^{-k}$$

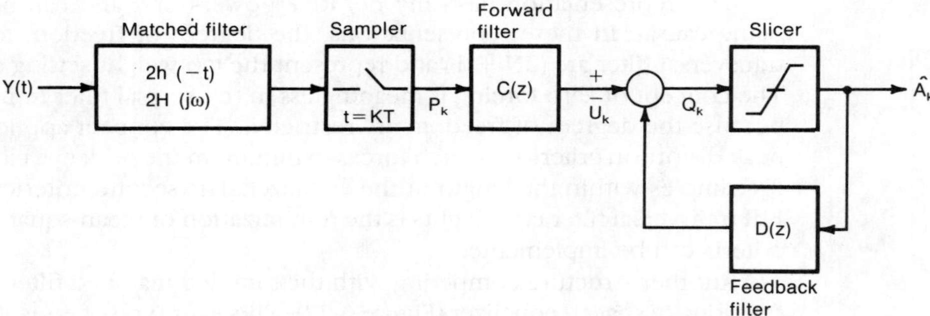

Figure 6-23. The DFE receiver.

Two types of DFEs are the zero forcing DFE (ZF-DFE) and mean-square error DFE (MSE-DFE). In the optimization of DFEs, the criterion chosen can be the noise power or the noise power and the ISI. Error propagation can be a problem. In the derivation of the DFE tap weights, the possibility is ignored and input to the feedback filter is assumed to be correct. MSE criterion is generally used when the signals are assumed to be slowly varying. Based upon this criterion, the MSE gradient algorithm exists. An optimum MSE coefficient vector is sought out by stochastic variation of the coefficients. This algorithm is termed the stochastic gradient (SG) algorithm, and the combined iterative algorithm, the minimum mean-square error based upon the stochastic gradient (or slope), is called the MSEG algorithm. These algorithms converge fairly dependably and the equalizer performance is well documented in most cases of noisy and pretty severe channels.

Timing Recovery

The subscriber clock is derived from the received signal. Subscribers do not have access to their own source of timing for clocking the transmitted date (Ahamed and Singh 1986) or for scanning the received data during an appropriate window of time as the data is being received.

In practice, the subscriber-transceiver channel unit has to rely on the transition characteristics in the signal that is received. The equalizer generally precedes the timing recovery circuit (TRC). If the equalizer is functioning correctly, it restores both the amplitude and the channel distortion. If the EC is functioning correctly, it removes a large proportion of the echoes. Thus, the signal at the TRCs is relatively clean and the transitions are reasonably well placed.

The functional requirement of the TRC is to reestablish the clock at which the data was originally encoded at the central office and supply it to the local subscriber circuits to be used for data scanning and for transmitting the subscriber data. Some of the other circuits that use the recovered clock are decision feedback equalizers (DFEs), finite impulse response filters (FIRs) (Rabiner and Gold 1975), and tapped delay lines (if any).

DFEs and FIRs for echo cancelers depend upon the clock, and the TRC depends upon the accurate functioning of the DFEs and ECs. To break the potential deadlock that leads to a no-win data communication situation, the subscriber circuits need to undergo a training sequence before they can function at all. Most ISDN channels resort to this procedure for a finite duration lasting from a fraction of a second to many seconds depending upon the system and training sequences. These training procedures first ascertain clocking functions under ideal conditions (such as transmitting an alternate binary sequence with a maximal zero-one transition). Next, they send single and/or well-defined pulse sequences so the equalizer can remove any residual tails from the recovered signals. Then they permit the subscriber to be activated so that the ECs may remove most of the reflected signals from the received signals, and so on.

The basic methodology in the recovery of time at the subscriber is simple. The partially processed received signal has a certain number of amplitude transitions. Such transitions carry a definite timing stamp at the transmitter. This timing information may get attenuated, distorted, and dispersed as it travels down the digital subscriber lines. However, the subscriber transceiver has enough device capability to compensate for the line effects. Hence, the recovery of the subscriber clock becomes that of using the reasonably accurate timing stamps to generate a periodic and well-defined clock. The performance of this circuit is measured as the amount of jitter (generally in degrees or minutes) that appears in the recovered clock (see Figure 6-24).

Numerous established filtering techniques are available. The most common class of circuits, known as *phase-locked loops*, exist especially for this purpose. Their function depends upon reinforcing the harmonic of the signal to be recovered in the input of a high-gain operational amplifier. These high-quality, high-gain operational amplifiers perform to extract the harmonic of interest (i.e., the transmitted clock at the central office) and effectively block everything else. Because their mode of oscillation is pure, crystal oscillators are used often by making their natural frequency of oscillation correspond to the right ISDN

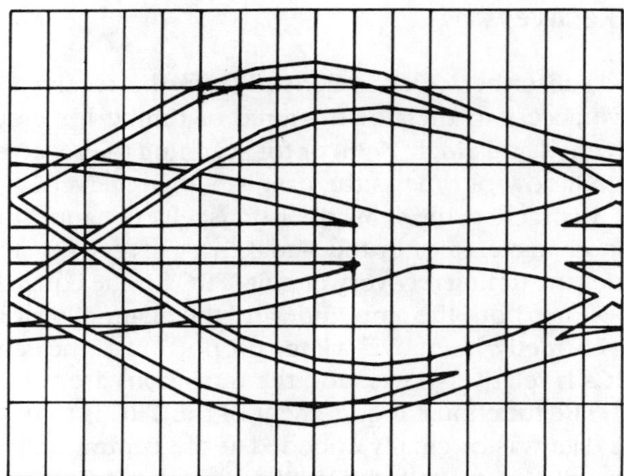

Figure 6-24. The uncertainty of the TRC depicted by the width of the vertical line at maximum eye height.

rate. System designers have successfully designed every type of TRC, ranging from circuits that use RC filters, analog filters (active and passive), digital filters, and high quality crystals. Such filters can be conventional, feedback or feedforward.

Transmission Requirements

The two most seriously competing technologies for the transmission of ISDN data during the eighties were fiber optics and twisted wire pairs. Fiber optics has proved to be extremely viable in most network environments. Numerous vendors have made the systems available to the system designers to multiplex, transmit, recover, demultiplex, and redistribute ISDN data in the local networks.

Fiber Optic Systems

One of the more dominant and widely accessible fiber optic systems in the subscriber loop plant in the United States is the Fiber SCL-96 (designed and developed by the predivestiture Bell System) during the early eighties.

This particular system links up to 96 remote terminals to a central office. Reduced power and size requirements with inherent immunity to crosstalk and electromagnetic inductive interference makes the repeaterless fiber optic systems desirable to the subscriber and in the distribution plant. This particular system operates in the 1.3 μ wavelength region. The dispersion is minimal and permits the use of light-emitting diodes (LED) as opposed to the injection laser diodes (ILD) which tend to have temperature-sensitive characteristics. At the receiver side, positive intrinsic negative diodes (PIN) opposed to the avalanche photodiodes (APD) offer wider temperature stability. During the early eighties, a range of about 20 km was envisioned with the lightguide cable having a graded refractive index profile. The core diameter of 62.5 μ and an outside cladding diameter of 125 μ was selected. Modest data rate at DS2 (6.314 Mb/s) was attempted. With N grade fiber, the loss was estimated at 0.70 db/km and 1.06 db/km or 1.8 db/km with the M or the L grades of the fiber.

The more recent designs promise significantly improved commercial systems. For example, the optoelectronic IC devices have been successfully tested at 1.2 Gb/s over 52 km with an InGaAsP laser diode and three FET drivers. This system uses InGaAs PIN photodiode and low-noise amplifier with 4 GaAs FETs and 5 GaAs Schottky diodes and a resistor on a 1X1 mm chip. Far higher rates are foreseen in the near future. More recently, the thrust toward extending the fiber to the homes of subscribers has prompted significant and viable designs. The Broadband Local Access Architecture envisioned by BOCs has a capacity of up to 560 Mb/s to the home via remote electronic facilities capable of video distribution and broadband packet-handling capability. The remote electronics facility is serviced by fiber feeders operating around 2.4 Gb/s from broadband central offices distributed throughout the metropolitan areas. Lower rates of 240/140 Mb/s are obtained by demultiplexing the higher bit rates to individualized customers. Other smaller systems for carrying high-speed data can be assembled by the components manufactured by vendors of fiber optic diodes and laser sources, fibers, detectors, and pin diodes.

Twisted Wire Pair Systems

For ISDN data traffic at the Basic rate (2B+D) using full-duplex ECs, the vendors of VLSI chips have introduced chips for the AMI code. These vendors are expected to introduce VLSI chips for the more widely accepted 2B1Q code in the near future.

The OSI layer and interface definition play an important role in the choice of components (and the appropriate VLSI chips) for ISDN data transmission facility in the subscriber loop environment. The four basic interface points (R, S, T, and U) are depicted in Figure 6-25.

When an ISDN terminal is connected to the physical transmission line, three (S, T, and U) of the four interface points are necessary. Between terminal S of the data equipment TE1, accepting data in the ISDN format, and the physical endpoint of the transmission line, interface point U, there are two other components (NT2 and NT1) necessary. NT2 (network termination 2) handles the multiplexing/demultiplexing, channel separation, and terminal control functions for the ISDN terminal(s) connected to NT2. NT1 (network termination 1) handles the physical layer requirements, such as electrical, mechanical, level, timing recovery, etc., functions.

Data at the physical medium is received from the transmission line at the U interface by NT1 and forwarded into NT2 for local distribution at the customer's premises. Data is also received from NT2 as a multiplexed bit-stream and forwarded into the transmission line. In general, the functions of NT1 (between interfaces U and S) include line maintenance, performance monitoring,

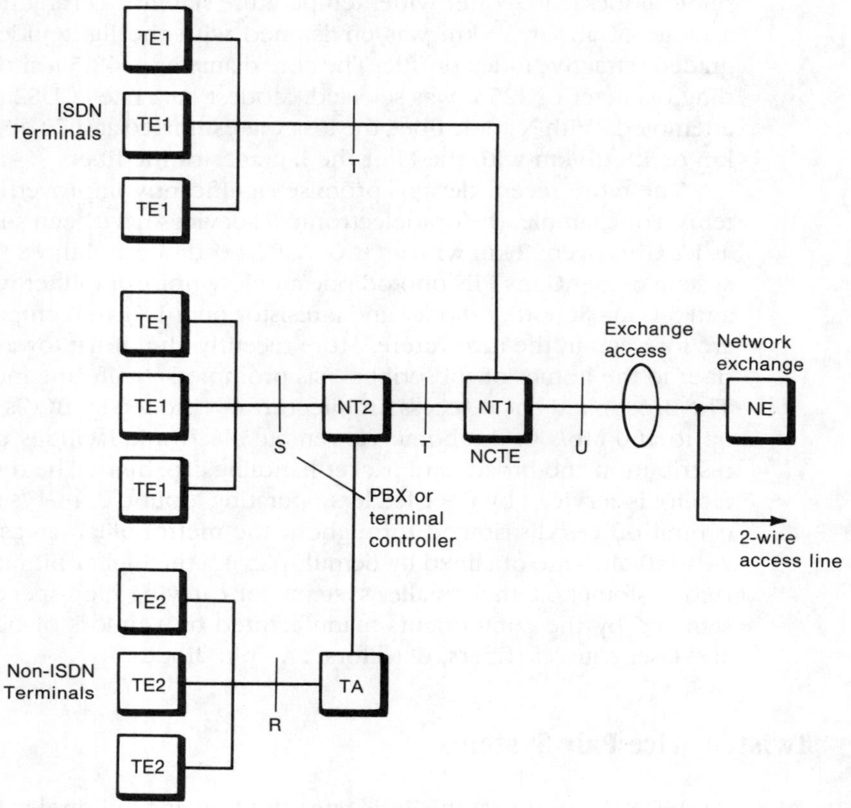

Figure 6-25. ISDN reference configuration showing the four points at R, S, T, and U.

and isolation of the transmission technology from the T interface point. Similarly, the functions of NT2 include the control of the many possible terminals that may share a common physical medium. Concentration and maintenance functions also become associated with NT2. One typical example of NT2 is PBX. The exchange may provide many local lines for internal users, it may seek out an outside line when the user uses an appropriate code (typically a 9-prefix to the telephone number string), and it may distribute incoming calls to the appropriate extension.

When non-ISDN terminals (i.e., terminals that do not conform to the ISDN standards for B- and D-channels, electrical and mechanical interfaces, etc.) have to function in the emerging ISDN environment, TAs (see Figure 6-25) are necessary. A TA may be used between the interface points S or T and one or more non-ISDN terminals. An immense variety of these TAs will become essential to accommodate the data devices presently available in the ISDN network.

In the United States, the vendors and network designers tend to strongly adhere to the CCITT guidelines and standards. In particular, the generic requirements published by Bell Communications Research spell out the translation of the CCITT standards to the actual device, hardware, and software requirements from the various vendors that supply the systems to be incorporated in the emerging ISDN. Such requirements on systems from the vendors of the ISDN switches and central offices promise a degree of consistency of services, interconnections, and exchange of information between the network users.

Conclusions

The transmission aspects in ISDN start out with a detailed study of the loop environment carrying the high-speed data between the digital central offices or data-switching centers of the emerging ISDN network and the customers. Numerous types of customers have been identified in our society. The data needs of businesses can be significantly different from the data needs of individual subscribers. The data needs of governmental agencies can be quite different from those of education campuses, and so on. For this reason, the transmission aspects in ISDN have been addressed by the data rates and specialized needs of the customers. These special needs are declared at the time data service is initiated and may be modified from time to time.

The provision of services at high speeds is not foreseen as a problem since the telephone network handles high-speed data communication effectively between central offices. Trunk transmission facilities are highly evolved in the U.S. Furthermore, the evolving fibernets offer ample bandwidth for high-speed communication ranging from a few megabits per second to a few hundred gigabits per second. However, the transmission of data at intermediate rates ranging from 80 (B+D) kb/s to 384 (5B+D), even 1.544 Mb/s (23B+D), or the Primary rate over the widely distributed telephone network providing access to every home is a unique challenge. Systems have been designed and are being tested currently to verify the conformity to CCITT standards. Systems and component vendors in the telecommunications industry have developed VLSI chips that accomplish subfunctions satisfactorily, even though extensive network testing is not complete. Some of the RBOCs are offering ISDN-like services more and more frequently.

References

Agazzi, O., D. A. Hodges, and D. G. Messerschmitt. 1982. Large scale integration of hybrid-method digital subscriber loops. *IEEE Trans. on Communications* COM-30:2095–2108. Also see, O. Agazzi, D. G. Messerschmitt, and D. A. Hodges. Nonlinear echo cancellation of data signals. *IEEE Trans. on Communications* COM-30:2421–33.

Ahamed, S. V. 1982a. Simulation and design studies of the digital subscriber lines. *Bell System Technical Journal* 61, no. 6:1003–77 (July–August).

———. 1982b. *Minimal Delay Rate Change Circuits*. U.S. Patent 4,316,061. Assignee, Bell Telephone Laboratories.

———. 1984. *Burst Error Correction Using Cyclic Block Codes*. U.S. Patent 4,488,302. Assignee, Bell Telephone Laboratories.

———. 1987. A computer aided design environment for the local lightwave communication systems. *IEEE, Fifth International Workshop on Integrated Electronics and Photonics in Communication* (October 21–23), Research Triangle, North Carolina.

———. 1988. The integration of fiber optic simulations with integrated circuit design. *Proceeding of the 1988 IEEE Military Communications Conference*. Paper No. 2.3, October 23–26. San Diego, California.

Ahamed, S. V., P. P. Bohn, and N. L. Gottfried. 1981. A tutorial on two-wire digital transmission in the loop plant. *IEEE Special Issue on Communications* COM-29, no. 11:1554–64.

Ahamed, S. V., and V. B. Lawrence. 1987. An intelligent CAD environment for Integrated Services Digital Network (ISDN) components. *Proceeding of the IEEE International Workshop on Industrial Application of Machine Vision and Machine Intelligence*. Paper No. 02, February 2–4. Roppongi, Tokyo, Japan.

Ahamed, S. V., and R. P. S. Singh. 1986. Physical and transmission characteristics of subscriber loops for ISDN services. *IEEE ICC-86* (June 22–25).

AT&T Bell Laboratories. 1982. *Transmission Systems for Communications* Fifth Edition. Winston-Salem: Western Electric Company.

Bell Communications Research. 1987. Characterization of Subscriber Loops for Voice and ISDN Services. Science and Technology Series, ST-TSY-000041 (June).

Bosik, B. S., and S. V. Kartalopoulos. 1982. A time compression multiplexing system for a circuit switched digital capability. *IEEE, Trans. COM*. (September).

Davis, P. C., J. F. Graczyk, and W. A. Griffen. 1979. Design of an integrated circuit for the T1C low power line repeater. *IEEE Journal of Solid-State Circuits* SC-14:109–20.

Elrefaie, A., and M. Romeiser. 1986. Computer simulation of single-mode fiber systems. *Optical Fiber Communications Conference* (February).

Gresh, P. A. 1969. Physical and transmission characteristics of customer loop plant. *Bell System Technical Journal* 48:3337–85 (December).

Lechlieder, J. W., and R. A. McDonald. 1986. Capability of telephone loop plant for ISDN basic access. *Proceeding of ISSLS 86* (September 29–October 3).

Manhire, L. M. 1978. Physical and transmission characteristics of customer loop plant. *Bell System Technical Journal* 57:35–39 (January).

Miller, M. J., and S. V. Ahamed. 1987. *Digital Transmission Systems and Networks, Volume I, Principles*. Rockville, Maryland: Computer Science Press.

———. 1988. *Digital Transmission Systems and Networks, Volume II, Applications*. Rockville, Maryland: Computer Science Press.

Rabiner, L. R., and C. M. Gold. 1975. *Theory and Application of Digital Signal Processing*. Englewood Cliffs, New Jersey: Prentice Hall, Inc.

Rao, T. N. 1976. Application of new linear integrated circuits to a single channel carrier system. *IEEE International Conference on Communications* 3:48.20–48.23.

Werner, J. J. 1984. An echo-cancellation-based 4800 bit/s full-duplex DDD modem. *IEEE Journal on Selected Areas in Communications*. SAC-2 no. 5:722–30.

Chapter 7

Managing Networks

Paul J. Brusil
Lee LaBarre

Chapter 7

ORGANIZATIONS INCREASINGLY RELY ON DATA AND telecommunications networks to conduct their business. Commensurate with their communication needs, they demand a certain quality of service from their networks in terms of communications bandwidth and delay, error rate, transparency, reliability, and the ability to adapt to users' changing needs without disruption of service. The network management problem is to ensure that the networks provide the requisite quality of service and adaptability. The solution to the network management problem includes provision of a set of tools for configuring, monitoring, and controlling networks, a set of procedures for using these tools, and humans to effect the procedures.

The network management problem should properly be placed in the context of a distributed processing environment which attempts to provide transparent access to geographically dispersed network resources. Within such an environment, it is necessary to manage the communications subsystem resources, resources of the connected subscriber devices (operating systems, peripheral devices, etc.), and application resources. Initial developments of a multivendor distributed processing environment have led to transparent process-to-process communications based on standard protocols. It is only natural that the initial network management efforts described in this chapter are concentrating on the definition and development of tools for management of the communication network (i.e., all hardware and software (protocols) needed for remote process-to-process communications). In this chapter, the term network management will be used to reference only management of the communications portion of the network. However, these same basic tools are applicable to the management of subscriber device resources and application resources of the distributed processing environment.

A growing number of organizations depend on products from multiple vendors, and transmission services across a catnet of multiple carriers, to provide for their data communication networking needs. This dependence has fostered the development of a set of standard data communication protocols to allow interoperability in the multivendor, catnet environment. However, to ensure interoperability, the protocol standards must be augmented with a standard set of tools for managing multivendor data communication resources.

The communications needs of many organizations usually extend beyond data communications to include telephony, video, and other transmission requirements. Indeed, data communications networks often use many of the same resources as telephony networks. Thus, organizations need an integrated, interoperable approach to managing all their multivendor networks—data communications, telephony, video distribution, or others.

Critical to assuring such interoperability both within and across networks is the development of commercial networking and network management products conformant to publicly available, internationally accepted standards.

This chapter presents a standards-based perspective on network management. Specifically, it describes network management from the perspective of the network management standards efforts in the international OSI community.

The organization of international standards bodies and a description of the process of developing standards is given in Appendix D at the back of the book. Appendix E provides details of various efforts to develop implementation specifications based on the standards. Acronyms associated with various standards organizations are defined in the Glossary of Acronyms, also located at the back of the book.

Standardization and Commercialization Process

The process of developing interoperable, multivendor, standards-based products is summarized in Figure 7-1. It is a multistep process, no one step of which by itself is sufficient to assure interoperable products. This figure indicates the relationships among the various organizations that contribute to this process.

Requirements for network management standards and subsequent products are developed by a number of user-oriented groups, as indicated in the figure. These requirements are fed into, and drive, the network management standardization activities in several international bodies. These bodies typically concentrate on standards for specific environments (e.g., local or long haul) or for particular protocol suites. Some of the bodies develop standards from the perspective of end-systems attached to transmission facilities, whereas others carry the banner of the communication service providers. In particular, ISO and the CCITT are developing standards for computer communications management in WANs based on the OSI protocols. The Internet Activities Board (IAB) is developing standards for computer networks based on the Transmission Control Protocol/Internet Protocol (TCP/IP) environments. IEEE is developing standards for LAN management. CCITT is also developing standards for telephony and ISDN network management.

Once standards are developed for OSI, other organizations develop specifications based on those standards. These specifications identify the options that must be supported from within the standards, implementation details outside

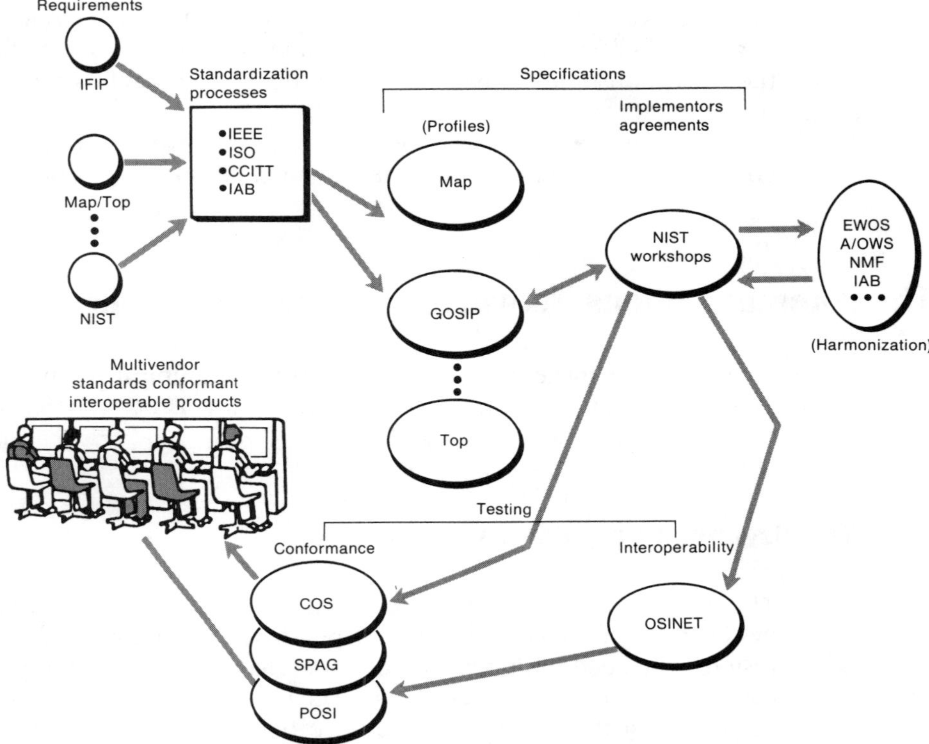

Figure 7-1. Standardization/commercialization process.

the scope of the standards but required to facilitate interoperability, and the particular profile(s) or subset of layered protocols that must be supported. Such specifications for industrial automation, office automation, and government sector networking products are being developed by MAP, TOP, and GOSIP, respectively.

Many of the above OSI-based specifications are based on publicly developed agreements derived by consensus among users, vendors, system integrators, and the like at the international open forums conducted under the aegis of the NIST Workshop for Implementors of OSI. To assure consistency across agreements that may be undertaken in regional forums, such as European Workshop for Open Systems (EWOS) and Asian/Oceania Workshop (A/OWS), or that are being developed to serve other constituencies by forums such as DARPA's IAB and the OSI NMF vendor consortium, the National Institute of Standards and Technology (NIST) Workshop coordinates with these various organizations to foster alignment and harmonization.

Products implemented according to the above specifications must then be tested. Corporation for Open Systems (COS), as well as its European and Japanese counterparts—Standards Promotion and Application Group (SPAG) and Promotion of OSI (POSI), respectively—develop and conduct tests against reference implementations to certify that products based on these specifications do in fact conform to the standards that these products purportedly implement. In addition, different vendors conduct multivendor tests, using vehicles such as the NIST-sponsored OSINET, to demonstrate interoperability of separately implemented products.

Only after completion of these processes can true multivendor, standards-compliant, interoperable products become available.

The Communications Network Management Problem

First, let's investigate the constraints on the communications network management problem in the context of the organizational and technical environment of the network(s) to be managed.

The Organizational Environment

The widespread availability of low-cost computing and networking products has led to organizations' increased dependence on automation. This in turn has fostered the need for increased network reliability and flexibility to accommodate growth and further technological change. However, with divestiture, users of WANs lost the reliability of carrier-provided network management. At the same time, organizations' computing and communications needs were now best served by competitive multivendor offerings.

Acquisition of computer systems and networks to interconnect them often grew out of an age of organizational "fiefdoms," whereby each division in an organization procured its own resources to meet its own needs. Not only did the heterogeneity of procured products, subsequently interconnected across divisions, spawn numerous technical problems associated with retrieving management information and/or effecting management control actions, but turf battles often occurred between divisions. That is, with boards that provide networking services typically integrated into a computer and connected to its backplane, the border between a network and an attached end-system became cloudy. The procurer and owner of the computer (and its networking board), often felt the resources were "bought and paid for" and consequently did not appreciate the request of another party—the network manager—to manage and consume some of those resources. Furthermore, network administrators often became faced with integrating multiple proprietary management systems in the LAN and WAN environment.

In the short term, these and other organizational issues were often dealt with by new administrative procedures and/or fiats that were brought on by the incorporation of networking, internetworking, and network management into the organization. The long-term effect of such administrative partitioning was to drive the need to develop standardized approaches for managing network resources within domains and for coordinating management between domains. This is discussed in more detail later.

The Technical Environment

Early networks often worked quite well with minimal network management capabilities because users depended on the carriers and major computer vendors to manage their WANs. Later, when LANs were developed to serve tens to hundreds of terminal users in local campus environments, often only a single communications channel and a single suite of proprietary vendor products were supported. Accordingly, network maintenance staff could be readily trained to support the small number of proprietary, single-vendor products in the LAN environment.

Current networks are much more complex, as illustrated by Figure 7-2. The development of the microprocessor has led to the availability and proliferation of low-cost, intelligent devices, such as workstations and personal computers, to be networked. The dramatic increase in the number and intelligence of user devices and user applications has resulted in significant changes in the volume and characteristics of the network traffic. Devices within the network, such as packet switches, concentrators, and gateways, also became more intelligent. Simple terminal-to-host protocols for device-to-device connectivity have been supplemented by complex host-to-host protocols for process-to-process connectivity.

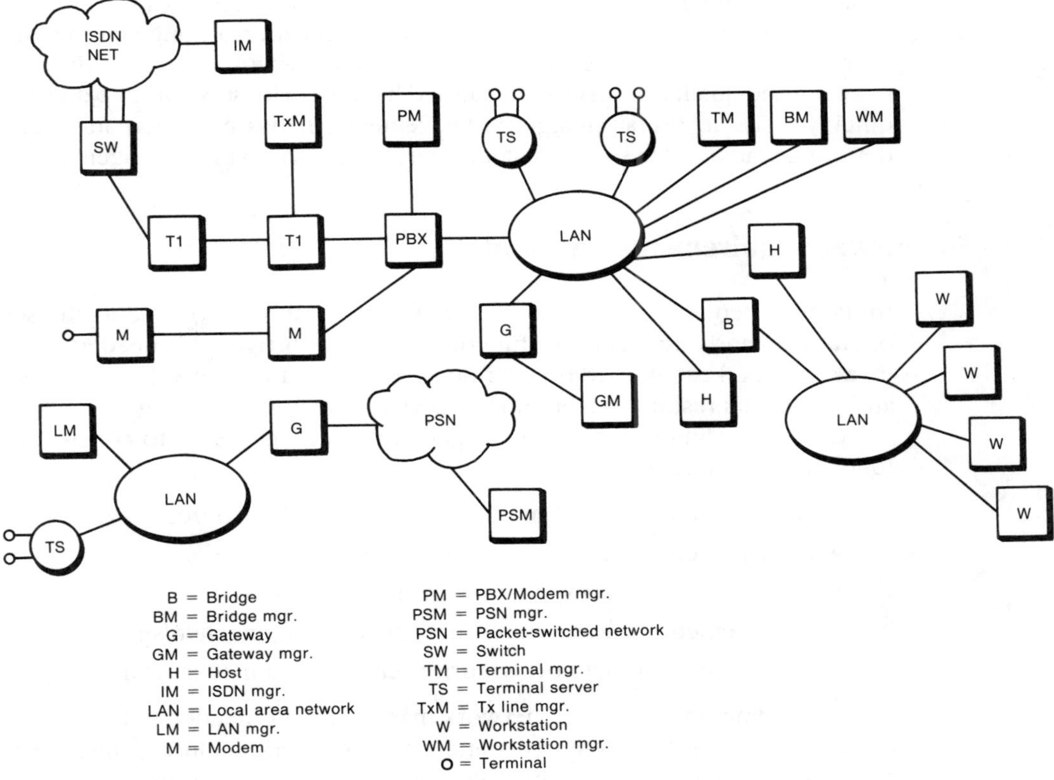

Figure 7-2. The generalized networking environment.

Local campus environments are now served by extended LANs consisting of simple LANs interconnected via data link layer bridges, network layer routers, and upper layer protocol or application layer gateways. Extended LANs are interconnected by WANs, which may typically consist of a multi-interconnected internet of network layer gateways, Tx multiplexers, and ISDN switches. End-system host computers and servers for terminals, printers, disks, and the like may be connected directly to a LAN or WAN or both.

Multiple subnetwork architectures have emerged to overcome geographic or bandwith limits of network products, to cater to differing user quality of service requirements, and to facilitate incremental growth. A typical network may contain many subnets of different technologies as a result of uncoordinated fiefdom acquisitions within an organization. Different subnets within the environment typically use network components from different vendors. These subnetworks usually must be connected to allow communications throughout the organization. Fortunately, through standardization efforts (e.g., OSI and TCP/IP standards) or de facto standards due to marketplace dominance (e.g., IBM's SNA), the number of physical technologies and protocol suites has been sufficiently constrained so that communications interoperability is possible—usually requiring bridging or gatewaying techniques.

Thus, the evolution in technology has allowed the development of extremely large, complex, concatenated, extended networks featuring multiple protocol, multiple channel, and multi-interconnected networking components from heterogeneous vendors to provide communication among heterogeneous user end-systems. However, in such an environment, it has become difficult to maintain the quality of service demanded by network users and to plan for and quickly adapt to users' changing requirements. It has become paramount to develop standards for sophisticated, interoperable network management.

Functional Requirements and Tools

In its most general form, network management can be modeled as the set of operational and administrative functions and supportive tools needed to bring up a network, keep it operational, fine-tune its operation, account for its usage, and protect its resources from unauthorized usage or tampering.

Correspondingly, network management can be modeled to consist of the following five functional areas:

- management of the configuration of network resources
- management of network component and resource faults
- management of network performance
- management of network resource accounting mechanisms
- management of network security services and mechanisms

Expanding on this model, network management is needed to bring up and/or reconfigure end-users systems and entire subnets, including intermediate systems such as gateways and bridges, and to administer their use of names and accompanying network address associations. It is needed to keep the subnets and the networking aspects of end-systems functioning by being able to detect failures and errors in order to isolate and correct communication faults. It is also needed to tune communication performance and improve network effectiveness by diffusing or circumventing communication bottlenecks. Lastly, network management is needed to monitor and control the efficacy of protection mechanisms to ensure the continued protection of communications paths as well as the network management information needed to manage the communication resources associated with these paths.

To support these functional requirements, network management must have tools to define and unambiguously identify the information to be managed, and to define and execute the specific operations (e.g., read, modify) permitted on this information. Furthermore, since the management decision-making processes and the network resources described and managed by this information are often geographically dispersed, network management must have tools for communicating between these processes and the network resources. Lastly, there must be tools for locating distributed instances of this information.

Network Management as a Feedback Control Problem

The essence of the communications network management problem then is to provide and maintain a quality of service commensurate with user communications needs. The quality of service is characterized by a set of metrics, which include indications of service availability, delay, throughput, incidence of security breaches, and so on. The major job of network management is to take network measurements, estimate the quality of service metrics from these measurements, and, to the extent that the estimated metrics deviate from the values desired by the users, initiate and sequence control actions, which may include reconfiguration, to maintain the desired quality of service. This can be considered as a variant of a stochastic estimation and feedback control problem, as portrayed in Figure 7-3.

Network Management Models

This section presents an approach for developing network management solutions. It is, in fact, the approach taken by many of the standards bodies participating in network management. First, a basic framework is developed. It provides a high-level overview or expectation of the solution. In the case of standards development, this overview scopes the standardization activities. It identifies what is, and what is not, being standardized.

Then, more detailed models are developed. These models refine the basic framework, concentrating on those aspects of the framework that are undergoing standardization. The models presented here include

- organizational
- functional
- information

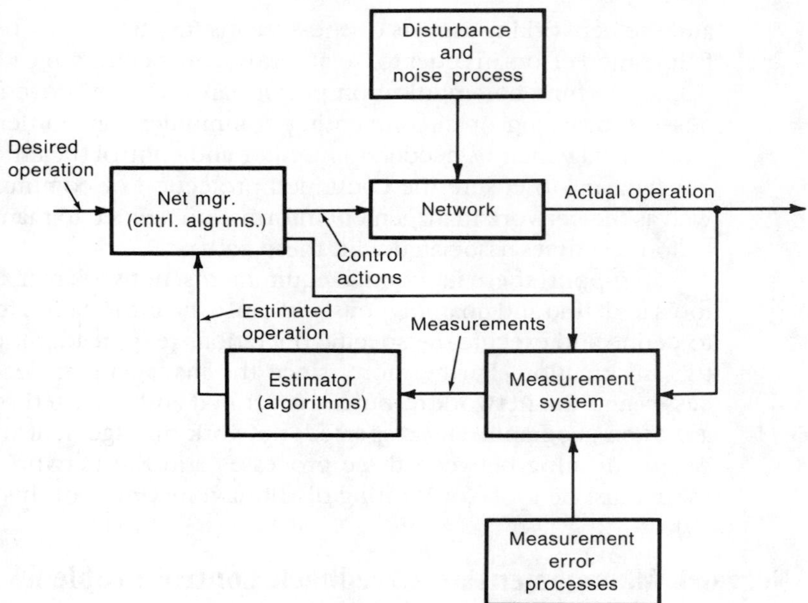

Figure 7-3. Network management—a stochastic estimation and control problem.

Although these models are being developed in the ISO community, they are applicable to, and are being used by, other communities, such as TCP/IP's Internet community and CCITT's telephony network community.

Basic Framework for Standard Network Management

Key to the development of standards for network management is agreement on the basic abstract model, or framework, for network management, as illustrated in Figure 7-4. The basic framework contains a manager system and one or more systems to be managed. Management is treated as a distributed application with components residing within a manager system (managing processes) and managed systems (agent processes).

Management activities are effected by manager processes communicating with remote agent processes to manipulate managed objects contained in the managed systems. Defined for each managed object are attributes (e.g., counters, thresholds, etc.), valid operations on the object, and notifications the object may emit. Both manager and agent processes must have the same shared conceptual view of the managed objects in terms of valid operations and notifications that may be emitted. A managing process may monitor or control one or more agent processes. An agent process manages the associated managed objects. That is, an agent process performs management operations such as reading or modifying attributes of a specific object or set of objects, as requested by a managing process, and may return a response to the managing process. Agent

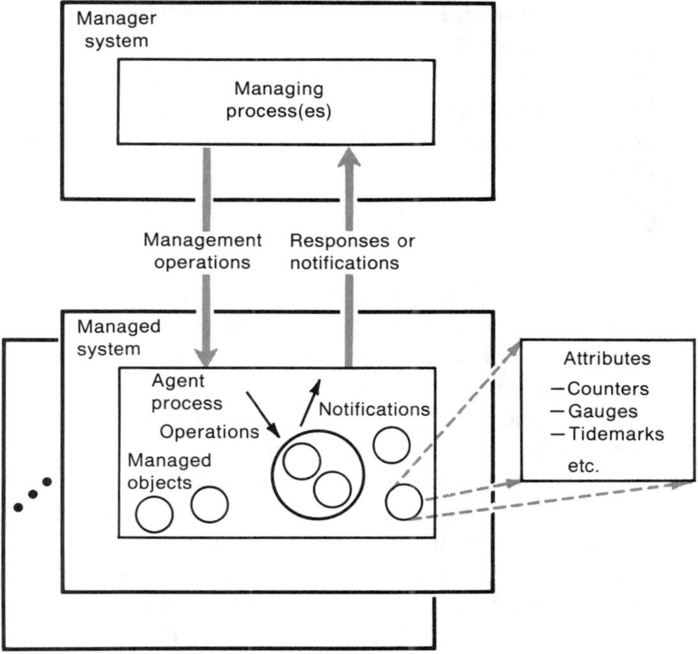

Figure 7-4. Basic network management framework.

processes may also forward notifications (events) asynchronously generated by managed objects.

As illustrated by the basic network management framework, the essentials of network management must include definitions of the data being managed, the operations that can be performed on these data, and the protocols supporting the remoting of these operations across networks. Thus, the network management tools most essential to undergo standardization include

- a common framework for describing network management concepts in terms of the logical components that take part in management (Figure 7-4) and an application of that model to the layered protocol architecture
- a set of communication services and related protocols to transfer management operations and responses as well as notifications between managing and agent processes
- a common structure for the management information
- detailed specifications of the managed objects and their attributes, the management operations permitted on them, notifications they may emit, and how the definition of the managed object relates to the behavior of the real entity it describes
- a mechanism for unambiguously identifying managed objects and associated attributes and events

Descriptions of the standards associated with these above tools are provided later in this chapter in the section entitled "Standards."

How management, per se, is accomplished is not standardized. That is, the algorithms for processing network resource observations, manipulating them to decide if management control actions are necessary, and deciding how to effect and sequence any resulting control actions to accomplish a complex management scenario are not standardized. Vendors are free to use their ingenuity to develop competitive edges in management decision-making capabilities and performance, in the efficacy and sophistication of the network manager's man/machine interface, and so on. Thus, the standards are designed to expedite the commercialization of interoperable network management products without stifling vendor creativity or product differentiation, since, at a minimum, all vendors would use the same standard tools to allow network resource observation and to allow management control action dissemination.

In refinement of the basic network management framework, standards bodies also developed additional models describing in more detail network management from several perspectives. An organizational model describes ways in which management can be administratively distributed. A functional model describes what management services are available to management users, and in the process, defines requirements for definition of the managed objects and the attributes and operations they must support. An information model provides guidance for identifying and defining the managed objects and their associated management information. With the aid of these models, the standards developers were able to refine what portions of the network management solution should undergo standardization. Let's take a closer look at these models.

Organizational Model

The network management for a large internet of interconnected WANs and LANs (Figure 7-2) will normally be partitioned into a number of management domains for reasons of scale, security, or accounting, or to provide administrative autonomy over an organization's resources. As depicted in Figure 7-5, each management domain has a managing process which monitors and controls the managed objects associated with agent processes in the end-systems and intermediate systems in its domain. The management domains may overlap each other as shown in Figure 7-5, one may be contained within another, or they may be disjointed. When management domains overlap, special conditions may apply.

Each domain manager may contain both managing and agent processes. This enables them to interact with other domain managers in either a managing or agent process role to form either hierarchical (superior/subordinate) or peer manager-to-manager relationships for global network management across the entire networking environment.

The administration of a management domain is performed by an administrative authority. This authority may be a public organization offering communication services, e.g., telecommunication administrations, or a private organization.

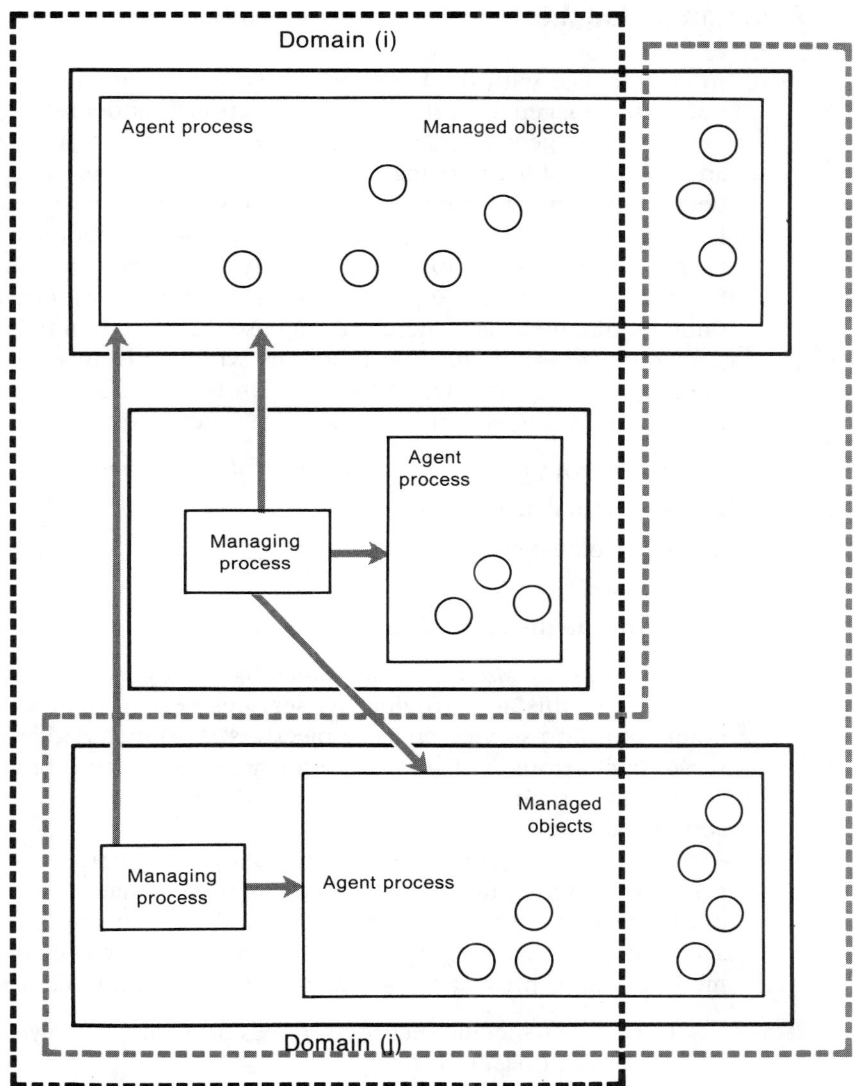

Figure 7-5. Concept of management domains.

The administrative authority is responsible for creation, modification, and maintenance of

- managed objects
- relationships among managing and agent processes of distributed management applications
- relationships among agent processes and managed objects within corresponding managed systems
- security mechanisms for access to managed objects and processes of the distributed management applications

Functional Model

In consonance with the high-level functional requirements to be satisfied by network management solutions, the functional model refinement of the basic network management framework defines five specific management functional areas (SMFAs) of network management. These functional areas are a convenient decomposition of the network management problem into areas based on fulfilling a specific management purpose. This allows network management requirements for each SMFA to be more easily identified, and for functions to be defined to meet those requirements. In some cases, different SMFAs have the same requirements and therefore may use the same functions to satisfy them.

Fault Management. The functions within this area provide the services needed to detect, isolate, and correct problems in disabled network components. Supporting fault management are functions to

- control the sending and logging of received event (e.g., error) reports
- manipulate event logs
- execute diagnostic tests
- trace faults
- initiate the correction of faults

Performance Management. Somewhat analogous to fault management, the functions in this area provide the services needed to measure and maintain communication service quality objectives. Also included are functions to observe, track, store, and analyze performance information associated with network components operating either under normal or controlled (artificially stimulated) conditions.

Security Management. A security policy, i.e., the rules governing the conditions for intercommunication, is implemented by selecting and configuring security services, and by monitoring and supervising their operation. In accordance with a security administration's security policy, security management functions provide the services to monitor and to control

1. the layer-specific security services provided by a layer to ensure the security of data transfers
2. the overall, system-specific security services, such as sending of security events and their logging and audit trails, that are not provided by specific layers
3. the layer-specific mechanisms, such as encipherment, that operate on data to secure their transmission

Accounting Management. The functions supporting this area provide the services to identify and/or negotiate mechanisms for collecting, and associating charges with, information regarding communication resource usage. The communication resources for which usage information can be maintained may include resources within both end-system and intervening networks. In addition, services are provided to activate accounts and monitor account-relevant information.

Configuration Management. Configuration management requires functions to control the configuration of network, system, or layer entities. Supporting this area are functions to

- create, delete, examine and change sets of management information that describe parts of a system
- examine and be notified of changes in the state of the system, to monitor overall operability and usage of the system and give or withhold permission for the use of specific objects
- examine the relationships among various parts of the system, to see how the operation of one part of the system depends upon or is depended upon by other parts

Information Model

The information model refinement of the basic network management framework considers all information to reside in a Management Information Base (MIB) which is a "conceptual repository of Management Information." Information within a system which can be referenced by the management protocol is considered to be part of the MIB. Conventions for locating and uniquely identifying the MIB information allow specific MIB information to be referenced within the management protocols so that it can be operated upon.

The communications and data processing resources to be managed are called managed objects. They include, for example, protocol state machines, layers, connections, and physical devices such as modems. An abstracted view of these objects which represents their properties as seen by management is called a managed object abstraction. This abstraction is not a different object, but simply a constrained view of the same object. For the rest of this chapter, we use the term managed object to refer to the managed object abstraction.

Managed objects for a specific protocol layer are called (N)-layer managed objects. Those that are relevant to multiple layers or to the system as a whole are called system-managed objects.

Structure of Managed Objects

Objects with similar characteristics are grouped into object classes. Each object is an instance of an object class, and an object class may be a subclass of another object class (its superclass). The subclass inherits the characteristics of the superclass from which it is derived, and may contain additional properties. The superclass/subclass hierarchy forms the inheritance tree.

Managed objects (see Figure 7-4) are characterized by

- their attributes, e.g., counters on messages sent or received, number of retransmissions, etc.
- operations which can be performed on them
- notifications which they can emit and be reported on by the agent process to one or more managers

An object's attributes are the smallest entities that can be manipulated using the management protocol. An attribute has an associated value, which may have a simple or complex structure. Each attribute must have at least one operation defined for it, e.g., read or modify.

The definition of a managed object includes specification of the set of management operations that can be performed upon it and the effect of these operations on the object and its attributes. The conditions under which each operation is valid and the set of possible ways that each operation may fail are included in the specification.

Also included in a managed object's specification is whether or not the managed object may emit notifications which can be reported by the agent process to the managing process, or which can be logged. Examples of ways in which notifications may be triggered include: occurrence of errors, defined thresholds being exceeded, timers elapsing, etc. Crucial to the success of any management system is the ability to control if, when, and where notifications are reported.

An object of a particular class may also be regarded as a member of some or all of the superclasses of that class. This capability, called *polymorphism*, allows a managed object class to be extended in such a way that it can be considered to behave as one of its superclasses. An object that is derived from a standard managed object, and contains new standard or proprietary extensions, will behave as its superclass, except for the extensions. This capability allows interoperation between managers that understand the superclass and agents that understand the subclass, or vice versa, at the level of the superclass.

Identification of Managed Objects

Managed object identifiers consist of two components: one which identifies the managed object class to which they belong, and another which identifies the specific instance of their class. Both identifier components are based on hierarchical tree structures. The managed object class identifier is based on a registration hierarchy, and the managed object instance identifier is based on a containment hierarchy. The registration tree is also used to assign identifiers to attributes, events, and anything else which needs a registered identifier.

The *registration hierarchy* is determined by the registration tree, the root and upper levels of which are defined in the ISO/CCITT Abstract Syntax Notation One (ASN.1) standard (ISO 1988b). The identifier represents a path which traverses the tree from the root node to the node to be identified. It is composed of a sequence of integers that represent the arcs of the tree, and is known as an ASN.1 Object Identifier. Figure 7-6 shows the first few levels of the tree, hypothetical assignments for the ISO transport and connection-oriented network service (CONS) as indicated by dotted lines, and part of the subtree assigned to the TCP/IP internet. For example, the identifier for the TCP protocol is {1.3.6.1.2.1.6}.

A *containment hierarchy* occurs when managed object instances of one class contain other managed object instances of the same or different classes. An object instance that contains another object instance is called the *superior object instance*; an object instance that is contained in another object instance is called a *subordinate object instance*. A subordinate managed object is contained in one and only one superior managed object. That is, the hierarchy of

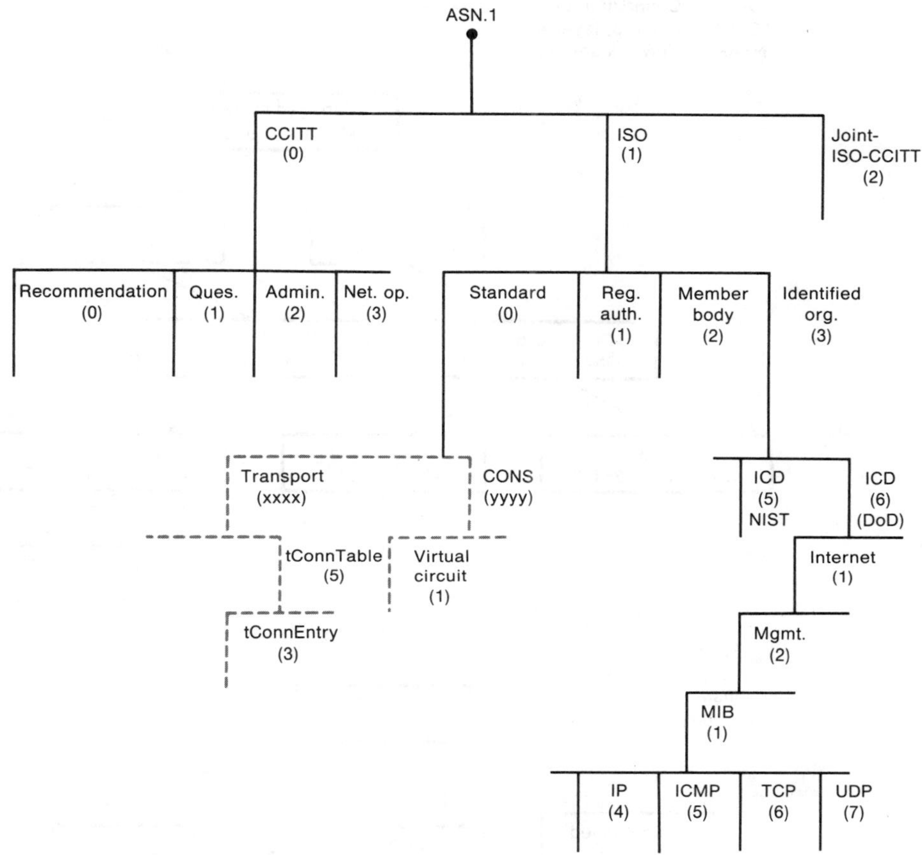

Figure 7-6. An example registration hierarchy.

superior and subordinate managed objects forms a tree known as the *containment tree*, often referred to as the *naming tree*. An example containment tree is illustrated in Figure 7-7.

Associated with each object class is a distinguished attribute, which value serves to differentiate instances of objects of the same class that are contained within the same managed object instance. This distinguished attribute constitutes the object's *relative distinguished name (RDN)*. The unique name of an object instance is formed by concatenating in a sequence the relative distinguished names of its superiors in the naming tree, starting at the root and working down to the managed object to be identified. The entire sequence of RDNs is called a distinguished name. Figure 7-7 and Table 7-1 illustrate this concept.

Standards

The heterogeneity of the organizational environment, the multivendor nature of the technological environment, and the necessity of developing tools to sat-

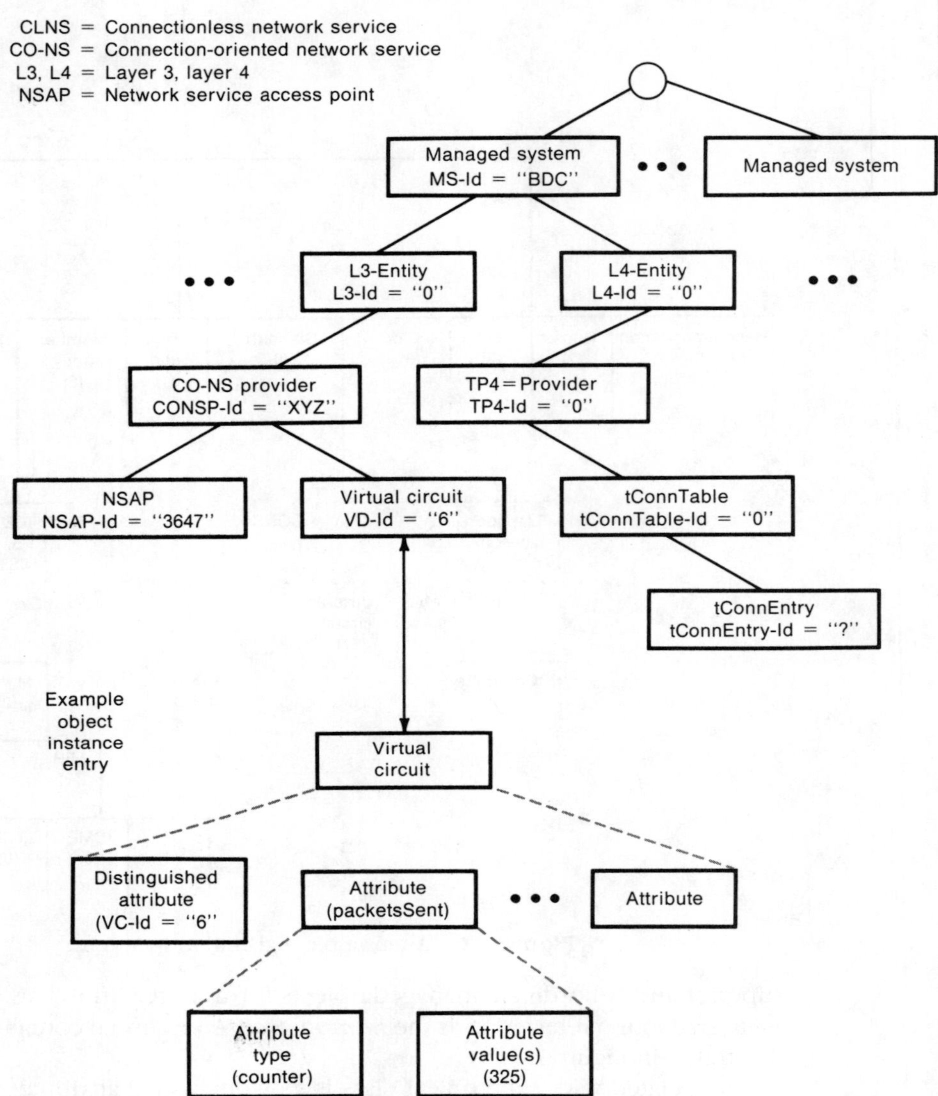

Figure 7-7. Example containment tree and entry.

isfy these functional requirements naturally lead to the need for standards to foster interoperability.

Standards provide cost-effective tools to manage across the diverse range of vendor products and carrier services. Network management based on common public definitions of the most useful network management tools assures worldwide interoperability while lowering networking life-cycle costs. By mandating such standards, multivendor interoperability of diverse end-systems and networking components is thus facilitated across the various fiefdom procurements within an organization, as well as across different procurement phases associated with the same group in an organization. Across the organization, procurements are simplified in that they may all be based on the same standard.

Table 7-1. Object Instance Naming for Figure 7-7

Relative Distinguished Name	Distinguished Name
{MS-Id = "BDC"}	{MS-Id = "BDC"}
{L3-Id = "0"}	{MS-Id = "BDC", L3-Id = "0"}
{CONSP-Id = "XYZ"}	{MS-Id ="BDC", L3-Id = "0", CONSP-Id = "XYZ"}
{VC-Id = "6"}	{MS-Id ="BDC", L3-Id = "0", CONSP-Id = "XYZ", VC-Id = "6"}

Furthermore, the life-cycle costs associated with procurements are lowered for a variety of reasons. That is, the existence of a standard and the reality of a competitor implementing the standard tends to increase the size of the pool of vendors implementing the standard. This competition improves the price performance ratio associated with network management products; either prices drop or capabilities/performance increase or both. With the availability of alternative, standards-based vendor equipment, upgrade costs thus tend to be lower. Lastly, because of the reduced variation in the number of network management tools, there is downward pressure on training and maintenance costs.

This chapter discusses standards in the context of the ISO network management standards. The concepts therein are the most fully developed, have international consensus, and are applicable to other communities that use layered protocols, e.g., the TCP/IP community. The ISO network management standards, as described in the next sections, are organized along the following lines: OSI management structure, management information, and management communication services. These standards provide the network management tools previously summarized.

OSI Management Structure

The OSI management structure is the basic network management framework described earlier (ISO/IEC 1989k, 1988c). This structure accommodates management from several perspectives: protocol, layer, and systems.

In brief, protocol management consists of those protocol-internal mechanisms needed to control a particular instance of communication. An example is flow-control windows on a particular transport layer connection. Protocol management is described within the protocol's standard, and is not discussed further herein. Layer management is associated with multiple communication and/or protocol instances at a specific layer. It consists of those activities needed to manage all OSI resources associated with a particular layer, e.g., network layer-routing mechanisms. Systems management consists of those activities needed to manage the OSI resources associated with several protocol layers in an open system. Systems management and layer management are considered in more detail in the next two sections.

Systems Management

An application of the basic network management framework to a layered protocol architecture, as exemplified by OSI protocols, is illustrated in Figure 7-8. Note that the modules described here are only conceptual and are not meant to imply an actual implementation. The model applies equally well to other layered protocols. For example, in the TCP/IP Internet's long-term approach to network management (Warrier and Besaw 1989), the presentation protocol is constrained to be the lightweight presentation protocol specified in Rose (1988), the session protocol is null, the transport protocol is the Internet's TCP (Postel 1981c) or UDP (Postel 1981a), and the network protocol is the Internet's IP (Postel 1981b).

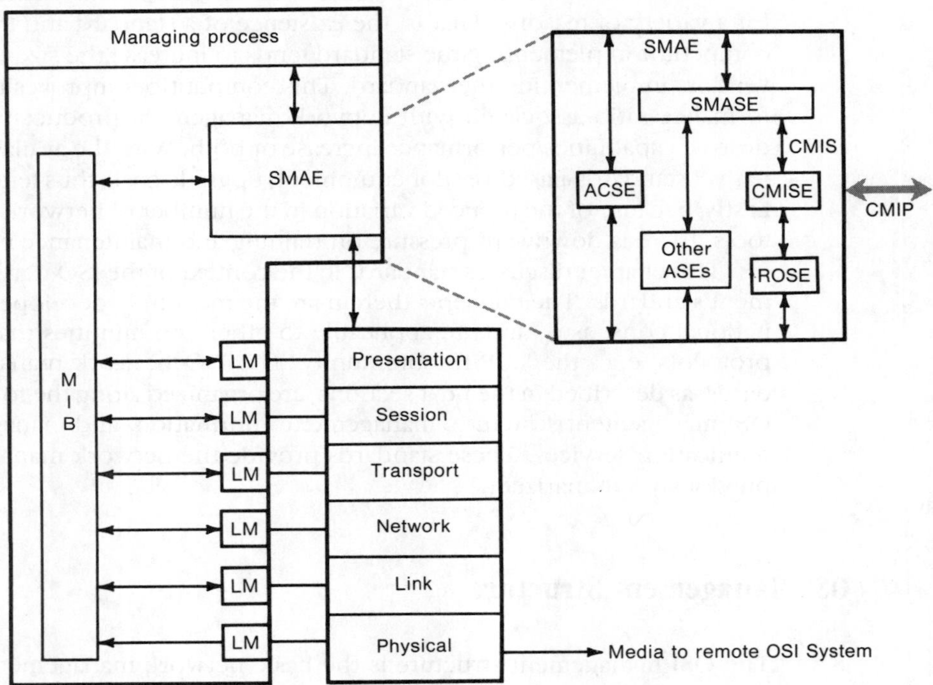

Figure 7-8. Architectural model of OSI management.

As shown in Figure 7-8, manager systems contain the suite of communications protocols and the management application process called a managing process. Managed systems (not shown) also contain the suite of communications protocols and a management application process, which in this case is called the agent process. Managing and agent processes contain application entities for communications and modules for accessing managed objects. A system management application entity (SMAE) is responsible for communications. Layer management modules (LMs) provide access to the managed objects associated with each protocol entity. The MIB contains information for each communication protocol entity, as well as for each system as a whole.

An SMAE consists of an association control service element (ACSE) and a systems management application service element (SMASE). The ACSE is used to establish application layer connections, so-called "associations," with other SMAEs. Once this is done, the SMASE is used to exchange information between the associated SMAEs.

The SMASE defines the behavior of the management process, together with identification of the semantics and abstract syntaxes of the specific management information to be exchanged between management processes. The layer standards and system management standards specify the classes of managed objects and their behavior and attributes.

The SMASE relies on other ASEs to effect communications. Typically, the services of the common management information service element (CMISE) are used. The management information exchange protocol for effecting CMISE services is the common management information protocol (CMIP). CMIP is a symmetrical protocol. It makes no assumption about which management process initiates, terminates, or controls the communication link. (The asymmetry between "managing" and "agent" processes is strictly a characteristic of relationships between management applications, not one of protocol.) To obtain needed transaction-oriented, communication services, CMIP uses the services provided by ROSE (Remote Operations Service Element).

For some management information communication situations, it may be desirable for an SMASE to use the services of ASEs other than CMISE, e.g., transaction processing (TP), or file transfer, access, and management (FTAM).

Taken as a whole, an SMAE ultimately relies on the services of the underlying protocol layers to communicate with other peer SMAEs.

In summary, the manager process may receive inputs from local administrative personnel or their (potentially AI-based) software agents, from local LMs, and/or from remote agent processes and LMs. Decisions made by the manager process are either effected by local mechanisms to the local managed objects, or they are communicated to remote agent processes via SMAEs.

Layer Management

Sometimes management activities must occur to assure continued operation of a particular layer throughout the network and across multiple instances of communication. For example, at the network layer, routing information is dynamically exchanged using protocols specific to the network layer. Data link layer protocols that use token passing (ANSI FDDI, IEEE 802.4 Token Bus, IEEE 802.5 Token Ring) must manage the token, detect faults, and automatically recover without requiring assistance from systems management applications. The protocols and managed objects specific to layer management are described in the standard specific to the layer.

Management Information

There are two aspects of the standards-defining management information: the structure of management information (SMI) and the managed object descriptions that apply to real resources. Details of the former are given in ISO/IEC (1989i, 1989a, 1989b, 1989h). Examples of the latter appear in ISO/IEC (1988d, 1988e) and IEEE (1988).

Structure of Management Information

The SMI standardization activities began reaching the initial draft proposal (DP) level of standardization in late 1988. Other parts of the SMI standard as well as working drafts of the standards associated with the definition of managed objects for some of the lower layer protocols are anticipated to reach the initial DP level of standardization in 1989.

The SMI describes

- the information model (ISO/IEC 1989i)
- templates used for defining managed object classes, attributes, and the containment hierarchy (ISO/IEC 1989h)
- definitions of support-managed object classes (ISO/IEC 1989a) and generic attributes (ISO/IEC 1989b), including their syntax, behavior, and valid operations

The managed object class template includes

- the name and unique registered identifier for the object
- mandatory attributes of the object class
- the superclasses from which the object is derived (inheritance)
- the set of superclasses to which the object is polymorphic
- the object class's distinguished attributes
- valid operations on the object, e.g., CREATE, DELETE, and specific ACTIONS and events
- the specific behavior of the object
- optional attributes, behaviors, and operations

The attribute template includes

- the name and unique registered identifier for the attribute
- the attribute syntax and semantics
- the range of valid values for the attribute
- valid operations on the attribute

The containment hierarchy is defined by a name-binding template which includes

- the object class name
- the name of the superior object class
- the name of the distinguished attribute used to create the relative distinguished name of the object

Support-managed object classes and generic attributes are types of object classes and attributes which may in principle be components of managed objects of a wide variety of classes. Example support objects might be discriminator objects that control the filtering of events reported to a remote manager or entered into a log. Example generic attributes include counters, gauges, and tidemarks. These object and attribute types may be used as components in the definitions of specific managed object classes defined to represent real resources, such as those defined for protocol entities.

Managed Object Definitions

There are two basic types of managed objects: those associated with protocol layers (layer objects) and those that are not associated with any protocol layer or that span several layers (system objects).

Examples of system objects and attributes include system time, the name of the manufacturer of a specific network node, the state of a node, the access control and event control tables associated with a node, etc.

The transport layer's retransmission timer, the network layer's routing table update timer, counters on protocol data units sent and received, and counts on various types of errors and thresholds on those errors are examples of layer objects and attributes.

Layer objects and attributes for a LAN MAC protocol can be drawn from IEEE 802.3. The emerging IEEE 802.3 layer management information standard (IEEE 1988) defines parameters for layer initialization, counts on transmit and receive frames, and thresholds for error detection.

Management Communication Services

Management processes communicate with each other by invoking Management Services. Remember, the standard defining these services is the CMIS (ISO/IEC 1988a, 1988k, 1988m), and the OSI standard protocol defined to provide the CMIS services is the CMIP (ISO/IEC 1988b, 1988l, 1988n).

CMIS relies on the ACSE (ISO 1988a) and the Remote Operations (RO) service (ISO 1987) for basic communication services. Recall that ACSE is used to establish and terminate application-to-application connections, called associations. RO provides a request/reply service over the association established by the ACSE. Requests are associated with replies by an invocation identifier. RO also provides for linking multiple replies to a single request. RO has a parameter for indicating which CMIS operation is carried in the RO request or reply.

The following services are provided by CMIS:

- initialization services—to exchange information about managed objects, management functions, and CMIS services supported by each end of the association established by ACSE
- information transfer services
- synchronization and linked-reply service

Information transfer services provide management operations services which

- create and delete managed objects (CMIP CREATE and DELETE operations)
- retrieve attributes of managed objects (CMIP GET operation)
- cancel retrieval services (CMIP CANCELGET operation)
- modify attributes of managed objects (CMIP SET operation)
- perform actions that may be specific to a managed object, such as initiating a diagnostic self-test and reporting the results (CMIP ACTION operation)

and notification services, which transfer events emitted by managed objects to remote managers (CMIP EVENT-REPORT operation).

Synchronization and linked-reply service provide for

- synchronization of an operation across multiple objects (best effort or atomic)
- multiple replies to be returned as a result of a single request and linked with that request (provided by RO)

Some services have "modes," both confirmed and unconfirmed. Confirmed services require the remote management process to send a response to indicate receipt and success or failure of the operation. Unconfirmed services do not use responses.

Sometimes a single service request may be applied across many managed objects. CMIS provides the capability of selecting which objects are to be operated on through a process of *scoping* and *filtering*. Scoping identifies which managed objects are candidates for selection (by specifying the root of a subtree in the containment hierarchy) and how many levels down the subtree are to be searched. Filtering is the application of a set of tests to each of the scoped (candidate) managed objects to extract a subset.

Management Functional Areas

For convenience, the requirements to be satisfied by OSI management standards have been partitioned into the same five SMFAs previously described in the functional model: Fault Management, Performance Management, Security Management, Accounting Management, and Configuration Management.

The partitioning of network management requirements into five areas is merely a convenience to develop requirements. Indeed, SMFAs have overlapping requirements, and management information and functions applicable to one SMFA are often applicable to another SMFA. For example, the management service control function (ISO/IEC 1988j) for controlling event reporting is applicable to all SMFAs. Other common functions are also emerging (ISO/IEC 1988f, 1988g, 1988h, 1988i, 1989c, 1989j). Similarly, counters on messages transmitted or received are examples of management information useful to Performance,

Accounting, and Fault SMFAs. In addition to the common system management functions referenced above, which are just beginning to be standardized, ISO is publishing the SMFA requirements in five separate documents (ISO/IEC 1988o, 1989e, 1989g, 1989f, 1989d). The management information is specified in documents appropriate to the resources to be managed.

Registration Mechanisms

The top levels of the registration tree for creating and registering ASN.1 OBJECT IDENTIFIERS for managed objects, attributes, events, etc., are described in the ASN.1 standard. However, all the formal mechanisms for becoming a registration authority, i.e., being given a branch in the registration hierarchy and authorization to administer the attached subtree, are not in place. In addition, the rules for a registration authority are unclear. Standards organizations are currently addressing the problem.

Use of Protocol Operations

An example of management operations will help clarify how the tools described in the previous sections can be applied to the manipulation of management information. The following is an example protocol exchange between a manager and an agent, using a pseudolanguage for management messages. It uses the registration tree in Figure 7-6 and the containment tree in Figure 7-7 for identification of objects. All messages are encapsulated in lower layer data units (PDUs), which are not shown.

The manager first establishes an association with the agent in the managed system. The association-information field in the A-Associate-request will contain all necessary information for addressing the agent process, and for parsing the data exchanged over the association. The user-information field contains a bit string that includes indications of which operations the manager is capable of requesting and performing. The access-control field is used for security—in this case it contains a simple password, "witches brew." The A-Associate-Response user-information field contains a bit string that includes indications of which operations the agent is capable of requesting and performing.

```
                                      -- Create a manager/agent association

A-Associate-Request {

    association-information      {...}
    user-information             {
         CMIS-functional-units          {'01011010101010101110B'}
         access-control          {"witches brew"}
                             }
                    }
```

```
A-Associate-Response        {
    user-information             {
        CMIS-functional-units              {'101001010101010101110B'}
                                  }
                     }
```

Management requests and responses are carried as arguments of RO protocol data units. The RO PDUs contain an invokeId parameter which is used to relate responses to requests. The RO PDUs also contain an operation-value field which indicates which CMIP operation is contained in the PDU (m-GET in this example).

The first request of the manager is to get the attribute "packetsSent" on virtual circuit "6." No scoping or filtering is applied. Therefore, this request applies to the baseManagedObject (virtual-circuit) only. The result is returned with the attribute "packetsSent" having the value "325." The current time (including data) is also returned.

```
                                   --First management request

RO-Invoke {
    invokeId                101,
    operation-value m-GET (3),
    argument  {
        baseManagedObjectClass      { virtual-circuit (1.0.yyyy.1) }
        baseManagedObjectInstance {MS-Id="BDC", L3-Id="0",
                                    CONSP-Id="XYZ",VC-Id="6"}
        attributeIdList  {
            attributeId     {packetsSent}
                          }
            }
        }
                                   --Response to first management request

RO-Result {
    invokeId                101,
    operation-value m-GET (3),
    argument {
        baseManagedObjectClass      { virtual-circuit (1.0.yyyy.1) }
        baseManagedObjectInstance {MS-Id="BDC", L3-Id="0",
                                    CONSP-Id="XYZ", VC-Id="6"}
        currentTime     "19890105223015.42000z"
        attributeList    {
            {attributeId    {packetsSent},
              attributeValue  325)
                          }
            }
        }
```

The second request of the manager is for the agent to return the values of "packetsReceived" and "packetsReceivedWithError" from all transport connection table entries (tConnEntrys) that have retransmitted more than 5 packets ("retransmittedPkts" > 5). In this request, the scope is set to include only those object instances that are one level below tConnTable (the baseManagedObject in the containment tree) to include all instances of tConnEntry. Filtering is applied to all instances of tConnEntry. That is, the agent must examine each instance of tConnEntry to see if the attribute "retransmittedPkts" is greater than 5. In this example, only one such instance of the managed object tConnEntry satisfies the filter criterion, and therefore only one tConnEntry is returned as the response. If multiple tConnEntry instances had satisfied the filter criterion, then "packetsReceived" and "packetsReceivedWithError" for each tConnEntry instance would be returned as a separate management response.

```
                              --Second management request

RO-Invoke {
    invokeId                102,
    operation-value m-Get (3),
    argument  {
        baseManagedObjectClass    { tConnTable (1.0.xxxx.5) }
        baseManagedObjectInstance {MS-Id="BDC", L4-Id="0",
                                   TP4-Id="QRS", tConnTable-Id="0"}
        scope     oneLevel (1),
        filter    { (retransmittedPackets > 5) }
        attributeIdList  {
              attributeId     {packetsReceived},
              attributeId     {packetsReceivedWith Errors}
                         }
              }
         }

                              --Response to second request

RO-Result {
    involkeId               102,
    operation-value m-Get (3),
    argument  {
        baseManagedObjectClass    { tConnEntry (1.0.xxxx.5.3) }
        baseManagedObjectInstance {MS-Id="BDC", L4-Id="0",
                                   TP4-Id="QRS", tConnTable-Id="0",
                                    tConnEntry-Id="12"}
        currentTime       "198901052232.23000z"
        attributeList   {
             (attributeId     {packetsReceived},
              attributeValue  323),
```

```
                    (attributeId {packetsReceivedWithErrors},
                attributeValue  2)
                                  }
                    }
            }
```

Finally, the manager closes the association.

```
                                        --Close the association

A-Associate-Release {
     user-information    { reason normal }
                         }

A-Associate-Response       {
     user-information      { reason normal }
                         }

                                 --The management association is closed
```

Commercializing Standard Products

Remember, once the international standards discussed above have stabilized, a whole other set of organizations and activities is initiated in order to bring interoperable, multivendor products to the marketplace (see Figure 7-1). For example, profiles and specifications must be developed to delineate which options within the standards are to be implemented. Multivendor implementation agreements are needed to guide vendors in their detailed implementations of the specifications. Interoperability demonstrations of multiple vendor implementations need to take place. Conformance tests need to be developed and conducted to certify that vendor products conform to the standards they presumably implemented. These activities tend to be initiated at about the time a standard reaches DIS status. As these activities progress, any deficiencies in the standards and requirements or suggestions for new features are fed back to the standards bodies as the standards progress to full IS (International Standard) status. Also during this time, to prove and validate solutions to specification and implementation agreements issues, prototypes are often built by impartial parties so that their findings can be fed back to the specifications and implementation agreements processes. Often such prototypes can be used to determine realistic performance bounds that can be used in acquisition of products. Once these activities have all reached fruition, vendors can build interoperable products and users can write procurement packages to acquire these products. The network management community is just now beginning to gear up for this commercialization phase.

There are several major network management specification activities underway. Three are driven by users. User groups from the MAP/TOP efforts (representing an enormous consortium from the industrial and office automation communities) and the GOSIP efforts (one representing the USA government and a second representing the United Kingdom's government) are developing network management specifications based on emerging ISO standards. A fourth specification activity is being driven by vendors. Under the auspices of the IAB, specifications are being developed for TCP/IP-based networking components. Despite differences in the communication protocols to be managed in the TCP/IP community (i.e., they are non-ISO), the long-term network management specifications are based on ISO network management standards.

All these groups are defining, for their own constituencies, network management specifications based on ISO standards. Their differences are reflected in what the standardization level was/is/will be of the standards to which their specifications apply. MAP/TOP network management specifications are based on early ISO WDs (Working Drafts) and DPs. The TCP/IP and GOSIP network management specifications are mutually based on more mature ISO WDs, DPs, and DISs. The GOSIP specifications will evolve as other ISO DISs and ISs emerge. The TCP/IP specifications, fulfilling an interim need until ISO networking components are fielded, may have no reason to upgrade their specifications as more mature ISO network management standards emerge. The MAP/TOP group's specifications apparently will be frozen until the mid 1990s, at which time they may be upgraded, or conceivably the final GOSIP network management specification may be endorsed. Details of these specification efforts are given in Appendix E.

Integrated Network Management

Our previous discussions on network management standards and the commercialization of products based on these standards focus on management in a single domain. The ISO standard network management organizational model, however, accommodates multiple domains of management. In fact, corroborating the need for multiple managers and multiple domains of management are the following:

- the complexity of today's networks
- the need to be able to scale these networks and their management capabilities to meet user needs
- the natural administrative partitioning of network resources within an organization
- the reality of multiple monitoring centers for accounting across interconnected networks
- the reality of manager products strictly oriented to specific carrier services
- the reality of manager products strictly oriented to specific vendors' particular network component product lines, such as terminal servers or bridges

Multiple management domains have associated with them yet other classes of network management needs and problems. Tantamount are both the need to integrate potentially autonomous, heterogeneous managers and the problem of arbitrating conflicting management decisions among such managers. These needs become more crucial as users begin demanding the elimination of "war rooms" consisting of many uncoordinated, inconsistent, noninteroperable, management systems consoles. Correspondingly, the multiple manager arbitration problem becomes more acute when multiple, virtual, separately managed, voice, and data communications services share the same transmission facilities.

At this point, very little further work addressing interdomain management issues is underway in the data communication standards community. However, several vendors are developing and/or marketing interdomain management solutions.

In the next section we consider the marketplace-driven, vendor activities oriented toward ad hoc, multidomain solutions, the needs for standard tools for manager-to-manager interactions, and interdomain management issues that need to be considered by the community in more detail.

Vendor Activities

Several vendors have begun addressing what they perceive to be perhaps the largest, timeliest, most important needs of the network management marketplace—the integration of multiple, heterogeneous management systems. Such integration permits an end-to-end view of network services when the services used are provided by several domains within a network or within an interconnected catnet.

Prominent among the vendors addressing these needs are the largest computer and carrier providers. Products such as IBM's NetView and NetView/PC, Digital's EMA (Enterprise Management Architecture) management director, Hewlett-Packard's OpenView, AT&T's UNMA (Unified Network Management Architecture) management workstation, Cincom's (Software Development Pty. Ltd.'s) NET/MASTER, Bolt Berenek and Newman's Automated Network Management System, and the like are beginning to address aspects of interdomain management.

Common among their approaches are the following notions:

- They focus primarily on that part of the manager/manager integration problem dealing with manager-to-manager interconnectivity.
- They allow management users a consistent view of their management capabilities as if these capabilities were provided by one system, even though these capabilities are often provided by many, diverse, heterogeneous, management subsystems.
- They concentrate on integrating the monitoring/reporting of management objects/events across individual management subsystems.
- They accommodate tiered integration architectures that permit hierarchical management authorities.
- They support management services functionally similar to the more mature ISO SMFA's, namely configuration and fault management.
- They rely on translations and mappings to interface the native management communication protocols, structure, and naming of management information, and managed objects implemented in different management subsystems with those inherent to their own network management implementation.

- They permit management users to build their own management applications that drive, or create presentations from, their integrated network management system.
- They use a modularized, building-block approach to facilitate easy accommodation of unforeseen variations in the environment being managed, the relationships between managers, the network management communication protocols, etc.

The other major initiatives in the network management vendor community that will impact the marketplace of the 1990s are the formations of numerous vendor alliances. To tackle users' needs for interoperability among heterogeneous managers and/or to create/challenge marketplace dominance, several companies have been bonding together in numerous, multivendor alliances.

Prominent among these alliances is the OSI Network Management Forum (NMF), a corporation consisting of members from certain computer vendors, carriers, telecommunication vendors, and others. To accelerate the commercialization of interoperable products that permit integrated, multidomain management, the NMF is developing manager-to-manager interaction agreements, accelerating the development of applicable standards, and developing a multivendor demonstration of management equipment built to these agreements.

Other examples of multivendor alliances include Cincom/AT&T, Cincom/Nixdorf, Apple/DEC, and DEC with numerous third parties such as Digital Communication Associates, CODEX, and HP with numerous third parties. The Cincom/AT&T pact permits integration of OSI and SNA network management. The Cincom/Nixdorf alliance will tie the SNA network management marketplace with products for UNIX operating systems. The Apple/DEC network management link-up will allow managers of Apple (Macintosh-Appletalk)/Digital (VAX-DECnet/OSI) internets to view DECnet resources with AppleTalk network management tools and vice versa, pass network management event reports from AppleTalk management systems to those of DECnet, and monitor and control components of AppleTalk for VMS and the AppleTalk/DECnet gateway. Furthermore, DEC's agreements with third-party vendors will expand DEC's ability to manage non-DEC equipment when such equipment is included in, or interacts with, DEC environments. Finally, via a Network Management Alliance, HP is allowing other vendors to use the network presentation services.

Manager/Manager Standards

Communication from one application to another often occurs by using standard networking resources in several domains. For example, these domains may include

- local, departmentally managed LANs
- organizationally managed, campus-wide, backbone networks
- privately managed, carrier-provided, local exchange networks
- privately managed, public internets or private interexchange networks

Manager/manager standards are thus needed to facilitate commercialization of low-cost, interoperable managers that support interoperation and integration of the several possible, heterogeneous vendor and provider managers managing the various standard networking resources in the several domains encountered from one end of the communication path to the other. In essence, such standards would afford "universal" vendor alliances, thereby obviating the current need for vendors to make specific alliances with other vendors in order to support the joint development of vendor-to-vendor management translations/mappings.

While the ISO Systems Management Overview standard (ISO/IEC 1989k) accommodates multiple domains of management, little additional standards development activities are currently underway to address multiple domain management. It is purported that CMIP, together with other existing ISO application layer protocols, such as FTAM, VTP (Virtual Terminal Protocol), and RDA (Remote Database Access) will be sufficient to handle all manager-to-manager communication needs. However, a plethora of other issues, such as the definitions of the managed objects/attributes to be exchanged between managers, additional SMI structures/enhancements that may be needed for these managed objects, and manager/manager arbitration policies, as well as those issues examined in more detail in the next section need to be considered by standards developers.

Future Activities

The work required to assure the availability of useful, interoperable, multivendor network management products is far from done. Several issues remain to be addressed within the standards, vendor, and user communities. Some of the more important issues are those associated with

- decision making
- stability
- reliability
- human interface
- security
- implementation concerns
- standards timeliness
- manager-to-manager integration

Decision Making

To date, much of the focus of network management activities has been on developing tools for identifying and communicating management information between managers and devices they manage. To a large extent, this work is now, or will soon be, coming to fruition. Efforts are now beginning to shift to determine how to manage networks and, consequently, how to use the standardized tools to provide network management functions.

As a first step, the management decisions that need to be made, either manually by network management personnel or automatically by intelligent management decision-making processes, must be identified.

Issues associated with understanding the roles of systems management (i.e., coordinated management of the entire communications protocol stack within a managed system) versus layer management (i.e., the autonomous tuning of individual protocol layers across many nodes) need to be articulated and studied. Mechanisms for coordinating and negotiating equitable compromises between these two potentially divergent perspectives must be defined.

The rules on how to manipulate observations about network operations in order to decide what is an appropriate control action are the management decision-making algorithms. These algorithms also decide when to initiate a control action, how multiple control actions must be sequenced, and how to synchronize changes across all distributed instances of managed objects associated with certain network resources.

Several other issues associated with decision-making algorithms need to be examined. For example, what should be the roles of AI and expert systems in decision-making algorithms? What are the tradeoffs between manual-driven algorithms versus automatic ones? In certain circumstances it is conceivable that once an initial event reporting threshold/trigger is crossed, volleys of highly correlated event reports, with little additional information to the network manager, will be generated. Mechanisms should be considered for controlling the flow of event reports so that the manager is not overrun with event reports (and the network is not flooded with management communications).

Still other issues associated with decision-making algorithms include the following: What are the useful network operations metrics relevant to the decision-making processes? What network operations measurements are necessary to compute these metrics? How accurately can/must these metrics reflect the actual operation of the network? Since measurements/observations of network-related events and operations may need to be made at any and all protocol layers, and since instantiations of these protocol layers are distributed across the network environment, it may be impossible to make observations on all distributed instances of the same protocol at one instant in time. Furthermore, because of the variable time delays that are likely to exist between observations made on resources associated with one protocol layer and observations made on resources associated with another protocol layer, it may be impossible to obtain a temporally consistent snapshot of network operations from which metrics can be estimated. Are the protocol layer measurements currently being proposed by standardization bodies appropriate for these metrics? Are there particularly crucial measurements that, in somewhat of a mathematical analogy, can be considered as "maximum eigenvectors" (i.e., knowing only their values is sufficient for the management decision-making algorithm to make the "correct" decision "most" of the time).

Official standards-making bodies generally frown on standardizing algorithms. On the other hand, organizations procuring several network managers from different vendors need to consider whether or not they should specify particular management algorithms that must be supported by the equipment they buy. Of particular concern to some organizations may be the necessity of heterogeneous managers to decide to take identical control actions if they are each presented with identical sets of observations about network operations.

Stability of Decision-Making Processes

Another important issue is understanding the stability of the management decision-making algorithms. Instability in network management can arise from several factors.

First, because network management can be modeled as a feedback control process, the inherent delays between the times at which network operation measurements are made and the times at which resulting management control actions are effected by the management decision-making algorithms can create an unstable network management control system. Furthermore, the network management system is not simply a single feedback path-control system. Rather, it has multiple, parallel feedback paths, e.g., at least one feedback path from each network node to the network manager. In addition, each feedback path may have its own delay characteristics.

Second, nonlinear control algorithms can foster instability. In particular, nonlinearities in network management decision-making algorithms can arise from the kinds of hysteresis that may be introduced by network management operations' event-reporting mechanisms triggered both by upperbound and lowerbound threshold crossings. That is, certain events might be reported either when the value of a specific network observation rises above an upperbound threshold or falls below a specific lowerbound threshold. The regimes under which instabilities associated with such nonlinearities can arise need extensive investigation.

Lastly, relatively autonomous managers, such as independent layer managers within one network or independent subnet managers in a concatenated system of several subnets, can make conflicting decisions that can set management instabilities into motion. For example, each manager, having a particularly biased view of the state of network resources, will likely try to make decisions that benefit the resources it manages (such as transport layer entities) rather then to benefit the entire system of distributed instances of multiple, interrelated protocol layers. More specifically, the issues to be examined include how likely is it for autonomous managers within a networked system (a), to make conflicting decisions that sacrifice the good of the entire networked system in favor of the good of the subset of the network objects they manage, or (b), to engage in deadlock battles of inconsistent, suboptimal decisions, wherein one manager tries to undo the decision of another, and vice versa, and vice versa, ad infinitum.

Understanding the stability regimes associated with such extremely nonlinear control systems with heterogeneous feedback delay characteristics is at the cutting edge of contemporary control theoretic principles and is therefore difficult to ascertain. It is unlikely that typical network management systems will lend themselves to closed-form stability equation solutions; and, without further developments in control theory principles and tools, stability analyses of such systems may, in fact, be totally intractable.

Reliability of Management

Those management decisions that are particularly crucial for assuring acceptable network operations need to be identified. What then needs to be considered is whether or not to provide fault tolerance for those associated critical, core management decision-making processes and mechanisms. Furthermore, mechanisms for supporting continued network operation during periods of the absence of network management functionality should be examined.

Human Interface

Organizations procuring several network managers from different vendors, or from different product lines from a single vendor, may wish to have common, specific, ergonomic properties of the man-machine interface (MMI) between network management personnel and the network management decision-making processes. In particular, organizations may find it desirable to standardize MMI display icons, icon usage rules, icon color meanings, and so on across the multiple vendor network management products they buy. The efficacy of standards covering such topics needs further examination. Traditionally, standards bodies have not considered user interface standards, although recent trends such as in IEEE's POSIX (Portable Operating System Interface) standardization effort may be changing such tradition.

Security

Open management requires hostility protection. That is, with management concepts and services being standardized and publicly available, potentially serious network vulnerability issues arise. Hostile "attacks," whether overtly conspicuous or insidiously inconspicuous, upon the network management system can be as effective in destroying network services as active physical aggression on the network. For example, an intruder spoofing as a network manager can alter a router's routing tables thereby destroying communications as effectively as cutting cables.

Security and protection issues that need to be examined include the following. Should management communications be encrypted? What type of mechanisms are sufficient to control access to the management system? What types of mechanisms should be considered to authenticate the validity of the person or process that makes a request of the network management system?

Implementation

Vendors will be faced with a multitude of implementation issues. Regarding CPU requirements for network management, vendors need to determine the processing power required for network management implementations. This is particularly an issue for existing communication products implemented on fixed, specific CPUs. When network management is to be incorporated into these products, implementers will need to understand how much less processing power will be available for applications and/or communications.

A corollary of this is understanding what load will be placed on the network due to communications that are specific to network management. This impacts how much communication bandwidth and/or communications duty cycle is available for normal application-to-application communication.

Additionally, there are several issues associated with distributing network management functionality. Looking from the perspective of the network manager, can the distribution of network management functional areas, such as fault management and performance management, into several distributed processors be as efficient as centralizing network management functionality into one processor? If network management functional areas are distributed, are there synchronization problems among the concurrent distributed instances of the network management functionality? What is the impact of communication delays between distributed management functionality, as well as between management decision-making processes and management agents; will these delays create instability problems, as hypothesized earlier in this chapter, in the inherent feedback control systems established via network management?

While efficiency is an issue for many, for others effectiveness and reliability of management control actions may be more important. For example, management agents may be intermittently out of contact with their managers: satellites may be out of sight of their managing ground stations or packet radios may be in communication null spots. For network management decisions and actions not requiring real-time reaction, network managers may choose to support delayed, reliable delivery of management communications. How should such services be implemented for these situations? Should management communications be transferred via electronic mail protocols such as X.400?

Standards Timeliness

Users are clamoring for network management products. Many realize the benefits of products based on complete, mature standards and are in a position to wait for these products, but the full suite of network management standards will not be mature until the 1990s. Some users will not be able to postpone their procurements until then. For these users, the timeliness associated with network management standardization is creating problems.

Users who immediately need network management must rely on proprietary solutions. Even the emerging "OSI management" products touted by some vendors are, in effect, proprietary. That is, although the implemented management protocols are based on early ISO standards, the syntax, semantics, and identification of manageable information do not necessarily reflect what will be in the eventual standards governing these topics. Many of the users who buy today will eventually be faced with issues of transitioning to future products totally based on standards. Remember, key among these issues will be how to provide interoperability among the older proprietary/pseudostandard products and the new standard products. An organization may choose to assure such interoperability either via technical or administrative means. For example, all network management products could be interconnected and could interoperate via network management translating/mapping gateways; or, maintenance staff could be trained for all products and manual interoperability could be mandated.

Manager-to-Manager Integration

Let's look at a sampling of the issues associated with manager-to-manager integration across multiple management domains. The issues considered here include intermanager coordination, management extensibility, and intermanager translations/mappings. Other issues that span both single and multiple domains of management, such as issues associated with the stability of management decision-making algorithms, are considered in the next section.

Intermanager Coordination. Multiple domains may be related in several ways. For example, they may be disjoint, overlapping, nested, hierarchical, or concatenated.

Different management issues are associated with each kind of multiple domain structure. For example, consider some of the issues accompanying overlapping domain management. First, when a network resource can be simultaneously managed by more than one manager, each manager may potentially make conflicting decisions on how to change attributes associated with the shared resource. Each manager may make decisions that benefit its own domain rather than the union of the overlapping domains. Thus, managers can make conflicting decisions regarding the shared resource; and, they may engage in deadlock battles, each trying to effect its own suboptimal decision inconsistent with the suboptimal decision of the other. Unless conflict resolution issues are addressed, serious instability problems can arise. The values of the shared resources' management attributes will oscillate as each manager continues to try to install its perception of the appropriate value.

Management Extensibility. Perhaps one of the most pragmatic challenges for the network management implementer community is to build network management systems that are extensible and facilitate the amalgamation of heterogeneous management products into a totally integrated management solution. When this is accomplished, it is conceivable to obtain any individual product's management capabilities via any other management product.

It would be desirable then that such products were compatible, in the management sense. The challenge is to design network management solutions that are interoperable with a plethora of heterogeneous products:

- products (such as MAP/TOP ones) that implement early versions of network management standards
- interim products that are based in part on more mature, but still evolving, standards and in part on concepts that are ahead of the standards
- products based on standard non-OSI protocols, e.g., TCP/IP products managed using SNMP or CMOT, and products that use the IEEE 802.1 protocol

- future products (such as those corresponding to the final NIST agreements and tested by COS conformance tests) that are based on stable and complete standards
- proprietary network management products (such as NetView)
- so-called "partial stack" products (e.g., modems, bridges, and routers which may not have all the higher layer communication protocols typically associated with standards-based network management products

Although it seems that total interoperability under such constraints may be nothing more than a pipe dream, what should at least be identified and exploited is the common ground that can be established among the individual, heterogeneous management components.

Lastly, network-related resources are but a small subset of the items that need to be managed in a total distributed processing environment. It would be extremely beneficial to extend standardized, network-managementlike facilities and services into the network-attached computers' heterogeneous operating systems and applications environments. In fact, some of the computer manufacturers are beginning to design such totally all-encompassing management capabilities that integrate the management of their computing and networking resources. Significant standardization work needs to be initiated and progressed if ultimately such distributed systems management is to span multiple vendor products.

Intermanager Translations/Mappings

To interface standard and proprietary network management systems, translators and mappers are often planned to be used to interface between heterogeneous network management command languages, protocols, managed objects definitions, etc. This is often referred to as a *proxy* mechanism. Such conversions/mappings are rarely perfect. The inherent imperfections and imprecision of these translating mechanisms will have ramifications on management decision-making processes. The extent of the decision-making "errors" attributable to such translation mechanisms needs to be understood so that appropriate compensations can be proposed and investigated.

Summary

Network management has become recognized as one of the most complex problems facing the networking community. Solutions based on internationally accepted standards, and implementation specification based on those standards, are now emerging. These standards and specifications provide the basis for interoperable network management products that will replace today's proprietary ones.

References

Case, J., M. Fedor, M. Schofferstall, and J. Davin. 1988. RFC 1098. A simple network management protocol (August).

IEEE. 1988. P802.3LM-88/7. Layer Management Draft L (November).

ISO. 1987. ISO 9072-1. Information processing systems—Text communication, remote operations: Model, notation and service definition. Gloucester (November).

———. 1988a. ISO 8649. Information processing systems—Open systems interconnection, service definition for the association control service element.

———. 1988b. ISO 8824. Information processing—Open system interconnection—Specification of abstract syntax notation one (ASN.1). Geneva (March).

ISO/IEC. 1988a. JTC1/SC21 DIS 9595. Information processing systems—Open systems interconnection—Management information service definition—Common management information service (August).

———. 1988b. DIS 9596. Information processing systems—Open systems interconnection—Management information protocol specification—Common management information protocol (October).

———. 1988c. ISO 7498-4. Information processing systems—Open systems interconnection—Basic reference model—Part 4: OSI management framework.

———. 1988d. JTC1/SC6/WG2. Specification of transport layer management information. Editor, S. DiCecco (November).

———. 1988e. JTC1/SC6/WG2. Specification of network layer management information. Editor, S. DiCecco (November).

———. 1988f. ISO/IEC DP 10164-1. Draft Proposal, Information processing systems—Open systems interconnection—Systems management—Part 1: Object management function. Sydney (December).

———. 1988g. ISO/IEC DP 10164-2. Draft Proposal, Information processing systems—Open systems interconnection—Systems management—Part 2: State management function. Sydney (December).

———. 1988h. ISO/IEC DP 10164-3. Draft Proposal, Information processing systems—Open systems interconnection—Systems management—Part 3: Relationship management function. Sydney (December).

———. 1988i. ISO/IEC DP 10164-4. Draft Proposal, Information processing systems—Open systems interconnection—Systems management—Part 4: Error reporting and information retrieval function. Sydney (December).

———. 1988j. JTC1/SC21/WG4 N3299. Draft Proposal, Information processing systems—Open systems interconnection—Systems management—Part 5: Management service control function. Sydney (December).

———. 1988k. ISO/IEC 9595/PDAD 1. Information processing systems—Open systems interconnection—Management information service definition—Common management information service, Addendum 1: CancelGet (December).

———. 1988l. ISO/IEC 9596/PDAD 1. Information processing systems—Open systems interconnection—Management information protocol specification—Common management information protocol, Addendum 1: CancelGet (December).

———. 1988m. ISO/IEC 9595/PDAD 2. Information processing systems—Open systems interconnection—Management information service definition—Common management information service, Addendum 2: Add/Remove (December).

———. 1988n. ISO/IEC 9596/PDAD 2. Information processing systems—Open systems interconnection—Management information protocol specification—Common management information protocol, Addendum 2: Add/Remove (December).

———. 1988o. JTC1/SC21/WG4 N3312. Information processing systems—Open systems interconnection—Fault management, Working Document. Sydney (December).

———. 1989a. ISO/IEC DP 10165-2. Information processing systems—Open systems interconnection—Structure of management information—Part 2: Definition of support management objects (January).

———. 1989b. ISO/IEC DP 10165-3. Information processing systems—Open systems interconnection—Structure of management information—Part 3: Definition of management attributes (January).

———. 1989c. JTC1/SC21/WG4 N3309. Information processing systems—Open systems interconnection—Systems management—Part 7: Log control function, Working Document. Edited Sydney output (January).

———. 1989d. JTC1/SC21 N3311. Information processing—Open system interconnection—Configuration management overview, Working Document. Edited Sydney output (January).

———. 1989e. JTC1/SC21 N3313. Information processing—Open systems interconnection—Performance management functional area specification, Working Document. Edited Sydney output (January).

———. 1989f. JTC1/SC21 N3314. Information processing—Open system interconnection—Accounting management functional area specification, Working Document. Edited Sydney output (January).

———. 1989g. JTC1/SC21 N3315. Information processing—Open systems interconnection—Management information services definition: Security management service definition, Working Document. Edited Sydney output (January).

———. 1989h. ISO/IEC DP 10165-4. Information processing—Open systems interconnection—Structure of management information—Part 4: Guidelines for the definition of managed objects (February).

———. 1989i. ISO/IEC DP10165-1. Information processing systems—Open systems interconnection—Structure of management information—Part 1: Management information model (April).

———. 1989j. JTC1/SC21/WG4. Information processing systems—Open systems interconnection—Systems management—Part 6: Confidence and diagnostic testing function (scheduled for DP in October).

———. 1989k. ISO/IEC DP 10040. Information processing systems—Open systems interconnection—Systems management: Overview (April).

McCloghrie, K., and M. Rose. 1988. RFC 1066. Management information base for network management of TCP/IP-based internets (August).

Postel, J. 1981a. RFC 768. User datagram protocol (September).

———. 1981b. RFC 791. Internet protocol (September).

———. 1981c. RFC 793. Transmission control protocol (September).

Rose, M. 1988. RFC 1085. ISO presentation services on top of TCP/IP-based internets (December).

Rose, M., and K. McCloghrie. 1988. RFC 1065. Structure and identification of management information for TCP/IP-based internets (August).

Warrier, U., and L. Besaw. 1989. RFC 1095. The common management information services and protocol over TCP/IP (CMOT) (April).

Chapter 8

SNA: Current Requirements and Direction

R. J. Sundstrom
J. B. Staton III
G. D. Schultz
M. L. Hess
G. A. Deaton, Jr.
L. J. Cole
R. M. Amy

Chapter 8

SINCE ITS ANNOUNCEMENT IN 1974, SYSTEMS NETWORK Architecture (SNA) has evolved in terms of its functional content, configurational flexibility, and network management services. This chapter briefly traces this progress to the present and examines the more recent advances in greater detail, including known requirements for enhanced application and transaction services, for additional provisions for very large networks, for continuing adaptation of small-system and transmission media advances, for inclusion of additional management capabilities, and for further integration of network standards—all of which will shape future SNA developments.*

Fifteen years have passed since IBM introduced SNA as the blueprint for the design of its communication products and for interconnecting them within networks. Introduced to meet an evident need for a long-term strategy for interconnecting disparate products, SNA has performed this role with notable success. This success can be measured by various indices: first, by the ever-growing number of SNA products of various manufacture and their enthusiastic acceptance in the marketplace; second, by the recognition in the industry of SNA as a pacesetter for functional richness and completeness; and third, by the facility of the architecture to meet new requirements and adapt to new technologies in an evolutionary fashion. An earlier paper traced the early years in a comprehensive manner (Sundstrom and Schultz 1980).

Evolution of SNA

In 1974, SNA began as a simple tree-oriented single-host network. Today, it has evolved to support multiple, independent, mesh-configured networks separately administered but interconnected by gateways into composite networks. End users can communicate freely with application programs anywhere in

*This chapter was originally published in the *IBM Systems Journal*, 6 no. 1 (1987).

these composite networks without being aware of the network configurations. Some of the major highlights in the progress of SNA are shown in Figure 8-1.

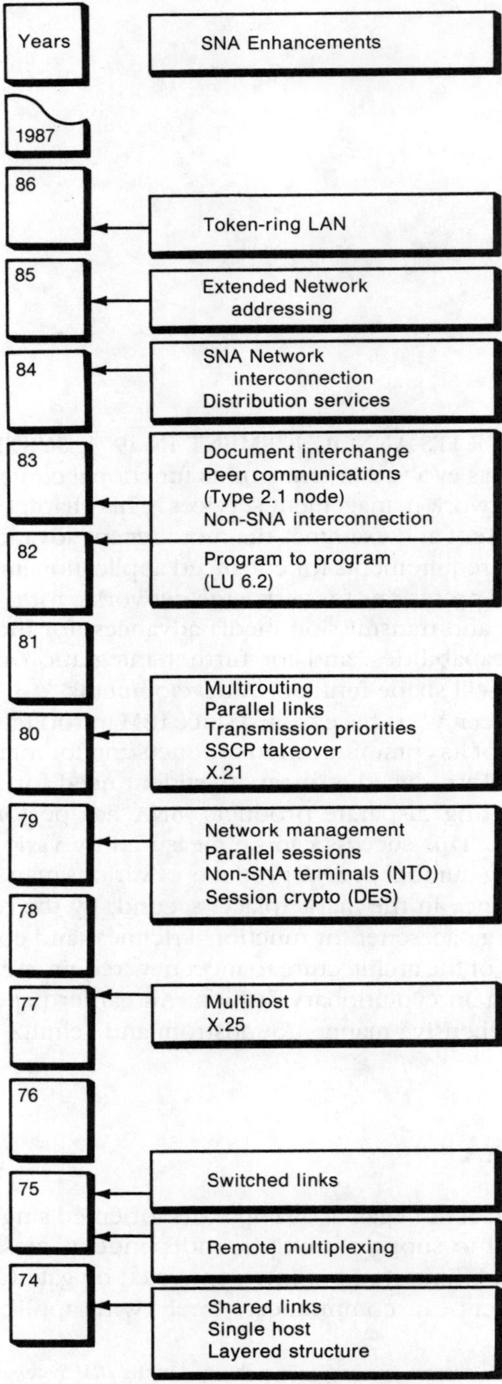

Figure 8-1. SNA evolution.

When SNA was introduced in 1974, it was supported by a single operating system, Disk Operating System/Virtual Storage (DOS/VS), running on a single host connected to terminals through a front-end communication controller. At that time, the only SNA terminals available were on the IBM 3600 Finance Communication System used in banking. Host programs communicated with the 3600 controller.

Within a year, SNA coverage was expanded to include remote communication controllers, the Multiple Virtual Storage (MVS) environment, and supermarket and retail point-of-sale controllers and their terminals. Still, SNA remained a nonswitched-line system only—a situation that changed in 1976 with the addition of switched-line capability.

In 1977, with the release of IBM's Advanced Communication Function (ACF) products, more general networking function became available. SNA allowed multiple host trees to be interconnected, using single links to connect front-end communication controllers. This capability opened the way for a terminal to access application programs in multiple host processors. Also in 1977, IBM introduced its initial support for the X.25 standard for public packet-switched networks. We discuss this in greater detail later.

With the basic networking in place, it was time for more emphasis on incorporation of network management services to monitor and control the network. This focus, which began in 1979, continues to the present. The need for such services increases according to the complexity of network configurations and the criticality of network reliability, availability, and serviceability to the users of the network. With businesses increasingly relying on their network operations and with the scope of their applications widening, network management services have taken on greater importance as the architecture and implementing product set have been extended.

In 1979, IBM also enhanced session capabilities to allow parallel sessions between two application subsystems such as the Customer Information Control System (CICS) and the Information Management System (IMS). Another new session feature at about that time was the support of the National Bureau of Standards' Data Encryption Standard (DES) for session cryptography. In addition, SNA capability to handle non-SNA terminals was significantly advanced by the inclusion of the Network Terminal Option (NTO) software product on the Network Control Program (NCP) in the IBM 3705 Communication Controller.

In 1980, major extensions were made to SNA configuration flexibility and to its transport services. Improvements included multirouting, parallel links between nodes, priority transport, and global congestion control within the network; fully meshed connectivity within the backbone transport network was introduced.

The 1980s brought the following advances:

- Advanced Program-to-Program Communication (APPC)—or LU 6.2—has introduced new, peer-oriented capabilities for communication between application programs.
- SNA Low-Entry Networking (SNA/LEN)—or node type 2.1—provides direct (one-hop) peer communication for small systems.
- Document Interchange Architecture (DIA) and Document Content Ar-

chitecture have extended SNA support for applications within the office environment.

- SNA Distribution Services (SNADS) provides a store-and-forward, or asynchronous, distribution service to SNA that complements the synchronous delivery support of sessions between two end-users.
- SNA Network Interconnection (SNI) and extended network addressing (ENA) have enhanced SNA routing and configuration flexibility, particularly for large networks.
- The IBM Token-Ring LAN, in conformance with national and international standards, provides high-speed communication for interconnecting information processing equipment at a local site, such as a building or campus.

These and other recent advances will be discussed in more detail in following sections.

In summary, some of the major evolutionary trends in SNA have been the following:

- increasing configuration flexibility, particularly to exploit advances in transmission technology
- a burgeoning set of SNA products from IBM and other suppliers
- greater attention to network management services
- inclusion of network standards as these have become available
- widening support for non-SNA devices
- expansion of routing and transport services to keep pace with installation of ever-larger networks
- increasing function available to end-users

The steady development of SNA has been tempered all along by a concern for compatibility of past products with new SNA releases. The care taken is manifested by the continued operation of older SNA terminals under newer releases of SNA. This migration sensitivity is one of the hallmarks of SNA evolution.

VTAM-NCP Transport Network

In our survey of the directions that will shape the SNA of tomorrow, we start with the Virtual Telecommunications Access Method (VTAM) and NCP transport network. VTAM and NCP are two of the first three SNA products (along with the 3600 Finance Communication System). They provide the SNA transport network and many of the control and service functions needed to operate SNA networks. Later additions to the VTAM-NCP transport network include SNI and ENA.

SNI

SNI was announced in November 1983: it provides for the interconnection of autonomous SNA networks through gateways consisting of specialized interconnection logic in VTAM and NCP. SNI is appropriate for intercompany communication, for companies experiencing mergers and acquisitions, and for situations where independence of company divisions is needed. It enables two or more networks to merge for the purpose of user communication but to be independently managed and controlled.

To maintain the integrity of the component networks, constraints are built into the gateway to prevent one network from disrupting an adjacent network or gathering information to which it should not have access. Flow control prevents one network from flooding its neighbors with more traffic than they are prepared to handle. Names (e.g., of logical units, discussed later) and routing addresses are also independently assigned. To resolve potential conflicts in name assignment, the NetView program product provides an optional name-aliasing facility. The SNI extensions to SNA are described in detail in Benjamin et al. (1983) and IBM (1985e).

Because each of the independent networks can use its full SNA address space, SNI can also be used to configure networks larger than would otherwise be possible. Each network can allocate a pool of addresses available as local aliases for destinations in other networks; dynamic assignment can result in using them as needed, thereby sharing the pool over a large number of destinations in other networks. Thus,, SNI provides the network interconnection function and, at the same time, possible relief from the addressing constraints some users were experiencing. This is why SNI was provided prior to a more direct solution to the addressing problem (which is our next topic).

As SNA networks grew in size, a requirement arose to extend the original 16-bit address space. These 16-bit addresses were partitioned into two pieces: a subarea address that identified the destination subarea node (containing VTAM or NCP), and an element address that was used by the destination subarea node for routing—for example, to the correct VTAM application program or to the intended terminal. In a particular SNA network, the subarea address can be chosen to be any size from one to eight bits; the remainder of the 16 bits is then used for the element address. In theory, over 64,000 destinations could be addressed; in practice, this number could not be achieved because the subarea/element split has to be uniform throughout the network, and the optimum split varies from node to node.

ENA

In September 1984, IBM announced ENA, which provides for 23-bit addresses, thereby allowing over eight million destinations in a single SNA network. The subarea portion is fixed at eight bits (the previous maximum for subarea addresses), and the element portion is fixed at 15 bits (the previous maximum for element addresses). These sizes were chosen because they were already accommodated by the existing routing tables.

We view this extension as an interim step and recognize the need to provide much larger subarea addresses. This next step would be relatively easy in the architecture from an addressing perspective because space exists for 48-bit addresses in SNA formats, but it would raise more serious problems with the routing schemes. Under the current SNA routing implementation, generating and storing routing tables becomes increasingly difficult as the network grows in size.

Today, if you have a large SNA network and want to add a new subarea node to it, you must first decide where to locate the new addition and what links should connect it to the existing network. Then, usually with the help of an IBM program such as Routing Table Generator (RTG) or Network Design and Analysis (NETDA), you design the routes of the enlarged network. Once this work is completed, you load the new routing tables into the subarea nodes of the network through a system definition process. This procedure lends itself to very efficient routing because all the routes are predefined to the network, but, because of definition time and complexity, it limits what can be done to accommodate unanticipated changes in the network configuration, such as the addition or deletion of a link or node. Such changes are likely to occur more frequently as the size of the network increases.

In addition to supporting very large networks, SNA has a requirement to make all networks easier to install and change. One of our long-term SNA design directions is to reduce, and, wherever possible, to completely eliminate, system definition.

One potential solution is to have a route-activation message carry a description of the route that the session will use through the network. This routing information could be created in an off-line process, such as is done to create the coordinated routing table used today. But since the routing information would be stored at each source node, rather than in each intermediate routing node, routing information could be updated independently at each node without having to stop the operation of the network.

The route-activation message could be routed using the list of nodes and links that was provided at the originating node. At each intermediate routing node, a temporary entry could be created in a routing table, for the life of the session, that related the link by which the route-activation message arrived and the local addressing information generated at the predecessor node for use on that link with the link the route-activation message was to be routed across (based on the routing information received in the message) and addressing information locally generated for use on that successor link. Thus, subsequent session traffic could be routed quickly by using the link and local address information to index the routing table, and would not have to carry the list of nodes and links defining the route.

This routing could be made more dynamic by having the network update itself through an exchange of node and link characteristics whenever a change occurs in any of these parameters. The network could then use the most current topology information to compute the best route between two points at the time the route was requested. This route computation could also consider a class of service requested by the user; this is how users specify to the network whether they need, for example, the least-cost route, the route with the least delay, or the route with the greatest bandwidth.

This dynamic routing capability could address a number of current requirements for SNA networks. First, it would permit larger networks, since the difficulties with the current route-generation process could be eliminated and intermediate nodes could store routing information only for currently active routes, not for all potential routes. Second, it would allow networks to be installed and changed more easily by reducing the workload now experienced in doing coordinated system definition. Third, it would be an important step toward fostering continuous operation, since a network need not be taken down for the purpose of updating routing tables. Further discussions of dynamic routing for SNA networks can be found in Eisenbies and Smetanka (1984) and in Jaffe et al. (1983).

The need for continuous operation runs deep in SNA and is worthy of more discussion here. A number of features currently available in SNA can be used to increase the availability of networks and to insulate its users from outages. These include the following:

- pause and retry logic in SDLC
- multilink transmission groups
- multiple routes
- parallel sessions
- host control-point (system services control point or SSCP takeover)
- distributed processing

Pause and retry logic in SDLC allows SDLC links to remain operational across periods of transient errors on the links. Multilink transmission groups allow bundling a number of SDLC links into a single logical link. The sender schedules data traffic for the first available link in a group, and the receiver reorders received messages, if necessary, to maintain the FIFO (first-in first-out) property of the logical link. Individual links can be dynamically added to or deleted from a transmission group without disrupting the ongoing flow of information; a transmission group fails only when the last operational link in the transmission group fails.

Networks can be configured with multiple predefined routes so that if the route serving a session fails, that session can be reestablished over an alternate route.

SNA currently allows multiple simultaneous (parallel) sessions to be established between host application subsystems such as IMS and CICS. These sessions can traverse different routes through the network and, where supported, comprise a resource pool; when a transaction program needs to communicate with a partner program at another host, the first available session with the desired class of service can be assigned from that pool. Should one session fail, other sessions in the pool will continue to provide session connectivity with the partner subsystem.

SSCP takeover provides protocols in the hosts and NCPs for detecting failure of controlling hosts and informing their backup hosts.

With distributed processing, application programs and data are moved closer to the user and the user can often continue working uninterrupted by link or node failures in the communication network (and experience improved response times under normal operation).

Although SNA today provides numerous functions that can be used to configure highly available networks, further requirements exist in this area. For example, while SNA provides multiple routes, should a route fail, the sessions it carries are deactivated prior to possible reactivation over a backup route. A desirable extension is to have the network perform this route switch without disrupting the sessions.

Another requirement is to provide for backup application subsystems. However, just having a backup application subsystem ready to start taking over the moment the primary application subsystem fails will not always be sufficient. Some critical application programs can support thousands of simultaneous users; it could take a number of minutes for the backup application subsystem to reestablish and resynchronize all the user sessions. To reduce the recovery time for these critical applications, a need exists to preestablish the backup sessions and have them available for immediate use should the primary application subsystem fail. For IMS applications, this capability has been announced as the Extended Recovery Facility (XRF). At the time that IMS support of XRF was announced, IBM also stated that the general direction of its development effort is to provide XRF capability for CICS.

Small Systems

Thus far, we have been focusing on the VTAM-NCP transport network. We now examine SNA requirements and directions from the perspective of the peripheral nodes of the SNA network. In the past, these peripheral nodes have been predominantly display terminals, printers, and remote job entry stations. With the steadily decreasing cost of mini- and microprocessors and storage, more and more of the peripheral nodes are small *systems* such as personal computers, distributed processors, intelligent workstations, and office systems. These small systems, because of their more general nature, have greater connectivity requirements than traditional terminal devices.

One requirement is more flexible session connectivity. Figure 8-2 shows the way sessions can be connected in SNA networks today. Host application subsystems can have sessions with other host application subsystems and with outboard terminals and small systems. The host-to-host connections can employ parallel sessions. These parallel sessions can be used to increase transaction bandwidth (each session can serve one active transaction), to provide for a distinct class of service selection, and to improve performance and availability by fanning out traffic across different routes between the hosts. Peripheral nodes, however, are currently limited to a single session per logical unit (LU), and that session must be with an LU in a subarea node, e.g., a host application subsystem such as CICS or a transaction-routing LU such as Network Routing Facility (NRF) in a communication controller. A requirement exists for small systems to enjoy the session connectivity that hosts enjoy today, namely the ability to use parallel sessions and to have direct session connectivity with any other destination in the network.

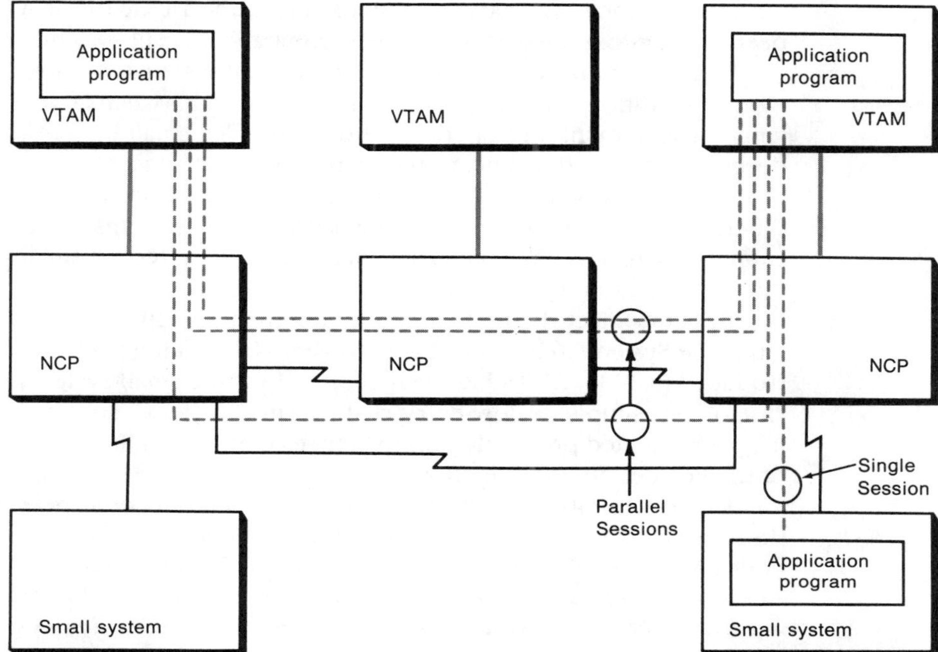

Figure 8-2. SNA session capability today.

These small systems also have requirements for communication outside the VTAM-NCP environment. One simple but important form of communication is direct peer-to-peer: just two nodes and a link between them. Although this configuration is the simplest possible, it is increasingly important because of the current trend in the communications environment toward high-connectivity, multiaccess facilities such as LANs, X.25 networks, and ISDNs.

In 1983, a new peripheral node type, node type 2.1, was incorporated into SNA to provide this peer-to-peer form of communication. Initial IBM implementations of this new protocol, called Low-Entry Networking, are available on the following systems:

- System/36 System Support Program
- System/38
- System/88 APPC
- APPC/PC
- Series/1 Realtime Programming System
- IBM 3820 Page Printer
- IBM LAN Print Manager Program

Direct peer-to-peer communication had been available earlier on IBM SNA products such as 8100/DPPX and previous releases of the 5520 Administrative System. The newer node type 2.1 protocols provide the capability to carry LU

6.2 sessions (including parallel sessions) and demonstrate the SNA direction for peer-to-peer communication between compatible small systems.

In designing networking solutions for small systems, it is important to recognize the differences in operating environments between large and small systems. Procurement and operational decisions for small systems are generally decentralized and dynamic, resulting in frequent change. Yet, technical support from systems programmers and network operators is far more limited. Another difference affecting design decisions is that small systems typically need not support the high traffic volumes of large systems; moreover, small systems have more stringent entry-cost requirements.

To better meet the networking requirements of customers with small systems, the System/36 Advanced Peer-to-Peer Networking (APPN) feature was introduced in 1986. APPN has been designed for the small-system environment; ease of use, simplicity, low-entry cost for small systems, configuration flexibility, peer-oriented protocols, and tolerance of node and link failures were some of the key design considerations.

The System/36 APPN feature extends the direct peer-to-peer communication provided by low-entry networking and attaches type 2.1 nodes as end nodes to the APPN network. Figure 8-3 shows the two types of nodes in an APPN network: *network nodes*, which provide session-level intermediate routing and other functions such as directory services, and *end nodes*. (Either type of node can be attached directly as a traditional *peripheral node* through a *boundary function* to the SNA backbone transport network of subarea nodes.) End nodes in APPN networks have the same session connectivity as network nodes. This session connectivity includes the ability to use parallel sessions and to have session connectivity with any other node (network or end) in the network. Thus, APPN provides the same session connectivity that has been recognized earlier as a requirement for the VTAM-NCP transport network.

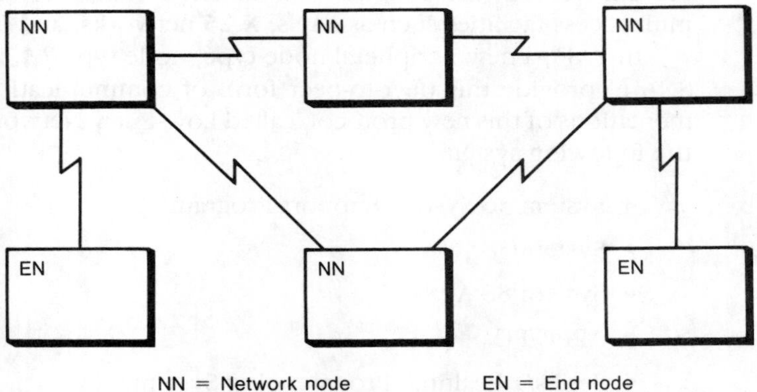

Figure 8-3. A System/36 APPN network.

APPN is a nonhierarchical, peer-oriented scheme that uses dynamic topology update and route-determination protocols similar to those discussed earlier as requirements for the large-system environment. A dynamic, distributed directory allows destination LUs to be found without predefining the location of each LU; later, we discuss this further. These two features, dynamic route determination and a dynamic LU directory, provide for ease of installation and of frequent network changes by eliminating the need for coordinated network definition of this information. Further discussion of the requirements for networking in a small-system environment and of the APPN solution appears in Baratz et al. (1985).

The evolution of small-system networking can hardly end with standalone networks; we anticipate a requirement to connect these networks of small systems to the high-capacity transport networks as shown in Figure 8-4. These connections should allow sessions between small-system A, for example, and an application in one of the System/370 hosts; they should also allow small systems to communicate peer-to-peer across the SNA backbone networks (for example, from A to G) and share the high-capacity links that often are in place.

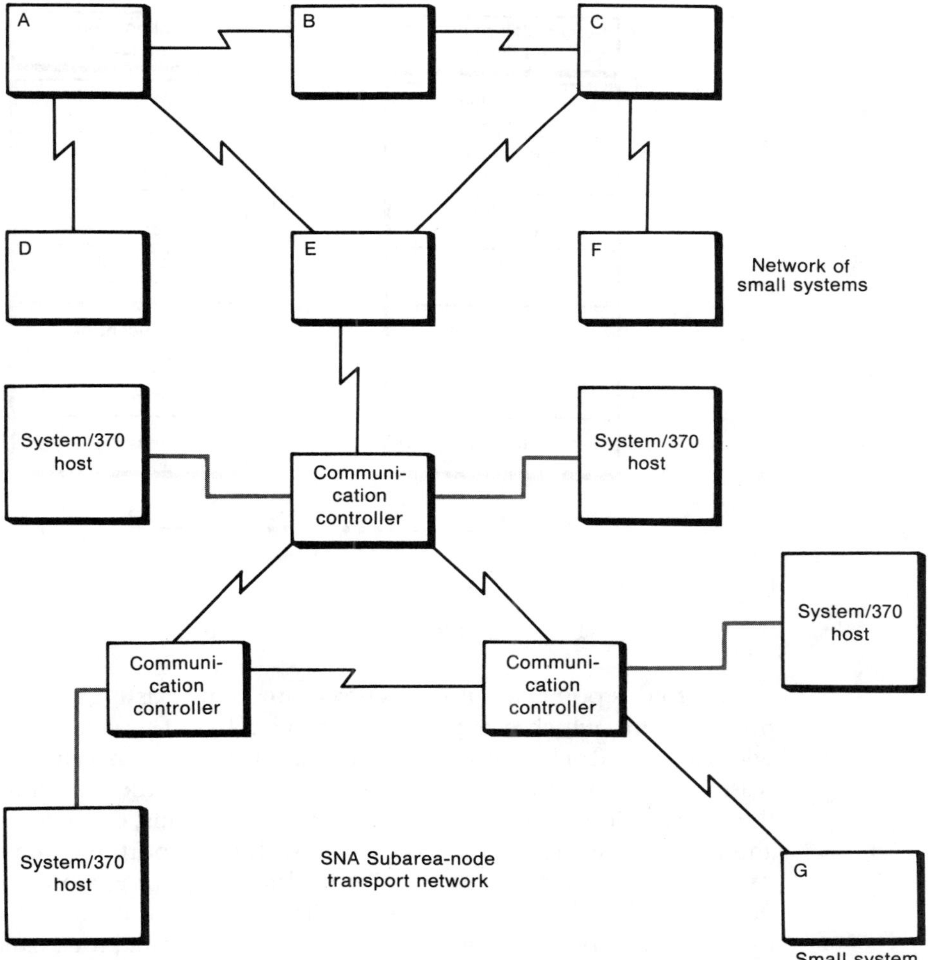

Figure 8-4. Combined network of small systems and large systems.

Provision must also be made for managing networks of small systems. These network management techniques should be consistent with the network management functions that are in place for SNA backbone networks so that when networks of small systems are connected to networks of large systems, the entire consolidated network can be centrally managed.

Logical Units

The LU has a central role in SNA, namely as the intermediary between the transport network and the people, devices, and application programs using or attached to the network. Figure 8-5 shows the position of the LU in the layered structure of SNA.

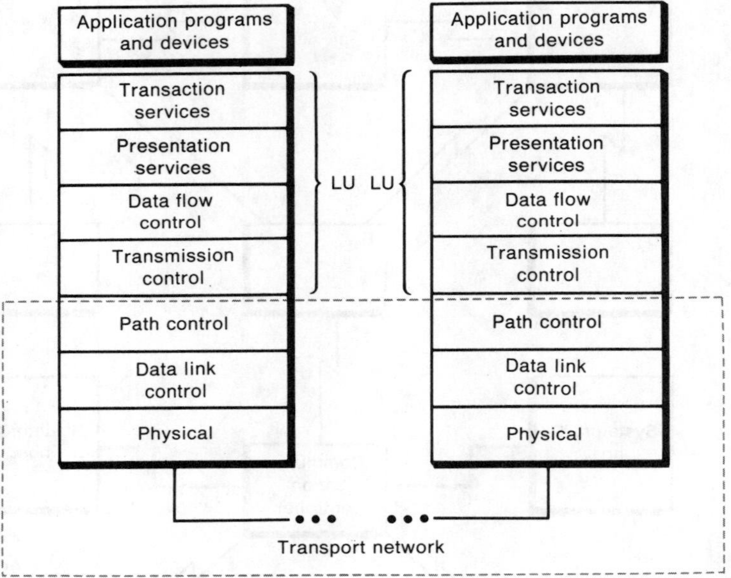

Figure 8-5. Role of the LU.

Up to this point, we have discussed functions existing mainly in the transport network, which provides global protocols and services such as network-wide flow control and routing. By contrast, the LU is concerned primarily with session protocols for paired end-users. LUs serve as the attachment points for the ultimate destinations of data (application programs, data bases, and devices) and provide the end-to-end session protocols in support of communication between these network resources. Whereas the transport network provides global flow control so that links and intermediate nodes in the network are not overloaded, the LU provides end-to-end flow control so that, for example, an application program does not send data to a printer faster than the printer can handle it. Other functions include session cryptography, name-to-address translation (using a distributed directory services capability of the network), and blocking and subdividing message units for efficiency in transmission and buffer usage by the LU.

A number of LU types are defined in SNA, with the earlier ones (LU types 1, 2, and 3) optimized for asymmetric host-application-to-device communication. With today's trend toward personal computers, office workstations, and other small systems, new communication requirements exist at the LU level as well as at the transport network level. The key requirement at the LU level is for general program-to-program communication. A single set of protocols is needed for all types of communication, including host to host, host to small system, and small system to small system. It should provide a range of functions suited to such products as the IBM Personal Computer and the IBM 3820 Page Printer at the low end, and CICS and the System/38 at the high end. The protocols should also provide a new base for device support, allowing for flexible function distribution between devices and host applications.

To meet these requirements, a new LU type, 6.2, was introduced in 1982 as APPC. Initial IBM implementations included CICS, Print Services Facility, 8100/DPPX, and the systems previously listed that provided node type 2.1 support. LU 6.2, as well as other SNA protocols, is widely available from other vendors. An important contributing factor in the development of APPC was the availability of powerful microprocessors in the outlying terminals, allowing these units to handle their end of a peer LU-LU session. Making use of this capability is a good example of exploiting advances in technology.

To support a broad range of distributed applications across any set of LU 6.2 products, LU 6.2 defines a set of generic commands, *verbs*, implemented by each LU 6.2 product in its own syntax but with common semantics, that application transaction programs can use to communicate, independent of the details of the underlying configurations and protocols. The services (e.g., session allocation, sending, receiving) provided by these verbs are defined in IBM (1985f).

LU 6.2 was designed to include SNA-defined transaction programs such as those for SNADS and DIA (discussed later), to serve device- or product-specific transaction programs such as those used to communicate with the IBM 3820 Page Printer, and to be used by user-written transaction programs. Users can provide their own transaction programs on LU 6.2 implementations such as CICS, System/36, System/38, and APPC/PC (a general LU 6.2 and node type 2.1 product for the IBM Personal Computer), which can be programmed by the customer. Such implementations are said to have an *open* application program interface (API); implementations such as Scanmaster I, in which the LU 6.2 implementation is limited to serving only prepackaged transaction programs, are called *closed-API* products.

To meet the low entry cost and the high function requirements, LU 6.2 has a base set of functions and a limited set of options. Every open-API implementation supports the base and may also support any of the option sets. One option, implemented by CICS, can synchronize updates to multiple data bases so that all updates either succeed or fail together as an atomic unit of work. Closed-API products need provide only the functions used by their coupled transaction programs.

LU 6.2 has been enhanced with the addition of option sets for transaction program security. The foundation of these protocols is a two-way verification exchange used to check the identity of the session partner. This verification is accomplished by having each LU generate and transmit a random number, and having the partner LU return that value encrypted under a shared session password. Verifying the identity of the session partner by determining whether it can correctly encrypt a random value protects against a "playback attack" (using data obtained from a previous session through illicit monitoring), since the password is not sent over the network. Later, when a transaction program initiates a conversation with a remote program using the session, it can include a user identification and a user password. Because of the trust established in the earlier verification, these fields need not be encrypted; they are used by the receiver to verify that the conversation initiator has the authority to gain access to the requested resource, such as a file or transaction program. Transaction programs with very high security requirements can additionally transmit fully encrypted data (including the user identification and user password) throughout their sessions. Further information on LU 6.2 can be found in IBM (1985d), Gray et al. (1983), and Sundstrom (1984).

In the next sections, we explore the progress in the transaction services layer, the top layer of SNA.

SNA Distribution Services

SNADS, made available in 1984, consists of a set of IBM-supplied transaction programs that use a network of LU 6.2 sessions to provide a store-and-forward distribution capability in an SNA network. The LU 6.2 base provides a synchronous, connection-oriented, logically point-to-point service for application programs, analogous to a telephone service. SNADS builds on this basic service to provide a distribution capability analogous to a mail service, wherein distributions can be made, possibly to multiple destinations, without the need for active sessions between the endpoints.

SNADS provides, at a user's request, the asynchronous transport of data such as documents and files supplied by that user to one or more other users. The service is provided by a network of nodes called *distribution service units*. A distribution typically begins at one such node and may spread out to many, as copies are fanned out at the appropriate point in the network and forwarded toward the specified destination users. Each move from one node to the next complies with formats and protocols defined for SNADS and the lower layers of SNA. When failures or planned outages occur in the network, SNADS allows material to be stored at distribution service units for later forwarding when the network resources are available. SNADS frees the user of concerns about network resource availability, and is particularly appropriate for batch-oriented, one-way flows found in such applications as document distribution, file transfer, and job networking.

A full-service distribution service unit can support multiple users and multiple applications and provide intermediate store-and-forward routing services on behalf of other distribution service units. The architecture describes how a distribution service unit can be optimized to a particular application, user, or role in a network. For example, a printing device could be defined as having a receive-only single-addressee role in the network. In this way, low-cost basic implementations can be provided in one release, and their functions and role expanded in subsequent releases, without inconveniencing session partners in the network.

SNADS provides its users with defined user names to identify the senders and recipients of distributions. The user names are location-independent, thereby allowing users to move from one node to another without changing their names. The current location of a user is found by reference to a SNADS-defined directory. Movement of a user from one node to another need be reflected only in the directories of the user's old and new nodes. Updating other directories in the network can proceed on a schedule determined by a network administrator.

The route taken by a distribution through a network is determined not only by the location of the recipient, but also by other properties of the distribution request. Depending on integrity requirements, the amount of data, and the priority of the request, different routes may be selected through a network.

SNADS defines a full set of actions to be taken in various error situations. If a distribution cannot be delivered, feedback to the originator specifies exactly which recipients were omitted and why.

SNADS is currently implemented in a number of products that will use it primarily for document distribution; these are the Distributed Office Support System/370 (DISOSS/370), System/36, System/38, 8100/DPPX, Series/1, and 5520 Administrative System. Because document distribution is the most common application in these first implementations of SNADS, the initial SNADS formats were designed to be compatible with those in DIA, one of IBM's architectures for the office. Further information about SNADS exists in Housel and Scopinich (1983) and IBM (1984).

Architecture for the Office

To handle situations generic to the automated office, IBM has developed architectures specific to this important application: DIA (Schick and Brockish 1982; IBM 1983c; Cordell 1984) and Document Content Architecture (Cordell 1984; IBM 1983a, 1983b).

Document Interchange

Like SNADS, DIA, introduced in 1982, is also part of the transaction services layer of SNA. It provides a set of protocols that define how several common office functions are performed cooperatively by IBM products. These include the filing, searching, and retrieving of documents and memos as part of the document library services of DIA. The document distribution services of DIA provide for the sending and receiving of documents or memos via SNADS or an underlying LU 6.2 session, and include listing items pending receipt, canceling or sequencing their delivery at the recipient's request, and allowing access to software mailboxes and files by other authorized users. The formatting and processing of documents are defined in application processing services. The implementation status of DIA is similar to that of SNADS, but also includes IBM PC, Displaywriter, and Scanmaster implementations.

Document Content

A vital component of the office architectures is the Document Content Architecture, which provides the formats for describing the form and meaning of objects that are managed by DIA. Currently, two forms are implemented: Final-Form Text and Revisable-Form Text.

Final-Form Text provides primitive format controls within a data stream in a generic fashion to allow device-independent document presentation. This provision allows the sender of a document to control the formatting and print integrity of a document at its final destination without knowing the print device characteristics of the destination. Revisable-Form Text allows interchange of documents in a form that is suitable for revision. Text processing indicators are included with the text, and may themselves be revised.

While the two current types of Document Content Architecture are a good beginning, others are needed to describe the mixing of information types within a document, such as text, graphics, image, and voice annotation data. An architecture serving mixed data would allow documents that integrate a variety of data types to be exchanged by future office workstations.

Directory Services

One of the design goals of SNA has been to insulate the user and the user's application program from the characteristics of the communication network and to allow workstations and application programs to be moved among processors without impacting other workstations and application programs that communicate with them.

To achieve this design goal, SNA has distinguished between resource names and their addresses. A name is a relatively stable identifier that users can apply to remote workstations and application programs (typically those with which they want to interact via a session). By contrast, an address can vary according to operations decisions made in the network. Users and their application programs access resources by name. The system uses the name as a key to a directory that provides the current address of the requested resource.

In early SNA networks, the directory tables were defined in the SSCP in a single System/370 processor. The control point acts as a mediator in LU-LU session initiation, translating names to addresses and checking resource availability. The use of a central directory in the control point simplified the management of the directory for additions, deletions, and changes.

With the introduction of multiple-host networks in 1977, the control points cooperated in providing directory services, with each control point being responsible for the detailed address information on a subset of the LUs in the network; each control point knew all LU names and the associated control point that could resolve a specific name to an address. Successive designs of the control point have reduced the amount of coordinated predefinition of resources by eliminating redundancy among the directories in different control points. Starting with the SNI release of SNA, a control point could perform a trial-and-error search of other control points for LUs not found in its own directory; this could further reduce the number of control points that need to be updated when new LUs are brought on line.

In SNADS, a user directory is referenced to determine the distribution service unit (address) of an intended recipient. SNADS products have implemented their directories, which are manually maintained, as part of the distribution service unit, rather than in the control point.

Two trends stress the current design point of manually maintained directories; as networks become larger, the frequency of directory updating increases and the number of directories that must be consistently maintained grows; furthermore, the trend toward peer connectivity among small systems requires that small systems also maintain directories, whereas they may formerly have depended upon a large host directory. Both trends result in many more directories and increased update activity in a network, and point to a growing need for the directories to be automatically and dynamically maintained.

The System/36 APPN feature has introduced the ability to register LUs only at their local (home) directories. Automatic searches of the various directories throughout the APPN network result in eventually finding the LU if an active path to the LU is available. Once found, the location of an LU can be stored in cache memory so that searches need not be repetitive.

Management Services

The previous sections of this chapter discuss the advances in the functional richness and configuration flexibility allowed by SNA. SNA users can connect multiple SNA networks, small systems to large systems, and various other devices, all within the same, composite network. The actual attachments may be over various transmission media (e.g., telecommunications links, System/370 channels, X.25 networks, LANs), using equipment from many different suppliers. This configurational flexibility exacts a price in making the network more complex to manage. It places strenuous requirements on the architecture to allow for such things as nondisruptive change, immediate and simple notification of problems, and high availability. The goal for SNA is to allow full end-to-end management of a network, including the telecommunications and non-SNA equipment.

Management services, also known as network management or communications network management (see also Chapter 7, "Managing Networks"), include the monitoring and controlling of a network. The requirements for managing an SNA network fall into four major management services categories:

- problem management
- performance and accounting management
- change management
- configuration management

Problem management is the function of managing a problem from its detection through its resolution. The steps of problem management are

- problem determination
- problem diagnosis
- problem bypass and recovery
- problem resolution
- problem tracking and control

Performance and accounting management is the process of quantifying, measuring, reporting, and controlling the usage, responsiveness, availability, and cost of a network. Change management is the planning, control, and application of changes (additions, deletions, and modifications) to the resources of a network. Configuration management is the control of information necessary to both logically and physically identify network resources and indicate their relationships to one another.

Components in SNA

The management services functions are represented in the architecture (IBM 1986a) by a management services component in the control point, in the physical unit (PU),* and in the individual layers of SNA. This structure provides a framework by which the aforementioned requirements can be satisfied.

Each layer of SNA (see Figure 8-5) is responsible for controlling the resources associated with that layer. This control is accomplished through a component called *local management services*. For example, routing information that is used for problem management is gathered by the local management services component in path control. Once gathered, this information is sent to the management services component in the PU.

PU management services is responsible for gathering local management services information to its node or attached links, performing some services such as reformatting and time-stamping the data, and sending the information to the control point for processing. Control point management services is re-

*A PU is an addressable entity, like the SSCP or LU. One PU exists in each node for local control and to represent the node to a control point (SSCP) in a host processor if one is currently controlling the PU. In a type 2.1 node, a control point exists to perform local control and provide required PU services for a remote SSCP.

sponsible for collecting management services data from the network, analyzing the data, and taking the appropriate action based on that analysis.

Trends

The release of multihost support in SNA focused more attention on problem determination. Network Problem Determination Application (IBM 1985c) was introduced in 1979 to help the network operator perform problem determination. Initially, statistics were kept at each node and collected by a host computer. The Network Communication Control Facility (NCCF) (IBM 1985a) was also introduced in 1979 to allow a network operator to interact with each such host in a multiple-host network to control testing and data collection and to examine the data.

The Network Problem Determination Application allowed a person with access to the host to look at the statistics and attempt to diagnose problems in the network. Today, each SNA node is responsible for its own error analysis to determine whether a problem exists and whether recovery action can be performed. If a problem exists that cannot be resolved locally, the node sends an Alert signal to the host to indicate that a component in the network is unavailable and that intervention is required. The Alert contains a general classification of the problem, a description of the probable cause of the problem, identification of the failing resource, and any additional details pertaining to the problem. The Alert mechanism allows immediate notification of problems in the network in order to foster quick and easy problem determination. Statistics are still kept by each node and collected at a host for problem trend analysis.

Subsequent enhancements to problem determination have focused on the communication links. In 1986, another Alert-like signal called Link Event was announced for management of the attachment to the IBM Token-Ring Network, and Link Problem Determination Aid 2 (LPDA-2) was announced for enhanced management of the IBM modems. Link Event is similar to Alert, but differs in that the node reporting the problem cannot provide a probable cause of the problem, possibly because of a lack of configuration knowledge at that node. In this case, configuration knowledge at the host is required to complete problem determination. LPDA-2 allows for more comprehensive diagnostics and increased configuration flexibility with the new IBM modems.

In accordance with the previously stated goal of managing the entire system, SNA management services have recently been extended to the PBX environment to include supports of Alerts from the ROLM Computerized Branch Exchange (CBX). This is a step toward providing centralized management for both data and voice equipment.

In 1984, SNA management services were extended in the category of performance management. Network Logical Data Manager (NLDM) (IBM 1985b) introduced the support of response-time monitoring, which allows the network operator to validate certain predefined end-user service levels for specified LU-LU sessions. Response time is measured by the time elapsed between the instant an LU recognizes a request from its end-user and the instant it receives the reply from the session-connected partner LU to which it sent the request. The predefined values can be changed dynamically by the network operator. The response-time values can be sent unsolicited upon threshold overflow or can be solicited by the network operator.

The network operator can request a summary of the response-time data for a specific LU over a user-defined period of time, detailed data for a specific session for a single collection period, and the long-term trend for a specific LU.

In addition, management services (and NLDM) have been extended to capture information about logical resources. Data captured by the control point on logical resources include

- session start information
- normal session termination information
- abnormal termination information (e.g., sense data)
- virtual route information

This information is available for sessions that were started through the assistance of single or multiple control points.

With the introduction of SNA network interconnection, a session can be established wherein the endpoints of the session reside in different networks. In this case, additional session information is required for problem management. Retrieval of session information includes the gathering of session control-block information from gateway nodes (NCPs) for cross-network sessions.

Future Requirements

The requirements for SNA management services increase as SNA protocols and telecommunications complexity continue to advance; management services will need to be an integral part of each SNA enhancement. Common solutions are sought, whether for the management of small or large systems, interconnected via SDLC, X.25, or LANs, and whether transporting voice or data.

A trend in both IBM SNA products and SNA management services has been to provide more granular monitoring and control of network components. Hence, such products are the 586X series of modems and the 3710 Network Controller offer extensive problem management features integral to their design. In turn, the architecture allows telecommunication links, for example, to be monitored and controlled at the level of their most basic subsystems: component adapters, modems, line concentrators, and transmission media. This provision has vastly improved problem management in SNA networks.

In the future, similar attention to other management services categories will be vital. For example, the ability to nondisruptively effect changes to the network from a central location is a key requirement. SNA Distribution Services could be used to distribute microcode and software updates to many nodes at the same time. This distribution might include installation instructions, such as when to install the change, and back-out instructions in case of failure. Additionally, management services must keep pace with other SNA capabilities such as peer-to-peer communication and networks of small systems. Requirements such as centralized management must be maintained regardless of the network reporting structure (i.e., hierarchical or peer-to-peer). Of course, the location of the central facility may be affected by the time of day or system backup status.

As SNA strives to provide full end-to-end network management, inclusion of integrated voice and data, and management of a multivendor environment, more comprehensive management services become paramount. A more generic management services architecture, for example, could facilitate a greater integration of non-SNA products into SNA management services. An existing manual describes the current formats and protocols involved in managing the components of an SNA network (IBM 1986a).

Local Area Networks

Even as architectural solutions for improved connectivity continue at the higher layers of SNA, the announcement of the IBM Cabling System in 1984 and the Token-Ring Network in 1985 provided major improvements in dynamic connections at the physical and data link control layers. The first product supporting the Token-Ring Network was the IBM Personal Computer. Subsequently, support was added to the IBM 3174 Communications Control Unit, the 3725 Communication Controller, and the 3270 PC. The System/36 can attach to the Token-Ring Network via support in the IBM PC AT.

When first announced in 1984, the Cabling System allowed an SNA network to be physically reconfigured without running new coaxial cable to specific locations in a building. By introducing a structured wire approach and wiring closets to prewire a building with either twisted-pair copper conductors or optical fibers, today's workstations can be moved from office to office by simply plugging them into a wall and reconfiguring them at a conveniently located wiring closet.

Although ease of reconfiguration is a desirable goal, the ultimate objective is to eliminate entirely the need for manual intervention by a systems professional when moving a workstation from one office to another. This objective was accomplished in 1985 with IBM's announcement of the Token-Ring Network on the Cabling System.

The Token-Ring Network consists of the wiring system, a set of communication adapters *(stations)*, and an access protocol that controls the sharing of the physical medium by the stations attached to the LAN. The IBM Token-Ring Network is based on the IEEE standard for a token-ring LAN. The token-ring LAN (IEEE Computer Society 1985) is one of several LAN standards developed by the IEEE 802 committee and submitted to the ISO. (Other IEEE standards include one for CSMA/CD on baseband cable and a token-bus standard on broadband cable. Each of these IEEE standards is also being processed by ISO.) A token-ring LAN is unique among these LANs, in that the nodes are physically connected serially by a transmission medium, such as twisted pairs or optical fiber. Access to the transmission medium is controlled through the use of a unique bit sequence *(token)* that is passed from one station to the next. When a station has a message unit *(frame)* to transmit, it modifies the token to a frame by changing the bit pattern of the token to a start-of-frame sequence; the frame is then transmitted.

When the station has completed frame transmission, and after appropriate checking for proper operation, it initiates a new token so that other stations have an opportunity to gain access to the ring (Andrews and Schultz 1982).

An important part of the token protocol is the ability of a station to reserve the token for use at a specified priority. It ensures that the next token issued will be at the highest priority requested, and allows a station to gain faster access to the ring for frame transmission than would otherwise have been possible.

To ensure that a token is always available on the ring, one station is elected as the *token monitor*. The function of the token monitor is to detect error conditions in token operation such as a continuously circulating frame or the absence of a token on the ring. The capability to be a token monitor resides in each station, and is determined by an election process when normal token operation is disrupted (Bux and Grillo 1985; Bux et al. 1983; Strole 1983).

Several advantages exist in choosing a token-ring configuration for a LAN, including ease of fault isolation, performance stability under load, the use of predominantly digital, rather than analog, engineering, and its potential to use optical fiber technology (Saltzer, Pogran, and Clark 1983).

To take full advantage of the peer-to-peer connection capabilities inherent in a shared physical medium, a station on the Token-Ring Network could use the data link control, called a *logical link control (LLC)*, as defined by the IEEE 802.2 committee for LANs. This LLC employs the asynchronous balanced mode of operation (like that in high-level data link control, or HDLC) when a link connection is established, thereby allowing either station to send data link commands at any time, and to initiate responses independently of the other link station. This mode provides for a balanced type of data transfer between two link stations that operate as equals on a logical point-to-point link (Carlson 1982). The number of logical links sharing the same ring equals the number of distinct pairs of communicating stations.

When a token ring reaches its capacity, either physically, in terms of the number of stations it is capable of supporting for the required distance, or when the bandwidth is exhausted and the performance is not acceptable, a *bridge* can be added to combine two token rings into one logical ring. A bridge is a device that copies a frame from one ring and transmits it on the other. Bridges can be used to combine a number of small rings to preserve the integrated connectivity in an establishment while providing better fault independence and performance (Bux et al. 1983). Locating stations on a ring, or on multiple rings connected by bridges, can be performed dynamically by broadcasting requests for specific station addresses. Once the station is located, routing data through bridges can be done efficiently by including the routing information to the destination station with each frame. By this action, bridges are allowed to copy frames from one ring to another based on routing information in the frame format, without building, referencing, and maintaining complex tables. Thus, expansion of the LAN to include additional rings need affect only the connecting bridge and can be transparent to all other stations.

In April 1986, IBM announced extensions of the token-ring support allowing multiple token rings to be interconnected via bridges to form logically composite LANs and to include connection to System/370 computers through the IBM 3725 Communication Controller and its related software. Up to eight token rings can be connected to host processors through a single controller. Special gateways are not required to connect to the full SNA backbone network because the LAN requires only the functions of the physical and data link control layers of SNA, not the higher layers such as path control. These layers remain independent of the LAN, just as they are for alternative lower layers. Additional network management support was also announced whereby an IBM Personal Computer on a ring may be used to monitor errors, perform problem determination, and interact with an operator wanting to evaluate ring status. Later in 1986, support for exchanging such network management data (via Alert signals) to NPDA in a host processor was also announced.

The introduction of the Token-Ring Network demonstrates again that the layered structure of SNA allows the inclusion of new technology in a nondisruptive fashion; supporting the new physical and data link control layers for the token ring had little effect on the rest of the architecture.

The long-term effects of the IBM Token-Ring Network on SNA could be far-reaching. Improving dynamic connectivity and reducing system generation requirements in SNA products become even more important when physical connectivity in an establishment creates the possibility of a "hot-pluggable," fully meshed network. That is, once an SNA workstation is plugged into an office wall, it can have immediate physical access to all SNA workstations and other SNA nodes attached to the Token-Ring Network. To translate this physical access into intelligent communication requires a consistent application program interface and a set of protocols allowing peer attachment to workstations and mainframe computers. Thus, LU 6.2 and node type 2.1 protocols in SNA will become even more important.

Link Subsystems

Initially, SNA supported terrestrial links, slow-speed satellite links, and channel attachments; soon it added public telephone network dial capability. Other link-level options that have since been added to SNA include packet-switched virtual circuits using X.25, high-speed satellite links, and the previously described LANs. ISDN is on the horizon and is being examined as a requirement for SNA.

Recommendation X.25 defines a packet mode interface for attaching DTE—such as host computers, communication controllers, and terminals—to packet-switched data networks (PSDNs). CCITT introduced X.25 in 1976 and updated it in 1978, 1980, and 1984. IBM products that offer X.25 capability comply with the 1980 version of the interface; some products provide an option supporting the 1984 version of the interface. IBM recognizes the requirement for additional products to support the 1984 version. A PSDN provides connectivity to other DTEs using X.25 virtual circuits. Permanent virtual circuits provide fixed connectivity between DTEs, whereas switched virtual circuits provide dynamic connectivity using virtual call setup and clearing capabilities. The X.25 interface also defines user facilities such as interface parameter negotiation, reverse charging, and closed user groups (CUGs).

Having participated in the development of X.25, IBM announced the capability in 1977 for attaching several DTE products to PSDNs in Canada and France. One of the early products was a network interface adapter, the IBM 5973, a stand-alone unit that is a converter between the link control protocol of SNA nodes—SDLC—and the X.25 protocols. This adapter allowed most IBM products that communicate with System/370 hosts to use X.25. Initially, the communication controller (IBM 3705) for SNA System/370 hosts used a special software adaptation for X.25. In 1980, an X.25 program product for the communication controller was introduced, allowing packet-switched communication with other SNA products and connections with non-SNA DTEs.

The IBM direction with respect to X.25 has been to integrate the interface into SNA products where required, so that the customer can choose the most economical communication medium (Deaton and Hippert 1983). If network tariffs favor X.25, one can choose packet-switched services; otherwise, traditional switched or nonswitched services can be used. By the end of 1986, 24 IBM products had been announced supporting the X.25 interface in more than 30 countries. Table 8-1 lists a broad sample of the IBM products that have X.25 capability. IBM (1985g) contains additional information about IBM's X.25 SNA products.

Table 8-1. IBM Products That Support X.25

Product Type	**IBM Product**
Communication controller	3705/3725/3720 (all with NPSI)
Processor	Series/1 (RPS, EDX), 4361, 9370, System/36, System/38, System/88, 8100
Personal computer	5150, 5160, 5170
Licensed program or PRPQ	XI (for DCE function on 3725/3720) TPNS, X.25 NPSI (for DTE function on 3705/3725/3720)
Network interface adaptor	5973-L02
Display station	5251-12
Display control unit	3174, 3274, 5294
Finance controller	4701
Network controller	3710
Computerized branch exchange	ROLM CBX

All SNA products that offer an X.25 1980 interface conform to an IBM-defined specification for attachment of SNA products to PSDNs (IBM 1986c). The most recent enhancement to this specification is called Enhanced Logical Link Control (ELLC). Sometimes virtual circuits are interrupted by the PSDN, causing inconvenience to the users of certain products. This inconvenience is reduced with the implementation of ELLC in low-end computers and terminals that provide a dynamic packet error detection and recovery procedure across one or more PSDNs between SNA nodes.

An IBM SNA X.25 interface specification has been published to describe aspects of the CCITT 1984 recommendation to be supported in SNA (IBM 1986b). Some of the new functions in the 1984 recommendation that have been included in the SNA X.25 1984 interface specification are

- multiple links between the DTE and the PSDN
- redirecting a virtual call by the PSDN from the called DTE to an alternate DTE
- hunt groups that allow the network to assign a call to one of several target DTEs
- an address extension capability that allows a DTE on a private packet-switched network to call a DTE on a public PSDN, and conversely

The SNA nodes we discussed are DTEs that attach to packet-switched networks. Some customers have the need for equipment from different vendors to communicate with one another over packet-switched networks. If the customer has a mix of SNA traffic and non-SNA traffic, the SNA backbone network can be used to carry the non-SNA traffic. The capability to add a PSDN appearance of the X.25 interface to SNA has been announced as a special SNA adaptation (IBM 1986d). In such a configuration, the SNA network provides X.25 permanent virtual circuit, virtual call, and user facility services to using X.25 DTEs. The SNA traffic and the X.25 traffic share the common SNA backbone network. Another feature of the adaptation, called X.25 SNA Interconnect (XI), is a gateway capability to allow X.25 DTEs on a public PSDN or another private PSDN. See Figure 8-6.

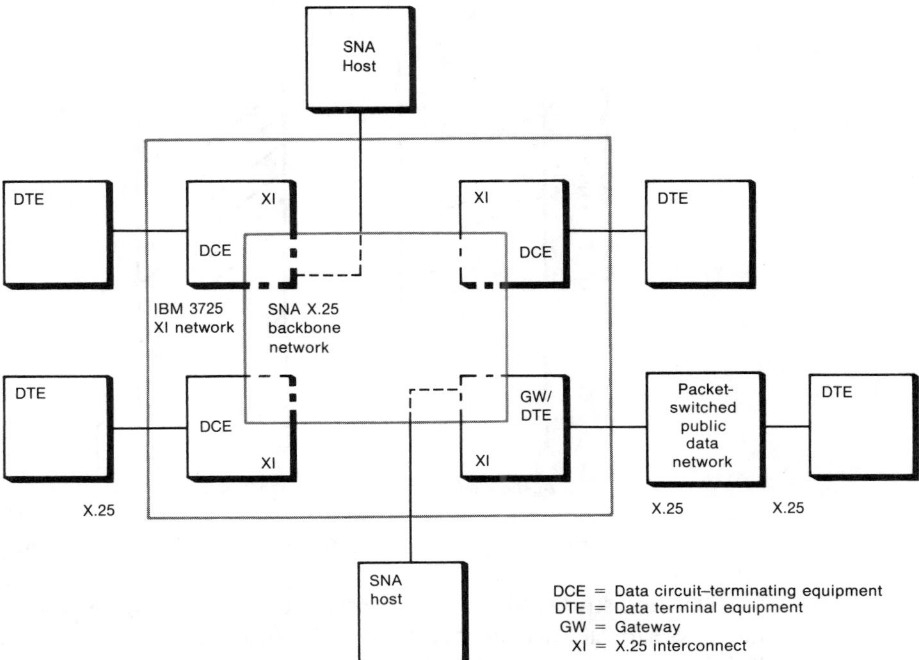

Figure 8-6. X.25 SNA interconnect.

A key aspect of X.25 is that it is an interface specification, not a network architecture. The internal operation below the X.25 interface, such as routing, flow control, and management services, is not specified by standards. Inclusion of an X.25 DCE capability and related network services within SNA is a relatively straightforward and natural step.

Some users find it advantageous to send their SNA traffic over satellite circuits. Because most communication satellites are in geostationary orbits above the equator at an altitude of about 23,000 miles, the delays in sending information from one earth station to another are long compared to those for a terrestrial circuit that connects the same two points on the earth's surface. Consequently, communication protocols must be designed to accommodate the long propagation delay of satellite circuits. Figure 8-7 shows the effects of delay on a link-level protocol that allows the transmitter to have up to seven unacknowledged message units in transit. In the terrestrial case, acknowledgments return to the transmitter in time for it to continue sending new messages, allowing efficient use of the link. In the satellite case, the transmitter stops to wait for an acknowledgment because of the longer propagation delay, and unused time is introduced on the link.

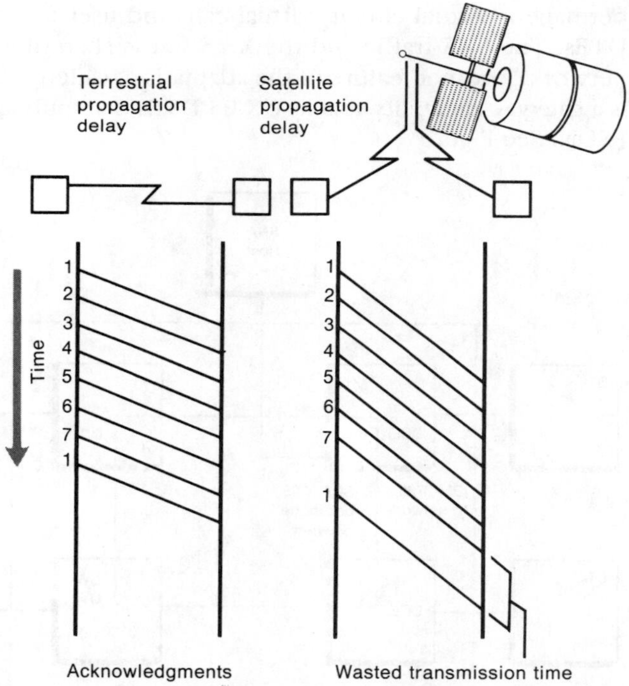

Figure 8-7. Effects of delay on a link-level protocol.

Detailed studies show that interactive and batch applications can use satellite links satisfactorily at speeds up to 19,200 bits per second when the satellite link is attached to an SNA peripheral node (Deaton and Franse 1980a, 1980b). The 3710 Network Controller provides satisfactory performance over satellite links at speeds up to 64,000 bits per second when the satellite link connects the 3710 to a 3725 or 3720 Communication Controller (using SDLC with a modulus of 128). Batch and interactive traffic are carried satisfactorily at link speeds up to 256,000 bits per second over satellite links connecting SNA 3725 and 3720 Communication Controllers. A special adaptation is available that allows two SNA 3725s to communicate over satellite links at speeds up to 1,344 million bits per second.

At satellite speeds above 256,000 bits per second, special consideration must be given to the types of protocol and the value range of protocol parameters at several architectural layers of the system (Andrews 1983; Brodd and Donnan 1983). Because high-speed satellite and terrestrial circuits are becoming more widely available, a requirement exists to enhance SNA to accommodate them. Capabilities such as support for larger link-level sequence numbers (an SDLC modulus of 128) have been added; selective retransmission of information and other protocols optimized to the high-speed or long-delay environment, or both, are being studied.

The rapidly approaching feasibility of high-speed digital communication (in units of 64,000 bits per second) will have significant impact on both data communication and telephony, and will open possibilities for interactive video applications in the foreseeable future. The ISDN standardization of the user-to-network interfaces for these applications has been going on for several years within CCITT. In Europe, many countries already offer digital network services on "pre-ISDN" networks. These networks use a CCITT X.21-like interface for signaling and data transfer at 64,000 bits per second. Some of them use slower speeds for signaling. IBM's requirement is to connect SNA DTEs to many of these networks. As ISDN evolves around the world, IBM will adapt SNA to take advantage of these and other new digital network services to meet customer requirements.

IBM has consistently represented the needs of data communication applications in the standardization effort and continues to cooperate actively in the development of a single set of worldwide standards. The CCITT ISDN Recommendations of 1984 and the interim Recommendations approved in 1986 are significant steps in the advancement of these new digital transmission services.

SNA and OSI

IBM recognizes the widespread interest on the part of users in interconnecting networks using different communication architectures. IBM supports such interconnection and publishes extensive information about SNA, including formats and protocols, which facilitates the interconnection of other systems to IBM SNA networks.

The widespread interest also gave rise to the OSI standards project (Day and Zimmerman 1983), whose aim is to provide communication protocols for interconnecting systems of different communication architectures, such as SNA and a system of another architecture.

From the start, IBM has been involved in the OSI work, contributing experience about layered communication architectures and also increasing understanding of advances elsewhere in that area. Clearly, some capability for interconnecting heterogeneous systems is desirable. From a vendor's perspective, a single international protocol for interconnecting heterogeneous systems is preferable to a number of national protocols.

IBM has stated that for industrial communications, it supports the National Bureau of Standards specifications of OSI Transport layer class 4 used over IEEE 802.4 LAN. The capability was demonstrated at the National Computer Conference in July 1984. More recently, at the Autofact Conference and Exposition in November 1985, IBM introduced file transfer and directory server programs that support the OSI-based Manufacturing Automation Protocol (MAP).

IBM Europe has developed native OSI software that provides System/370 support for selected functions in the OSI 4 (Transport) and 5 (Session) layers. The Open System Transport and Session Support (OTSS) program makes OSI Session layer services available to IBM host application programs that need to communicate with programs in a system implementing another architecture. This represents a further step in IBM's commitment to provide products capable of system interconnection in conformance with OSI standards.

Additionally, OSI protocols could be supported in SNA for protocol conversion; that is, we could transform SNA protocols to and from OSI protocols through conversion code in a host to allow attachment to other networks that use existing network architectures. Indeed, as reported in Shukuya, Yamaguchi, and Kobayashi (1985), Yamaguchi and Sy (1985), and Shiohara, Sy, and Yamaguchi (1985), IBM Japan, in cooperation with Nippon Telegraph and Telephone (NTT), has judged the use of OSI as intermediate protocols to be a viable way to interconnect SNA networks with networks that use DCNA protocols.

The OTSS and Open Systems Network Support (OSNS) products work in conjunction with the VTAM, NCP, and NPSI SNA products to provide OSI Session layer services over an X.25 network. While SNA remains IBM's strategic network architecture, IBM will continue to evaluate standards and develop timely, OSI-compatible products based on customer and business requirements. See also Aschenbrenner (1986) for further information on IBM's activities related to OSI.

Conclusions

SNA has evolved continually and will do so as long as new technology, applications, and requirements unfold. The layered structure of the architecture and of the implementing products allows this process to be natural and nondisruptive.

Some of the historical trends have been cited in the preceding sections. For example, the network management services provided in SNA networks have been an ongoing concern. Moreover, recently announced extensions in this area not only supply greater function for SNA networks but facilitate managing non-SNA, multivendor, and voice network components.

These extensions provide users the ability to manage mixed SNA and non-SNA networks using a single consistent framework and a proven set of network management products. The framework involves a *focal point*, which consists of a set of products that provide centralized management application support for all network components; *entry points*, which are those products that can transmit formatted network management information (such as Alert data) to the focal point about themselves as well as attached communication devices; and *service points*, which provide comparable network management support for IBM Token-Ring Networks, ROLM CBXs, selected PBXs, and non-SNA components for which entry-point support may not exist. Examples of products providing support for a focal point are NetView, Distributed Systems Executive (DSX), Network Performance Monitor (NPM), and INFO/MANAGEMENT. Examples of entry points are the System/36, System/38, 3720, 3725, 3174, System/88, Series/1, and 3708 Network Conversion Unit. An example of a service point is NetView/PC, which also provides an application program interface (API/CS) for communicating with the NetView product in System/370; various application programs can work with NetView/PC to provide problem determination and Alert management for the IBM Token-Ring Network, the IBM PC Network, and the ROLM CBX.

Configurational flexibility and accommodation of larger networks have been another continuing concern. Besides the generalized topology and larger address space now available through SNA network interconnection (SNI) and extended network addressing, specific offerings such as the IBM 3720 Communication Controller and the 3710 Network Controller, which offer a remote link concentration capability, have resulted in cost-performance advantages. Of course, the Low-Entry Networking capability allows the flexibility of peer communication without host mediation, while the System/36 APPN feature builds on this further, allowing multihop System/36 configurations.

Additional offerings have resulted in the extension of SNA capabilities into areas that are important to many customers, such as for SNADS and document services in an office environment (DIA and Document Content Architecture). Another example is the inclusion of VTAM as an integral component of the native virtual machine (VM) environment, thereby enhancing performance of SNA network operation from the VM viewpoint. A more recent example of increased transaction services supported in the SNA environment is the introduction of Distributed Data Management (DDM). DDM is designed (using LU 6.2 sessions for transport) to fit within the local data management of a system so that access to remote files is transparent to the application program. Currently, CICS can provide file-server support for System/36 and System/38 in this way, while System/36 and System/38 can provide both file-access and file-server support for another System/36 or System/38.

Continuous network operation needs, as served by the extensive list of capabilities mentioned earlier—from link, route, and session parallelism and redundancy to well-defined backup and takeover support—will foster ever more features that promote high availability. Advances in route dynamics and distributed directories will also play a significant role in meeting requirements in this area. The whole matter of reducing the static nature of network definition is a consuming interest; a long-term goal is to eliminate the need for static definition entirely.

Another area of traditional concern to customers is non-SNA device support. One technique, using format envelopment, was incorporated into the Non-SNA Interconnection (NSI) program product on the NCP, which allows Binary Synchronous Communication (BSC) remote job entry terminals and BSC network job entry subsystems to communicate through an SNA network and share the SNA links. Another technique employs protocol conversion. Here, besides the long-time NTO support for pre-SNA terminals in the NCP, new capabilities such as that in the IBM 3174 Communications Control Unit, which allows SNA and non-SNA terminals to communicate with SNA and non-SNA hosts, continue to enhance SNA coverage in this important area. In general, the trend here has been to perform protocol conversion to SNA as close to the non-SNA interface as possible, in order to gain quickly in the operation the SNA benefits of resource sharing and network management.

Of course, one of the most visible areas of non-SNA protocol support is national and international standards. IBM will continue to play a leading role both to cooperate in formulating such standards and to include support for such standards in SNA products subject to appropriate business decisions. This chapter has cited several examples of such standards, such as the CCITT X.25 and the more recent IEEE LAN standards, that have been integrated into SNA.

Finally, SNA will continue to exploit advances in technology as they appear. Here, a known requirement is to extend the peer-to-peer operation in SNA. This need follows from developments both in processor design—especially in small systems—and in transmission technology, such as for LANs, satellites, PSDNs, and ISDN. Other developments, not yet evident, will affect future requirements. The process will continue and undoubtedly be the cause of much interesting evolution of SNA for a long time to come.

References

Andrews, D. W. 1983. Throughput efficiency of logical links over satellite channels. *Proceedings of the Satellite and Computer-Communications Symposium*, Versailles (April 27–29). Amsterdam: North-Holland Publishing Co.

Andrews, D. W., and G. D. Schultz. 1982. A token-ring architecture for local-area networks—An update. *Proceedings COMP-CON Fall 1982*. IEEE Computer Society, Los Angeles.

Aschenbrenner, J. R. 1986. Open systems interconnection. *IBM Systems Journal* 25, nos. 3/4:369–79.

Baratz, A. E., J. P. Gray, P. E. Green, J. M. Jaffe, and D. P. Pozefsky. 1985. SNA networks of small systems. *IEEE Journal on Selected Areas in Communications* SAC-3, no. 3:416–26 (May).

Benjamin, J. H., M. L. Hess, R. A. Weingarten, and W. R. Wheeler. 1983. Interconnecting SNA networks. *IBM Systems Journal* 22, no. 4:344–66.

Brodd, W. D., and R. A. Donnan. 1983. Data link control requirements for satellite transmission. *Proceedings of the Satellite and Computer-Communica-*

tions Symposium, Versailles (April 27–29). Amsterdam: North-Holland Publishing Co.

Bux, W., F. H. Closs, K. Kümmerle, H. J. Keller, and H. R. Müller. 1983. Architecture and design of a reliable token-ring network. *IEEE Journal on Selected Areas in Communications* SAC-1, no. 5:756–65 (November).

Bux, W., and D. Grillo. 1985. Flow control in local-area networks of interconnected token rings. *IEEE Transaction on Communications* COM-33, no. 10:1058–66 (October).

Carlson, D. E. 1982. Bit-oriented data link control. *Computer Network Architectures and Protocols*. P. E. Green, Jr., ed. New York: Plenum Press.

Cordell, R. 1984. Rock-solid office architecture. *Computerworld on Communications* 21–23 (October 3).

Day, J. D., and H. Zimmerman. 1983. The OSI reference model. *Proceedings of the IEEE* 71, no. 12:1334–40 (December).

Deaton, G. A., and D. J. Franse. 1980a. Performance analysis of computer networks that access satellite links. *ICCC-80 Conference Proceedings*, Atlanta. Amsterdam: North-Holland Publishing Co.

———. 1980b. Analyzing IBM's 3270 performance over satellite links. *Data Communications* 9, no. 10:117–32 (October).

Deaton, G. A., Jr., and R. O. Hippert, Jr. 1983. X.25 and related recommendations in IBM products. *IBM Systems Journal* 22, nos. 1/2:11–29.

Eisenbies, J. L., and T. D. Smetanka. 1984. An automatic topology update scheme for SNA networks. *Proceedings of the Seventh ICCC*. Amsterdam: North-Holland Publishing Co.

Gray, J. P., P. J. Hansen, P. Homan, M. A. Lerner, and M. Pozefsky. 1983. Advanced program-to-program communication in SNA. *IBM Systems Journal* 22, no. 4:298–318.

Housel, B. C., and C. J. Scopinich. 1983. SNA distribution services. *IBM Systems Journal* 22, no. 4:319–43.

IBM. 1983a. *Document Content Architecture: Final-Form-Text Reference*, SC23-0757.

———. 1983b. *Document Content Architecture: Revisable-Form-Text Reference*, SC23-0758.

———. 1983c. *Document Interchange Architecture: Concepts and Structures*, SC23-0759.

———. 1984. *Systems Network Architecture Format and Protocol Reference Manual: Distribution Services*, SC30-3098.

———. 1985a. *NCCF General Information Manual*, GC27-0429.

———. 1985b. *NLDM General Information Manual*, GC27-0657.

———. 1985c. *NPDA General Information Manual*, GC34-2111.

———. 1985d. *SNA Format and Protocol Reference Manual: Architecture Logic for LU Type 6.2*, SC30-3269.

———. 1985e. *SNA Format and Protocol Reference Manual: SNA Network Interconnection*, SC30-3339.

———. 1985f. *SNA Transaction Programmer's Reference Manual for LU Type 6.2*, GC30-3084.

———. 1985g. *X.25 SNA Guide*, GG24-1568.

———. 1986a. *SNA Format and Protocol Reference Manual: Management Services*, SC30-3346.

———. 1986b. *The X.25 1984 Interface for Attaching IBM SNA Nodes to Packet-Switched Data Networks—General Information Manual*, GA27-3761.

———. 1986c. *X.25 SNA Interconnection: DTE/DCE Interface Description*, GH19-6520.

———. 1986d. *X.25 SNA Interconnection: X.25 SNA Network Supervisory Function General Information Manual*, GH19-6572.

IEEE Computer Society. 1985. *Token-Ring Access Method and Physical Layer Specifications*, IEEE Standard 802.5. ISO/DIS 8802/5.

Jaffe, J. M., F. H. Moss, and R. A. Weingarten. 1983. SNA routing: Past, present, and possible future. *IBM Systems Journal* 22, no. 4:417–34.

Saltzer, J. H., K. T. Pogran, and D. D. Clark. 1983. Why a ring? *Computer Networks* 7:223–31.

Schick, T., and R. F. Brockish. 1982. The document interchange architecture: A member of a family of architectures in the SNA environment. *IBM Systems Journal* 21, no. 2:220–44.

Shiohara, M., K. K. Sy, and M. Yamaguchi. 1985. A study of the protocol conversion between SNA LU 6.2 and OSI session/transport layers. *Proceedings of the 30th Annual Convention, IPS Japan*. Information Processing Society of Japan, Tokyo (March). In Japanese.

Shukuya, S., M. Yamaguchi, and Y. Kobayashi. 1985. A study of OSI subsets from LU 6.2 functional viewpoints. *Proceedings of the 30th Annual Convention, IPS Japan*. Information Processing Society of Japan, Tokyo (March). In Japanese.

Strole, N. C. 1983. A local communications network based on interconnected token-access rings: A tutorial. *IBM Journal of Research and Development* 27, no. 5:481–96.

Sundstrom, R. J. 1984. Program-to-program communications—A growing trend. *Data Communications* 13, no. 2:87–92.

Sundstrom, R. J., and G. D. Schultz. 1980. SNA's first six years: 1974–1980. *Proceedings of the Fifth ICCC*, Atlanta (September). Amsterdam: North-Holland Publishing Co.

Yamaguchi, M., and K. K. Sy. 1985. A comparison of various gateways for SNA-OSI interconnection. *Proceedings of the 30th Annual Convention, IPS Japan*. Information Processing Society of Japan, Tokyo (March). In Japanese.

Chapter 9

Digital (DEC) Network Architecture

Radia Perlman

Chapter 9

THIS CHAPTER DESCRIBES PHASE V OF THE DIGITAL Network Architecture (DNA), Digital Equipment Corporation's proprietary network architecture. Much of it is identical with that of the ISO standard protocols, in many cases because ISO protocols are derived from DNA protocols. Phase V DNA is designed to be compatible with systems that are compliant with ISO and compatible with Phase IV DNA systems.

This chapter emphasizes the concepts involved in the protocols, rather than details of the protocols, and so we avoid exact packet formats but list interesting information included *in* a packet. For exact details of particular protocols, the proper reference is the protocol's specification.

DNA defines a means by which computer systems can communicate with each other. DNA partitions the problem of intercomputer communication into a set of layers, and defines the function of each layer, the protocols and algorithms through which each layer accomplishes its function, and the interfaces through which a layer receives services from the layer below. Additionally, DNA defines the mechanisms through which the network can be managed.

DECnet is the family of communications products, both hardware and software, which implement the DNA architecture. DECnet products were first delivered in 1976, and there have been five major phases, each bringing new capabilities. Phase I, the initial phase, allowed directly connected systems to communicate over a variety of devices, with the only systems supported being the RSX family of operating systems for the PDP11 computers. Phase II extended the capabilities to a wider variety of computer systems. Phase III added forwarding capabilities and automatic distributed route calculation. Phase III also introduced the capability of managing systems in the network remotely (i.e., message exchange between the system and the manager would take place over the network). Phase IV allowed for vastly larger networks by extending network addresses to 16 bits, with a two-level hierarchy. It also incorporated protocols for utilizing circuit-switched and virtual circuit-switched connections, such as communication across X.25 networks and protocols for efficiently exploiting the connectivity provided by LANs. It defined a virtual terminal protocol, through which remote access to any computer on the network from any other computer on the network became possible. It also defined capabilities for interconnection between DNA and SNA, and for transparent access of X.25 networks through a DECnet network.

The current phase is Phase V. The major additional capabilities are

- integration of OSI standards
- support for much larger networks than were possible with Phase IV
- a Naming Service, which allows efficient sharing of critical shared information, such as the mapping between human readable names of network resources, and their network addresses

DNA Goals

Throughout its history, DNA's goals have been

1. To be general purpose. A network architecture should be designed so that a wide range of applications can be supported. New applications, as they are designed, should be easily built upon the network architecture. Likewise, a wide range of communications facilities should be supported, and new technology should be easily incorporated without major change to the architecture.
2. To be scalable. The network architecture should efficiently support small as well as large networks.
3. To not constrain topologies. The network topology should be chosen based on factors such as the physical location of computer systems, the availability of communications facilities, and traffic patterns. The network architecture should not constrain the topology.
4. To require minimal human intervention. The network should, whenever possible, self-configure without manual intervention. For instance, it should automatically compute routes as events occur which alter the network topology, such as the addition of new nodes or links or the failure of nodes or links.
5. To be robust. The network should continue to operate even if nodes or links fail. Similarly, network services should be distributed to avoid single point-of-failure vulnerabilities.
6. To make use of standards. Many networks require interconnection of systems from many different vendors. Thus, conformance to OSI standards is critical.
7. To be manageable. Although the network can self-configure some functions, other functions cannot be automatically managed, for instance, the choice of a human-sensible character string to act as a name of a node. In addition, although care is taken to choose default settings for parameters that will operate in a wide variety of conditions, human intervention is sometimes required to "tune" the settings to make the best

tradeoffs (for instance, cost/performance or efficiency/responsiveness) for a particular situation. The network architecture should allow for nodes to be managed remotely, across the network.

DNA Layers

DNA is strictly layered, and follows very closely the layering in the OSI Reference Model (Zimmerman 1980). Layering allows a moderate amount of independence between layers, so that individual layers can be replaced as new standards emerge or hardware or software implementation of standards become available, without affecting the other layers. A certain amount of efficiency might be gained by collapsing several layers, but the gains of generality, ability to conform to evolving standards, and debuggability make strict layering well worth potential performance disadvantages.

One departure from standard OSI layering is that DNA offers two options above the Transport Layer (see Figure 9-1). One option is DNA Session and DNA Application Layers. The other option is OSI Session, Presentation, and Application Layers. The reason for this split is for compatibility with previous DNA Applications built upon the DNA Session service, as well as applications that are not currently standardized by OSI. However, the DNA architecture is structured so that it will be easy to support new upper layer OSI standards as they become available.

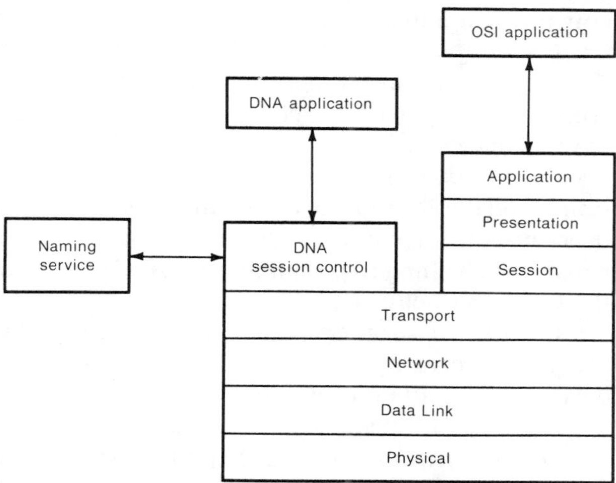

Figure 9-1. DNA layers.

The layer at level n is known as the n-layer. The n-layer uses the services of the (n−1)-layer, and provides services to the (n+1)-layer. Adjacent layers communicate through an interface. The n-layer provides its added functionality by cooperation with other n-layer entities. Communication with other n-layer entities is done through a protocol. There are nine layers.

Physical Layer. The responsibility of the Physical Layer is to transmit unstructured bits of information across a link. It deals with such problems as size and shape of connectors, assignment of functions to pins, conversion of bits to electrical signals, and bit-level synchronization. Many mature Physical Layer standards exist, and most are easily supported within the DNA architecture.

Data Link Layer. The responsibility of the Data Link Layer is to transmit chunks of information across a link. It deals with such problems as checksumming to detect data corruption, orderly coordination of the use of shared media, as in a LAN, and addressing when multiple systems are reachable, as in a LAN.

Network Layer. The responsibility of the Network Layer is to enable any pairs of systems in the network to communicate with each other, though the network itself is not fully connected. In other words, the Network Layer must find a route and systems along the path must forward packets in the appropriate direction. The Network Layer deals with such problems as route calculation, packet fragmentation and reassembly (when different links in the network have different maximum packet sizes), and congestion control.

Transport Layer. The responsibility of the Transport Layer is to establish a reliable communication stream between a pair of systems. It deals with errors that can be introduced by the Network Layer—such as lost packets, duplicated packets, packet reordering, and fragmentation and reassembly—so that the user of the Transport Layer can deal with larger sized messages and less efficient Network Layer fragmentation and reassembly might be avoided.

DNA Session Layer. The responsibility of DNA Session is to facilitate the initiation of connections. It deals with such problems as human-friendly name to machine-friendly address translation, access control, and system-specific conversation initialization functions.

DNA Application. Many DNA applications are available in Phase V, such as file access and transfer, network virtual terminals, electronic mail, SNA interconnection applications, computer conferencing, videotex, and remote network management.

OSI Session. The responsibility of OSI Session is to offer services above the simple full duplex reliable communication stream offered by Transport, such as dialogue control (enforcing a particular pattern of communication between systems) and chaining (combining groups of packets so that either all or none in the group get delivered).

OSI Presentation Layer. The responsibility of OSI Presentation Layer is to provide a means by which OSI applications can agree on representations for data, thus providing those applications with a means to transfer information without loss of the application semantics.

OSI Application. Many OSI applications are currently, or soon to become, standard, such as FTAM (File Transfer, Access, and Management Services), and VT (Virtual Terminal Services).

Because data cannot flow directly between n-layer entities (other than the Physical Layer), communication between n-layer entities is accomplished by passing information across the interface down to the (n−1)-layer, which packages the information, adding control information necessary for the performance of the (n−1)-layer service, and passes the information down to the next lower layer (see Figure 9-2).

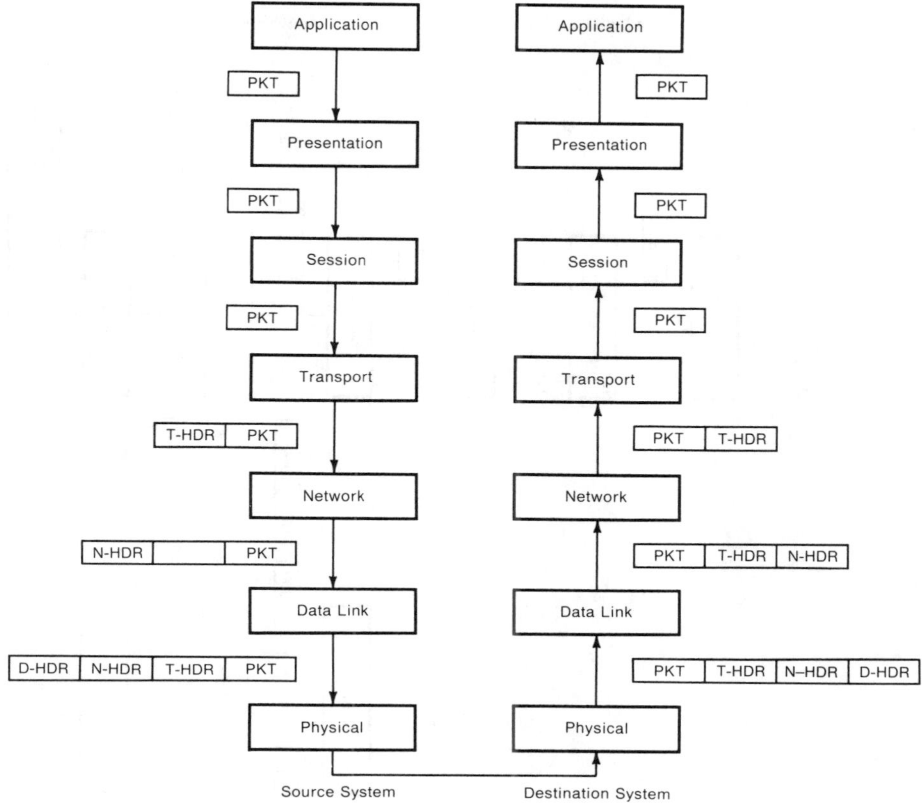

Figure 9-2. Communication between layer entities.

When computers are not directly connected, information must pass through one or more "intermediate systems," which forward the information (see Figure 9-3). In the figure when the intermediate system's Network Layer receives the information, it ascertains, based on the control information attached to the packet by the source system's Network Layer, that the packet is not destined for its own node but must rather be forwarded on. Thus, instead of removing the control information and passing the packet up to the Transport Layer, the Network Layer passes the packet back down to the Data Link Layer.

Physical Layer

There are two types of links that can connect systems, the point-to-point link, connecting exactly two systems, and the multiaccess link, connecting multiple systems.

There are two types of multiaccess links, the LAN and the *multipoint link*. The LAN has many attachments and any pair of stations attached can communicate. In addition, there is usually the capability for a single transmitted packet to be received by multiple recipients. Protocols for dealing with LANs will be further discussed in the section on the Data Link Layer. In the multipoint link,

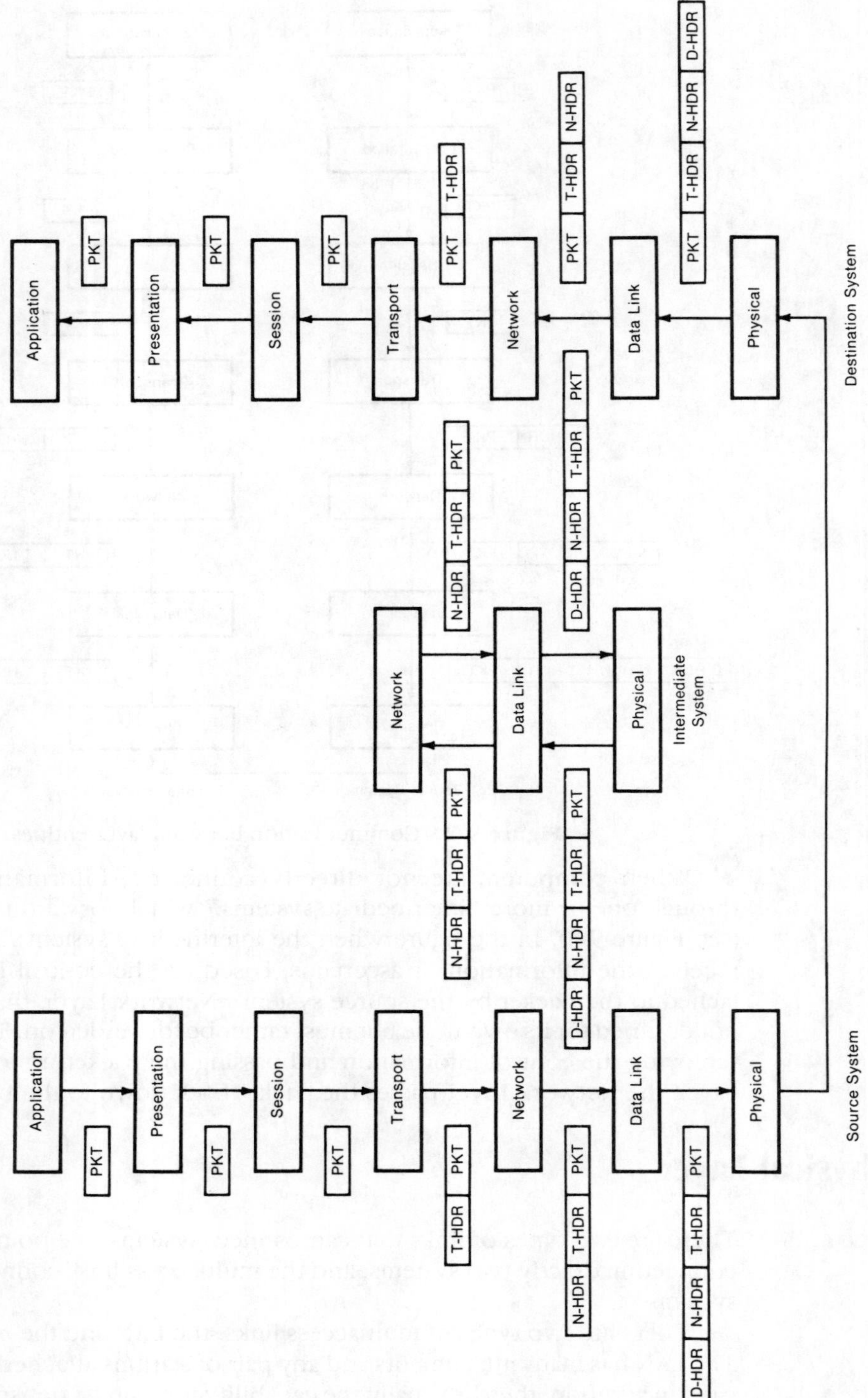

Figure 9-3. Communication through an intermediate system.

access to the shared media is controlled by a *master station*, with the other stations being *tributaries*. A tributary station does not transmit unless polled by the master station. This type of device can also be supported by the DNA architecture, but is based on older technology and is becoming less common.

DNA can easily support any Physical Layer protocol. Standards for point-to-point links currently supported by DECnet products include EIA RS-232, EIA RS-423, CCITT V.24. Standards for LANs which are currently supported by DECnet products are based on the Carrier Sense Multiple Access with Collision Detect (CSMA/CD) standards, both the original Ethernet design and the current ISO 8802-3 standards. There are several implementations of CSMA/CD within DECnet, including the original 8802-3 standard, the ThinWire standard (802.3 10BASE2), and a broadband implementation.

In CSMA/CD, "Multiple Access" means many (usually hundreds) of stations can be attached, and "Carrier Sense" means that a station listens before transmitting and defers if the medium is currently being used by another transmitter. "Collision Detect" means that a station listens while transmitting to detect if another station has also decided to transmit. In the event of a collision, each station waits a random amount of time before retrying. The CSMA/CD standard calls for *exponential backoff* which means that after each unsuccessful transmission (i.e., each collision), the time interval from which a random time is selected is doubled.

Details of particular Physical Layer standards currently being supported by DECnet products are not very significant to understanding the DNA architecture because, due to DNA's modular structure, any Physical Layer standard can be supported by an implementation and fit well into DNA, provided that the characteristics of the Physical Layer standard resemble one of the main types of links already supported. These types of links are

- static point-to-point link—a direct link between two systems that is kept operational at all times
- LAN—a multiaccess link enabling pairwise communication between any connected stations, as well as multicast capability (i.e., transmission of a single packet to multiple recipients)
- dynamically established link—a point-to-point link that is connected and disconnected automatically by the network (often, the network automatically determines the destination attachment point)

The handling of these generic types of links will be discussed at length in the section on the Network Layer. Standards such as FDDI (a LAN) and ISDN (dynamically established link) can be easily supported by the DNA architecture and easily added to implementations.

Data Link Layer

The purpose of the Data Link Layer is to transmit packets of information between adjacent stations. The meaning of "adjacent" is quite fuzzy in this context, since sometimes information is moving between systems through an intermediate system (IS), a computer attached to the network that, in addition to initiating and receiving traffic, also forwards traffic. However, because the intermediate system is transparent to the end systems (ES), the end systems are considered adjacent. An example of this situation is a bridge connecting two LANs (described further in the section on Bridges).

Most Data Link Layer protocols designed for point-to-point links perform the following functions:

- structuring the bit-stream service provided by the Physical Layer into packets
- attaching control information to packets, including a checksum so that the receiver can detect data corruption, and packet numbers so that damaged packets can be retransmitted

Thus, point-to-point Data Link protocols tend to provide a *reliable* delivery service, i.e., in normal operation all packets are delivered without loss, duplication, or misordering. However, when synchronization between the end stations is lost, due to failure of either station or the connecting link, packets may be lost or duplicated. It is safest to assume, then, as the DNA Network Layer assumes, that the Data Link Layer provides a *datagram service*, i.e., that most packets arrive undamaged, that data corruption is detected with very high probability, but that some possibility of lost, duplicated, misordered, or corrupted packets exists.

In contrast, most Data Link protocols designed for LANs provide a datagram service. Packets are not numbered or acknowledged. The assumption on a LAN is that error rates are sufficiently low that error recovery can be performed at a higher layer without loss of efficiency. However, Data Link Layer protocols for LANs need additional mechanisms to deal with addressing, because there are multiple potential recipients of a packet.

Point-to-Point Protocols

The most popular Data Link protocol designed for point-to-point links is the *bit-stuffing* class of protocols. With minor differences, the protocols in this class include HDLC and LAPB. To delimit messages, a bit-stuffing protocol uses the flag consisting of six 1s inside a pair of 0s. Inside the message, the possibility of six adjacent 1s is prevented by having the transmitter "stuff" an extra 0 after any occurrence of five adjacent 1s. Then the receiver, after receipt of five adjacent 1s, checks to determine whether the next received bit is 0, and if so, removes the 0.

A *sequence number* is contained within each packet. The standard size of the sequence number field is three bits, but some bit-stuffing protocols allow the use of *extended sequence numbering*, which allows the sequence number field to be seven bits long. This is particularly important on high-delay links such as satellite lines, since the number of not-yet-acknowledged packets the transmitter is allowed to transmit must be less than the sequence number space, and indeed, cannot be more than half the sequence number space if the receiver can keep packets received out of order. For instance, the receiver receives packets 1 and 2, loses 3, and receives 4. If the receiver holds onto 4 while waiting for 3, the transmitter cannot transmit a packet with a sequence number more than n/2 (where n is the size of the sequence number space) greater (modulo n) than the unacknowledged packet with the lowest sequence number.

Another point-to-point protocol supported by DECnet products is Digital Data Communications Message Protocol (DDCMP). Functionally, DDCMP is similar to HDLC. It uses a particular start-of-message character to delimit packets, but unlike HDLC, it does not modify the data to prevent the start-of-message character from occurring within the data. Instead, the header of the packet contains the size of the packet. In the event of bit errors on the link, the two ends can become missynchronized, because the receiver can find start-of-message characters inside the data. However, the protocol is designed so that resynchronization will occur quickly.

Although the bit-stuffing protocols are more popular, DDCMP has the advantage that it can work on a wider variety of lines. Since the bit-stuffing protocols add single bits at somewhat random points in the data stream, bit-stuffing protocols really only work well on synchronous links.

LAN Protocols

Because LANs have low error rates, retransmission of damaged packets can be done solely at a higher layer without loss of performance. Thus, there is no need for numbering messages and providing acknowledgments. LAN Data Link Layer protocols are usually very simple—the control information basically consists of addressing and checksum. Messages are not numbered, or acknowledged, by the LAN Data Link Layer protocol.

The ISO 8802 series of standards define three types of LANs (8802-3 defines CSMA/CD, 8802-4 defines a token ring, and 8802-5 defines a token bus), plus management protocols and LAN interconnection protocols.

Additionally, 8802-2 provides for building a connection-oriented Data Link Layer protocol upon the basic datagram service. When this is used, the control information in data packets is extended to include the information found in point-to-point Data Link protocols, such as message numbers and acknowledgment numbers. DNA does not use this form of LAN Data Link Layer because its use complicates the lower layer protocols, and does not eliminate the need for end-to-end error recovery done by the Transport Layer.

Thus for DNA, the LAN Data Link header consists of

Dest

Source

Length

DSAP

SSAP

Ctl

user data
Pad
CRC

Source and Destination Addresses

Dest and Source are each 48-bit quantities. One bit of an address is reserved to distinguish *group* or multicast addresses from *individual* addresses. With a group address, multiple stations may be "listening," and will receive packets with that group address as destination. With an individual address, the usual case is that there is only one recipient. However, it is possible for a station to listen "promiscuously," so that it would receive all packets transmitted on the LAN, regardless of their destination address. This capability is useful for purposes such as network monitoring, and for bridges.

An additional bit out of the 48-bit address distinguishes addresses that were assigned by IEEE, and therefore guaranteed to be unique, from addresses that are *locally assigned*. No global authority defines how local addresses are chosen or used. In Phase V, DECnet products normally use only globally assigned addresses, since this relieves the customer from the responsibility of ensuring that all addresses in a network are unique.

Length Field

The necessity for the *length field* arises because of the CSMA/CD technology. To ensure very high probability of successful packet delivery, the 8802-3 standard requires that packets be sufficiently long so that, if a collision occurs, the transmitter is aware of that and will retransmit the packet. Thus, there is a minimum packet size equal to the number of bits that can be transmitted during a round trip delay on the LAN. An example of the worst case scenario for which a round trip delay is required in order to detect collision is this: A transmitter on one end of the network begins transmitting, and, just before the packet reaches the other end of the network, a transmitter on the other end of the network begins transmitting, not realizing its packet is about to collide with an already transmitted packet. After the collision occurs (slightly less than one LAN-length after the first transmitter initiated transmission), it requires another trip across the LAN for the news of the collision to reach the first transmitter.

Because there is a minimum legal length for packets, packets that are smaller than this length must be padded to minimum length. Thus the length field is required to extract the real data from the packet on packets that were not larger than minimum length.

Multiplexing Fields

The 8802 standards allow the possibility of multiple upper layer protocols to coexist on the LAN, and even coexist on the same system, sharing the services of the Data Link Layer concurrently.

The original Ethernet standard provided for a single field for this purpose, the *protocol type field*. It was 16 bits long, and administered by Xerox Corporation. Every manufacturer wishing to design protocols to run over the Ethernet was required (if they wished to be compliant with the Ethernet standard) to apply to Xerox for a protocol type number for each protocol using the Ethernet Data Link protocols.

When the CSMA/CD standard was adopted by IEEE, it modified the control information, so instead of a single 16-bit protocol type field, there are two 8-bit fields—*destination service access point* (DSAP) and *source service access point* (SSAP). Breaking the field into two parts allows numbering of protocols within machines to be done independently. At first this seems flexible, but it makes autoconfigurability difficult.

The 8-bit SAP addresses have defined structure. One bit is defined to be individual or group, just as with the 48-bit address. This gives the capability to define a SAP that would be received by multiple protocols. Another bit is defined to be globally administered or locally administered. This distinguishes SAP addresses assigned by IEEE, and therefore guaranteed to be unique, from locally administered SAP addresses. As with locally administered station addresses, no standard specifies how locally administered SAP addresses would be chosen, or used.

Given that 2 bits out of the 8 bits are predefined, the global authority which assigns SAP addresses only has 6 bits left, or 64 possible SAP addresses. With such a limited number, they cannot give addresses to proprietary protocols. Instead, only national or international standards can be assigned SAP addresses. When such standard protocols are being utilized, the same protocol will be in the destination station as in the source station, and as such, the DSAP and SSAP addresses in the packet will always match. Thus, globally assigned SAP addresses really do function like the protocol type field in the original Ethernet standard.

To work around the problem of the very limited SAP size, and the inability for proprietary protocols to acquire a globally assigned SAP number, a single SAP number was globally assigned and known as the *Subnetwork Access Protocol*, or SNAP SAP. When the SNAP SAP value is present in the DSAP and SSAP fields, an extra field is present beyond the base 8802-3 header, known as the *protocol ID*. This field is 5 bytes long.

The original Ethernet specification called for a 2-byte protocol ID field. That may have been sufficiently long. However, it was noted that the remainder of the header was an odd number of bytes, so for certain implementations for which headers of odd bytes were inconvenient, the committee standardizing the SNAP SAP use suggested the protocol ID field be 3 bytes long instead.

Another proposal suggested that by making the protocol ID at least 4 bytes long, assignment of protocol IDs by a global authority could be done automatically with the assignment of addresses. When station addresses are needed, application is made to the IEEE, which assigns a block of addresses for which 3 bytes are assigned by IEEE and 3 bytes are unspecified. In this way, each address block assignment gives 2**24 addresses. If the protocol ID field were longer than 3 bytes, a protocol ID block would be added, again with the same 3 bytes specified and the remaining bits assigned by the holder of the address block.

Because there were good reasons for making the length of the protocol ID field odd and good reasons for making the length of the protocol ID field more than 3 bytes, the committee agreed to make the length of the field 5 bytes.

Migration from Ethernet to 8802-3

The 8802-3 standard is very similar to the original Ethernet standard, but it is not identical. Since the same physical hardware can support either standard, stations built to the original Ethernet standard can coexist on the LAN with stations built to the 8802-3 standard.

Fortunately, there is a method to distinguish packets in Ethernet format from packets in 8802-3 format. The Ethernet standard did not have a length field, and instead had the protocol type field where the 8802-3 standard has the length field. Since the only legal packet lengths are less than 1,500 bytes, any packet with a value greater than 1,500 in the length field can be assumed to be in Ethernet format. (Xerox did not assign any protocol types less than 1,500 to make this distinction possible.)

Bridges

LANs are really multiaccess links—the word "network" implies that all stations that wish to communicate reside on the LAN, and that the LAN is the entire universe. Although in limited cases this may be true, LAN technology has the following restrictions:

1. geographic—limited physical size
2. traffic—all traffic on a LAN must share the same medium, thus the total aggregate traffic bandwidth is limited when the entire network consists of a single LAN
3. number of stations—limited number that can attach to a single LAN

These restrictions often create the need to interconnect LANs into a larger network.

Usually interconnection of links is the function of the Network Layer. However, some stations originally designed for LANs have not implemented any Network Layer protocol, in which case it is not possible for that station's traffic to be forwarded by a Network Layer relay (a *router*). If all stations have implemented a Network Layer protocol, but they do not agree on a single Network Layer protocol, it might be possible to interconnect the LANs with a multiprotocol router. However, such solutions can be inconvenient, especially if any of the protocols might evolve.

One method of interconnecting LANs that works regardless of whether the stations have implemented a Network Layer protocol is through a Data Link Layer relay, or bridge.

The basic idea, which created the possibility of a transparent relay, is a box which attaches to two LANs, listens promiscuously on each, and forwards each packet received onto the other LAN.

The next refinement was to observe that the bridge could learn, based on the source address of transmitted frames, on which LAN each station resided. Then, if the bridge has learned that a station resides on the bridge's left, and later the bridge receives a packet for that station on its left, the bridge need not forward the packet.

Initially, the bridge, B, does not know the location of any station. Now assume that station A, on B's left, transmits a packet for station Q, also on B's left. The source address equals A, and the destination address equals Q. From this information, B will conclude that A resides on its left, and since it has no information about the location of Q, B will forward the packet, since Q might reside on B's right.

Now assume that Q transmits a packet for station A. Bridge B will learn, based on the source address (Q), that Q resides on its left. Also, since A is the destination address and B has already learned that A resides on its left, B will not forward the packet.

With this form of automatic "learning" of destination address, bridges forward packets only when necessary, and local traffic remains localized to the LAN.

A bridge might interconnect more than two LANs. The same idea applies. Instead of remembering the location as right or left, the bridge remembers source addresses for each link. When the destination station's location is known to a bridge, the bridge forwards the packet only to the appropriate link, or does not forward the packet at all if the packet was received on the link from which the bridge learned the station's address (see Figure 9-4). This design also extends to paths consisting of multiple bridges. In fact, this design works for any tree topology.

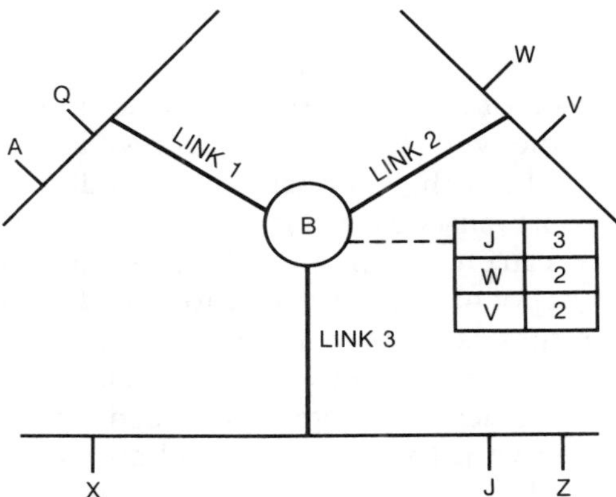

Figure 9-4. Three-port bridge.

In Figure 9-4, Bridge B1 cannot distinguish how far away stations are and treats all stations reachable through a particular link as equivalent. This behavior has the desired effect, i.e., that packets reach the destination station and that once the destination station's location has been learned by the bridges, no unnecessary forwarding of traffic for that station is done. Traffic to that station remains localized only to the LANs between the source and destination.

However, this design does not extend to arbitrary topologies. In particular, there can be no redundancy in the topology. For instance, if a station on the top LAN transmits a packet (assume a destination address not yet learned by the bridges), all three bridges will receive it, and store it for forwarding on the bottom LAN. Then, as each bridge successfully forwards the packet onto the bottom LAN, it is received by the other two bridges, and stored for forwarding onto the top LAN. This process will continue forever. Not only will the packet loop forever, but each time a copy of the packet is transmitted, two more copies of the packet are created.

Thus, the transparent bridge idea will not work with loops in the topology because

- Certain packets will loop forever.
- In certain topologies, looping packets also proliferate exponentially.
- Bridges will not be able to learn the location of source stations because packets from a source station can arrive from multiple directions.

For this reason, the standard also includes a *spanning tree* protocol, that is, a protocol run by the bridges which continuously computes a loopfree subset of the topology. The basic bridge data packet-forwarding occurs on the loop-free subset of the topology computed by the spanning tree.

Transparent bridges that automatically learn station locations and automatically compute a spanning tree were originally designed and built by Digital, and have been adopted as standard 8802-1.

Network Layer

The purpose of the Network Layer is to accept a packet from the Transport Layer, together with a destination address, and deliver the packet across a "reasonable" route with "reasonable" probability.

The route must be reasonable in the sense that it need not be optimal. Various factors can create nonoptimal routes. For instance, knowledge of the better route might not have had a chance to spread throughout the network before the packet finishes its journey. Another example is due to *hierarchical routing*, in which the size of the network necessitates the computation of approximate routes. This is described later in the section, "Hierarchical Networks."

The Network Layer in DNA and also specified in ISO 8348, "Connectionless-mode Network Service," is a datagram service. The Network Layer may lose, duplicate, or corrupt packets, and packets may be delivered to the destination in a different order than they were generated by the source. Services such as detecting corruption, recovering from lost packets, and reordering packets are done by the Transport Layer.

Recall that the two main types of systems implementing the Network Layer are the ES, which generates and receives packets but does not forward them, and the IS, which, in addition to generating and receiving packets, also forwards them.

There are two main reasons for creating two types of systems. First, it is desirable to allow systems to attach to the network with minimal effort. Thus, the ability to have a very simple ES protocol allows the vast majority of the nodes in the network to be implemented at less cost. Any complexity that can be moved from the ES to the IS will reduce the overall cost of the network because there are so many more end systems than intermediate systems.

Routing algorithm complexity grows much faster with the number of intermediate systems than with the number of end systems. Thus, networks of greater size can be implemented with the ES/IS distinction than could be implemented if all nodes were identical.

There are six tasks the Network Layer must perform:

1. Systems must ascertain the identity and type of their neighbors.
2. ESs on LANs must specify a LAN destination address on packets. This might be one of the ISs on the LAN or the destination system itself. The ES must somehow become aware of when it needs to send a packet to an IS. If a packet must be forwarded through an IS, the ES must choose an IS, preferably one on the best path toward the destination. If the destination resides on the same LAN as the source, the source must somehow become aware of this, as well as become aware of the LAN address of the destination. (We assume the source already knows the Network Layer address of the destination, but the Network Layer address does not necessarily contain the Data Link Layer address.)
3. ISs must exchange enough control information so that it is possible for them to compute routes.
4. ISs must compute routes.
5. ISs must forward packets. This is complicated by the fact that the network supports heterogeneous link types. In particular, different links might have different maximum packet sizes. Thus, an IS might have to fragment a packet if the link onto which it is to be forwarded is not capable of carrying a packet of that size. A fragmented packet is reassembled by the destination ES.
6. The problem of congestion must be handled.

In the following sections, we discuss all these problems in detail.

The current ISO standards specify a data packet format and protocols for neighbor handshaking between ESs and ISs. They do not yet specify protocols between ISs necessary for computing routes. Digital has proposed this standard, based on Phase V DNA. This proposal has been accepted by both ANSI and ISO as base text for progression to an eventual International Standard.

Neighbor Handshaking

On point-to-point links, ascertaining the identity of one's neighbors is fairly simple. Each node periodically transmits a special "Hello" message identifying itself, including such information as its node type, its Network Layer address, and how frequently it will be transmitting Hellos. Usually on point-to-point links, the Data Link Layer is aware of when communication with the other system has failed and will inform the Network Layer. However, even if the Data Link Protocol offered a datagram-type service, knowledge that the neighbor was no longer reachable (as a neighbor—perhaps some other path through the network still can reach the node that was previously a neighbor) can be inferred from lack of receipt of Hello messages from that node. (Note that we are assuming here that connectivity on a point-to-point link is two-way.)

On LANs, handshaking becomes more complex. First the LAN offers a datagram service. Second, in order to communicate with a node, one needs a LAN (Data Link Layer) address to which that node is listening. And one of the most important goals of DNA is that it be autoconfiguring. Thus, there must be no necessity for a manually maintained data base listing potential neighbors on the LAN. Instead, especially for End Systems, it must be possible to buy an off-the-shelf ES, plug it into any LAN, and have it operate.

Another goal of the LAN handshaking protocol is to minimize work for the ES. It is undesirable to force the ES to perform a lot of calculation, use a lot of storage, or receive a lot of control packets.

The LAN protocol finds neighbors through the use of multicast addresses. One used by the Network Layer is listened to by all ESs. The other address is listened to by all ISs. The reason for using two addresses is so that ESs can be simpler and have less overhead in terms of receipt of control messages. In this way, it is not necessary to know beforehand the identity of potential neighbors. Instead, all that is necessary is knowledge of the two multicast addresses, which are valid on any LAN, in any DNA (or ISO) network.

ESs issue their Hellos to "All Intermediate Systems." ISs issue their Hellos to both addresses. In this way, the ESs keep a data base consisting of the identity of all the ISs, but they need not keep a data base consisting of all the ESs, nor do they need to receive all the Hellos issued by ESs (a blessing, because there may be at least twice as many more ESs than ISs).

Knowledge that a neighbor is no longer functioning, or that the link to the neighbor is no longer functioning, is not automatically ascertained by the Data Link Layer. Instead, neighbors must periodically issue Hellos. Since the LAN is a datagram service, some Hello messages may be lost. Thus, a node cannot assume the link to a neighbor is down merely because one Hello time interval has passed within receiving a Hello from that neighbor. Instead, some multiple of the Hello time interval must pass without receipt of any Hello messages from the neighbor before the node can conclude connectivity to the neighbor has been lost. The Hello timer could have been a networkwide constant, but instead, it is set node by node. Because the Hello message contains the Hello timer (the frequency with which the transmitted node will issue Hello messages), neighbor nodes will know how often to expect to hear Hello messages from that node.

Based on Hello messages, then, ISs hear from and keep a data base of all nodes on the LAN, together with information about each, such as whether it is an IS or an ES. ESs only hear from and keep a data base of all the ISs on the LAN.

"Next Hop" on the LAN

End Systems must specify an immediate next destination when transmitting packets onto a LAN. The protocol to accomplish this must

- minimize endnode complexity
- allow operation when the entire network consists of a single LAN with no ISs (all the nodes on the LAN are ESs)
- minimize extra traffic on the LAN, for instance, due to having an ES transmit traffic through an IS, and having the IS forward the traffic back onto the LAN

The algorithm followed by the ESs which accomplishes the goals above is:

1. Endnodes keep a data base of all the ISs on the LAN.
2. ESs keep a cache of destinations to which they have recently communicated, and for which they have some knowledge of proper LAN address for use as Next Hop. The method by which ESs discover this information is through receipt of "Redirect" messages from ISs. Another method by which information is entered into the cache is by receipt of a Hello message from another ES. Entries in the cache are removed after a specified amount of time (the time the entry should be kept is specified in Redirect and Hello messages), when required due to lack of space, or when the Network Layer is informed by the higher layer that traffic may not be reaching the destination.
3. When an IS receives a packet to be forwarded, and the forwarding decision made by the IS is to forward the packet back onto the LAN (either to another IS closer to the destination or to the destination itself, if the destination resides on the LAN), the IS forwards the packet but additionally transmits a Redirect message to the node from which the IS received the packet, informing it of the more appropriate Data Link address to use for Next Hop.
4. When an ES transmits a packet onto a LAN for destination D, if D is in its cache with Next Hop N, the ES transmits the packet with Data Link Layer address N. Otherwise (D is not in the cache), the ES transmits the packet to any IS. However, if there is no IS, the ES transmits the packet to the multicast address "All End Systems." All ESs receive the data packet, but drop the packet after examination if the Network Layer address does not specify them as the destination. The ES that is the destination address will accept the packet and transmit its Hello message directly to the Data Link address specified as source address in the received packet.
5. If ES A receives a Hello message from another ES, B, with Data Link Layer destination address specifying A, A enters B into its cache, with Next Hop the Data Link Layer address from which the Hello message was received.

This algorithm assures correct operation when no IS is on the LAN, but performance will be impacted due to the necessity for all the ESs to receive all the broadcast data traffic. Thus, even when the entire network consists solely of a single LAN, it is still beneficial to have at least one IS attached to the LAN.

Intermediate System Control Traffic

In this section we'll describe how ISs calculate a path to the destination specified in a packet header. Each link in the network is assigned a *cost*. The cost of a path is the sum of the costs of the links. The best path is considered to be the path with smallest path cost.

If all links were equivalent, they would all be assigned the same cost. However, when heterogeneous links are used (different delays, different bandwidths), it is desirable to assign different costs to different types of links. If the traffic matrix is known, the link costs can be configured to optimize the traffic flow for a particular traffic pattern.

DNA's routing is hierarchical, with the network partitioned into subnetworks to facilitate much larger networks than would be possible with a flat structure. However, when we first describe the algorithm, we'll describe it in terms of a flat structure (for simplicity), and then we'll explain how the hierarchy works.

The raw information by which ISs compute routes consists of *Link State Packets (LSPs)*. An LSP basically contains the ID of the node which generated the LSP, together with a list of neighbors of that node. Each LSP is broadcast throughout the network, and every IS keeps the latest LSP from every other IS in the network. New LSPs are generated periodically, as well as when the information in them changes due to new neighbors—neighbors to whom connectivity has been lost—or link cost changes.

Included in the LSP is a *sequence number* that enables nodes to decide, given two LSPs from the same source IS, which LSP is newer. Each time the source IS generates a new LSP, it increments the sequence number.

When an IS receives an LSP generated by source IS "S," it examines its data base for another LSP from S. If no such LSP exists, the received LSP is accepted as being *new*. If an LSP exists, the sequence number of the one from memory is compared against the sequence number of the received LSP.

1. If the received LSP is deemed newer, the one from memory is overwritten, and the received LSP is propagated to all neighbors except the one from which it was received.
2. If the received LSP is deemed older, the one from memory is transmitted to the neighbor from which the older LSP was received.
3. If the received LSP is deemed equal to the one in memory, it is acknowledged and dropped.

On LANs, LSPs are multicast to All Intermediate Systems so that one copy of an LSP can be transmitted, instead of one copy for each neighbor IS on the LAN. Individual acknowledgments are not transmitted on a LAN because that would necessitate every IS on the LAN to send an acknowledgment to every other IS on the LAN for every LSP. Instead, a special packet, known as a *Sequence Numbers Packet*, summarizing the Link State data base is broadcast periodically. It contains the sequence numbers of all the LSPs in the data base.

Computing Routes

Given the Link State data base, there is sufficient information from which to compute routes. The basic algorithm was devised by Dijkstra (1959). However, it has been modified to account for LANs and computation of equal cost paths.

Once routes are computed, a *forwarding data base* is constructed, consisting of the proper neighbor (or set of neighbors in the case of multiple equal cost paths) to forward packets to, for each destination.

Forwarding Packets

An IS forwards a packet based on the information in the forwarding data base. Additional complexity arises because of

- congestion
- generation of Error Reports and Redirects
- fragmentation

If too many packets are already queued onto the outgoing link, the packet is dropped. Networks which do not drop packets either prereserve buffers for each conversation, which is not efficient when traffic is bursty, or are prone to deadlocks. Backpressure is another alternative to dropped packets, but it creates the problem that the entire network can become slowed due to a single bottleneck.

When congestion is building, so that a packet encounters queuing delays, but is not yet severe enough for the packet to be dropped, DNA's Network Layer sets a flag in the packet. The destination node is aware then that packets are arriving via a congested path. Next, the Network Layer at the destination node informs the Transport Layer at the destination node, which piggybacks the information that the path is becoming congested on packets that are flowing in the reverse direction.

As a result of receiving a data message to forward, an IS might need to send a Redirect (if the IS is forwarding the packet onto the same LAN from which the packet was received) or it might need to send an Error Report packet to the source (if the packet must be dropped due to unknown destination, bad format, or congestion).

If the packet is to be forwarded onto a link that cannot handle such a large packet, it is fragmented. Given that packets can be duplicated, with individual pieces traveling over different paths and possibly fragmented into different sized chunks, the reassembly task at the destination ES can be complex. To assure that the destination can have a memory-efficient reassembly algorithm, fragmentation must be performed on 8-byte boundaries.

Reassembly

Enough information must exist in each fragment of a packet so that the destination can reassemble a complete packet. Thus, each fragment must contain control information identifying to which packet it belongs. The information which identifies a packet consists of

- the Network Layer source address
- the Network Layer destination address
- a *Packet Identifier field*, which is a counter incremented by the source each time a packet is generated and which will (we hope) not wrap around during a packet lifetime

Additionally, it is convenient for the destination node if, upon receipt of any fragment of a packet, it can determine the size of buffer into which the packet should be reassembled. Each fragment contains the total length of the original packet with an offset at which this fragment starts. The total length must appear in every fragment because there is no guarantee that a specific fragment, such as the first, will arrive at the destination first.

Performing the bookkeeping in the buffer allows the destination to reassemble the packet without allocating more memory for the operation than the size buffer required for the assembled packet. Kept in each *hole* (a section of the packet for which data have not yet arrived) is information such as pointers to adjacent holes and the length of the hole.

Hierarchical Networks

Routing algorithms break down if the network is overly large due to memory requirements, bandwidth requirements, and algorithm settling time, which all grow with the size of the network. Creating hierarchical networks builds networks larger than the routing algorithm can manage.

In a hierarchical network, the network is partitioned into subnetworks. Routing within a subnetwork is known as *Level 1 Routing*, which is concerned with all the nodes and links within the subnetwork.

Routing between subnetworks is known as *Level 2 Routing*, which is concerned with paths to subnetworks, but not with the internal dynamics of subnetworks.

Assuming each subnetwork is no bigger than the routing algorithm can manage, Level 1 Routing succeeds in maintaining routes within each subnetwork. Assuming that the number of subnetworks does not grow overly large, Level 2 Routing succeeds in computing routes between subnetworks.

When hierarchical routing is employed, hierarchical addressing becomes critical. It must be possible, based on the destination address, for a Level 1 IS to determine whether the packet should be routed within the subnetwork (i.e., via Level 1 Routing) or whether the packet should be routed to the nearest Level 2 IS, which will infer the identity of the destination subnetwork from the address and route the packet to it.

Another instance for hierarchy in networks is when different sections of the network really are autonomous, i.e., when that subnetwork is a *domain*. With hierarchy, this allows different domains to operate different Level 1 Routing algorithms and offers some protection from problems in one domain from leaking into others.

DNA actually offers three levels of hierarchy. The bottom two levels are dynamically computed, and the top level is done with fixed tables. The top level is fixed to support autonomous domains—DNA does not place any requirements of protocol in other domains. Because ISO currently does not have a standard for interdomain protocols and algorithms, fixed tables allow DNA domains to communicate with non-DNA ISO domains.

Dynamically Established Data Links

As stated earlier, there are two basic types of links supported by the Network Layer. One is a multiaccess link, like a LAN. The other is a point-to-point link.

Sometimes the point-to-point link is a direct connection between two nodes, as with leased lines or private lines. Sometimes the links are provided by connection-oriented facilities such as X.25 networks. Such a link is known as a *Dynamically Established Data Link*. It is desirable in some cases for the network to establish and tear down connections automatically, rather than leaving them up at all times because

1. Usually such connections are charged for connect time in addition to traffic sent. Therefore, it is expensive to keep a connection up when there is no traffic to send.
2. Sometimes, such as when the link is actually an attachment to an X.25 network, there are so many potential neighbors (i.e., any other station on that network can be called) that the Network Layer cannot possibly keep track of all possible destinations, nor keep calls to all possible destinations up at all times.

In such cases, the link is considered to be *Dynamically Assigned*, and the Network Layer determines the address to which the call should be established based on the Network Layer address.

An ISO address contains the following information:

IDP

DSP

The IDP (Initial Domain Part) has some structure associated with how addresses are allocated. Basically, the high-order part of the IDP defines a particular network, such as a particular X.25 network, and the remainder of the IDP specifies a particular address within that network. The DSP (Domain-Specific Part) is unspecified by ISO, but allows for further addressing following the attachment point. For instance, if a private network consists of separate pieces with each piece attached to a particular X.25 network, the IDP allows the Network Layer to reach the particular piece of the private network, and the DSP allows the Network Layer to reach a specific node within that piece.

DNA has defined the structure of the DSP to be the following:

LOC-AREA

ID

SEL

The IDP offers a level of hierarchy, and the LOC-AREA offers another level of hierarchy. Thus, DNA provides for a three-level hierarchy, allowing networks of virtually unlimited size. DNA does not automatically compute Level 3 routing—rather, it is done through fixed tables.

ESs need not know their own IDP and LOC-AREA. Instead, they need only know their own IS. When an ES hears a Hello from an IS, it infers the remainder of its address. In this way, an ES will automatically configure into any portion of a DNA network.

For example, suppose S wishes to communicate with D. First S obtains D's Network Layer address (see section on Naming Service), which contains the point of attachment of "piece 2" into the common carrier network.

Assuming S is an endnode, S launches the packet to an IS. The IS in "piece 1" recognizes that the packet belongs to a different domain, and routes the packet to a level 2 IS. The level 2 IS recognizes that the destination is some attachment point on the common carrier net and routes the packet to the particular level 2 IS that attaches to the common carrier network. That level 2 IS extracts the attachment point of piece 2 from the address, and places a call on the common carrier network to that address, thereby establishing a connection to the level 2 IS on piece 2. When that level 2 IS receives the packet, it routes it via level 2 routing to D's domain, and then level 1 routing routes the packet to D.

Autoconfiguration

One of the primary goals of DNA is that it be easy to use, that an off-the-shelf system can plug into any DNA network and operate correctly (as an ES). It is important that adding ISs be easy as well, but it does not have to be quite so easy as adding an ES into the network.

In order to meet this goal, Phase V DNA requires ESs to have a unique 48-bit ID, whether or not they will attach to a LAN. Given that a system has a unique 48-bit ID, the rest of its address is configured automatically. When an ES establishes communication with an IS, the IS informs the ES of the remainder of its address (its IDP and its LOC-AREA). If the ES does not hear from an IS, it uses a default value for those portions of its address.

DNA's three-level hierarchical structure supports networks of virtually unlimited size (millions of nodes), as well as supporting interconnection of autonomous networks between ISs of different domains (due to the third level of hierarchy which makes no requirement for exchange of protocol messages other than user data traffic). In addition, a primary goal of DNA's Network Layer has been the ability to automatically assimilate ESs, making the management of a domain with hundreds of thousands of nodes practical.

Transport Layer

The Transport Protocol standardized by ISO actually consists of five classes of protocol, actually five distinct protocols with a common message structure and certain other similarities. Class 0 is the simplest protocol, giving the least functionality and assuming the most service from the Network Layer. Class 4 is the most general protocol, offering the most services and assuming only a datagram service from the Network Layer. Since class 4 is the most general protocol, it is expected to be the most widely used. In this chapter, we concentrate on class 4. From this point, when we say, "Transport," we mean "Class 4 Transport."

The Transport Layer assumes the service by the Network Layer is a datagram service. Thus, it assumes that with high probability, each packet will arrive at the destination, but

1. With high probability, packets may arrive at the destination in a different order than in which they were transmitted. (Packet reordering can occur with high probability when multiple equivalent paths to the destination exist, because DNA attempts to optimize throughput by splitting traffic between equivalent lowest cost paths.)
2. With medium probability, packets may be lost and never arrive.
3. With low probability, packets may arrive damaged.

The only constraints that the Transport Layer places on the Network Layer are that

1. Each individual packet independently has a nonzero probability of delivery across the network (assuming connectivity to the destination exists).
2. The Network Layer accepts (and delivers) packets of reasonable minimum size.
3. The Network Layer guarantees, within acceptable probability, a maximum packet lifetime in the network (so that wraparound of Transport counters is not a problem).

The service provided by the Transport Layer is a connection-oriented, reliable service. Once connection is established with a process at another machine, packets are delivered in the order transmitted, without loss, duplication, or corruption. The Transport Layer provides this service by numbering messages, adding a checksum to discover corruption, reordering packets at the destination, acknowledging packets, and retransmitting damaged or lost messages.

Flow Control

It is wasteful for the Transport Layer to transmit packets, only to have them dropped at the destination Transport Layer for lack of buffer space. Allocating more buffer space at the destination does not solve the problem, because the problem might be that the Transport Layer user has stopped receiving its messages (e.g., when the application is a printer which has temporarily stopped until someone reloads it with paper). In such a case, there will never be enough storage at the destination, since there is virtually an unlimited amount of data that can be transmitted while the receiving process is not accepting new data.

ISO's Transport Layer thus has a protocol which enables the destination to ascertain when buffers are available at the destination. This is known as a *credit mechanism*. The receiver sends a certain number of credits to the transmitter, which is allowed to transmit that many packets to the receiver. As the receiver acknowledges packets, it returns credits for additional packets.

ISO's Transport allows for credit reduction. Although previously it might have allowed the transmitter many buffers, it may subsequently find those buffers needed for other processes. (It had employed *optimistic flow control*, meaning that it had offered credits on the assumption that resources would become available.)

Retransmission Timer

Transport assumes a packet was lost if some time elapses before the transmitter receives an acknowledgment to that packet.

The value of that timer must be determined dynamically and constantly adjusted, because the characteristics of the network (i.e., end-to-end delay) vary greatly depending on location of the destination within the network and congestion within the network. If the retransmission timer is too short for a particular destination, packets will be erroneously assumed lost and needless retransmission will occur, congesting the network with nonuseful packets. If the retransmission timer is too long, throughput and responsiveness are degraded when packets are lost because it takes longer than necessary to notice and recover.

Thus, the round-trip delay is constantly measured and adjusted on a per-packet basis, using a weighted average scheme.

Congestion

When the Network Layer has more traffic than it can carry, it must drop packets. When congestion occurs, it is desirable for the users of the Network Layer, i.e., the Transport Layer entities, to notice the problem and reduce demand on the network.

The DNA Network Layer informs the Transport Layer when congestion is building by setting a bit in packets that encounter some congestion (but, of course, not so much congestion as to require being dropped). When the destination Network Layer receives packets with the congestion indication, it informs the receiving Transport Layer, which accordingly lowers the credit window, causing the transmitter to transmit fewer packets.

Also, when the source Transport Layer fails to receive an acknowledgment to a packet, it assumes the packet was dropped due to congestion, and voluntarily lowers its window (the number of outstanding unacknowledged packets allowed), gradually increasing it as acknowledgments occur.

DNA Session Layer

DNA Session is responsible for bridging the gap between the service provided by the Transport Layer and the service required by DNA applications. Its functions include

- matching incoming calls to processes
- managing calls
- managing and enforcing system-specific access control
- translating between human-friendly names and machine-friendly Network Layer addresses
- selecting the appropriate upper layer protocols for a conversation

Conversations are established by having an application process at one system request a connection, through the Session Layer, specifying the application at the destination machine. The Session Layer issues a "Connect Request" to the destination machine, with information included in the Connect Request packet specifying the destination process. The Session Layer at the destination machine executes a system-dependent algorithm to ascertain if an existing application process corresponds to the request—or perhaps starts up such a process based on the request—and passes the connection request to that newly started process.

The most interesting aspect of DNA Session is its use of the Naming Service, which performs name-to-Network-Layer address-mapping for the Session Layer, although the Naming Service is also directly available to applications and can store any information which maps character strings into attributes.

DNA's Naming Service is similar to the telephone system's White pages, which maps names into addresses and telephone numbers. Like the telephone system, it

- is partitioned
- is hierarchical
- is replicated
- enforces access control
- encourages local caching

Since the data base of telephone clients is too large to conveniently fit into a single book, the telephone system provides many different directories. To find a particular telephone user, one has to look in the correct directory. Likewise, the Naming Service data base is assumed too large to fit into a single directory, so there are multiple directories.

With the telephone system, to find a particular telephone number, one would first specify the country in which the telephone user was located, then the state, then the city. One could not simply ask the telephone information service for a number in Oakland, because a city of that name exists in most states in the U.S. You'd need to know that the desired directory was U.S./Wisconsin/Oakland.

Likewise, DNA's Naming Service is hierarchically structured. Information is stored in directories, structured into a tree. To find a particular object stored in a directory, one needs to specify the complete path from the root to the desired directory, and then specify the name of the object.

With the telephone system, more than one copy of each directory exists. This is important for several reasons:

- availability—if there were only one copy of a particular directory, and that copy was unreachable for some time, nobody would be able to find telephone numbers that were in that directory and no updates would be possible during that time
- robustness—if the single copy of a particular directory were damaged or lost, the telephone company would have to go through some highly inconvenient mechanism for reconstructing the data base, such as calling possible telephone numbers and asking whoever answered for their name and address
- efficiency—it is convenient to have copies of directories near where they are most likely to be used (i.e., for an occasional lookup in a different state, it is reasonable for people to make a phone call and call information, but for local numbers, it is preferable to have a directory right in each home)
- scalability—if there were only one location that everyone had to reference to find and update numbers, the traffic near that location would be too great, and the location would not be able to keep up with all the requests

As with the telephone system, the Naming Service is replicated, with each directory having many copies. Some of the copies (the vast majority) are read-only (like the phone book in one's home). Other copies can accept updates, such as new entries, deletions of existing entries, or modification of existing entries.

Just as the telephone system keeps certain "unlisted" numbers that are not publicly available, parts of DNA's namespace can be protected from anyone except authorized users. In addition, just as the telephone system encourages individuals to remember or write down frequently used numbers (rather than calling directory assistance), DNA's Naming Service encourages local caching of information.

Unlike the phone system, DNA Naming Service guarantees uniqueness of names—the telephone system does not demand that you choose a new name if you move to another town, ask for telephone service, and find that there is already a John Smith in that town. However, their willingness to allow several John Smiths in a town does create problems, and higher layer mechanisms must sort out the confusion. It is sometimes necessary to call several John Smiths before finding the correct one.

Internal operation of the Naming Service is interesting as well. To allow high levels of partitioning and replication, the Naming Service provides only loose consistency guarantees. In other words, until enough time has passed since an update occurred so that the update can have propagated to all replicas, there is no guarantee that the update will become "permanent" in the data base. In the case of conflicts, time-stamps determine which update takes effect. For example:

1. In the case of two stations each doing an INSERT of an object of the same name into two different replicas of a directory, the INSERT with the earlier time-stamp takes effect and the one with the later time-stamp is ignored.
2. In the case of two stations each doing a MODIFY of the same attribute of an object of the same name with two different replicas of a directory, the MODIFY with the later time-stamp takes effect. If two different MODIFYs of the same object in different replicas occur, in which the MODIFYs are updating different attributes of the object, both take effect.
3. In the case of two stations each doing a DELETE of the same object with two different replicas, the object is merely deleted with no ill effects.

To keep replicas reasonably consistent, the directories periodically perform a "skulk" operation, in which all updates since the last skulk are gathered and distributed to all replicas.

A station attached to a LAN does not need to know the address or location of the Naming Service. Naming Servers periodically advertise their presence. A station that wishes to find a Name Server (i.e., a station that has just booted), listens for the advertisement by listening to a multicase address on a LAN—or to speed the process up, solicits via another multicast address on a LAN.

Network Management

Most systems have controls available to the user. For instance, a TV set has an ON/OFF switch, a volume control, and a channel selector. These controls should not have a factory set default and must be readily accessible to the user. A second set of controls, for instance, for the brightness and tint, are also available to the user but are less easily accessible because they should be modified less often and by someone with slightly more knowledge. Inside the set, there are various potentiometers that should be modified only by an experienced repairman. Other parameters might be read-only, for instance, a warning light that might come on when a battery is low.

Likewise, the protocols in a network have various parameters. Whenever possible, reasonable default values are set so that the user has minimal work in order to operate the network. Network Management defines which parameters are available within each module, the syntax of the parameter (character string, integer within a certain range), and whether it is read-only or read/write. Control and monitoring of parameters enables the network manager to maintain the network (discover malfunctioning components), monitor its performance (discover the need for extra capacity), or "tune" the network (for instance, to optimize cost/performance tradeoffs for a particular situation). For certain conditions, "events" are automatically recorded by Network Management. These events can be logged locally or sent remotely to an event collection system.

Additionally, Network Management defines downline load protocols to enable systems to be loaded with new software, or to enable diskless workstations to boot with information stored at some remote location in the network.

Application Layer

Many applications are available in DECnet:

- file access and transfer
- remote terminals
- electronic mail
- gateways
- time service
- computer conferencing
- videotex
- distributed queuing

With file access and transfer, files can be accessed remotely in the same manner as if they are stored locally, even across heterogeneous file systems. Files can be created, deleted, modified, and renamed remotely. Remote directories can be listed.

Remote terminals allow users to type at their local system, as if they are typing at the remote system.

Users can send and receive messages with electronic mail, which supports the X.400 suite of protocols and supports a highly reliable store-and-forward system of mail delivery. Store-and-forward mail is critical in the case where source and destination are personal workstations that only infrequently connect to the network. With store-and-forward mail, the source of the mail attaches to the network, deposits the mail, and disconnects from the network. At some point in the future, the destination may connect to the network and receive the mail.

With DECnet's SNA Gateway application, DNA provides application protocols for communicating with systems conforming to IBM's SNA protocols, including 3270 terminal emulation, printer emulation, remote job entry, DISOSS data exchange, file transfer and data access, and various user programming interfaces (see Figure 9-5). In addition, programs in a host DNA system can gain access to an X.25 PSDN, even if the PSDN is only reachable remotely over a DNA network (see Figure 9-6).

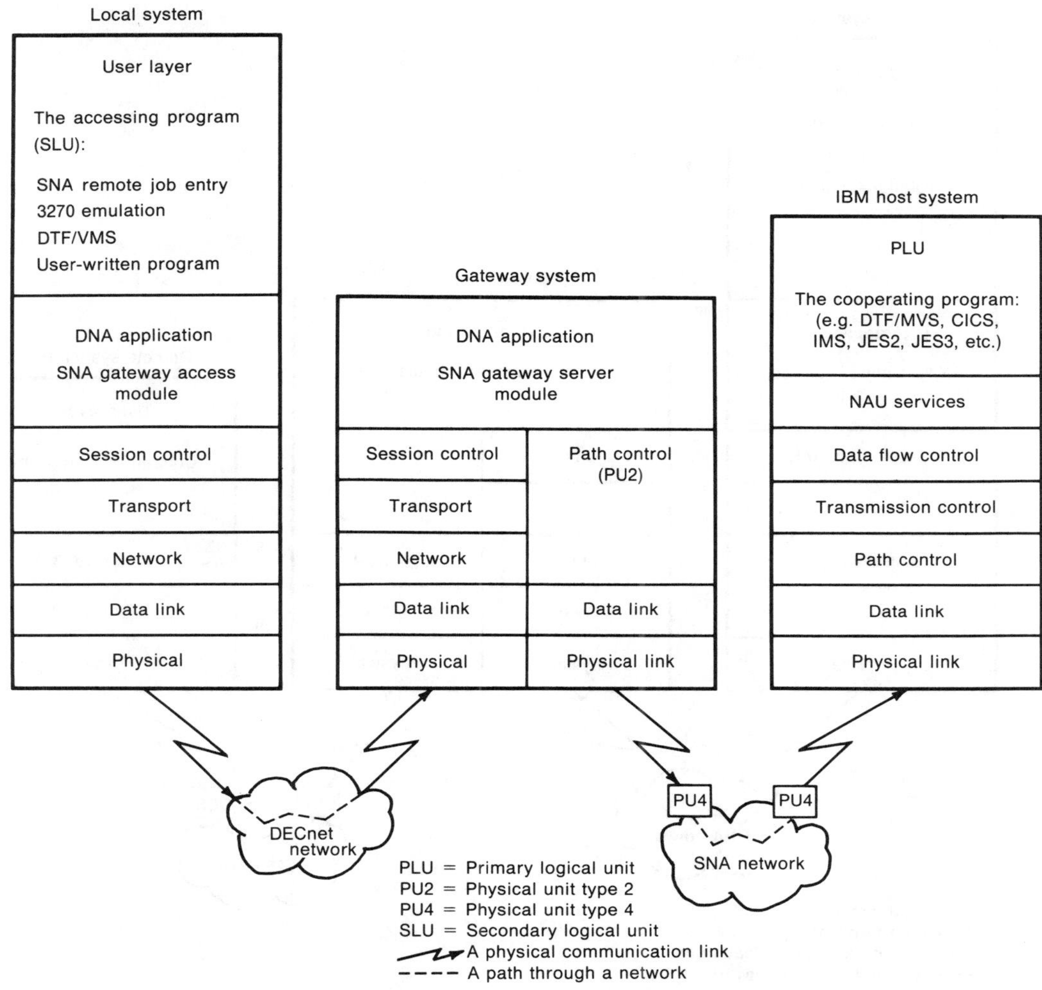

Figure 9-5. The gateway system.

In certain distributed protocols, it is important for different systems to have synchronized clocks. The degree of skew between systems that can be tolerated depends on the application. For instance, with the Naming Service, which uses the Time Service, clock skew of minutes between systems is tolerable.

DNA's Time Service is an architecture for providing and maintaining correct time in a distributed system. A collection of time servers collaborates to maintain synchrony of time. Their protocol accounts and corrects for clock skew and faulty servers.

A system on a LAN need not know the address of the Time Service. Rather, as with the Naming Service, contact between client and server is done through well-known multicast addresses that are constant, regardless of which LAN systems reside on it or which DNA network systems reside in it.

With the "Notes" facility, any number of "conferences" can be set up. A

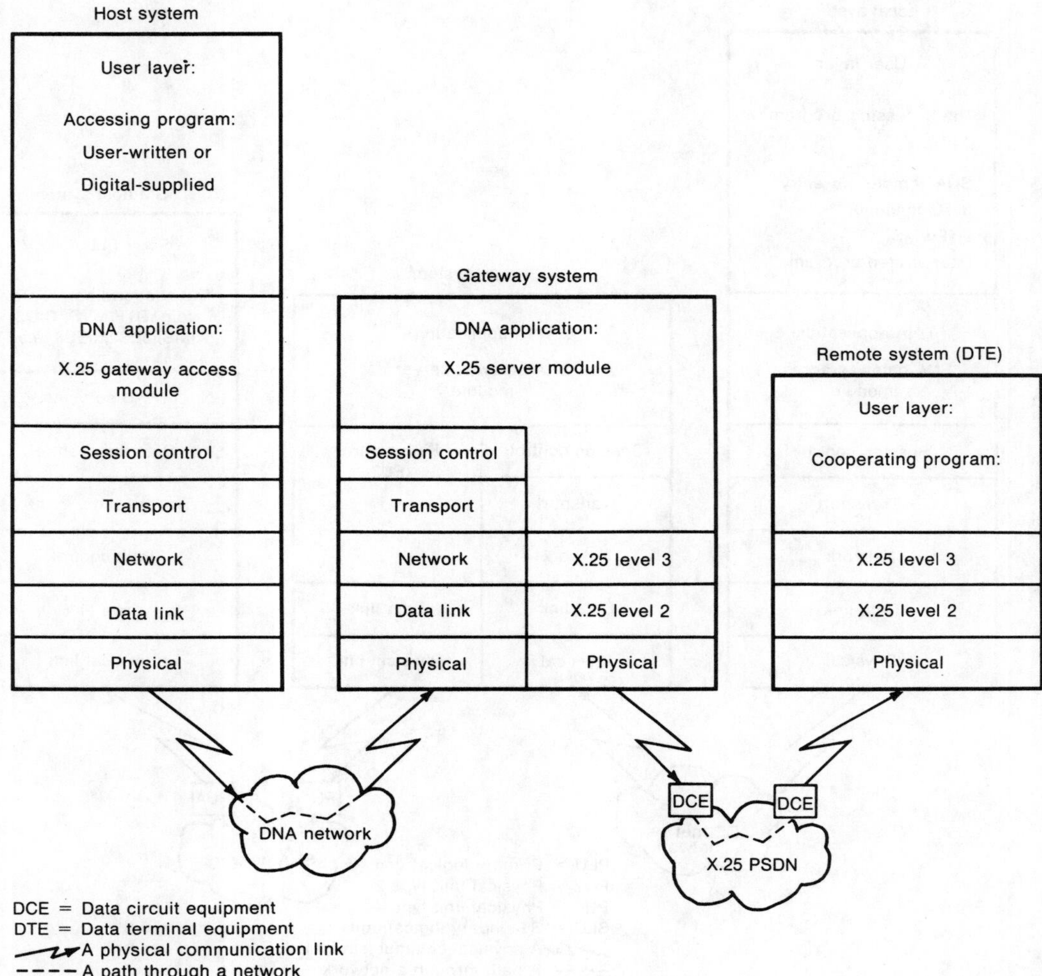

Figure 9-6. The X.25 gateway system.

conference is generally about some topic of interest, such as comments and bug reports about a specific program. It can be completely open or there can be restrictions about which users can write and/or read the conference.

The structure of a conference consists of a sequence of notes, with "replies." Typically, if a user wishes to add something which is really a new topic or new question, he adds a note. If a user wishes to respond to a note, he adds a reply to a note. Thus, the directory of a specific conference will list, for each note, its title and the number of replies to that note.

Videotex offers storage and retrieval of information. It assumes video terminals, and has a simple user interface. Users can display, print, and save information.

When multiple servers, such as printers, exist and a user does not care which server processes his job, the distributed queuing service queues the job to a general purpose queue, which hands jobs to servers as they become available.

In addition, DNA supports many of the OSI standard applications, and plans to support others as they become standards, such as FTAM (ISO 8571 parts 1 to 4), RTSE (Reliable Transfer Service) (ISO 9072 parts 1 and 2), Message Handling System (ISO 8883 and 9065), and Management Information Services (ISO 9595 and 9596).

Bootstrapping

In this section, we present an example of *bootstrapping*, i.e., buying an off-the-shelf diskless workstation with DNA software and plugging into a DECnet.

We assume that the newly purchased system is already configured by the manufacturer with a unique 48-bit ID. Shortly after attaching to the DECnet, either by attaching to a LAN or attaching to a point-to-point link to a router, it will hear a Hello message from an IS (a router). Included in the Hello is the IDP and LOC-AREA in which the ES has attached. This gives the ES its entire Network Layer address.

However, the ES will need a unique name as well. This name must be unique within a Naming Service directory, but need not be unique across a network because, by definition, since the complete name includes the directory, uniqueness within a directory guarantees networkwide uniqueness.

The manager of the directory into which this new node will reside can set up the directory to be world-writable, in which case the new user will propose a name to the Naming Service, and will be told whether the name is in use or not. If the directory is not world-writable, the user would need to obtain a name through someone with access to the directory who would also register the name on behalf of the user.

Once a system has a name, it can register its address with the Naming Service. Other users can look up the name in the Naming Service, obtain the address, and then contact that user. In the case of a diskless workstation, which would boot knowing only its unique ID, its load server would load the relevant software, including the system's name (the load server would keep a list of ID/name correspondence for its clients).

Summary

Networks in the future will grow much larger due to two factors:

1. More nodes will be required to support the same number of users.
2. More users will need to be supported.

Low-cost workstations act as separate nodes in a network. In the past, a host computer supported many individuals connected through simple terminals. In this way, a single network node represented many individuals. Some applications, in particular network mail, need to work across entire organizations, and even between organizations.

To succeed in the 1990s, a network architecture must be able to support networks of hundreds of thousands or millions of nodes, and support interconnection of heterogeneous subnetworks. The subnetwork heterogeneity is caused by the necessity of interconnecting networks that evolve with different protocol suites, or by interconnecting the networks of mutually suspicious organizations.

Four factors are necessary to support large networks:

1. Network protocols must be designed from the start to support millions of nodes. Patches to protocols designed to support, at most, hundreds of nodes will not support networks of the size required in the future.
2. The protocols must be robust. In many network designs, a single faulty node can bring down the entire network.
3. Network nodes must be remotely manageable. It will not be feasible to require individuals to be present at all sites for the purpose of managing the nodes.
4. The network must, to as large an extent as possible, be autoconfiguring. As individuals retain control over their own workstations, it must be possible for an individual to acquire a workstation, plug it into the network, and operate.

In addition, conformance to standards will be increasingly more important as people come to expect applications such as electronic mail to work across organizations. The suite of protocols standardized by ISO, and to which DNA conforms, will allow global networking in the near future.

References

Zimmerman, H. 1980. OSI reference model—The ISO model of architecture for open systems interconnection. *IEEE Transactions on Communication* COM-28, no. 4:425–32 (April).

Dijkstra, E. W. 1959. A note on two problems in connection with graphs. *Numer. Math*. 1:269–71.

Appendixes

Appendix A

CCITT and ISDN

This appendix describes the organization and activities of the International Telegraph and Telephone Consultative Committee (CCITT) and the U.S. participation therein, particularly as they relate to the ISDN. It summarizes the functions, structure, and membership of the CCITT, a permanent organ of the International Telecommunication Union (ITU). It also describes the considerable involvement of the United States in the work of the CCITT and shows how U.S. contributions are channeled through the U.S. CCITT organization. The driving force behind this increased U.S. participation in international standards development is the changing international market for services and equipment. This is particularly true for ISDN. The U.S. telecommunications industry is showing great interest in the development of ISDN, and (through the U.S. CCITT organization) is making major contributions to the international standardization efforts.

For more detailed information, see Cerni (1982), from which much of this summary was taken.

The ITU and the CCITT

The ITU is a specialized agency of the United Nations. As an international treaty organization, it consists of some 157 member nations that signed the ITU convention. The ITU functions through seven organs (see Figure A-1):

- the Plenipotentiary Conference
- the Administrative Council
- the Administrative Conferences
- the General Secretariat
- the International Frequency Registration Board (IFRB)
- the International Radio Consultative Committee (CCIR)

- the International Telegraph and Telephone Consultative Committee (CCITT)

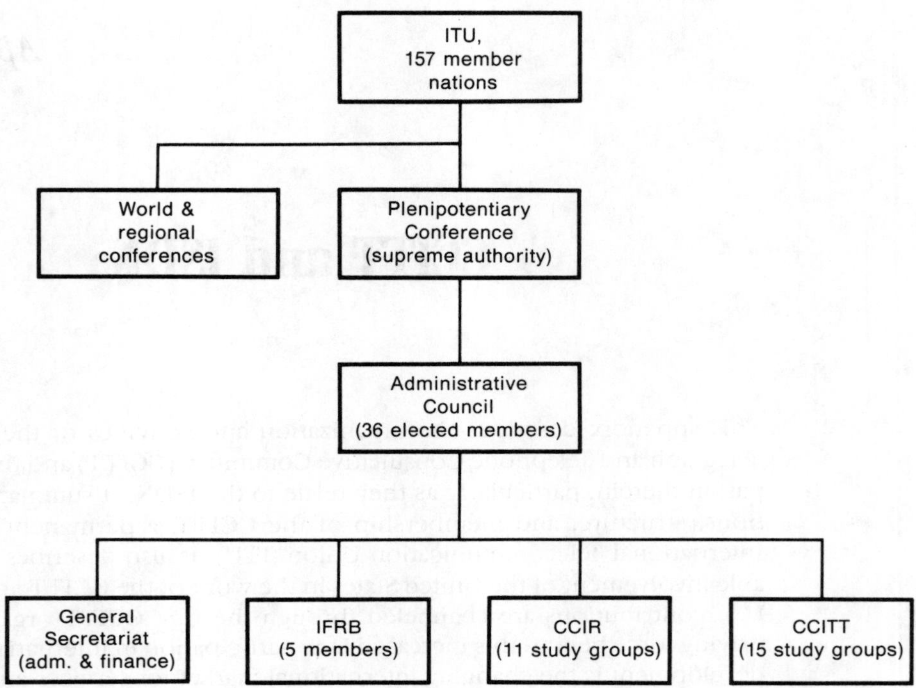

Figure A-1. The International Telecommunication Union.

Since it is the CCITT that is in the process of developing Recommendations (or standards) for ISDN, that organization is described here.

The CCITT, conducting work through fifteen technical Study Groups, other committees, and special autonomous groups, attempts to promote and ensure the operation of international telecommunication systems. This is done by issuing Recommendations (or standards) for end-to-end performance, interconnection, and maintenance of the world networks for telephone, telegraph, and data communication. Certain tariff and operating principles are also established by the CCITT.

Full membership in the CCITT is offered to the administrations of all members of the ITU and to any recognized private operating agency (RPOA) with a member's approval. RPOAs are private or government-controlled corporations that provide telecommunication services (e.g., AT&T in the United States). They are nonvoting members of the CCITT that act as principal advisors to national administrations. Limited participation is extended to certain other international organizations, e.g., the International Standards Organization (ISO), and to scientific or industrial organizations.

Study groups provide the means for developing Recommendations that are issued as a basis for voluntary international standards. The fifteen Study Groups for the 1981–1984 study period are listed in Table A-1. Study Group XVIII, entitled "Digital Networks" is primarily concerned with ISDN during the 1981 to 1984 study period. Other groups covering related fields such as Data Communication Networks, Telephone Switching and Signaling, and Telephone Transmission Performance are also involved in various aspects of ISDN.

Table A-1. Titles Designated to the Technical CCITT Study Groups (1981–84)

Group Number	Title
Study Group I	Definition and operational aspects of telegraph and telematic services (facsimile, teletex, videotex, etc.)
Study Group II	Telephone operation and quality of service
Study Group III	General tariff principles
Study Group IV	Transmission maintenance of international lines, circuits, and chains of circuits; maintenance of automatic and semiautomatic networks
Study Group V	Protection against dangers and disturbances of electromagnetic origin
Study Group VI	Protection and specifications of cable sheaths and poles
Study Group VII	Data communication networks
Study Group VIII (and XIV)	Terminal equipment for telematic services (facsimile, teletex, videotex, etc.)
Study Group IX (and X)	Telegraph networks and terminal equipment
Study Group XI	Telephone switching and signaling
Study Group XII	Telephone transmission performance and local telephone networks
Study Group XV	Transmission systems
Study Group XVI	Telephone circuits
Study Group XVII	Data communication over the telephone network
Study Group XVIII	Digital networks

Recommendation development starts, in theory, with the Plenary Assembly which normally meets every three years. This body draws up a list of technical communication subjects, or "Questions," the study of which would lead to improvements in international communications in many cases. Questions also result from the overflow of work done in the previous study period. Questions are entrusted to an appropriate study group in the interval before the next assembly, the study period. (See Appendix B for a copy of the key Question concerning ISDN. Eighteen other questions relating to the ISDN have been entrusted to various CCITT study groups.)

The work of the study groups is brought to a close when final reports are presented to the plenary assembly. These final reports contain the draft Recommendations and amendments developed by the group as well as general information about the work and the status of each question. The plenary assembly examines the study group reports, approves new or revised Recommendations, and selects and assigns questions for the next study period.

The U.S. CCITT

The U.S. participation in the work for the CCITT is channeled through the U.S. CCITT organization, whose function is to do preparatory work for the international CCITT meetings and is advisory to and under the jurisdiction of the Department of State. Delegations to the international CCITT meetings are under the aegis of the Office of International Communications Policy, Bureau of Economic and Business Affairs in the State Department.

The U.S. CCITT organization is structured as shown in Figure A-2. The National Committee constitutes a steering body and has purview over the agenda and work of the four study groups and of the Joint Working Party (JWP) on the ISDN as indicated in the figure. Each of the four study groups, A to D, covers the work of several relevant international CCITT study groups.

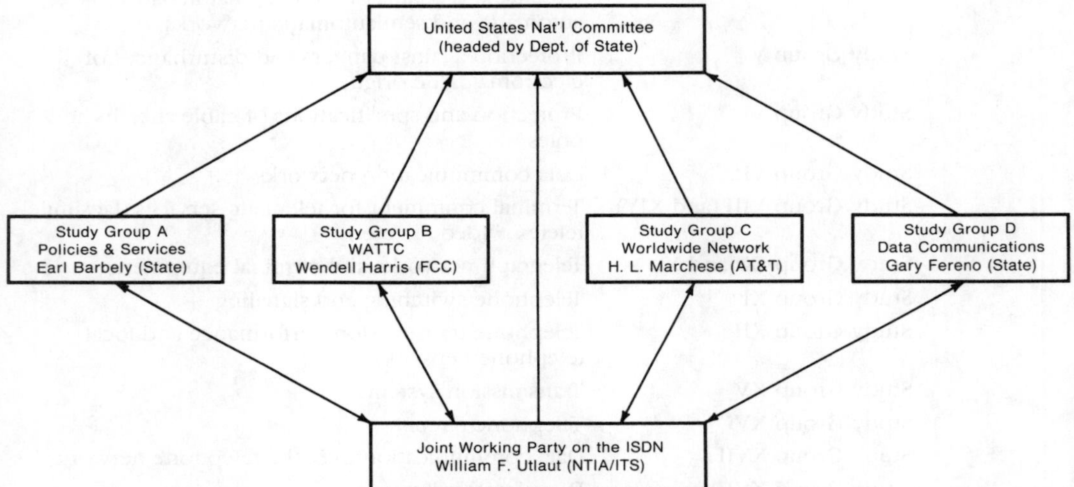

Figure A-2. The structure of the U.S. CCITT and chairmen for 1984–1988.

The JWP on the ISDN was established by the National Committee in May 1981. It contains members of all four study groups in recognition of the probable impact of the ISDN on existing telegraph, telephone, and data services. The JWP is concerned mainly with the contributions from the United States to Study Group XVIII pertaining to the ISDN. The groups' functions also include reviewing contributions of other countries to Study Group XVIII, approving U.S. positions with respect to these contributions, and maintaining liaison with the appropriate U.S. Study Groups studying such Recommendations.

Each of the U.S. Study Groups meets at the discretion of its chairman and meetings are usually keyed to the agenda of international meetings. The dates of each meeting and proposed agenda are announced to the public both in the Federal Register and in a Department of State release at least fifteen (working) days prior to the convening of a meeting. These meetings are open to the public.

The four main functions of the U.S. CCITT are

1. to offer to the U.S. telecommunication industry, in general, a forum for participation in the standards-making process
2. to serve as an arena for discussion and debate in its study group activity, preparatory to the development of U.S. positions and contributions
3. to provide, through this discussion and debate, guidance for delegates at the international meetings
4. to serve as a pool of informed and interested personnel from the private sector that can be drawn upon to staff the U.S. delegations to the international CCITT meetings—these delegates assist and advise the official U.S. representation or head of the delegation

Membership in the U.S. CCITT covers a broad spectrum of U.S. industry, government agencies, scientific organizations, user groups, and standards groups such as the American National Standards Institute (ANSI) and the Electronic Industries Association (EIA). These members also participate in working groups to study assigned topics.

The contributions from the United States to the CCITT are not sent directly to Geneva from a member organization. Rather, the contribution is first passed through a formal chain of approval and coordination. The resultant approved contribution, depending on its content and source, may be either a "U.S." contribution or an "individual member" contribution. A U.S. contribution represents the position of the U.S. study group; an individual member contribution is usually more limited and keyed to the interest of one of the private organizations (presently 57) that are members of the CCITT. The vast majority of these individual contributions, past and present, have emanated from AT&T.

Figure A-3 illustrates the chain of approval for a U.S. contribution. The chain starts with a presentation of a draft contribution to the relevant study group by a U.S. CCITT member or an ad hoc committee appointed by the study group. The resultant discussion provides feedback to the contributor and lends understanding and support to the position expressed by the formal contribution. Upon approval, the document is sent to Geneva via the Department of State.

Figure A-4 illustrates the chain of approval for an individual contribution. This figure shows that the CCITT member organizations, although always encouraged to present their contributions to the relevant U.S. CCITT study group for discussion and feedback, are not obliged to do so under constraints of time or other factors, but may work through the study group chairman instead.

The purpose of this chain of approval, or system of coordination, is to avoid having highly controversial issues sent directly to Geneva from different quarters, which could lead to difficulties at the international CCITT meetings.

Many countries, and particularly the European countries, have been exerting strong pressures on the CCITT to produce basic Recommendations for the ISDN during the 1981 to 1984 study period. Development of such Recommendations is presently moving ahead but results are still changing. To present a status report in this dynamic environment is very difficult, and impossible to summarize here. The CCITT documents themselves must be constantly reviewed to stay up to date. The Draft Recommendations under development by Study Group XVIII will be submitted for approval to the next Plenary Assembly in 1984.

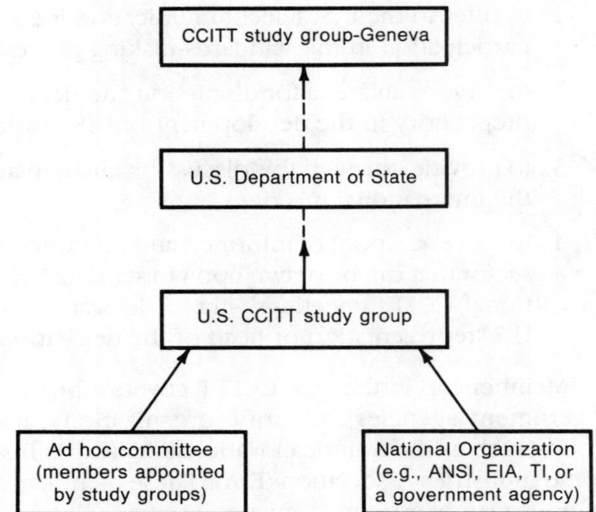

Figure A-3. Approval chain for U.S. contributions to the CCITT.

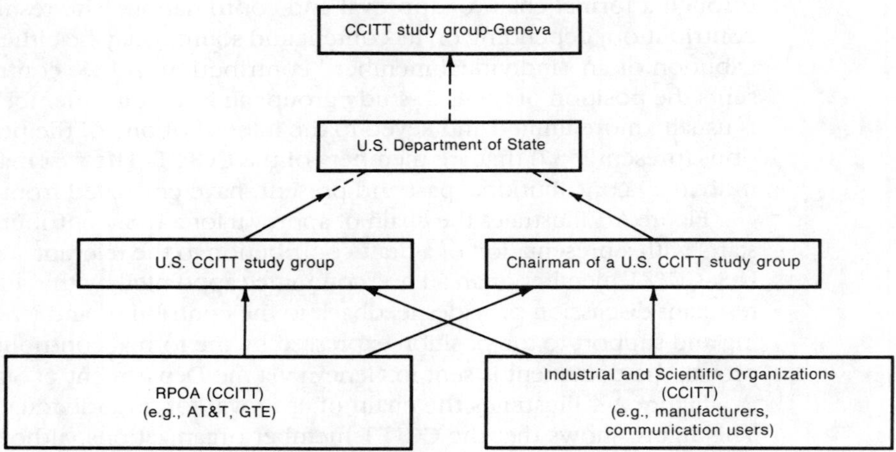

Figure A-4. Approval chain for individual-member contributions to the CCITT.

Reference

Cerni, D. M. 1982. The CCITT: Organization, U.S. participation, and studies toward the ISDN. *NTIA Report 82–101*.

Appendix B

Question 1, Study Group XVIII, 1981–1984

Question 1/XVIII—General network aspects of an Integrated Services Digital Network (ISDN) (continuation of part of Question 1/XVIII, studied in 1977–1980).

This question is concerned with overall studies related to the general features of future ISDNs capable of satisfying the requirements of many different services. Study Group XVIII will define the scope and framework of an ISDN and identify the services which may be incorporated in such networks. It will study the evolution of Integrated Digital Networks (IDNs) dedicated to specific services (e.g., telephony, data) towards an ISDN.

The objectives will be to define overall network and system principles which can form a basis for study and Recommendations by appropriate specialist CCITT Study Groups. The generic features appropriate and applicable to an ISDN will be identified together with optional service-dependent features applicable to part of an ISDN.

The study of the following five related aspects will take into account the considerations arising from studies carried out during the 1977–1980 study period as recorded in Annex A to this Question. In addition, the multiple aspects of this work require coordination between the various Study groups involved (e.g., Study Groups III, VII, XI, XV, XVI, XVII and XVIII).

Some of these Questions have to be studied initially by Study Group XVIII, with high priority, to enable other Study Groups to initiate or continue their work and to draft Recommendations within the current CCITT study period. In other cases Study Group XVIII needs information from other Study Groups in order to make progress in its own network studies.

Recommendation No. G.705 provides information and future developments of the ISDN.

Studies of ISDN aspects were carried out under Question 1/XVIII during the 1977–1980 study period and a partial reply to that Question is reproduced as Annex 1 to this new Question. Annex 2 records many points already identified and of relevance to the ongoing studies. Annexes 3 and 4 contain significant information which was not fully considered before the end of the study period. These Annexes are also of relevance to other new Questions of Study Group XVIII.

Note: The chairman and vice-chairmen of the Study Group involved (Study Groups III, VII, XI, XV, XVI, XVII, and XVIII) will jointly assess the progress made by the various Study Groups and initiate any steps necessary to expedite the work. This should take place at about the middle of the study period (e.g., beginning of 1982), with the chairman of Study Group XVIII acting as convenor for this coordination.

Considering

a) that the requirements of data transmission services and several new nonvoice services are being studied by CCITT (*Note*: In several countries, services-dedicated digital networks are already in service or will be installed for nonvoice services that may use part of the ISDN for access to this network.)

b) many countries wish to adopt a common strategy for extending the use of Integrated Digital Networks (IDN) beyond the telephony application for form Integrated Services Digital Networks

c) telephony service will constitute the major portion of the carried load on digital networks characterized by time-division transmission and switching and common-channel signaling

d) efficiency and economy of methods of access to the ISDN from customer terminals are significant factors in planning the local network

e) CCITT Recommendations on digital switching and interexchange signaling, which take into account the future evolution of the IDN for telephony toward the ISDN, are already available in the Q series and may form the basis for future Recommendations on ISDN.

Point A. Service Aspects

1. Which services should be taken into account in the establishment of network features of the ISDN?
2. What are the network features needed to support these services? Which network features should be regarded as general throughout the ISDN, and which should be classed as service-dependent for particular service applications? (*Note*: Among other network features, attention should be paid to charging so that adequate information could be made available for charging purposes.)
3. For which services, if any, should a change of service on an established connection be envisaged? What are the implications and requirements of such a feature?

4. What kinds of leased paths will be required in the ISDN when it is in widespread operation?

Note 1: Services should be identified which will supplant existing leased line services.

Note 2: Consideration should be given to the use of semipermanent connections, closed user group and hot-line features, remote switching units, etc.

Point B. Network Aspects

1. What are the principles in terms of network structure and systems architecture which define the ISDN and which form the basis for study of specific aspects?
2. Should layered protocols and functional layers be adopted for ISDN to form the basis of CCITT Recommendations? If so, what are the characteristics of this layering, and in which way is the concept of functional layers used with respect to subsystems, such as the signaling channels?
3. What are the implications of ISDN on numbering plans and service indicators for telephony and other services?
4. What methods of voice-band encoding other than standard PCM (see also Question 7/XVIII) and what forms of digital speech interpolation can be considered in relation to the evolution of the ISDN?

Point C. Customer Access

What are the principles in terms of network structure and systems architecture which define customer access to ISDN and which should form the basis of studies of related transmission, switching, signaling, and interface aspects?

Point D. Interworking

What are the principles which should form the basis for detailed study of the interfaces' interconnections and interworking between ISDN and service-dedicated networks?

The following specific points should be included in the studies:

i) At what point in the connection should special processing for interworking be accomplished (e.g., in the originating or terminating country)?

ii) What networks should be given preference to complete connections in a transit call situation?

iii) What special problems arise from the use of ISDN to provide interconnections of particular services (e.g., according to X.21, etc.) via different networks, and what restrictions or restraints should be placed on services or networks when interworking (e.g., to accommodate accounting, timing, and signaling features)?

iv) What methods should be recommended for accessing one network from another?

v) How should conversions be accomplished (e.g., data to data, voice to data)?

vi) What arrangements or procedures are needed to accommodate the accounting function for a connection involving mixed networks?

vii) What influence would different national applications of service integration have on the international network with regard to interworking?

viii) What special problems arise from the use of ISDN to interconnect networks carrying services to existing standard terminal interfaces?

ix) What are the possibilities of application of service bits allocated in primary PCM and higher order digital systems in national and international digital networks?

Point E. Guidelines to Facilitate Evolution toward ISDN

Which strategy should be followed in order to facilitate and speed up the establishment of a worldwide ISDN?

Note: It should be taken into consideration that, in the introductory period, it will be necessary to establish an all-digital network mainly for the needs of "business subscribers" who represent only a small percentage of the overall number of subscribers but who originate a substantial portion of traffic. It may be useful to create a digital "overlay network" in each country and to interconnect these national networks by digital links.

Appendix C

Open Systems Interconnection

The purpose of the Open Systems Interconnection Reference Model "is to provide a common basis for the coordination of standards development for the purpose of systems interconnection, while allowing existing standards to be placed into perspective within the overall Reference Model" (ISO 1982).

Use of the model permits an orderly process for analyzing existing standards and determining areas that need new standards.

The OSI Reference Model has a layered structure that permits the application of standards to interconnect dissimilar end-systems. This is done by making architectural layers modular in a way that permits software development according to functional definitions. The reference model has seven layers chosen so that no layer would be too complex and a number of layers would not become a problem in itself. Table C-1 shows the layers with a brief description of functions within each layer. The first three layers—Application, Presentation, and Session—are for end-user needs. The bottom four layers—Transport, Network, Data Link, and Physical—provide for moving of data.

Table C-1. Functional Layering of the OSI Reference Model

End-user Application Process	Function
Application	Provides access to OSI and selects communications to satisfy user needs
Presentation	Provides for data formats and code conversion so that "same language is spoken"
Session	Sets up and terminates interaction between end-users; manages dialog
Transport	Provides for data integrity between end-user systems
Network	Selects a route and directs data to another end-user
Data link	Transfers information to other end of communications link
Physical	Transmits bit stream to transmission media such as telephone lines

The functions that are listed are fulfilled by applicable standards. For example, RS-232-C would apply to the physical layer. Another standard is CCITT Recommendation X.25. It applies to the physical, data link, and network layers. The protocols associated with each standard reside in the terminals and nodes of a network.

Within the context of the reference model, a number of terms should be noted. Interconnection standards encompass *protocols*, referring to a set of rules for communication between similar processes (or peer layers) such as actions between computers or terminals, and *interfaces*, or more appropriately, "interactions," referring to a set of rules for communication between dissimilar processes (or adjacent layers) such as between a person and a terminal, or a terminal and a network. The ultimate user of OSI is the *application process (AP)*. It can vary from a simple keyboard program to a complex computer data base operation between end-users. The applications process serves user needs in government, including information systems such as Social Security and Internal Revenue, and private industry, including electronic funds transfer (EFT) for banking and recordkeeping for insurance.

According to Folts (1981), the OSI reference model fits into the overall communications scheme as follows. The OSI users are APs, "X" in end-system I and "Y" in end-system II. Each is located within its own local system environment.

When an AP in one end-system wishes to communicate with an AP in a distant end-system, the interconnection is performed by the OSI Environment (OSIE). The local system manager (LSM) provides the control for invoking the OSIE functions to create the interconnection for the desired communications.

The APs communicate through the application layer and the underlying layers along the path shown in Figure C-1. A peer protocol for each layer controls and coordinates the designated functions between communicating end-systems. A message generated in one local system enters the OSIE through a

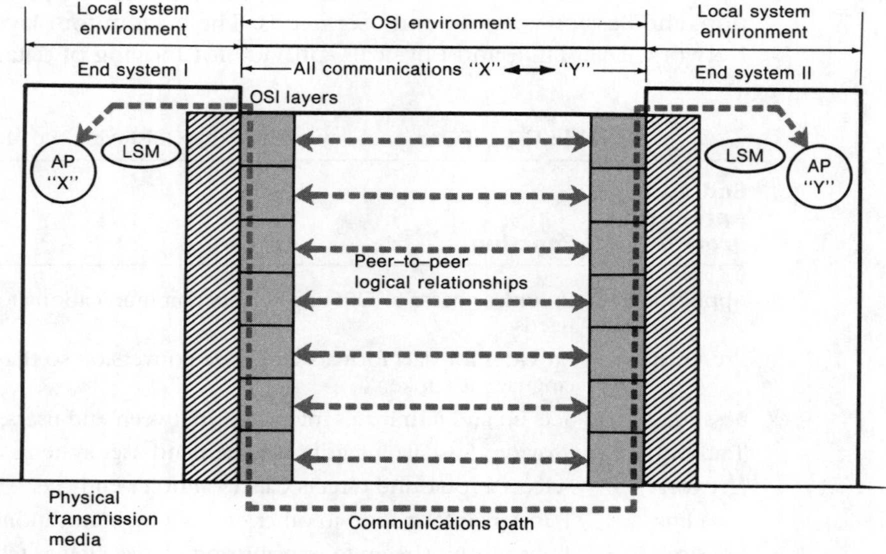

Figure C-1. Structured message flow *(Folts 1981)*.

window of the applications layer. After being processed by each of the seven layers, a formatted message traverses the transmission medium.

The interaction between the functional layers and the LSM is detailed in Figure C-2. The message (called a *data unit*) is appended with a control-header, containing information defined in a peer protocol, by each of the seven functional layers. The original message data unit, combined with the header of a specific layer, is viewed in the next layer as an integral data unit.

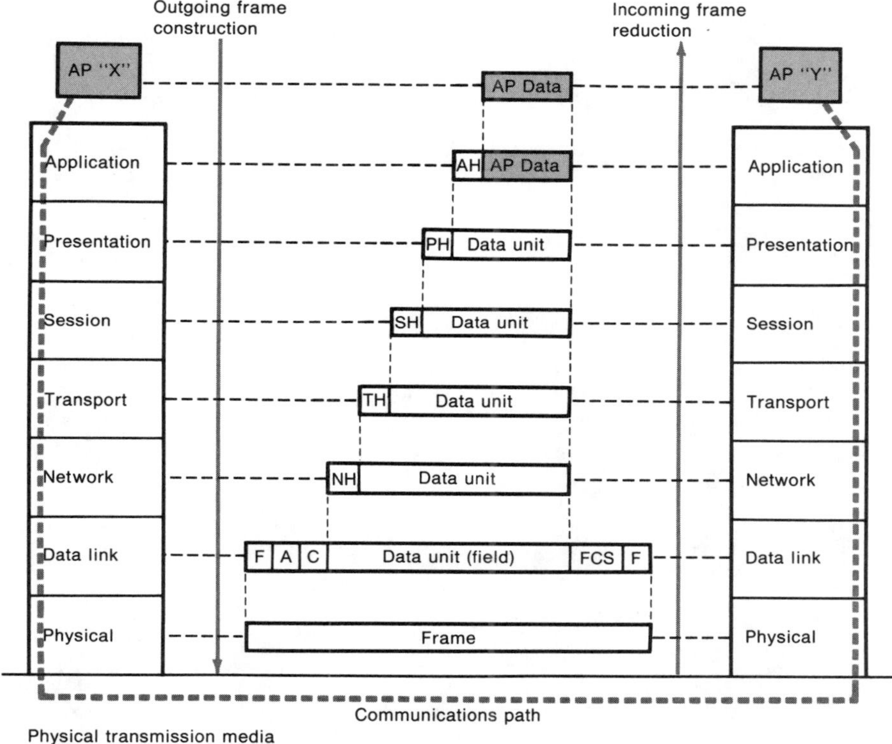

Figure C-2. Frame construction *(Folts 1981)*.

This is an example of basic OSI reference model communication. Ordinarily, there might be several intermediate nodes, with communication switches between endpoints. Various lower level layers may or may not be invoked as the data traverse the communications path at the intermediate node.

References

Folts, H. C. 1981. Coming of age: A long awaited standard for heterogeneous nets. *Data Communication* 10, no. 1 (January).

ISO. 1982. DIS 7498. Information processing systems—Open Systems Interconnection—Basic reference model.

Appendix D

Standardization Organization, Procedures, and Status

The development of standards for network management is far from complete. Given herein are descriptions of the organization among the various standards bodies participating in the development of data communications-oriented network management standards, the standardization process, how the various aspects of network management are partitioned among the various standards bodies, and the status of these various standards development activities.

Standards Organization

A simplified view of the organization of network-oriented standards bodies is shown in Figure D-1. ISO* and CCITT are the primary international bodies developing network management standards. Their concentrations are data communications network management and telephony network management, respectively.

The national standards bodies of several countries contribute to both international organizations. For example, the American National Standards Institute (ANSI) is the United States' delegate to ISO. The British Standards Institute is an example of another national body contributing to ISO. ANSI also contributes to CCITT, but it does so as a representative of the U.S. State Department, which is the CCITT representative. The European PTTs are examples of other national bodies contributing to CCITT.

Various technical bodies may contribute to the national standards bodies. For example, standards developed by the Institute of Electrical and Electronic Engineers (IEEE) are fed into ANSI to be progressed as international ISO stan-

*In particular, ISO/IEC/JTC1/SC21, i.e., SubCommittee (SC) 21 of Joint Technical Committee (JTC) 1 of ISO and IEC (the International Electrotechnical Committee).

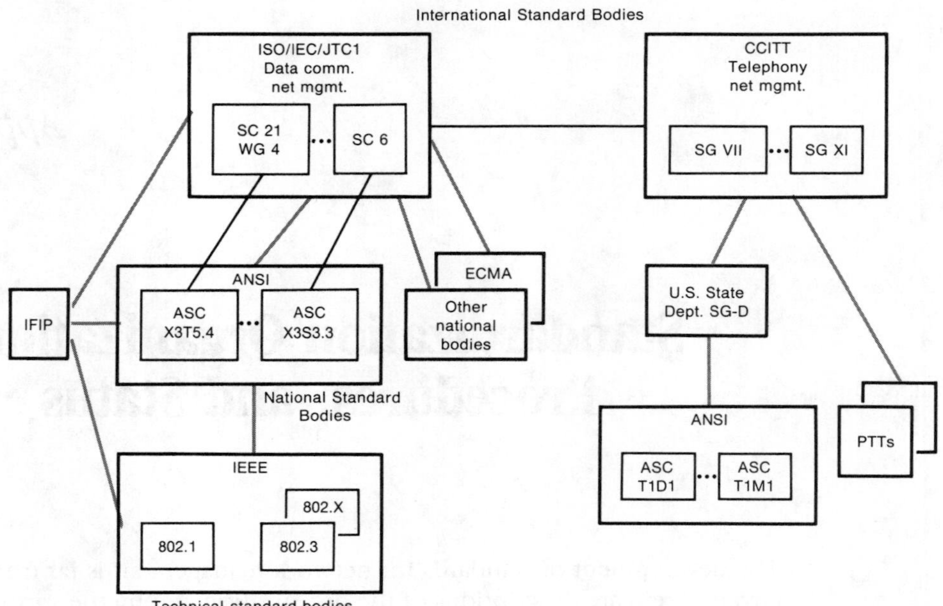

Figure D-1. Organization of the network management standards development committees.

dards. Similarly, the European Computer Manufacturers Association (ECMA) tends to feed European national standards bodies. IFIP does not develop standards, per se. Rather, as occurred with a variety of computer-oriented standards activities, IFIP tends to inject requirements into the formal standardization process. IFIP in fact has just started such an effort relative to network management requirements.

Within ISO, there are working groups from several subcommittees (SCs) that are developing network management-related standards. Parallel to these working groups, but at the national body level, are working groups of several ANSI Accredited Standards Committees (ASCs) acting as technical advisory groups to ISO. For example, ASC X3T5.4 contributes to the network management standardization efforts of working group (WG) 4 of ISO's SC21. In fact, it is the primary U.S. focal point for progressing the standards for all the network management tools. Similarly, ASC X3S3.3 contributes to the network management standardization activities within WG2 and WG4 of ISO SC6, while ASC X3T5.5 contributes to the network management activities of its parent groups in ISO. Similar pairings of ANSI ASCs to CCITT study groups also exist.

Standardization Process

The process of developing standards in ISO and CCITT are somewhat different. In ISO, after a proposed standard becomes recognized as a new work item, national bodies are asked to provide inputs regarding text for the eventual standard. Such inputs, after being coordinated internationally, become Working Drafts (WDs) of the eventual standard. These WDs then enter a three-step standardization process. The first, tentative level of standardization occurs when WDs are voted by the national standards bodies advising ISO to be stable enough to be sanctioned by ISO as having reached Draft Proposal (DP) status. As DPs evolve toward the next level of standardization, they may undergo potentially significant technical changes. Once they are technically stable, they are voted to elevation to the Draft International Standard (DIS) level. With primarily only editorial changes to improve understanding, DISs are then voted to be elevated to full International Standard (IS) status. At its fastest, this process tends to require at least three years for an IS to be created.

CCITT, on the other hand, develops standards (Recommendations), which are in effect for a four-year "study period." During this time, refinements to the standard are developed and, once consensus is reached, they will be incorporated into the standard to be in effect for the next four-year period.

Standards Partitioning/Status

The reference model for management is at the IS level. It is an Addendum to ISO's Basic Reference Model for Open Systems Interconnection (OSI). The standards associated with the services and protocol for management communication exchanges (CMIS, CMIP) are at the DIS level, with progression to IS expected to occur in the fall of 1989.

Descriptions of the five specific functional areas of network management are in various stages of standardization progression. The documents describing functions related to fault management and configuration management are draft proposals, with DIS status scheduled for 1989 and IS scheduled for 1990. Development of the security management functions, although underway, is hampered by the lack of mature security standards being developed within a different ISO WG. Work is just beginning in earnest for the performance management and accounting management functions. It is reasonable to expect that standards specific to these latter three management functional areas will not appear until the early 1990s, with DISs perhaps as early as 1990 and ISs in 1991. However, functions developed for the other functional areas, e.g., event reporting, log control, state management, object management, etc., are equally applicable to these areas.

The standards describing the identification of management information, as well as common structures pertinent to the management information, are intended to guide protocol layer standards in defining management information for the layers of which they are in charge. These standards will define the syntax of the management information, while each layer standard will define the semantics of the management information specific to its layer. Four DPs on SMI have been developed.

Finally, there is the effort to standardize the syntax and semantics of the management information. It is anticipated that there will be several standards documents emerging from this effort. That is, each of the communication protocol layers will have its own management information standards pertinent to the management information associated with the layer. It is likely that there will also be a standard pertinent to system management information, such as system time and access control tables, that is not specific to just any one protocol layer.

Work on these latter standards is in various stages of completion. It has been progressing under the aegis of ISO/IEC/JTC1/SC6 for the lower protocol layers (transport and below). It has just begun for the upper layers under charter to another ISO SC.

For the network and transport layers, working drafts for their management information, while still needing to be aligned with the structure of management information standard, are becoming mature. They are likely to progress to DP soon, with DIS elevation as early as 1990 and IS elevation thereafter. For the upper layers, the corresponding management information standards are not likely before the early 1990s.

The layer management information standards associated with layers below the network layer are being progressed by yet other groups. ANSI ASC X3T9.5 is developing layer management information specific to the lower layer protocols associated with the Fiber Digital Data Interface (FDDI) standard. For the lower layers associated with the IEEE standard LANs, the several IEEE 802 working groups responsible for the IEEE LAN standards are developing corresponding layer management information standards applicable to their layer. Thus, the IEEE 802.2 group is developing a working draft of the Logical Link Control (LLC) layer management information standard. Similarly, IEEE 802.3, 802.4, 802.5, and 802.6 are developing working drafts of the Media Access Control (MAC) layer management information standards associated with the CSMA/CD, token-bus, token-ring, and metropolitan area network MACs, respectively.

No formal schedules exist for completing the IEEE layer management information standards. The work is in various stages of completion. The 802.3 and 802.4 layer management information documents are quite mature; those associated with 802.2, 802.5, and 802.6 are still young. These documents all need to be aligned with the ISO structure of management information standard. Once approved as IEEE standards, they will need to progress to the appropriate ANSI ASC which can then progress them into the ISO international standards community. It is reasonable to expect that ISO ISs corresponding to these emerging IEEE standards are not likely to appear before 1990.

It should be noted the progression of all these management information standards will lag behind that of the standard pertaining to the structure of management information.

Influencing the future efforts of the international, national, and technical standards bodies will be a new IFIP working group—WG 6.6. Often, IFIP working groups tend to be prestandards organizations that investigate the need for standards. For example, the initial version of an OSI model and the need to standardize such a model arose from IFIP. Highlights of IFIP WG 6.6 areas of investigation include the following:

- examining the need to develop a common format, human presentation language to the users of network management systems

- investigating the need for a common man/machine interface and graphics displays for network management systems
- investigating the desirability of common data base management system support capabilities for network management systems
- investigating the need for standardized network management decision-making algorithms and the role AI could play in effecting these algorithms
- organizing a biannual symposium to bring together users, vendors, and standards makers to discuss the issues

IFIP WG 6.6 was commissioned too late to provide such impetus for the current network management standardization activities; however, their charter goes beyond the current work and instead focuses on the needs for advanced user requirements for network management systems.

Appendix E

Network Management Specification Efforts

There have been three OSI-based implementation specification efforts in the network management community: MAP/TOP, TCP/IP, and GOSIP.

MAP/TOP

In recognition of their constituency's immediate user needs for nonproprietary remote management capabilities in a multivendor networking environment, MAP/TOP, representing hundreds of vendor and user organizations, recently completed development of its version 3.0 network management specifications.

MAP/TOP envisions networks (primarily LANs) with heterogeneous nodes, some of which have the entire seven-layer ISO communication protocol stack implemented, while others contain only partial protocol stacks (e.g., link and physical layer protocols only). Since the ISO network management standards implicitly assume all network nodes being managed contain the full seven-layer protocol stack, the MAP/TOP network management conceptual framework goes beyond the ISO network management reference model. Accordingly, the management decision-making processes within the MAP/TOP manager(s) communicates with its (their) management agents in the MAP/TOP network nodes in different ways, depending on whether the network management agents reside in a full or partial stack node. In all cases, these processes use the network management communication services/protocol (CMIS/CMIP) defined in the ISO DP. In managing fullstack nodes, the CMIP uses the services of the entire seven layers of underlying communication protocols. In managing partial stack nodes, CMIP's communication service needs are mapped onto the services provided by the LLC protocol. Conceptually, this mapping is provided by a "thin protocol stack" between CMIP and LLC. This thin stack provides extremely little, if not null, communication capabilities corresponding to the missing intervening layers.

Where ISO network management standards existed, such as CMIS/CMIP, the MAP/TOP network management specifications stated the required standards' options that are mandatory for the networking products to be procured by these specifications. Where ISO standards did not yet exist, such as in defining the layer management information and defining its structure, MAP/TOP developed its own standards. In some cases, such as the management information associated with upper layer protocols, the MAP/TOP "standards" work preceded any ISO work. In other cases, such as the network and transport layer management information, the MAP/TOP and ISO work proceeded cooperatively and in parallel, and it is extremely likely that major portions of the MAP/TOP standards will become ISO standards. Although, in the long term, MAP/TOP is committed to specifications based on ISO standards. MAP has decided to keep its specifications stable until 1994.

TCP/IP

The TCP/IP community had similar constraints on the immediacy of their specifications for network management. The most pressing concern was for managing network layer gateways (routers) in the Internet. An approach was taken to satisfy the immediate requirements with an interim Simple Network Management Protocol (SNMP) (Case et al. 1988), with the long-term solution using the OSI management framework and protocols. The latter approach is referred to as CMIP over TCP (CMOT) (Warrier and Besaw 1989). Both protocols work with the same core MIB defined for the TCP/IP internet.

Having started later than the MAP/TOP effort, the TCP/IP community was able to use DIS and IS ISO network management standards for their long-term approach. They developed standards and specifications for the layer management information associated with the TCP/IP, non-ISO protocol layers.

Both TCP/IP-based and ISO-based components will coexist in networks for at least the next ten years. During this transition period, when both ISO network nodes and TCP network nodes coexist, a common set of CMIS communication services will be provided. For ISO nodes, CMIS services will be provided by CMIP over the entire seven-layer protocol stack. For TCP/IP nodes, a subset of CMIS services will be provided by SNMP for the short term, and for the long term, full CMIS services will be provided by CMIP over TCP/UDP transport layer protocols.

GOSIP

The United States government is developing its ISO network management specifications under the auspices of some twenty government agencies which have pooled their networking needs under the GOSIP umbrella.

The GOSIP specifications directly point to implementation agreements decided upon in the series of ongoing NIST Workshops for the Implementors of Open Systems Interconnection. NIST began this series of quarterly forums in 1983. These forums bring together users and vendors of ISO-based networking products. The workshops accept as inputs the specifications of emerging ISO protocol standards and from them generate agreements on the implementation and testing particulars of these protocols. These workshops have been expediting the development of ISO protocol products, and through multivendor demonstrations on OSINET (the Open Systems Interconnection Network), they are promoting the interoperability of independently manufactured OSI networking equipment.

The activities to formulate network management implementation agreements at the NIST workshops have recently started. The Network Management SIG (Special Interest Group) is spearheading the development of GOSIP network management implementation agreements over the next several years. Interim implementation agreements based on the most recent ISO, ISDN, and telephony network management standards are expected to be published as a Federal Information Processing Standard (FIPS), as early as late 1989, to be utilized in part by GOSIP. Final implementation agreements corresponding to a full complement of ISO network management ISs and DISs will follow through the early 1990s as the various ISO network management standards are finalized. It is anticipated that interoperability tests and demonstrations of separately developed implementations of the SIG's agreements will occur during the early 1990s.

The ultimate benefit of the NIST network management implementors' agreements is that conformance tests will be developed for these agreements by the newly founded Corporation for Open Systems (COS). COS was created in 1985 primarily by a consortium of OSI vendors. Its charter focuses on the development and conducting of conformance tests to certify that implementations of OSI protocols conform to the applicable OSI standards and specifications. COS has recently created a Network Management SubCommittee (NMSC) to accomplish COS's mission for network management conformance tests. A close collaborative working relationship exists with the NIST network management SIG. NMSC and the NIST NMSIG are jointly considering conformance-testing philosophies. The SIG is developing conformance-testing guidelines. The COS NMSC will begin developing their conformance test tools according to these guidelines once the corresponding NIST network management SIG implementation agreements are based on OSI standards at the DIS level.

References

Case, J., M. Fedor, M. Schofferstall, and J. Davin. 1988. RFC 1067. A Simple Network Management Protocol (August).

Warrier, U., and L. Besaw. 1989. RFC 1095. The Common Management Information Services and Protocol for TCP/IP (February).

Contributors

Robert F. Linfield was with the National Bureau of Standards in Washington, D.C., Corona, California, and Boulder, Colorado from 1948 to 1961. In 1961, he joined a group which started the Boulder Laboratory for DECO Electronics, Inc., which later was acquired by the Westinghouse Electric Corporation. He directed the Communications and Navigations Systems Section for the Westinghouse Georesearch Laboratory until 1974 when he joined the Institute for Telecommunication Sciences (ITS) in Boulder. He recently retired as the associate deputy director of the Systems and Networks Division of ITS and is responsible for projects dealing with switched networks for various government agencies. He currently is working as a consultant to the Institute. Mr. Linfield received a B.S. in engineering physics from the University of Colorado in 1956.

Donald V. Glen is a consultant at CyberLink Corporation, a telecommunication engineering firm for voice and data networks. He provides services for the connectivity of PCs, mainframes, and peripherals through LANs, ISDN, and proprietary networks using copper and fiber optic transmission media. Mr. Glen is a former staff member of the Institute for Telecommunication Sciences (ITS), National Telecommunications and Information Administration (NTIA), where he participated as a member of ANSI X3S3.7, a North American data communications standards committee, that has made contributions to packet switching, ISDN, and other standards. Other experience at NTIA includes evaluation of communication interference for the FAA, multiple satellite-hop testing of voice circuits for the FCC, testing of GOES satellite data links for NOAA, and developing electronic mail alternatives for the USPS. He has written numerous technical reports and articles as part of his work. Mr. Glen received a B.S. in engineering physics from the University of Colorado in 1959.

Evelyn M. Gray has been with the U.S. Department of Commerce Boulder Laboratories for 26 years. She worked first in the National Bureau of Standards Central Radio Propagation Laboratory and then in the successor organizations.

She is currently in the Institute for Telecommunication Sciences (ITS), the research and engineering arm of the National Telecommunications and Information Administration (NTIA). For many of those 26 years she was an editor for the Institute's technical reports and a principal reporter for in-house newsletters. She is currently a computer programmer. Ms. Gray received a B.A. in art history (1960) from the University of California in Berkeley and an M.A. in journalism (1979) from the University of Colorado where she was elected to Kappa Tau Alpha journalism honor society.

C. Anthony Cooper currently manages the Broadband Transmission Analysis District at Bellcore. From April 1984 to January 1987, he managed Bellcore's ISDN Technical Planning District, responsible for completing ISDN architecture plans, planning technical support of current services with ISDN, and providing technical support of ISDN Trials. Dr. Cooper joined Bell Laboratories in 1969 and has participated in a variety of projects pertaining to Network Planning. He went to AT&T General Departments in 1981 as a district manager with planning responsibility for Operations Systems and new technology applications. He returned to Bell Laboratories in 1983 with responsibility for Operations Systems Network (OSN) functional requirements and standards, and moved to Bellcore with this same OSN responsibility in January 1984. Dr. Cooper received his Ph.D. in electrical engineering from the University of Southern California in 1969. He has belonged to the Tau Beta Pi, Eta Kappa Nu, and Phi Kappa Phi honor societies and is a senior member of the Instrument Society of America and a member of the IEEE. He has published over twenty technical articles.

Syed V. Ahamed is a professor of computer science at the City University of New York, where his teaching interests include computer graphics and image processing, computer architecture, CAD/CAM, algorithms, networks, and MIS. He has authored or coauthored over 100 publications and holds several patents. Dr. Ahamed is a senior member of the IEEE. He received his Ph.D. and D.Sc. degrees in electrical engineering from Manchester University in England and his M.B.A. in economics from New York University.

Victor Lawrence joined AT&T Bell Laboratories in 1974 and was involved in research in digital signal processing. In 1986, he was appointed head of the Digital Techniques department, and in April 1988, he assumed responsibility as head of the Data Communication Research department. He served as technical program and general chairman for the first and fourth International Workshops on VLSI in Communications, and as technical program chairman for the first IEEE Workshop on Metropolitan Networks. He was associate editor for the IEEE Communications Magazine from June 1978 through July 1981 and associate editor, Digital Signal Processing for the IEEE Transactions on Circuits and Systems, from June 1981 to June 1983. He was special Rapporteur on coding for CCITT SG XVII in 1984. He is presently editor-in-chief of the IEEE Transactions on Communications. Dr. Lawrence has been adjunct professor at Columbia, Princeton, Rutgers, and Fairleigh Dickenson Universities. He delivered the 1986 Distinguished Chancellor's lecture series at the University of California at Berkeley. He was corecipient of the 1981 Guillemin-Cauer prize paper award, and corecipient of the J. Karp award for the best paper at Interface 1984. He holds seven patents and has published over 40 technical papers. He is coauthor of two technical books. Dr. Lawrence is a Fellow of IEEE. He received his B.Sc. in 1968 and his Ph.D. in electrical engineering in 1972 from the University of London.

Lee LaBarre is currently a lead engineer in the Distributed Processing Division where he consults on performance evaluation, OSI/TCP protocols, and network management for MITRE's Network Center. He has been active in many standards and specification efforts, including ISO, ANSI, IEEE, MAP/TOP, the NIST NMSIG, and the IETF. Mr. LaBarre organized, convened, and now chairs the IETF NETMAN Working Group which is developing the long-term approach to managing TCP/IP networks using the OSI network management framework and protocols. Mr. LaBarre received a B.S. in physics from SUNY College at Potsdam in 1969, and an M.S. in systems analysis from Clarkson University in 1972.

Paul J. Brusil joined the technical staff of the MITRE Corporation where he first concentrated his efforts on performance aspects of local networking. He then led the group chartered to develop network traffic and performance evaluation tools for capacity planning for MITRE's internal network. Dr. Brusil is a principal scientist for the Distributed Processing Division, where he provides technical direction for MITRE's Network Center and its Network Management Specialty Center. He organized, convened, and now chairs the Network Management SIG of NIST's Workshops for Implementors of OSI. He is also chairman of IFIP's First International Symposium on Integrated Network Management, and a contributor to ISO's Performance Management Standard. Dr. Brusil received a Ph.D. in systems analysis from Harvard University in 1973. His initial research into the application of signal processing to medical diagnosis and prediction was conducted as a Fellow of Harvard's Medical School.

Robert J. Sundstrom is currently manager of Communications Systems Architecture and the chairman of the SNA Architecture Maintenance Board. He is responsible for the architecture departments that are developing the VTAM-NCP transport network, small-systems networking, and logical unit 6.2 extensions to SNA. He received a B.S. in applied mathematics, and an M.S.E. and Ph.D. in computer, information, and control engineering from the University of Michigan in 1970, 1971, and 1974, respectively. Dr. Sundstrom joined IBM in 1974 and initially worked in the area of formal specification of communication architectures. Since that time, he has held development and management positions while contributing to the ongoing evolution of SNA. He is a member of the ACM and the IEEE Computer Society.

James B. Staton III joined IBM in 1978 at Research Triangle Park. He is currently on assignment to the European Networking Center in Heidelberg, West Germany, where he is developing prototype systems using OSI protocols. In 1981, Mr. Staton joined the SNA group, where he worked on several enhancements to SNA. He initially participated primarily on network management issues involving modems and communication links. Before his current assignment, he managed the Communications Architecture Department, which was responsible for the development of the communication protocols for the IBM Token-Ring Network and its integration into SNA. Prior to that, he helped design and develop version 2 of the Teleprocessing Network Simulator program product, which simulates networks and devices for performance and reliability testing. Mr. Staton received an A.B. in mathematics from Guilford College in 1972, an M.A. in mathematics from the University of North Carolina at Greensboro in 1974, and an M.S. in computer science from Ohio State University in 1978.

Gary D. Schultz joined IBM in 1965. His work assignments have included: telecommunications access method systems programming; participation in the specification of IBM's binary synchronous communication, along with design and review of its initial software and hardware implementations; development of a time-sharing system used by the University of North Carolina computer science department for a decade; mathematical modeling of buffer storage schemes and ad-tech programming of modern algorithms while in the IBM Research Division; and, since 1973, development of SNA, primarily in terms of its formal definition and external publication. Currently, he is a global reviewer of the architecture and chief technical editor of the growing library of SNA specifications. He has a B.S. in statistics from the University of Chicago and an M.S. in computer science from the University of North Carolina at Chapel Hill.

Matthew L. Hess joined IBM Canada in 1968 as a systems engineer. He specialized in performance analysis and the design of on-line systems. In 1976, he joined the telecommunications center in La Gaude, France, to study new public data network offerings, and continued this work when he came to Research Triangle Park. For the past seven years, he has participated in the development of SNA, particularly SNI and, more recently, SNADS, as project manager. Dr. Hess received a B.Eng. from McGill University, Montreal, Canada, in 1964. He received an M.Sc. in 1966 and a Ph.D. in 1968 from the University of Birmingham, England.

George A. Deaton, Jr. contributed to manned and unmanned satellite projects done under IBM contracts to NASA. He then became involved in the development of IBM commercial communication products and has since worked with the architecture and design of digital time-division systems, in high-speed loop communication systems, and in the development of computer-communication architecture for local area and wide area networks. Currently, he is manager of the Network Development Project Office, which has architecture and product coordination responsibilities for attachment interfaces and standards supported by IBM products for public data networks. Mr. Deaton has a B.S. in physics from Virginia Polytechnic Institute and has done graduate studies in physics and astrodynamics. He has written numerous papers on computer communication and lectures frequently on that subject.

Leo J. Cole joined IBM in 1979, working in Architecture and Telecommunications in Research Triangle Park. In 1980, he moved to Tampa, Florida, working in Network Design for the IBM Information Network. In 1982, he returned to Architecture and Telecommunications, where he is currently manager of Network Management Architecture. Mr. Cole received a B.S. from Syracuse University in 1979.

Robert M. Amy joined IBM in 1969 in technical market support, specializing in data communications at the Kalamazoo, Michigan, branch office. In 1974, he accepted an assignment in LSI and microcode simulation for the IBM 4341 development project in Endicott, New York. He became a part of SNA development in Raleigh in 1979 and later managed an architecture development group within that function. Currently, he is manager of Network Standards Development, with responsibility for IBM participation in standards activities related to the lower two layers of OSI, and has been concentrating on ISDN for the last three years. He participates in ANSI T1 and T1D1, as well as CCITT SG XI, and SVIII, on the subject of ISDN. Mr. Amy received a B.S. in physics from the University of Michigan in 1966.

Radia Perlman is a consulting engineer at Digital Equipment Corporation. She designed the spanning tree algorithm used by Digital's bridges and adopted for use by both IEEE 802 bridge standards (802.1's "transparent bridges" and 802.5's "source routing bridges"). She was also responsible for the design and specification of the Network Layer in Digital's Network Architecture, aspects of which have been adopted by ISO for use in the standard connectionless Network Layer. She has designed super-fault tolerant Network Layer protocols that continue to operate even in the presence of active sabotage. Dr. Perlman has taught as adjunct faculty at the graduate schools of Wang Institute and University of Lowell, and at the Wang Summer Institute. She is on the editorial board of *Computer Networks and ISDN Systems*. She received B.S. and M.S. degrees in mathematics from MIT and a Ph.D. in computer science from MIT.

Glossary of Acronyms

ABM Asynchronous Balanced Mode
ACD Automatic call distribution
ACF Advanced Communication Function
ACSE Association control service element
A/D Analog-to-digital
ADCCP Advanced Data Communications Control Procedures
ADM Asynchronous Disconnected Mode
ADPCM Adaptive differential pulse code modulation
AIS Automatic Intercept System
AM Administrative module
AMI Alterate mark inversion
ANSI American National Standards Institute
A/OWS Asian/Oceania Workshop
APD Avalanche photodiodes
API Application program interface
APPC Advanced Program-to-Program Communication
APPN Advanced Peer-to-Peer Networking
ARM Asynchronous Response Mode
ASC Accredited Standards Committee
ASCII American Standard Code for Information Interchange
ASM Abstract switching machine
ASN Abstract Syntax Notation
AT&T American Telephone and Telegraph
ATM Automatic teller machine
AU Access unit
AWG American Wire gauge
BCD Binary-coded decimal
BCUG Bilateral closed user group
BDLC Burroughs Data Link Control
BIT Binary digit
BnZS Binary (number) Zero Substitution
BOC Bell Operating Company
BRI Basic rate interface
b/s Bits per second
BSC Binary Synchronous Communication
BSE Basic Service Element
BSRF Basic Synchronization Reference Frequency
CAMA Centralized Automatic Message Accounting
CAPTAIN Character and pattern telephone access information network
CATV Cable television
CBX Computerized Branch Exchange
CCIR International Radio Consultative Committee

CCIS Common channel interoffice signaling
CCITT International Telegraph and Telephone Consultative Committee
CCS Common channel signaling
CEI Comparably efficient interconnection
CEPT (European) Conference of Posts of Telecommunication Administrations
CM Communication module
CMIP Common management information protocol
CMISE Common management information service element
CONS Connection-oriented network service
COS Corporation for Open Systems
CPE Customer premises equipment
CPU Central processing unit
CRC Cyclic redundancy check
CRT Cathode ray tube
CSA Carrier Serving Area
CSDC Circuit-Switched Digital Capability
CSDN Circuit-switched data network
CSMA/CD Carrier Sense Multiple Access with Collision Detect
CSPDN Circuit-switched public data network
CSU Channel service unit
CUG Closed User Group
D/A Digital-to-analog
DARPA Defense Advanced Research Projects Agency
DBM Data Base Manager
DCE Data Circuit-Terminating Equipment
DDCMP Digital Data Communications Message Protocol
DDM Distributed Data Management
DDS Digital Data System
DES Data Encryption Standard
DFE Decision feedback equalizer
DIA Document Interchange Architecture
DIS Draft International Standard
DISC Disconnect
DISOSS Distributed Office Support System
DLC Digital Loop Carrier
DMERT Duplex Multi-Environment Real-Time
DNA Digital Network Architecture
DNIC Data Network Identification Code
DOS/VS Disk Operating System/ Virtual Storage
DP Draft Proposal
DSAP Destination service access point
DSE Data switching units
DSL Digital Subscriber Line
DSP Domain-Specific Point
DSU Data service units
DSX Distributed Systems Executive
DTE Data Terminal Equipment
EBCDIC Extended Binary Coded Decimal Interchange Code
EC Echo canceler
ECMA European Computer Manufacturers Association
ECSA Exchange Carriers Standards Association
EFT Electronic funds transfer
EIA Electronic Industries Association
ELLC Enhanced Logical Link Control
EMA Enterprise Management Architecture
ENA Extended network addressing
ENIAC Electronic Numerical Integrator and Calculator
ERLE Echo-Return-Loss Enhancement
ES End system
ESS Electronic switching system
ET Exchange Termination
EWOS European Workshop for Open Systems
FAX Facsimile
FCC Federal Communications Commission
FCS Frame Check Sequence

FDDI Fiber Digital Data Interface
FDM Frequency division multiplex
FED STD Federal (Telecommunication) Standard
FEP Front-end processor
FEXT Far-end crosstalk
FIFO First in/first out
FIPS Federal Information Processing Standard
FIR Finite impulse response
FTAM File transfer, access, and management
FTSC Federal Telecommunications Standards Committee
GFI General format identifier
GOSIP Government OSI Profile
HDLC High-level data link control
HI-OVIS High interactive-optical visual interactive system
HU High-usage
IA International Alphabet
IAB Internet Activities Board
IAN Integrated Analog Network
IC Integrated circuit
IDN Integrated Digital Networks
IDP Initial Domain Part
IEEE Institute for Electrical and Electronics Engineers
IFIP International Federation for Information Processing
IFRB International Frequency Registration Board
ILD Interjection laser diode
IM Initialization Mode
IMS Information Management System
INIC ISDN Network Identification Code
I/O Input/output
IOP Input/output processor
IRC International Record Carriers
IS International Standard
ISDN Integrated Services Digital Network
ISI Intersymbol interference
ISO International Organization for Standardization
IST Interswitch Trunk
ITS Institute for Telecommunication Sciences
ITU International Telecommunication Union
JTC Joint Technical Committee
JWP Joint Working Party
LADT Local Area Data Transport
LAMA Local Automatic Message Accounting
LAN Local Area Network
LAPX Link access procedure, extended
LATA Local Access Transport Area
LCGN Logical channel group number
LCI Logical channel identifier
LCM Line concentrating module
LCN Logical channel number
LDS Logically disconnected state
LED Light-emitting diode
LGC Line group controller
LLC Logical link control
LM Layer management
LP Logical port
LPDA Link Problem Determination Aid
LSI Logical channel identifier
LSM Local system environment
LSP Link State Packets
LU Logical unit
MAC Media Access Control
MAN Metropolitan Area Network
MAP Manufacturing Automation Protocol
MCC Master Control Center
MCI Microwave Communications Incorporated
MF Multifrequency
MFJ Modified Final Judgment
MIB Management Information Base
MLP Multilink procedure
MMI Man/machine interface
MML Man/machine language
MSI Medium-scale integration
MVS Multiple Virtual Storage
NCP Network Control Program
NCS National Communication System

NCT Network Control and Timing
NCTE Network Channel Terminating Equipment
ND Network Default
NDM Normally Disconnected Mode
NEMOS Network Management Operations Support
NETDA Network Design and Analysis
NEXT Near-end crosstalk
NIST National Institute of Standards and Technology, formerly National Bureau of Standards
NLDM Network Logical Data Manager
NMF Network Management Forum
NMSC Network Management SubCommittee
NPA Numbering plan area
NPM Network Performance Monitor
NRF Network Routing Facility
NRM Normal Response Mode
NSI Non-SNA Interconnection
NT Network Termination
NTIA National Telecommunications and Information Administration
NTN Network Terminal Number
NTO Network Terminal Option
NTT Nippon Telegraph and Telephone
NUI Network Unit Identifier
ONA Open network architecture
OSDS Operating System for Distributed Switching
OSI Open Systems Interconnection
OSIE OSI Environment
OSINET Open Systems Interconnection Network
OSNS Open Systems Network Support
OTSS Open System Transport and Session Support
PABX Private automatic branch exchange
PAD Packet assembly/disassembly
PBX Private branch exchange
PC Personal computer
PCM Pulse code modulation
PDU Protocol data unit
PH Packet-handling
PIN Positive intrinsic negative
PLP Packet layer procedure
POP Point-of-presence
POR Plan of Reorganization
POS Point-of-sale
POSI Promotion of OSI (Group)
POT Point-of-termination
POTS Plain old telephone service
PRI Primary rate interface
PROTEL Procedure-Oriented Type Enforcing Language
PSDN Packet-switched data network
PSPDN Packet-switched public data network
PSTN Public-switched telephone network
PTT Post, Telegraph, and Telephone (organization)
PVC Permanent virtual circuits
QAM Quadrature amplitude modulation
RAM Random access memory
RBOC Regional Area Bell Company
RDA Remote Database Access
RDN Relative distinguished name
REJ Reject
RNR Receive not ready
R-O Read-only
RO Remote Operations
ROSE Remote Operations Service Element
RPOA Recognized private operating agency
RR Receive ready
RSA Rivest, Shamir, Adelman (algorithm)
RTG Routing Table Generator
RTR Real-Time Reliable
SABM Set asynchronous balanced mode
SAPI Service access point identifier
SDLC Synchronous Data Link Control
SF Single-frequency
SIG Special Interest Group
SLP Single-link procedure

SM Switching module
SMAE System management application entity
SMASE Systems management application service element
SMFA Specific management functional areas
SMI Structure of management information
SNA Systems Network Architecture
SNADS SNA Distribution Services
SNA/LEN SNA Low-Entry Networking
SNAP SAP Subnetwork Access Protocol Service Access Point
SNI SNA Network Interconnection
SPAG Standards Promotion and Application Group
SPC Stored program control
SSAP Source service access point
SSCP System services control point
SSI Small-scale integration
STP Signal transfer point
T1 ANSI Accredited Standards Committee of ECSA
TA Terminal adaptor
TCM Time compression multiplex
TCP/IP Transmission Control Protocol/Internet Protocol
TDM Time-division multiplex
TE Terminal equipment
TEI Terminal endpoint identifier
TOP Technical and Office Protocol
TP Transaction processing
TRC Timing recovery circuit
TSPS Traffic Service Position Systems
TST Time-space-time
TWX Teletypewriter Exchange Service
UDLC Universal Data Link Control
UNMA Unified Network Management Architecture
VAN Value-added network
VC Virtual calls
VDT Video display terminal
VLSI Very large-scale integration
VM Virtual machine
VSF Voice store-and-forward
VSM Virtual Switching Machine
VTAM Virtual Telecommunications Access Method
VTP Virtual Terminal Protocol
WAN Wide Area Network
WATS Wide Area Telephone Service
WD Working Draft
XID Exchange Identification
XRF Extended Recovery Facility

Index

O

T

C Programmer's Guide to NetBIOS
C Programmer's Guide to Serial Communications
SAMS
Data Communications, Networks, and Systems
Data Communications Testing and Troubleshooting

Digital Communications

Thomas C. Bartee, Editor-in-Chief

Communications professionals who must stay abreast of state-of-the-art technology will benefit from this comprehensive collection of data.

Nine leading experts have authored chapters on their specialties that reflect the most current information available in their fields.

Digital Communications is organized into nine chapters, each one concentrating on an important technical area. The chapters may be read in order, or separately.

Each chapter provides references that make this an excellent tutorial, reference, or introduction to the complex and amazing subject of digital communications.

Topics covered include:

- Fiber-Optic Transmission Technology and System Evolution
- Satellite Communications
- Integrated Services Digital Networks (ISDN)
- Computer-Based Messaging
- Electronic Mail Systems
- Cellular Networks
- Challenges in Communications for Command and Control Systems
- Digital Coding of Speech
- Video Teleconferencing

424 Pages, 7½ x 9¾, Hardbound
ISBN: 0-672-22472-0
No. 22472, $39.95

Micro-Mainframe Connection

Thomas Wm. Madron

Focusing on the organizational environment, this book explores the opportunities, technologies, and problems involved in implementing the transfer of data between the mainframe and the micro workstation—more comprehensively than any other book on the market.

Designed to help managers and technical support people design and implement micro-mainframe networks, it gives complete information about features, facilities, and requirements, including cost considerations.

Topics covered include:

- The Micro-Mainframe Link
- Features, Facilities, and Problems in the Micro-Mainframe Connection
- Micros, Mainframes, and Networks
- Local Area Networks in the Micro-Mainframe Connection
- Micros as Mainframe Peripherals: Mainframes as Micro Peripherals
- Micros and IBM® Mainframes in a Synchronous Network
- Asynchronous Devices in a Synchronous Network: Protocol Conversion
- File Transfer Protocols
- Data Extraction, Data Format, and Application Specific File Transfers
- Making the Micro-Mainframe Connection

272 Pages, 7½ x 9¾, Hardbound
ISBN: 0-672-46583-3
No. 46583, $29.95

PC LAN Primer

Kleeman, Anderson, Angermeyer, Fisher, McCoy, The Waite Group

PC LAN Primer explores the Token Ring—the grand strategy to tie together IBM® micros, minis, and mainframes with local area networks providing the communication feature. The book compares PC and Token-Ring Networks and provides a discussion of IBM's strategy for the future of PC LANs. Numerous hands-on examples of installation and operation are provided for administrators and users of local area networks.

Emphasizing PC LAN (micro to micro) and the Token Ring (mainframe/mini to micro), this primer is a valuable introduction and reference for anyone with an intermediate level of experience in PC DOS® 2.1 and 3.0.

Topics covered include:

- Local Area Networks
- IBM's Network Strategy
- The Token-Ring Network
- The PC LAN Program
- Network Naming Conventions
- Installing the Network Software
- Programming for the LAN
- Mainframe and LAN Communications

240 Pages, 7½ x 9¾, Softbound
ISBN: 0-672-22448-8
No. 22448, $22.95

Reference Data for Engineer Radio, Electronics, Computer, a Communications, Seventh Editi

Edward C. Jordan, Editor-in-Chief

Written by 70 professionals, this book was originally published as limited private edition used by e gineers, mathematicians, and phy cists at ITT. Forty years later, it has become a familiar and deper able reference for engineers worldwide.

In this completely updated seven edition, the title has been chang to reflect the range of disciplines included. The scope of coverage has been greatly expanded.

Topics covered include:

- International Telecommunication Recommendations
- Units, Constants, and Conversion Factors
- Filters, Simple Band-Pass Design
- Modern-Network-Theory Desig
- Rectifiers, Filters, and Power Supplies
- Optical, Analog, and Digital Communications
- Computer Communications Networks
- Satellite and Space Communi cations
- Broadcasting, Cable Televisio and Recording System Standa
- Switching Networks and Traffic Concepts
- Electroacoustics
- Computer Organization and Programming

1,368 Pages, 7½ x 9¾, Hardbou
ISBN: 0-672-21563-2
No. 21563, $69.95

Visit your local book retailer or call 800-428-SAMS.